Building An ASP.NET Intranet

Kourosh Ardestani

Brian Boyce

Matt Gibbs

Chad Hutchinson

Saurabh Nandu

John C Roth

Chandu Thota

Jonathon Walsh

Karli Watson

With additional material by Matt Gibbs

Wrox Press Ltd. ®

Building An ASP.NET Intranet

Trademark Acknowledgements

Published by Wrox Press Ltd,
Arden House, 1102 Warwick Road, Acocks Green,
Birmingham, B27 6BH, UK
Printed in the United States
ISBN 1-86100-749-3

Credits

Authors

Kourosh Ardestani
Brian Boyce
Chad Hutchinson
Saurabh Nandu
John C Roth
Chandu Thota
Jonathon Walsh
Karli Watson

Additional Material
Matt Gibbs

Commissioning Editor
Daniel Kent

Lead Technical Editor
Daniel Kent

Technical Editor
Gerard Maguire

Index
Andrew Criddle

Technical Reviewers

Marco Bellinaso
Natalia Bortniker
Mark Horner
Benny Johansen
Shefali Kulkarni
Sophie McQueen
John Timney

Production Team Leader
Abbie Forletta

Cover
Natalie O'Donnell

Proof Reader
Susan Nettleton

Managing Editor
Louay Fatoohi

Project Manager
Charlotte Smith

About the Authors

Kourosh Ardestani

Kourosh is a consultant, developer, and trainer focusing on .NET technologies in the enterprise. He has been working closely with ASP.NET and other .NET technologies since the preview release of the .NET runtime. Kourosh has a BSc in computer science along with a degree in business management. He is also certified in about a dozen IT certifications including MCSD, MCSE, MCDBA, MCSA, and CISSP. When not working with computers, Kourosh enjoys reading, playing music, and watching nature shows. He can be reached at kpaars@yahoo.com

Brian Boyce

Brian Boyce is Strategic Director at Alphatec Software Ltd, a UK-based software solution provider, specializing in financial and business intelligence systems. He loves snowboarding and skiing, and is a regular contributor to several .NET magazines.

I would like to dedicate this work to my fiancé Angela and our son Aidan, without whom my life would only be half complete. I would also like to thank my parents for their lifetime of love and support.

Chad Hutchinson

Chad Hutchinson lives and works in sunny Florida where retired Mainframe programmers migrate. He has been working professionally with C/C++, FoxPro, VB and other Microsoft related technologies for the last 10 years, specializing in COM/ActiveX technologies.

Lately, he has been programming mobile devices using VB and the .NET platform. In fact, it is not uncommon to see him in line at Starbucks, PocketPC in hand, administering some network remotely via ASP.NET and the mobile controls.

When tired of sitting in front of a monitor for days on end, Chad also enjoys the much-welcomed distractions of Painting and music.

I would like to thank the technical editors at Wrox for being so very helpful and patient with me. The editing staff at Wrox is very hard working and well informed. In particular, I would like to thank Charlotte for always being so sweet and thoughtful. I have worked with her on and off over the last couple of years and it has always been a pleasure.

Saurabh Nandu

Saurabh lives in Mumbai, India. He is the founder of the site http://www.MasterCSharp.com which concentrates on teaching C# and .NET. He worked on web technologies like DHTML/HTML, JavaScript and Flash 5.0 before he started learning Java. He was introduced to .NET by his friend Nanu Jogi and after being influenced by the power and flexibility of .NET he sticks to working as a freelance writer/reviewer on .NET and related technologies. He has recently won the Microsoft Asia Most Valued Professional award for his work in the online communities. He is currently working as a Technical Evangelist at YesSoftware Inc.

Firstly, I would like to thank Charlotte Smith, Daniel Kent and the Wrox team to get me on this project. Also a big thanks to the fellow authors and reviewers who made it possible to complete this book in such a short time.

I would also like to thank my friend Nanu Jogi without whose direction I would have never started working on the .NET Platform. Finally, I would like to acknowledge my family's support, especially my brother Pritesh who keeps me going all the time!

John C Roth

John is the president of iSpeakGeek Computer Consulting. John began his career like so many in the industry as "that guy who knows the computer stuff". Eventually, realizing that he could actually make a living having fun, John started programming full-time and he hasn't looked back in the decade plus (ouch!) since.

He considers himself fortunate in his career to have been able to fill the role of Senior Developer and Web Developer at Compaq, to teach both students and other instructors at institutions like the University of British Columbia and Kwantlen College, and to work with many other wonderful clients, big and small.

John can be reached by e-mail at john@ispeakgeek.com.

I'd like to dedicate my part of this book to three people who mean the world to me:

To my mom, for her unwavering love and support throughout the years. Mom, you are an amazing woman and I'm proud to be your son.

To Collin, one of the best friends anyone could ask for! Cousin, you've been an inspiration to me both personally and professionally – you're my alpha geek!

And to Andrea, who continues to be my best friend!

I'd also like to thank the great team at Wrox for all of their patience, their help, their patience, their support, and their patience... You're all a dedicated lot, but I'd especially like to thank Dan and Charlotte for the incredible work they put in to make this project come together!"

Photo credit: Greg McKinnon

Chandu Thota

Chandu Thota works as a Technical Lead for a Chicago based Channel Management Software Company. He has published several articles related to .NET and also founded an online .NET XML Web Services portal http://www.esynaps.com. He is also a co-author of the book "Understanding the .NET Framework (WROX Press)".

During his time off, Chandu likes to relax by listening to music, especially the Beatles and enjoying Spanish Tapas in Chicago's Cafe Iberico.

I would like to dedicate my work to the Divine Lord Venkateswara.

Jonathan Walsh

Jonathon Walsh is Chief Technology Officer with Management Information Disciplines, Inc., a software solutions provider headquartered in Indianapolis, Indiana. Jonathon has worked in the information technology industry for more than 8 years in varying capacities, but mostly as a consultant. His speciality is rapid development of enterprise-class solutions using Microsoft technologies.

Jonathon graduated as an Alfred University Scholar from Alfred University with a Bachelor of Science in Business Administration, majoring in Management Information Systems with minors in Computer Science and Economics. He has worked at several companies ranging from those in the Fortune 500 to small consulting companies. As a consultant, he has worked on some of the largest applications in the world and now helps organizations to understand, re-tool with, and use .NET to build solutions. Jonathon can be reached at jwalsh@midtechnologies.com.

Jonathon was a contributing author on *Visual Basic.NET and SQL Server 2000: Building and Effective Data Layer* (Wrox Press, ISBN: 1861007051) and was the Technical Editor for *MSDE Bible* (IDG Books, ISBN: 0764546813).

To my wife Lisa, my son Mason, and my daughter Madison, thank you for enduring the long hours and unyielding support with this and all my other endeavors. To Professor Frank G. Duserick, thank you for introducing me to the IT industry and for your unwavering patience. Finally, a special thank you to my parents, Larry and Peggy, who have always supported me no matter what.

Karli Watson

Karli Watson is an in-house author for Wrox Press with a penchant for multicolored clothing. He started out with the intention of becoming a world famous nanotechnologist, so perhaps one day you might recognize his name as he receives a Nobel Prize. For now, though, Karli's computing interests include all things mobile, and upcoming technologies such as C#. He can often be found preaching about these technologies at conferences, as well as after hours in drinking establishments. Karli is also a snowboarding enthusiast, and wishes he had a cat.

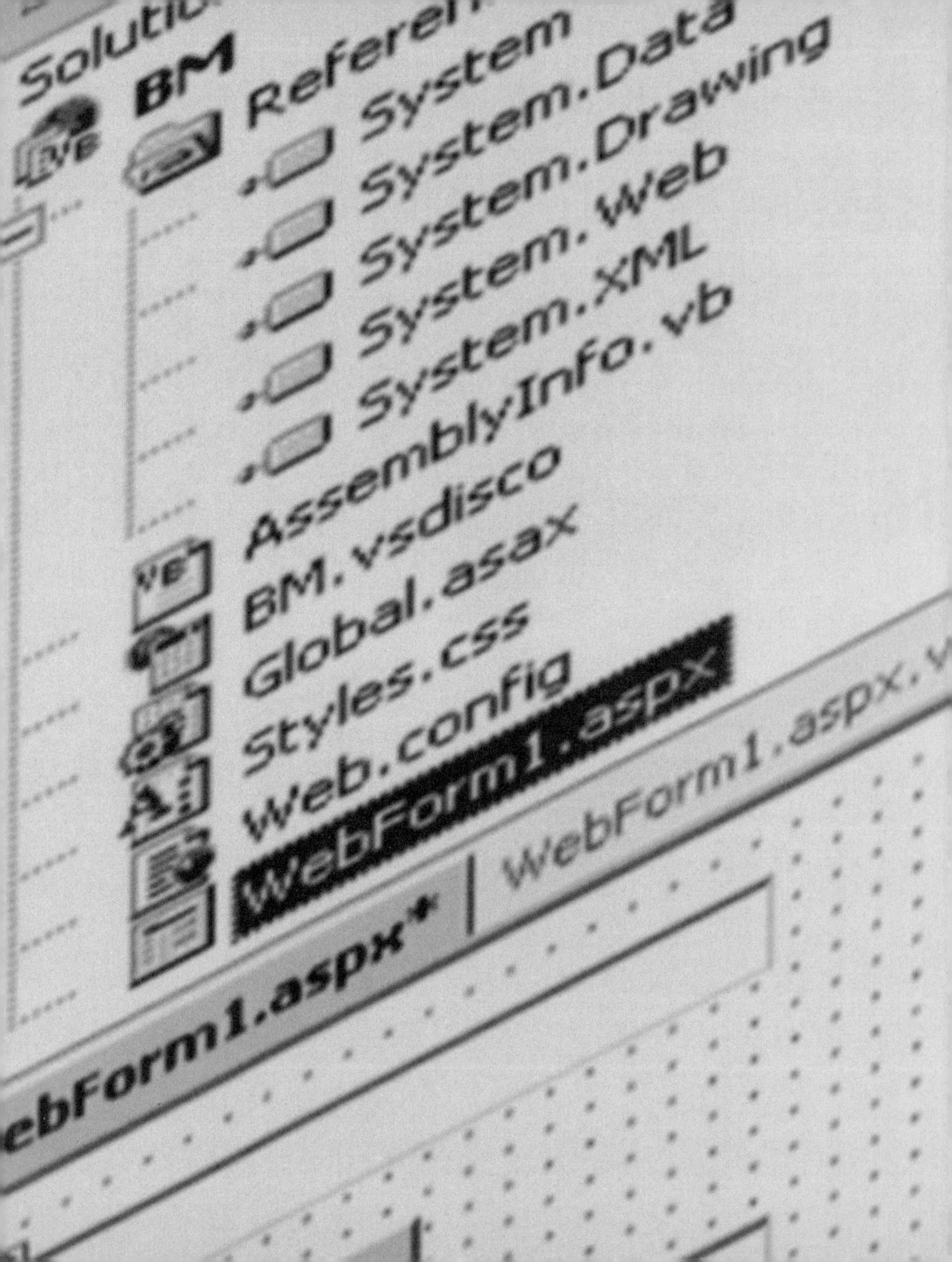

Solution
BM
Reference
System
System.Data
System.Drawing
System.Web
System.XML
AssemblyInfo.vb
BM.vsdisco
Global.asax
Styles.css
Web.config
WebForm1.aspx
WebForm1.aspx.v
WebForm1.aspx* WebForm1.v
ebForm1.aspx*

Table of Contents

Table of Contents

Table of Contents

Table of Contents

Solutio
BM
VB

References
System
System.Data
System.Drawing
System.Web
System.XML

AssemblyInfo.vb
Assembly
BM.vsdisco
Global.asax
Styles.css
Web.config
WebForm1.aspx

ebForm1.aspx*   WebForm1.aspx.v
WebForm1.aspx.v

Introduction

Do you want to know how you can use ASP.NET to build a modular Intranet? An intranet that could be used to share information within a small or medium sized organization? Well, congratulations, you've come to the right place!

Microsoft provides sample architecture for this sort of portal application, available at www.IBuySpy.com. Since they encourage developers to use this as a starting point for their own applications, we decided to take advantage of the functionality it offers. We will be taking this example and extending it to suit our needs, learning some valuable lessons in code reuse along the way.

Just as we used the IBuySpy example as the starting point for our Intranet, readers are encouraged to use the code in this book in their own applications - the modules we have created will slot into any implementation of the IBuySpy architecture, and let's be honest – no-one wants to re-invent the wheel, right?

What This Book Covers

The book starts by discussing general issues of Intranet development:

❑ **Chapter 1** looks at why developing Intranet sites is different from building sites for the Internet. There are some considerations that need to be addressed in order for Intranet projects to be successful.

The next three chapters look at the IBuySpy Architecture.

- ❑ **Chapter 2** provides a thorough explanation of the architecture and what it provides. It also explains why we decided to use the existing architecture rather than starting from scratch.

- ❑ **Chapter 3** shows how we can customize the IBuySpy example for our own purposes, creating our own Intranet site.

- ❑ **Chapter 4** discusses the importance of security in the Intranet, explains how security features are implemented in the IBuySpy architecture, and shows how to use two different types of authentication.

We then move on to discuss the modules that provide the actual content and functionality of our Intranet. We can use some of the IBuySpy modules as they are but others need some adjustment to fit our needs. The next two chapters show how to start with existing IBuySpy modules and make improvements and extensions.

- ❑ **Chapter 5** takes us on a walkthrough of the IBuySpy discussions module, showing some improvements that we can make along the way.

- ❑ **Chapter 6** starts with the IBuySpy events module and adds additional functionality to create our own version of the module.

Some of the modules we require for our Intranet differ sufficiently from any of the existing modules that our best route is to start from scratch. The remaining chapters of the book cover how we built these modules.

- ❑ **Chapter 7** looks at how we can build a content management system that allows users of the intranet to add information to be shared with other users

- ❑ **Chapter 8** covers document management - uploading existing documents such as Word files or Excel spreadsheets to the Intranet to be shared.

- ❑ **Chapter 9** describes a Human Resources Information System that stores information about company employees.

Data access is important to all of the modules that we built. It was important to use consistent data access techniques in the code that we wrote, so we created a common data access class to abstract database access.

- ❑ **Appendix A** discusses the common data access class

What You Need to Use This Book

To run the samples in this book, you will need:

❑ A suitable operating system: Windows 2000 (Professional, Server or Advanced Server edition) with Service Pack 2, or Windows XP Professional Edition.

❑ The .NET Framework SDK.

❑ Most of the examples in this book require either a SQL Server or MSDE database server.

Some of the examples in this book are developed using the Visual Studio .NET IDE, and for these, it is recommended that you have the VS.NET IDE installed, although it is not absolutely necessary.

We recommend that you also download the complete source code for the examples in this book, from http://www.wrox.com (see the *Customer Support and Feedback* section below).

Conventions

We have used a number of different styles of text and layout in the book to help differentiate between the different kinds of information. Here are examples of the styles we use and an explanation of what they mean:

Bullets appear indented, with each new bullet marked as follows:

❑ **Important Words** are in a bold type font

❑ Words that appear on the screen in menus like the File or Window are in a similar font to the one that you see on screen

❑ Keys that you press on the keyboard, like *Ctrl* and *Enter*, are in italics

Code has several fonts. If it's a word that we're talking about in the text, for example, when discussing the if...else loop, it's in this font. If it's a block of code that you can type in as a program and run, then it's also in a gray box:

```
public static void Main()
{
    AFunc(1,2,"abc");
}
```

Sometimes you'll see code in a mixture of styles, like this:

```
// If we haven't reached the end, return true, otherwise
// set the position to invalid, and return false.
pos++;
if (pos < 4)
    return true;
else {
    pos = -1;
    return false;
}
```

The code with a white background is code we've already looked at and that we don't wish to examine further.

Advice, hints, and background information come in an italicized, indented font like this.

> **Important pieces of information come in boxes like this.**

We demonstrate the syntactical usage of methods, properties (and so on) using the following format:

```
Regsvcs BookDistributor.dll [COM+AppName] [TypeLibrary.tbl]
```

Here, italicized parts indicate object references, variables, or parameter values to be inserted; the square brackes indicate optional parameters.

Style Conventions

We have used certain layout and font styles in this book that are designed to help you to differentiate between the different kinds of information. Here are examples of the styles that are used, with an explanation of what they mean.

As you'd expect, we present code in two different ways: in-line code and displayed code. When we need to mention keywords and other coding specifics within the text (for example, in discussion relating to an if...else construct or the GDI+ Graphics class) we use the single-width font as shown in this sentence. If we want to show a more substantial block of code, then we display it like this:

```
private void Form1_Paint(object sender,
                         System.Windows.Forms.PaintEventArgs e)
{
    Graphics g = e.Graphics;
    g.FillRectangle(Brushes.White, this.ClientRectangle);
}
```

Sometimes, you will see code in a mixture of gray and white backgrounds, like this:

```
private void Form1_Paint(object sender,
                         System.Windows.Forms.PaintEventArgs e)
{
    Graphics g = e.Graphics;
    g.FillRectangle(Brushes.White, this.ClientRectangle);
    g.DrawRectangle(Pens.Black, 10, 10, 50, 40);
}
```

In cases like this, we use the gray shading to draw attention to a particular section of the code – perhaps because it is new code, or it is particularly important to this part of the discussion. We also use this style to show output that is displayed in the console window.

Advice, hints, and background information comes in an indented, italicized font like this.

> **Important pieces of information (that you really shouldn't ignore) come in boxes like this!**

Bulleted lists appear indented, with each new bullet marked as follows:

- ❑ **Important Words** are in a bold type font.
- ❑ Words that appear on the screen, or in menus like the File or Window, are in a similar font to the one you would see on a Windows desktop.
- ❑ Keys that you press on the keyboard like *Ctrl* and *Enter* are in italics.

Customer Support and Feedback

We value feedback from our readers, and we want to know what you think about this book: what you liked, what you didn't like, and what you think we can do better next time. You can send us your comments, either by returning the reply card in the back of the book, or by e-mail to feedback@wrox.com. Please be sure to mention the book's ISBN and title in your message.

Source Code and Updates

As you work through the examples in this book, you may choose either to type in all the code by hand, or to use the source code that accompanies the book. Many readers prefer the former, because it's a good way to get familiar with the coding techniques that are being used.

Whether you want to type the code in or not, it's useful to have a copy of the source code handy. If you like to type in the code, you can use our source code to check the results you should be getting – they should be your first stop if you think you might have typed in an error. By contrast, if you don't like typing, then you'll definitely need to download the source code from our web site! Either way, the source code will help you with updates and debugging.

Therefore all the source code used in this book is available for download at http://www.wrox.com. Once you've logged on to the web site, simply locate the title (either through our Search facility or by using one of the title lists). Then click on the Download Code link on the book's detail page and you can obtain all the source code.

The files that are available for download from our site have been archived using WinZip. When you have saved the attachments to a folder on your hard drive, you need to extract the files using a de-compression program such as WinZip or PKUnzip. When you extract the files, the code is usually extracted into chapter folders. When you start the extraction process, ensure that you've selected the Use folder names under Extract to options (or their equivalents).

Errata

We have made every effort to make sure that there are no errors in the text or in the code. However, no one is perfect and mistakes do occur. If you find an error in this book, like a spelling mistake or a faulty piece of code, we would be very grateful to hear about it. By sending in errata, you may save another reader hours of frustration, and of course, you will be helping us provide even higher quality information. Simply e-mail the information to support@wrox.com; we'll check the information, and (if appropriate) we'll post a message to the errata pages, and use it in subsequent editions of the book.

To find errata on the web site, log on to http://www.wrox.com/, and simply locate the title through our Search facility or title list. Then, on the book details page, click on the Book Errata link. On this page you will be able to view all the errata that has been submitted and checked through by editorial. You will also be able to click the Submit Errata link to notify us of any errata that you may have found.

Technical Support

If you would like to make a direct query about a problem in the book, you need to e-mail support@wrox.com. A typical e-mail should include the following things:

❑   In the Subject field, tell us the **book name**, the **last four digits of the ISBN** (7493 for this book), and the **page number** of the problem.

❑   In the body of the message, tell use your **name**, **contact information**, and the **problem**.

We *won't* send you junk mail. We need these details to save your time and ours. When you send an e-mail message, it will go through the following chain of support:

1. **Customer Support** – Your message is delivered to one of our customer support staff – they're the first people to read it. They have files on most frequently asked questions and will answer anything general about the book or the web site immediately.

2. **Editorial** – Deeper queries are forwarded to the technical editor responsible for the book. They have experience with the programming language or particular product, and are able to answer detailed technical questions on the subject. Once an issue has been resolved, the editor can post the errata to the web site.

3. **The Authors** – Finally, in the unlikely event that the editor cannot answer your problem, he or she will forward the request to the author. We do try to protect the author from any distractions to their writing; however, we are quite happy to forward specific requests to them. All Wrox authors help with the support on their books. They will mail the customer and the editor with their response, and again all readers should benefit.

> Note that the Wrox support process can only offer support to issues that are directly pertinent to the content of our published title. Support for questions that fall outside the scope of normal book support is provided via the community lists of our http://p2p.wrox.com/ forum.

p2p.wrox.com

For author and peer discussion join, the **P2P mailing lists**. Our unique system provides **programmer to programmer**™ contact on mailing lists, forums, and newsgroups, all *in addition* to our one-to-one e-mail support system. Be confident that your query is being examined by the many Wrox authors, and other industry experts, who are present on our mailing lists. At p2p.wrox.com you will find a number of different lists that will help you, not only while you read this book, but also as you develop your own applications.

To subscribe to a mailing list just follow these steps:

1. Go to http://p2p.wrox.com/ and choose the appropriate category from the left menu bar.

2. Click on the mailing list you wish to join.

3. Follow the instructions to subscribe and fill in your e-mail address and password.

4. Reply to the confirmation e-mail you receive.

5. Use the subscription manager to join more lists and set your mail preferences.

Soluti...
BM
Refere...
System.Data
System.Drawing
System.Web
System.XML
System
AssemblyInfo.vb
BM.vsdisco
Global.asax
Styles.css
Web.config
WebForm1.aspx

WebForm1.aspx.v

ebForm1.aspx* | WebForm

1

Intranet Concepts

In this chapter we will learn about concepts surrounding intranets. We show how intranets came to be and how businesses can leverage intranets to their benefit. We will specifically explore the following topics:

- ❏ A brief history of the intranet
- ❏ Common issues when building intranets
- ❏ Common features of intranets

Finally, we will summarize what we covered before moving on to the next chapter.

What Do We Mean By 'Intranet'?

This book deals with building and using an Intranet site that would be useful to a small business (or a department of a larger organization). Before we can build and use one, it will be useful to define what we mean by an Intranet.

Sometimes, the word Intranet is used to refer to a network used by an organization that is secured so that only members of the organization can access it. At other times, Intranet is used to refer to a private web site available only to authorized users. We will be using the word in the second sense in this book. The site will we build might be available only on a private network or it may be accessed over the internet. Either way, the important thing is that it is designed only for the use of specific users.

In recent years, companies have found value in providing limited access to some of their intranet applications to trading partners, clients, and other organizations they are working with. These types of sites are called Extranets. They allow users from other organizations access to some of the providing company's Intranet applications. The Intranet we will build in this book will not be aimed at providing an extranet but it would be easy to adapt it in that direction.

Intranets - A Quick History

When Timothy Berners-Lee first conceived (Cira1990) the Hypertext Markup Language and Hypertext Transport Protocol (better known as HTML and HTTP, respectively) it is doubtful he could have predicted the magnitude of its effect. From that day to this, the technology has evolved from a simple way to track notes to what we now call the World Wide Web, or simply the Web. It did not take long for companies to begin using Web-based technologies as a new communications channel to customers. Initially, web sites tended to be what is called "brochure ware". That is, content was almost entirely static and in many instances electronically replicated company brochures and catalogs.

As with all things, the Web evolved over time in form and function. One of the first major innovations was the introduction of the dynamic content. Dynamic content allowed organizations to automate their product catalogs, take customer orders online, etc. The second major innovation was when companies began using HTML based applications internally. Up until then, intranets were composed of file sharing and, in some cases, client - server applications based on custom solutions.

Intranets followed a similar evolution as their external brethren. The first intranets were primarily static, providing employees such basic information as phone lists, company policies, and forms that could be replicated electronically and printed out. As businesses started to realize gains from rudimentary technologies, more and more advanced technologies were incorporated until we have present day intranets. Today's applications are interactive - allowing users to add information as well as view it.

The Role Of The Intranet

Today's intranets can play a number of roles within an organization:

- ❑ Centralization of data or information storage
- ❑ Decentralization of information authoring and ownership
- ❑ Access to information
- ❑ Facilitate communication

It is important to note that all the roles seek to achieve an overarching goal of improving the management of an organization's data and information.

Now, let's explore each role in more detail.

Centralization of Information

The first role of an intranet is to provide a centralized location of information and data storage. For small organizations this can be one physical and logical location. However, with large, multi-national companies the centralization happens across several physical locations but still has one logical location. This means that, although the storage of the data is physically separated, the information appears to users to be stored together. Information that is stored in the same logical location can more easily be harvested and aggregated.

Consider a scenario where a company has several offices spread across the country. Senior managers want to make informed decisions based on data from the offices. If each office has its own information repository, it takes significant time to identify, gather, and ship that data to the decision makers. However, if the information is in one repository, the information can be harvested in near real time and the decision is made. By reducing the time to gather the information and make a decision the company reduces the cost of making that decision.

Decentralization of Information Ownership

A related concept of centralization is the decentralization of information ownership. What we mean by this, is that although the information may be physically stored in a central place, the owners (including authors and even end users) can be physically dispersed. In other words, though a system or application may be served from one single location, those responsible for the information can be in several other locations. By doing this, those who are most intimate with the information or data can take operational ownership for it.

Access to Information

The second role of an intranet is to provide access to information. More specifically, intranets help to deliver the appropriate information to the appropriate people. This provides value to a business in that, if the right people are getting the right information in a timely manner, the better they are able to do their jobs. However, the opposite is also true. If an employee cannot find or have access to information they need, their productivity suffers.

Intranets are also being used to display data from legacy systems along side or incorporated with data from newer systems. This process can be invisible to the users themselves as they use only one interface to access the information they require.

Access to information tends to be the stickiest of issues when designing an intranet. Not all people require access to all the company's information, and in most cases, no one in the company should be able to access everything. For instance, human resources information should be accessible only to the human resources staff and very few others. There could be real workplace issues if personnel records, salary information, and reviews became public knowledge.

Communication

An intranet provides a business with the ability to communicate information en masse to its staff. For example, suppose a manager wants to send subordinates an announcement. The announcement could be posted on the intranet where all those who need to see it can access it. Another example of this is using intranets to facilitate communication between peers or teams. An intranet site can be used for hashing out ideas, a document repository, managing deadlines, etc. Using intranets tends to be more cost-effective than many other means. You can spread your message to your entire company without straining an overworked e-mail server.

Because of the increased communications afforded by intranets, designers and implementers must be cognizant of something called information overload. Information overload occurs when users get so much information and data they cannot sort through it to find the data they need.

For example, imagine yourself as the owner of a manufacturing company with several factories. As the owner, you would be concerning yourself with the aggregate business functions, talking to partners, and trying to sell more business. Now, suppose you wanted to look at productivity metrics for your company. If you have to cull through the information that each of the plant managers or manufacturing line managers use, it would take you a very long time to find the information you need to be effective. But, suppose you had the information aggregated for all the plants, you now have the information you need to make effective decisions.

An intranet can help to fight information overload by aggregating information and allowing users to find what they want, when they want it. It's much better to have information on demand than to receive hundreds of emails every day that must be digested and filed away.

Building An Intranet With ASP.NET

As intranets become increasingly integrated with companies' mission-critical operations, it is important to choose a technology that can enable intranet developers to create them quickly and effectively. There are lots of reasons why we chose ASP.NET for our intranet, but here are the main ones:

- ❑   Rapid development
- ❑   Control based approach
- ❑   Availability of a portal architecture

Rapid development is an issue because intranet projects often need to show real results fast. Fortunately, ASP.NET allows advanced functionality to be built very quickly indeed, especially when combined with Visual Studio .NET.

We wanted to use a **control based approach** because it is important that the intranet can be built in a modular fashion, allowing multiple developers to work on it both concurrently and at different times in the lifecycle of the intranet. ASP.NET server controls and user controls provide a well-defined way to create reusable and interoperable modules.

The final thing that made our decision was the fact that Microsoft provides the **IBuySpy portal architecture**, an example intranet-style site that can be freely used and adapted. This would give our development a head start. We will be looking at this architecture and what it provides for us in the next few chapters.

Differences Between Intranet and Internet Development

There are some important differences between developing public web sites and developing intranet sites. We'll briefly discuss these in order to set the scene for some of the decisions we will be making in the rest of the book.

Control of Browser Usage

One of the great things about creating an intranet is that the development team can often focus on building functionality for only one web-browser and not have to worry about the entire universe of available browsers. The reason for this is that most organizations have standardized on a single browser. This standardization translates into dollars in that developing for a single browser takes less time than developing for many.

Security

As with internet sites, intranet sites must also be secure. The difference between them is that an intranet's security focus is on allowing the appropriate people the appropriate access while internet sites have to deal with authentication of users that are unknown to the organization.

Intranets are at far less risk of malicious attack from outside than Internet sites because they are typically secured behind a company's firewall and have a known list of users. For users to connect to an intranet they must first connect to the network via VPN or similar technology and only then can access their intranet applications. This does not mean that security is not a priority - while the intranet has more layers of protection around it, the consequences of it being compromised are potentially very large. An intranet may contain sensitive information about the organization or may be critical to day-to-day operations.

Usability and Presentation

Given the nature of intranets, in that they are employee facing and not client facing, they typically have less graphics and artwork than an Internet site. This reduced amount of "branding" doesn't mean that less work should be done on the application's usability (usability can be thought of as ergonomics for web sites), but simply that a plainer, more functional interface can be used. Indeed, because the intranet will be a core source of information for employees during their day-to-day jobs, usability improvements can lead to real productivity gains.

Contact with Users

Users of an intranet application are known and can be reached, as they are part of the organization. This makes the chore of designing an effective intranet application easier because the designers can speak to all or most of the people using it. Internet site designs are based on focus groups, market research, and, in some cases, the whim of the designers.

Another way that contact with users helps to build an effective intranet application is that feedback can be easily culled from the user community with a fair degree of confidence in its accuracy and efficacy-whereas Internet sites have to sort through feedback (if there is any) to determine what needs to be changed.

It's Harder To See Examples of Intranets

Given the nature of intranets, it is difficult to talk about specific examples of what works and what doesn't. The primary reason for this is that intranets are proprietary and companies do not usually want to give out any possible competitive advantages that come from using their applications. This differs considerably from Internet sites where these sites are in the public domain and the good and bad features can be pointed out quite easily.

Challenges Of Intranet Development

As with any project, there will be problems during the creation of an intranet. We will discuss some of the more unique challenges associated with these projects and some of the common problems as they pertain to intranets.

Standards & Requirements Management

When a company begins to adopt intranets, one of the toughest issues to manage is the existence of "rogue" groups. Rogue groups are those that either develop their applications in a vacuum because they are not aware of any corporate standards or they are aware of the standards and they simply choose to ignore them. No matter which situation is the case, the end result is still the same. That end result being an application that does not look or perform in the same way as any of the others in the company. This becomes problematic because eventually your company ends up loosing money.

Users will become accustomed to a consistent look and feel. After the initial deployment of the intranet, those users will become pretty adept at navigating it to find and provide the information required for their daily tasks. If a rogue application is introduced with a different look and navigation scheme, on the users must learn a new system, which costs time.

A bigger problem with rogue groups is when they use a different technology than that used by the rest of the organization. The end result is typically an application that does not communicate with the rest of the organization's applications, or an 'information silo'. The information and data contained in these applications cannot be easily harvested or aggregated by the rest of the company's systems without special ad-hoc processes being created when the need arises. These processes will require some kind of staff (one person or many) to maintain and trouble-shoot as problems occur. This kind of resource expenditure can become very costly, especially when the application and processes are created with an obscure or non-mainstream technology.

The formation of an oversight group can help contain these issues as well as help in setting scope for the project. This group should be responsible for enforcing a common look and feel throughout the intranet site (easily achieved using Cascading Style Sheets) and standardizing on a common set of technologies used to build the site.

As mentioned before, this group should manage the scope and functionality of any current intranet development efforts to avoid a situation where conflicting requirements arise. Imagine the dilemma you might have when two Vice Presidents both require something and that those things are mutually exclusive. Whose "something" do you incorporate and whose do you leave behind? What makes it even more challenging is when the project manager decides to do both, even though they are mutually exclusive.

What is even more challenging than the previous situation is when you are attempting to gather business requirements and find that different groups perform the same task in different ways. In almost all these situations, the development team will not be able discern which method, if any, is the correct way of performing the task. These two situations can be easily remedied by an oversight group. It will be up to them to decide which functionality is in and the manner in which that functionality should be implemented.

Never Really Done

As a company develops an intranet, at some point the realization sets in that an intranet is nothing more than a collection of internal web sites, each with a specific task, and with a unified look and feel. After this realization sets in, the next question is, "When will we be done?" The short answer is that you will never be done.

A somewhat longer answer is that as your business evolves and technology evolves, you will continue to find valuable ways to apply that technology to your company's processes. This answer creates an interesting dilemma for those creating the applications. The issue centers on balancing the evolution of the intranet applications and keeping them stable. By 'stable', We mean an application that has been deployed, users have been using it, and your company is deriving value from it.

If your intranet is in a constant state of flux it is doubtful much value will be derived from it. As the intranet changes, users must re-acclimate to the new or changed applications, which can take significant time. Granted, adding new features doesn't usually have the same impact as modifying an existing feature, but is still measurable and should be taken into account.

However, if changes are not considered once in a while your company may forego an opportunity to further enhance its business processes and enhance value. For example, suppose you have an intranet package that allows you to manage projects. This application is deployed to the user community and is well received. Some time goes by and you find that a newer project management application is available with many new workflow features. This promises to be a great improvement. If you do not make the change to your intranet, you will never realize any of the gains made by the enhanced features.

In practice, this balance is achieved through breaking up an intranet into discreet tasks and projects. As each task or project is completed, a few months pass before the next iteration of that particular task or project is reexamined for enhancements and efficacy.

Changing Requirements

A common problem that faces all software development projects, not just intranet development, is that the requirements for the application continually change. Changing requirements can be very costly to the development team because of "false starts", unexpected code changes, and the like.

An offshoot of changing requirements is dreaded "scope creep". Scope creep occurs when minimal functionality is added to the project after the project has been defined, designed, and (in most cases) programming is in progress. Typically, this is not just one change, but several changes that alone do not seem to be major adjustments, but, taken as a whole require significant time and resources to build in. This is especially a problem for intranet projects because close contact with the users of the system can lead to many suggestions for improvements.

The only way to mitigate these issues is to have a well-defined development process and strong project manager. The development process should include phases for defining the requirements, building the technical designs, coding the application, and testing the application. A strong project manager is desirable so that changing requirements can be resolved quickly and scope creep be nipped in the bud early.

Requirements For A Good Intranet

We will be looking later at types of functionality that intranets will often contain. First, we should look at some overall features that will help make an intranet successful.

The areas we will look at are:

- ❑ Solid architecture
- ❑ Extensibility
- ❑ Manageability
- ❑ Security

Solid Architecture

Any good intranet will start with a good architecture. By this we mean the manner in which pieces of the site will interact with each other. A good architecture should provide for a stable application that performs well under everyday user load. Moreover, a good architecture will take into account how the site can be extended, managed, and secured.

Extensibility

In almost any case, once the initial effort to create the intranet has been completed, there will be requests to enhance, add, or otherwise alter functionality. By adding functionality we are extending the site. The best way to provide for this is by using a modular approach.

A modular system is one where all pieces of functionality are developed in discrete units. This allows for functionality to be altered, added, or removed without affecting the rest of the site. This approach also allows for the reuse of common functionality across the site.

Manageability

An intranet application should be easy to manage, not only by the developers but also by the end users. These users will typically have operational responsibility for it. The end users should be able to create, modify, and remove content easily from the site. This can be done using automated controls, such as expiration dates, or manually by directly editing the content. Remember, the goal is to provide value to the organization, not create an administrative nightmare.

Security

Finally, the site must have a well thought out security infrastructure in place. This means not only securing from the outside world but also providing a flexible enough security scheme that the appropriate people can get and are allowed to see the appropriate information (see the *Information Access* section earlier in this chapter).

Common Intranet Features

Now that we have spent some time understanding what an intranet is and what general challenges and features are involved in building one, lets move on to some common functionality that intranets offer. The features discussed below are by no means an exhaustive list, but certainly will give you a sense of the capabilities of an intranet.

Content Management

Content management is exactly like it sounds: it is the method by which content is managed in the intranet. Good content management allows the users to create content in a tightly controlled format. Users can add words, links to other pages, and graphics but this is done within predefined templates.

It also allows the intranet owners to define a workflow of building, checking, and publishing content. This is done mainly to avoid errors and to provide a method of checks-and-balances. In addition to managing the publication process, workflow also allows the users to decide when content will be published and for how long.

We will be building a content management module in Chapter 7.

Document Management

The ability to disseminate existing documents to the people in your organization is a natural fit for an intranet application and may have arguably been one of the first features. In the early days, end users could have downloaded documents, but it wasn't until later that users could effectively upload documents.

A good document management system allows the users to upload and download existing documents and provide some mechanism of managing different versions of that document. More advanced document management systems allow users to give permissions to other users to view or update their documents.

We will look at document management in more detail in Chapter 8.

Project Management

Another natural function of an intranet is providing project management. These applications give project team members a mechanism to communicate with each other. This communication could be the propagation of documents or take the form of message boards.

In addition to information dissemination, project management systems are used on for time entry and to track team members' progress. For teams that are geographically dispersed, these types of systems are fast becoming necessary rather than an attractive alternative to traditional mechanisms.

Moreover, the system can allow clients to access certain types of content such as client approved documents, the project finance, and similar information that would normally have be done via mail or fax machine.

Human Resources Information System

A human resources information system (or HRIS) allows a company to move much of their human resources functions from paper to electronic form. In this way a company can realize cost savings in that it no longer needs to print off forms that its professionals need. It also helps to automate tasks that were manually accomplished before.

An example of this is one that was mentioned earlier: the time entry functionality. Not only does the time entry functionality allow users to enter in the time against projects, but also track vacation days and holidays. Prior to this function being electronic, if a user wanted to take a vacation they would typically submit a vacation request to their manager who would then submit it to the HR staff. The HR staff would have to go through their records to see if the person making the request had enough vacation time to grant the request or not.

Now, the user can see how much vacation time they have used and make the appropriate request electronically. This request can then be acted upon by both the human resources department and the user's manager in parallel.

Another possible function of these systems is managing an employee's benefits. Again, the idea is to move a primarily paper-based system to electronic form in order to increase efficiency and reduce cost. Many companies now provide their employees electronic access to manage items such as their 401(k), direct deposit, and medical insurance.

One thing to keep in mind with these systems is that they are a storage area for personnel information and must be dealt with in confidence. For this reason, you will want to be sure that you have a reliable security architecture to keep prying eyes away from the information that they should not be looking at. We touch more on security in Chapter 4.

Shared Calendar

Shared calendars help to reduce confusion and aid in planning. Many companies employ several calendars for a variety of functions. They allow members of the organization to record when they are taking time off so that others can make appropriate plans. Another type of calendar is one used to manage the use of resources.

How often have you been on your way to a meeting and find another group in the conference room you were going to use? With a shared calendar you can reserve or schedule a conference room and once that reservation has been confirmed, others can now see that it is reserved and make alternative arrangements. Though the actual cost savings from such functionality is somewhat minimal, but it does provide significant impact in that it helps to reduce frustration and possible embarrassment.

We will be looking at shared calendar functionality in Chapter 6.

Contact Management

In the same vein as shared calendars are systems that provide contact management. A contact is a person or entity that you communicate with in your daily business activities. Efficiency is gained when everyone in an organization has access to the same list. First, it provides a single source of information for the whole organization to use and reduces redundancy. Second, by having one list, the system can allow the management of who "owns" which contact and when the contact was last called on. Finally, a contact management system allows the company the most efficient way to keep its information current.

Live Chat

One of the newer facilities of intranets is the concept of live chat. Using either a special page or a special program, users may communicate with each other in real time rather than the lags associated with e-mail or forums. The more advanced chat tools allow a company to store the chats for queries later (sometimes called back chat).

Some chat tools allow for application sharing so that users can work on a single physical document at the same time from different locations. This technology works well with another feature of robust chat tools – that being live audio and video. At this point though, the tool isn't so much a chat tool in the proper sense, but more of an organizational telephone.

The Future Of Intranets

As intranets continue to become a facet of everyday corporate life and continue to evolve to meet more demanding needs, we can only guess at what the future holds. For instance, intranet based information can be easily disseminated to mobile devices. As these devices' capabilities grow, so too will their role within the corporate intranet. Think of a salesperson who can get real-time warehouse information from there cell phone to determine if a particular product is in stock while they are at the client's office.

Moreover, corporations are moving more of their critical applications to their intranets. Will there ever be a time when we can access all of the information we want, no matter where we are? This is by no means certain, but we are definitely heading in that direction.

Summary

In this chapter we discussed how intranets are simply internal web sites and how that evolution occurred. We saw that these internal web sites play four major roles, all of which revolve around being more efficient and having effective information management.

- ❑ Centralization of data or information storage
- ❑ Decentralization of information authoring and ownership
- ❑ Access to information
- ❑ Facilitate communication

We also looked at some of the common features and applications within an intranet.

As we move forward in this book, these concepts will be built upon with the end result being a functional intranet application that you could take to create your own intranet.

Solution
BM Referen...
System
System.Data
System.Drawing
System.Web
System.XML
AssemblyInfo.vb
Assembly...
BM.vsdisco
Global.asax
Styles.css
Web.config
WebForm1.aspx

WebForm1.aspx.v

WebForm1.aspx* | WebForm1.aspx.v

ebForm1.aspx*

2

The IBuySpy Portal Architecture

In this book, we'll be using the freely available IBuySpy Portal as a starting point for our intranet development. This choice needs justification - and that is what we will do in the first part of this chapter. We'll look at both why we are modifying an existing intranet application rather than creating our own, and why we choose the IBuySpy Portal in particular.

Once we have covered the basics, we'll continue to look in more depth at the IBuySpy Portal, starting with how to install it. Next, we'll take a tour of its features, with an eye on how it fits in with the objectives outlined in the previous chapter.

Moving on from this we'll take a more technical look at the IBuySpy Portal architecture, looking at the files and types it consists of, how they function and fit together, and general principles behind the site.

Finally, we'll take a brief look at how security is handled.

Why use an existing architecture?

In the last chapter, we looked at all the things we are likely to want from an intranet, and there were quite a few of them! However, if we were to design an intranet from scratch, many areas would require a lot of work to obtain even the most basic functionality. There are also many important challenges to overcome, such as deciding how to handle authentication and authorization, what other applications we require on our servers, and so on.

Much of this is solved instantly if we take an existing intranet's architecture as a starting point. If someone else has already worked out how to handle security issues, how to achieve effective data storage, and so on, then we can get up and running much quicker. This doesn't mean that we can just take any existing intranet, though, since some architectures may not fulfill enough of our requirements, or may be very difficult to customize and extend.

What we want, then, is a well-designed intranet architecture that solves problems without creating new ones – an intranet architecture that we can easily tailor to our needs.

What does the IBuySpy Portal Architecture provide?

The IBuySpy Portal architecture is one that makes the grade. As we will see in this and other chapters, it simplifies the creation of our intranet while providing an excellent foundation for adding our own features. It also offers one other crucial advantage - it is free to obtain and no restrictions are placed on our usage of the code it contains!

We'll look at the specific features that are obtained from the IBuySpy Portal later, but first here's a list of key points:

- ❑ It makes use of well-established database technology via SQL server or Microsoft Data Engine (MSDE) database access.

- ❑ It is simple (and free) to install, with no tiresome and time-consuming registration forms to complete.

- ❑ It is built in a modular way, with several useful modules (such as modules for authentication, forums, and news articles) already in place, and it's also extensible, so we can add more as required.

- ❑ It is 100% customizable to whatever corporate look and feel you need, with whatever extra functionality you can dream up.

The application architecture follows a traditional n-tier model, with functional separation of classes that deal with presentation, business logic, and data access. However, as with many ASP.NET applications, the business logic does overlap slightly with the presentation, since ASP.NET pages are capable of sophisticated processing without affecting performance.

All database access is achieved via stored procedures, which also improves performance. Stored procedures are SQL queries stored as part of the database, which may be parameterized to add versatility. Since they are part of the database, the database server can perform additional optimization for us, such as using built-in caching. In addition, security is improved by using this method, since we can restrict access to stored procedures only, thus preventing malicious users from executing potentially harmful SQL queries. The result of this, as we will see later, is that we end up with very simple data access components that for the most part simply act as an interface for the stored procedures in the database, via ADO.NET.

To get a better idea of what is provided you can either look at the online version of the portal at http://www.ibuyspyportal.com/ or install it on your server. Since we will spend the rest of the book modifying the code for this application you may as well go right ahead and install it now.

Installing the IBuySpy Portal Architecture

IBuySpy Portal can be obtained from http://www.asp.net/ibuyspy/downloads.aspx. This download page also contains files for another example application, IBuySpy Store, which is a starting point for Internet e-commerce applications. However, we're not interested in this application here.

Before we download the application (or, as it is referred to on the web page for downloading it, the Solution Kit) we should ensure that our server is equipped to deal with it. The most basic requirement here is having the .NET Framework installed. We also need access to either a SQL Server database, or the free (but trickier to administer - see note below) MSDE data engine. MSDE is installed as part of the ASP.NET **quickstart** applications that are part of the .NET Framework.

> *If you only have MSDE installed then many administration tasks may only be carried out using command line SQL queries. Here's a tip: get the Enterprise Manager application from the MSDN SQL Server evaluation download - it'll make your life a lot easier and isn't limited by the 120 day trial license that applies to the SQL Server database download itself!*

The IBuySpy Portal also requires an installation of the ASP.NET Mobile Internet Toolkit, a link to which appears on the web page mentioned above. In this book, we won't be looking at the mobile device access of intranets, but it is worth remembering that IBuySpy Portal has been designed with this functionality in mind, and you may want to conduct your own research into this area.

> *For more information on the Microsoft Mobile Internet Toolkit, see ASP.NET Mobile Controls: Tutorial Guide: Adaptive Web Content for Mobile Devices with the MMIT, by Wrox Press, ISBN: 1861005229*

There are four different versions of the download for IBuySpy Portal, two for the VB.NET version of the code and two for the C# version. In this book we're using VB.NET, so we can ignore the two C# versions. The difference between the two VB.NET versions is that one of them (the VS.NET version) is intended for Visual Studio .NET users while the other (the SDK version) isn't. There is no difference in functionality between these versions, only that the VS.NET version uses the 'codebehind' model for all ASP.NET files, where the VB.NET code is contained in separate .vb files rather than being included in .aspx and .ascx files, and includes solution files for loading straight into the VS.NET IDE. The choice of which version you use is entirely up to you depending on which code model you prefer (and on whether you own a copy of VS.NET!). I prefer the codebehind model, so the screenshots etc. in this chapter will reflect this, but don't feel left out if you go for the other version, it really makes very little difference.

Now, a word of caution! When you run the installer program for the IBuySpy Portal Developer Solution Kit (whichever version you choose), it will present a dialog that warns about the risk of installing a new version when an existing version of the portal is present (even if the installer is being run for the first time):

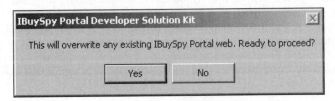

Modifications made to a previous installation can be lost if you ever run one of the four IBuySpy Portal installer programs at a later date. We'll come back to this point shortly, after we've seen what the installer program actually does.

The installer requires very little intervention - all we need to do is to select a folder to install to (the default, C:\PortalVBVS for the VS.NET version of the application, is fine) and a database instance to use to store the data used by the application. Since a new database will be added, we need the required database privileges to do this, although I won't go into details about this. Suffice to say that if you are logged in as Administrator, and are using a local SQL Server or MSDE instance you won't encounter any problems here.

After we select the database instance and click on configure it should only take a minute or two for everything to be set up for us. At this point, we can look at the installation log to ensure everything went smoothly - here's the one I ended up with (I've removed the date stamps for clarity):

```
[Checking system requirements]
[Pass] Detected the NetSDK version of MSDE.
[Pass] Determined SQL Server version (8.00.194).
[Pass] Detected .NET Framework.
[Pass] Detected Internet Information Server (IIS).
[Begin Sample Configuration]
[Pass] Created IIS virtual directory.: PortalVBVS
[Pass] Determined SQL Server version (8.00.194).
[Pass] Added ASPNET user to SQL Server.
[Pass] Executed SQL script.: PortalDB.sql
[Pass] Added aspnet user to database.: Portal
[Done]
```

The installer performs the following steps:

❑ It creates a new directory to hold the application (C:\PortalVBVS) and copies the portal files to it.

❑ It configures an IIS virtual directory pointing at a subdirectory of the directory created in the above step (C:\PortalVBVS\PortalVBVS), with the same name as this directory (PortalVBVS).

❑ It creates a new database in the selected database instance (called Portal) and populates it with data.

❑ It adds the user (local)\ASPNET to the database server and to the list of users with permission to access the newly created database (this is essential for ASP.NET applications since it is the account that they run under - the portal wouldn't be able to access the data without this step).

Now we can discuss what will happen if we rerun one of the installation programs at a later date. First, if we select the same directory to install to as before then files may be overwritten. Second, the database creation will fail. The result of this second problem is that the new installation will have access to modified data. Should we wish a completely new database to be installed we have to remove the existing database manually, or move it somewhere else if it contains data we wish to preserve. Unfortunately, no facility exists for specifying the database name to use during installation, which would solve this problem.

The root directory of the portal (C:\PortalVBVS) contains many of the files used during installation, including the SQL script used to generate the database, and the resulting log file. It also contains the End User License Agreement (EULA) for the portal code, and a directory with the files that are accessed via the IIS virtual directory for the portal, as mentioned above.

IBuySpy Portal Acclimatization

When you first open the IBuySpy Portal intranet site in a web browser, by either navigating to http://www.ibyspyportal.com/ or using your local copy at http://localhost/PortalVBVS/, you will be greeted with the following page:

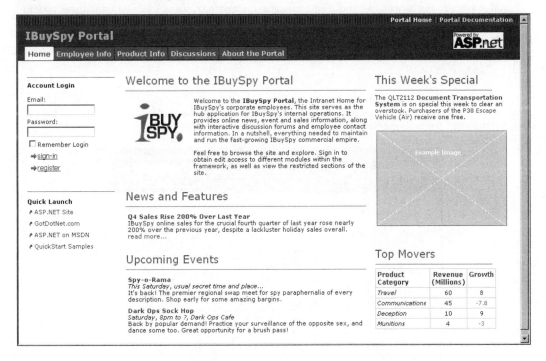

If you are using the online version then the Example Image frame on the right will contain an actual image - many of the bitmaps that make up the example application aren't included in the downloadable version to keep the size of the download to a respectable level. This doesn't affect the functionality at all.

This initial page illustrates much of the functionality of the portal. Starting from the top, we have a title bar containing a main heading, a collection of tabs, and a few other bits and pieces that don't concern us for now. The Home tab is currently selected, and the rest of the page makes up the Home page content.

The main body of the page is divided up into three columns - a large one in the middle and smaller ones on either side. Each of these columns contains content that is built up from individual modules, which may not be apparent at first since the modules are designed to use the same styles so they do seem to merge together in places. There are eight modules displayed on this page: two on the left (one for logging in and one for quick navigation), three in the middle (the welcome message, a news section, and an events section), and three on the right (the 'This week's Special' section, an image, and the 'Top Movers' section).

Logging In

The module on the top of the left column allows us to log on, or to create a new login. The IBuySpy Portal is initially configured to handle authentication in this way, using form-based authentication, although it is quite easy to switch to integrated Windows authentication if desired.

> *We'll look at this in a little more depth at the end of this chapter, before covering security issues thoroughly in Chapter 4.*

The initial installation comes with one existing user account called Guest with the e-mail address of Guest and the password of Guest. Users can add themselves to the intranet simply by clicking on the register link in the authentication module. Try this now:

When you click on the Register and Sign in Now link you'll be returned to the Home page with a few differences - the authentication module has disappeared, and the information at the top of the page has changed:

User information now appears, and a new Logoff link enables you to log off.

Once you are logged in you have access to more functionality, such as being able to contribute to discussions and so on, although the specific privileges granted is determined by an administrator. This granting of privileges is known as authorization (not to be confused with authentication, which is the act of verifying login information). In the IBuySpy Portal architecture, this is achieved by privileges based on groups, where a user may belong to any number of groups.

Initially, only one group is defined for us, a group called Admins whose members are intranet administrators. The user we start with, Guest, is a member of this group. If you log off your new Charles Darwin user and log on as Guest one effect of this is instantly visible:

A new tab has appeared: Admin. Through this tab, which is only available to users in the Admin group, we can perform administrative tasks, such as user account manipulation, and even complete reorganization of the intranet site.

It's not just administrators who can get this customized content; we can add any number of groups and tabs that only certain groups can see.

Exploring the Content

At this point, I'll ask you to put down this book and look around the default installation of the IBuySpy portal. Try to get a feel for the way things work - it's pretty much all self-explanatory. Explore the various tabs and the content on those tabs, add a discussion message or two, perhaps upload a document, and you'll find that the interface is intuitive and exciting. Don't fiddle around too much with the Admin tab for now - you may find yourself accidentally doing something you'll regret later!

When you're ready, come back and we'll take a closer look at how this application meets the objectives outlined in the last chapter.

Addressing our Objectives

In the last chapter, we outlined three broad objectives of an intranet site:

❑   Centralization of information

❑   Access to information

❑   Communication

The IBuySpy Portal certainly proves it's worth here. Information is centralized - document data is stored either in the portal database or through the web server virtual directories. Information is easy to access - the web interface and simple authentication exposes our data to all clients who can run a web browser, and we can expose some or all of the information over the wider Internet for remote access. Communication is made simple - the various modules that exist or can be added make it easy for staff to communicate in a variety of ways, from discussion groups, to articles, to shared documents.

We also pointed out several common features of intranets in the last chapter:

- ❑ Content management
- ❑ Document management
- ❑ Project management
- ❑ Forums
- ❑ Human Resources Information System
- ❑ Shared calendar
- ❑ Contact management

Several of these are already available with the existing modules (notably content and document management via the Admin tab, forums via the discussion group module, and contact via the contacts module). The portal architecture makes it possible to add all the rest, which is something we will be looking at in later chapters.

Corporate Identity

The IBuySpy Portal has a specific look and feel about it. This may not be exactly what you are looking for, but don't panic! In the next chapter, we'll see how we can completely customize the look and feel of the portal, using stylesheets and direct code modification. What is there now is purely a demonstration of what is possible, not a limitation on what you can do. The important point is that the backend functionality is solid, and you aren't likely to want to make too many changes to that.

Modules Supplied

The IBuySpy Portal architecture comes with ten modules, which form a starting point for our intranet development. The modules supplied are as follows:

Module Name	Module Description
Announcements	A list of text articles, showing a summary of the article and a read more link to get access to full text.
Contacts	A list of contacts.
Discussion	A discussion forum, divided into threads.
Documents	A list of documents, either uploaded to the server or linked to via URLs.

Module Name	Module Description
Events	A list of events, with date and location information as well as short descriptions.
Html/Text	A general purpose module for displaying HTML.
Image	A simple module for rendering an image.
Links	A list of hyperlinks.
QuickLinks	A list of hyperlinks rendered in a compact way.
Xml/Xsl	A module for displaying XML documents by transforming them with an XSL stylesheet.

These modules may be used several times in a single portal - a single page may even contain multiple instances of a single module. To achieve this, each module added to the portal is assigned a unique ID. This also enables multiple modules of the same type to store their data in the same database table, thus simplifying the data storage structure.

Tab Manipulation

The Admin tab allows administrators to manage the content of the IBuySpy Portal intranet by adding new tabs, deleting old ones, or modifying existing ones. Head to this tab now and edit the Employee Info tab by selecting it and clicking on the pencil icon shown below:

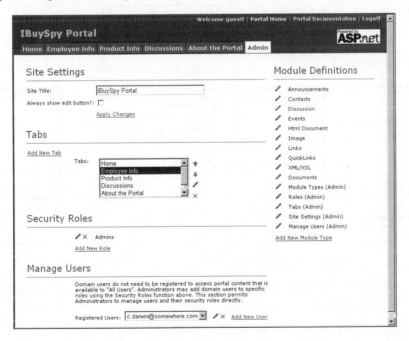

This takes us to a new screen that shows us tab properties as follows:

- ❏ The name of the tab
- ❏ What roles have access to the tab
- ❏ Whether the tab is shown to mobile browsers
- ❏ What name to use for the tab for mobile users
- ❏ What modules to show on the tab, along with their names and positions

The page also includes the facility to add new modules of a selected type, and edit module properties. If you select a module and click on the pencil icon, you'll be taken to a screen containing general module properties:

Module specific properties and module content can only be modified by subsequently navigating to the tab and editing the module via its own interface. The above module, Spy diary, is only editable by members of the Admin group.

Interestingly, no information is shown concerning the types of modules. Once a module is added the only way to glean this information with the default application code is to navigate to the tab containing the module directly and edit it. However, this information isn't crucial, as it's the functionality of modules that's important once they are added.

A Technical Look at the IBuySpy Portal Architecture

For the remainder of this chapter we will look in a little more depth at how the IBuySpy Portal architecture works, providing an insight into the customization techniques we will be using in the rest of the book.

First, a general overview. Users entering the intranet site are redirected by default.aspx to one of two other pages, DesktopDefault.aspx or MobileDefault.aspx. We'll concentrate on the former, as we're not looking in detail at the mobile aspect of this application in this book.

`DesktopDefault.aspx` is really a placeholder for the various modules that make up individual tabs in the application, which are in fact user controls stored in `.ascx` files. The authentication module, stored in `SignIn.ascx`, is displayed in all tabbed pages, but only if the user has yet to log in. Other modules are added depending on what tab is selected. `DesktopDefault.aspx` also contains one standard user control,- `DeskTopPortalBanner.ascx`, which is displayed at the top of the page. All these user controls are dynamically added to the page that the user sees when they request a given tab, that is, they are added to the content of `DesktopDefault.aspx` as this page is loaded.

Many of the `.ascx` files take their display information from data in the database, or use information in the database in some other way (such as authenticating login information). None of the `.ascx` files perform database access directly; instead they use data access classes stored in other `.vb` files to do this.

The general overview, then, looks like this:

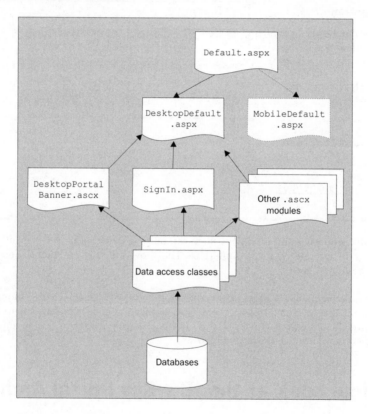

Database Structure

The content and arrangement of content within the IBuySpy Portal application is all stored in the portal database. In order to get to grips with what the code does we should look at this database to see what information it contains.

Table Name	Table Function
Announcements	Data used by Announcements modules.
Contacts	Data used by Contacts modules.
Discussion	Data used by Discussion modules.
Documents	Data used by Documents modules.
Events	Data used by Events modules.
HtmlText	Data used by Html/Text modules.
Links	Data used by Links and Quicklinks modules.
ModuleDefinitions	A list of the available modules, including a reference to the .ascx files that define them.
Modules	A list of what modules appear on what tabs, along with information about where they appear, what title to use, who can edit the module content, and so on.
ModuleSettings	Additional data for any modules that require it.
Portals	A list of the portals defined in the database (initially only one appears here - the default IBuySpy Portal).
Roles	The roles that users can be members of.
Tabs	The tabs that can be displayed in the portal, and which roles are allowed to view them.
UserRoles	A list of links associating users with roles.
Users	A list of users, with password and e-mail information.

The database also includes 66 stored procedures used by the data access objects in the application, for all functionality. This includes adding records, extracting records, and so on.

Initially, the sample portal content is configured as follows:

❑ The IBuySpy Portal is given an ID in the Portals table.

❑ A single role, Admin, is set up in the Roles table, and a single user, guest, is set up in the Users table. The guest user is set up as a member of the Admin role via an entry in the UserRoles table.

- ❏ The `ModuleDefinitions` table contains a list of the 15 modules: the ten sample modules listed earlier and five for administration.

- ❏ The `Tabs` table contains entries for each of the six tabs available to users.

- ❏ The `Modules` table contains information about all of the modules present on each of the six tabs in the `Tabs` table.

- ❏ The `ModuleSettings` table contains module-specific configurations.

- ❏ The remaining tables contain the data used by each module instance (remember that just one of these tables, `Announcements` say, contains data for all of the `Announcements` modules in the portal, identified by Module ID values).

All of the data in the database can be edited by hand if required, although there is nothing there that can't be modified using the tools on the **Admin** tab of the portal.

We shouldn't remove any of the tables themselves, but we might well add our own tables as we customize the portal.

Keeping Track of Things: the PortalSettings Class

The basic scheme described above centers on the fact that the `.ascx` user controls are added dynamically to a basic framework. In order for this to work in practice the user controls must be aware of certain information, such as the logged in user (if any). The `DesktopPortalBanner.ascx` control also needs to know what tabs to display, as well as which one is selected. Some other controls also have custom information that will be required when they render themselves.

To facilitate this, contextual information is stored whenever the portal receives an HTTP request. This information can then be accessed by any of the user controls, or other classes that make up the application. User information is stored in the standard `User` member of the `Context` object that is accessible by ASP.NET code, and other information is stored in an instance of a class called `PortalSettings`, which is defined as part of the application.

This information storage is carried out in the code for `global.asax`, which is the file that contains application, session, and request level event handlers. One event handler, `Application_AuthenticateRequest`, deals with authentication (as its name suggests!), and will be covered in more detail in Chapter 4. Another event handler, `Application_BeginRequest`, deals with creating a `PortalSettings` instance, placing it in the `Items` collection of the `Context` object for retrieval by whatever code requires it during request processing.

When an instance of the `PortalSettings` class is created, it extracts tab information from the database, including the names of the tabs, which user roles have access to each tab, and so on. It also uses information passed to it in its constructor to determine the currently selected tab (which is detected in `Application_BeginRequest` by looking at the `querystring` accompanying the web request - selecting a tab results in this information being sent to the server). Settings for individual modules are extracted from the database as and when required - individual modules can use the shared `PortalSettings.GetModuleSettings` method for this.

The code for `Application_BeginRequest` is as follows:

```
Sub Application_BeginRequest(ByVal sender As Object, ByVal e As EventArgs)

    Dim tabIndex As Integer = 0
    Dim tabId As Integer = 0

    ' Get TabIndex from querystring
    If Not (Request.Params("tabindex") Is Nothing) Then
        tabIndex = CInt(Request.Params("tabindex"))
    End If

    ' Get TabID from querystring
    If Not (Request.Params("tabid") Is Nothing) Then
        tabId = CInt(Request.Params("tabid"))
    End If

    Context.Items.Add("PortalSettings", New PortalSettings(tabIndex, tabId))

End Sub
```

Here you can see that the two `querystring` parameters `tabindex` and `tabid` (referring to the position and type of tab selected respectively) are extracted and passed to the `PortalSettings` constructor to initialize the object. The newly created object is stored as an item called `PortalSettings` in the `Context` object.

The `PortalSettings` class exposes the following public fields:

```
Public PortalId As Integer
Public PortalName As String
Public AlwaysShowEditButton As Boolean
Public DesktopTabs As New ArrayList()
Public MobileTabs As New ArrayList()
Public ActiveTab As New TabSettings()
```

Here `PortalId` and `PortalName` are taken from the `querystring` parameters, and the rest are extracted from the database. The global `AlwaysShowEditButton` field is used by many modules when they render, the `DesktopTabs` and `MobileTabs` fields are lists of properties of tabs that exist (including what roles they are available for, used when determining which tabs to display), and the `ActiveTab` field contains information about the currently selected tab.

`DesktopTabs` and `MobileTabs` are `ArrayList` fields that contain `TabStripDetails` instances. This simple class is as follows:

```
Public Class TabStripDetails

    Public TabId As Integer
    Public TabName As String
    Public TabOrder As Integer
    Public AuthorizedRoles As String

End Class
```

Each tab in the `Tabs` table is placed in an instance of this class, with fields as follows:

TabStripDetails Field Name	Description
TabId	The ID of the tab in the `Tabs` table.
TabName	The text to display for the tab.
TabOrder	Tabs with lower order number are displayed first.
AuthorizedRoles	The roles with access to the tab, in the form of a semicolon separated list of role names.

`ActiveTab` is an instance of the `TabSettings` class, defined as follows:

```
Public Class TabSettings

    Public TabIndex As Integer
    Public TabId As Integer
    Public TabName As String
    Public TabOrder As Integer
    Public MobileTabName As String
    Public AuthorizedRoles As String
    Public ShowMobile As Boolean
    Public Modules As New ArrayList()

End Class
```

Some of these fields are duplicates of the ones examined above. The rest of the fields are as follows:

TabSettings Field Name	Description
TabIndex	The position of the tab in the title bar.
MobileTabName	The text to display for the tab on mobile devices.
ShowMobile	Whether this tab should be displayed on a mobile device.
Modules	Which modules appear on the tab page.

The `Modules` field is very important, since it contains information about all the modules that exist on a tab. Without this data the page couldn't be rendered. `ActiveTab.Modules` is an `ArrayList` containing a `ModuleSettings` object for every object on the tab. The class definition of `ModuleSettings` is as follows:

```
Public Class ModuleSettings

    Public ModuleId As Integer
    Public ModuleDefId As Integer
    Public TabId As Integer
    Public CacheTime As Integer
```

```
        Public ModuleOrder As Integer
        Public PaneName As String
        Public ModuleTitle As String
        Public AuthorizedEditRoles As String
        Public ShowMobile As Boolean
        Public DesktopSrc As String
        Public MobileSrc As String

    End Class
```

All this information is extracted from the Modules table, using the current tab ID to get the relevant modules, except for DesktopSrc and MobileSrc, which come from the ModuleDefintions table for associated module type. The fields contain the following information:

ModuleSettings Field Name	Description
ModuleId	The ID of the module in the Modules table.
ModuleDefId	The corresponding ID of the module in the ModuleDefinitions table.
TabId	The ID of the tab that the module belongs to.
CacheTime	The amount of time to cache the module output for (0 in all cases for the default installation).
ModuleOrder	Modules with a lower number here are added to the tab page first.
PaneName	Where to display the module on the page (see next section).
ModuleTitle	The title to display for the module, if any.
AuthorizedEditRoles	Which roles have access to edit the content of the modules.
ShowMobile	Whether this module can be displayed on a mobile device.
DesktopSrc	The .ascx user control source code for the module when displaying on a desktop web browser.
MobileSrc	The .ascx user control source code for the module when displaying on a mobile web browser, if any.

Now we know what information is available to the rest of the application we can delve deeper into what happens when the main page is loaded.

DesktopDefault.aspx Architecture

We can get a better understanding of DesktopDefault.aspx by looking at the ASP.NET code for this page. The important section is the <table> element in the form body:

```
<table width="100%" cellspacing="0" cellpadding="0" border="0">
   <tr valign="top">
```

```
            <td colspan="2">
                <portal:Banner id="Banner" SelectedTabIndex="0" runat="server" />
            </td>
        </tr>
        <tr>
            <td>
                <br>
                <table width="100%" cellspacing="0" cellpadding="4" border="0">
                    <tr height="*" valign="top">
                        <td width="5">
                             
                        </td>
                        <td id="LeftPane" Visible="false" Width="170" runat="server">
                        </td>
                        <td width="1">
                        </td>
                        <td id="ContentPane" Visible="false" Width="*" runat="server">
                        </td>
                        <td id="RightPane" Visible="false" Width="230" runat="server">
                        </td>
                        <td width="10">
                             
                        </td>
                    </tr>
                </table>
            </td>
        </tr>
    </table>
```

Here the `<portal:Banner>` element is mapped to the `DesktopPortalBanner.ascx` user control (which we'll look at in more detail in the next section), and you can see the three columns in the form of three table cells with the names `LeftPane`, `ContentPane`, and `RightPane` respectively:

```
                <td id="LeftPane" Visible="false" Width="170" runat="server">
                </td>
                <td width="1">
                </td>
                <td id="ContentPane" Visible="false" Width="*" runat="server">
                </td>
                <td id="RightPane" Visible="false" Width="230" runat="server">
                </td>
```

These columns are populated as part of the `Page_Init` event handler in the code for this page. The code here uses the `PortalSettings` instance created earlier to get the information it needs. One of the first tasks of the code, then, is to retrieve this object from the `Context` object:

```
        ' Obtain PortalSettings from Current Context
        Dim _portalSettings As PortalSettings =
            CType(HttpContext.Current.Items("PortalSettings"), PortalSettings)
```

Next, the code handles some security issues, namely checking to see if the current user has been authenticated and if so whether access to the current tab is permitted. We won't look at this for now since we're covering security issues later.

The currently selected tab determines what modules are displayed. As we saw in the last section, information about these modules is stored in the `Modules` field of the `ActiveTab` field of the `PortalSettings` object that has just been extracted. The rest of the code examines this information and populates the three columns accordingly:

```
' Dynamically Populate the Left, Center and Right pane sections of the
' portal page
If _portalSettings.ActiveTab.Modules.Count > 0 Then

    ' Loop through each entry in the configuration system for this tab
    Dim _moduleSettings As ModuleSettings
    For Each _moduleSettings In _portalSettings.ActiveTab.Modules

        Dim parent As Control = Page.FindControl(_moduleSettings.PaneName)

        ' If no caching is specified, create the user control instance and
        ' dynamically inject it into the page.  Otherwise, create a cached
        ' module instance that may or may not optionally inject the module
        ' into the tree
        If _moduleSettings.CacheTime = 0 Then

            Dim portalModule As PortalModuleControl = _
                CType(Page.LoadControl(_moduleSettings.DesktopSrc), _
                    PortalModuleControl)

            portalModule.PortalId = _portalSettings.PortalId
            portalModule.ModuleConfiguration = _moduleSettings

            parent.Controls.Add(portalModule)

        Else

            Dim portalModule As New CachedPortalModuleControl()

            portalModule.PortalId = _portalSettings.PortalId
            portalModule.ModuleConfiguration = _moduleSettings

            parent.Controls.Add(portalModule)

        End If

        ' Dynamically inject separator break between portal modules
        parent.Controls.Add(New LiteralControl("<" + "br" + ">"))
        parent.Visible = True

    Next _moduleSettings

End If

End Sub
```

An interesting point, with consequences for customization as we will see in the next chapter, is that the `PaneName` information for a module is one of `LeftPane`, `ContentPane`, or `RightPane`, that is, it matches one of the columns on the page. The correct column is found using the `Page.FindControl` method, and used to add the module to.

When the module to add has a `CacheTime` setting of 0, the user control for the module is loaded using the `Page.LoadControl` method, which returns a `UserControl`, then converted to a `PortalModuleControl` (the base class for all modules user controls as we will see later). It is then initialized and added to the child controls collection of the column that the module will be displayed in. If `CacheTime` is not 0 then a `CachedPortalModuleControl` is used instead, and initialized with enough information to create the required module and cache rendering results.

> *The CacheTime setting actually means 'the amount of time, in seconds, to cache the HTML returned by this control'.*

This pretty much completes the discussion of `DesktopDefault.aspx`. The rest of the functionality of the portal is encapsulated in the user controls that are added to this page.

Tabs and the DesktopPortalBanner.ascx Control

The `DecsktopPortalBanner.ascx` user control appears at the top of `DesktopDefault.aspx`, and displays tabs along with some other information. This control uses the `PortalSettings` object stored in `Context` to find the tabs to display, and user login information to determine whether to display a **Log Off** link etc. The site title is displayed in a label called `siteName`:

```
<asp:label id="siteName" CssClass="SiteTitle" EnableViewState="false"
        runat="server" />
```

The ASP.NET code for the control also includes an `<asp:datalist>` control for displaying tabs:

```
<asp:datalist id="tabs" cssclass="OtherTabsBg" repeatdirection="horizontal"
           ItemStyle-Height="25" SelectedItemStyle-CssClass="TabBg"
           ItemStyle-BorderWidth="1" EnableViewState="false" runat="server">
    <ItemTemplate>
         
        <a href='<%= Request.ApplicationPath %>/DesktopDefault.aspx?tabindex=
               <%# Container.ItemIndex %>&tabid=<%# Ctype(Container.DataItem,
               TabStripDetails).TabId %>'
           class="OtherTabs">
           <%# Ctype(Container.DataItem, TabStripDetails).TabName %>
        </a>
         
    </ItemTemplate>
    <SelectedItemTemplate>
         
        <span class="SelectedTab">
           <%# Ctype(Container.DataItem, TabStripDetails).TabName %>
        </span>
         
    </SelectedItemTemplate>
</asp:datalist>
```

This control, called `tabs`, displays an array of `TabStripDetails` objects. It uses the position of the tab (as represented by `Container.ItemIndex`) and the ID of the tab (from `TabStripDetails.TabId`, extracted from `Container.DataItem`) to create a URL that users can use to navigate to the tab page. This URL is of the form:

```
(AppPath)/DesktopDefault.aspx?tabindex=(TabIndex)&tabid=(TabId)
```

This is the correct format used by the `Application_BeginRequest()` event handler we saw earlier, when these two parameters are used to initialize a `PortalSettings` object.

The code for this user control is very short, and only consists of a `Page_Load()` event handler. As before, this code needs to extract the `PortalSettings` object:

```
' Obtain PortalSettings from Current Context
Dim _portalSettings As PortalSettings = _
   CType(HttpContext.Current.Items("PortalSettings"), PortalSettings)
```

The name of the site is extracted from this object and used as the `Text` property of the `siteName` label we saw above:

```
' Dynamically Populate the Portal Site Name
siteName.Text = _portalSettings.PortalName
```

Next, we have some security code to check what other information to display on the banner (which we won't look at here), and finally the code to obtain an `ArrayList` of `TabStripDetails` objects to bind to the `tabs` datalist:

```
' Dynamically render portal tab strip
If ShowTabs = True Then

    tabIndex = _portalSettings.ActiveTab.TabIndex

    ' Build list of tabs to be shown to user
    Dim authorizedTabs As New ArrayList()
    Dim addedTabs As Integer = 0

    Dim i As Integer
    For i = 0 To _portalSettings.DesktopTabs.Count - 1

        Dim tab As TabStripDetails = _
            CType(_portalSettings.DesktopTabs(i), TabStripDetails)

        If PortalSecurity.IsInRoles(tab.AuthorizedRoles) Then
            authorizedTabs.Add(tab)
        End If

        If addedTabs = tabIndex Then
            tabs.SelectedIndex = addedTabs
        End If

        addedTabs += 1
```

```
        Next i

        ' Populate Tab List at Top of the Page with authorized tabs
        tabs.DataSource = authorizedTabs
        tabs.DataBind()

    End If

End Sub
```

This code simply extracts the `TabStripDetails` objects stored in the `PortalSettings` object and adds them to an `ArrayList` called `authorizedTabs` if the current user is in a role that the tab applies to. This `ArrayList` is then databound to the tabs datalist.

Apart from the security code, which we'll leave to Chapter 4, this functionality is pretty straightforward, and results in the tabbed banner we've seen several times already.

Module Structure

Earlier we saw that `DesktopDefault.aspx` added user control modules to three table cells called `LeftPane`, `ContentPane`, and `RightPane` using the following code:

```
Dim portalModule As PortalModuleControl = _
    CType(Page.LoadControl(_moduleSettings.DesktopSrc), _
        PortalModuleControl)

portalModule.PortalId = _portalSettings.PortalId
portalModule.ModuleConfiguration = _moduleSettings

parent.Controls.Add(portalModule)
```

The code in the `.ascx` file for the control is used to create a `PortalModuleControl` object, which then has two of its properties initialized before being added to the controls on the page. Specifically, the `PortalId` property is set to the `PortalId` value extracted from the `PortalSettings` instance used to create the page, and the `ModuleConfiguration` property is set to the `ModuleSettings` object that has previously been extracted from the `PortalSettings` object for this module.

These actions link the module controls into the IBuySpy Portal framework. Since all modules inherit from this `PortalModuleControl` class we should examine this class (which is stored in the `DesktopControls.vb` file) in more detail.

PortalModuleControl

The two properties used by the `DesktopDefault.aspx` above, `PortalId` and `ModuleConfiguration`, are simple - they simply wrap two private fields, an integer value in `_portalId` for `PortalId`, and a `ModuleSettings` value in `_moduleConfiguration` for `ModuleConfiguration`.

`PortalModuleControl` has three other properties: `ModuleId`, `Settings`, and `IsEditable`. The simplest of these, `ModuleId`, simply returns the `ModuleId` field of the stored `ModuleSettings` object. This could just as easily be achieved via the `ModuleConfiguration` property, but since this is a commonly used value, the IBuySpy Portal designers have seen fit to expose it directly.

`Settings` uses the shared `PortalConfiguration.GetModuleSettings` method discussed earlier to extract custom module configuration information from the database, in the form of a `HashTable`. This method is only called once, the first time the `Settings` property is accessed, at which point the returned `HashTable` is stored in the private field `_settings`. Subsequent attempts to access `Settings` have access to this cached version. This mode of operation ensures that as few database accesses as possible are used - modules that don't have custom configuration information won't even access the database once. The code to do this is as follows:

```
<Browsable(False), _
DesignerSerializationVisibility(DesignerSerializationVisibility.Hidden)> _
Public ReadOnly Property Settings() As Hashtable

   Get

      If _settings Is Nothing Then
         _settings = PortalSettings.GetModuleSettings(ModuleId)
      End If

      Return _settings
   End Get

End Property
```

`IsEditable` is a Boolean property that is used to determine whether the module is currently editable, a fact that is used by many controls to render an **Edit** button. There are two situations when this property will be `True`: either the current user will have edit permission granted directly on account of role membership, or the global `PortalSettings.AlwaysShowEditButton` is `True`. The latter case doesn't necessarily mean that the user can edit the content, they still require the correct permission to do this, but it does mean that the **Edit** button will be visible.

The code for this property makes use of a private `_isEditable` field to cache the result of the calculation of this value:

```
<Browsable(False), _
DesignerSerializationVisibility(DesignerSerializationVisibility.Hidden)> _
Public ReadOnly Property IsEditable() As Boolean

   Get

      ' Perform tri-state switch check to avoid having to perform a security
      ' role lookup on every property access (instead caching the result)
      If _isEditable = 0 Then

         ' Obtain PortalSettings from Current Context
         Dim _portalSettings As PortalSettings = _
          CType(HttpContext.Current.Items("PortalSettings"), PortalSettings)
```

```
            If _portalSettings.AlwaysShowEditButton = True Or _
              PortalSecurity.IsInRoles( _
               _moduleConfiguration.AuthorizedEditRoles) Then
               _isEditable = 1
            Else
               _isEditable = 2
            End If
        End If

        Return _isEditable = 1
    End Get

End Property
```

Initially, _isEditable is set to 0, so the logic in the middle of the above code is executed. This code results in _isEditable being set either to 1 if the PortalSettings.AlwaysShowEditButton property is True or the user is authorized to edit the module, or 2 otherwise. If _isEditable is set to 1 then the property returns a value of True, otherwise it returns False.

The advantage of doing things this way is that most of the code shown above only executes once, since _isEditable cannot be 0 after it has finished processing, only 1 or 2.

Editable modules generally display an Edit button using the DesktopModuleTitle.ascx user control.

DesktopModuleTitle.ascx

In order to get a common look and feel for modules, many of them use this user control to display a title and an Edit button. The ASP.NET code for this simple control is as follows:

```
<table width="98%" cellspacing="0" cellpadding="0">
    <tr>
        <td align="left">
            <asp:label id="ModuleTitle" cssclass="Head" EnableViewState="false"
                       runat="server" />
        </td>
        <td align="right">
            <asp:hyperlink id="EditButton" cssclass="CommandButton"
                       EnableViewState="false" runat="server" />
        </td>
    </tr>
    <tr>
        <td colspan="2">
            <hr noshade size="1">
        </td>
    </tr>
</table>
```

A label control (`ModuleTitle`) is used to display the title itself, and a hyperlink (`EditButton`) shows the Edit button. This button only appears if the control is editable, a fact that is determined in the `Page_Load` event handler for the control:

```
Private Sub Page_Load(ByVal sender As System.Object, _
                      ByVal e As System.EventArgs) Handles MyBase.Load

    ' Obtain PortalSettings from Current Context
    Dim _portalSettings As PortalSettings = _
      CType(HttpContext.Current.Items("PortalSettings"), PortalSettings)

    ' Obtain reference to parent portal module
    Dim portalModule As PortalModuleControl = _
      CType(Me.Parent, PortalModuleControl)

    ' Display Modular Title Text and Edit Buttons
    ModuleTitle.Text = portalModule.ModuleConfiguration.ModuleTitle

    ' Display the Edit button if the parent portalmodule has configured the
    ' PortalModuleTitle User Control to display it -- and the current client
    ' has edit access permissions
    If _portalSettings.AlwaysShowEditButton = True Or _
      (PortalSecurity.IsInRoles( _
          portalModule.ModuleConfiguration.AuthorizedEditRoles) And _
      Not (EditText Is Nothing)) Then

      EditButton.Text = EditText
      EditButton.NavigateUrl = EditUrl + "?mid=" + _
        portalModule.ModuleId.ToString()
      EditButton.Target = EditTarget
    End If

End Sub
```

This code sets the `Text` property of `ModuleTitle` label to a value extracted from the `ModuleSettings` object obtained from the parent module, and the `Text`, `NavigateUrl`, and `Target` properties of `EditButton` to values taken prom the parameters used in the ASP.NET code used to insert the control. The URL for `EditButton` also has an additional querystring parameter added, `mid` - which is set to the module `ID`.

User Controls

The code for the various module user controls varies quite a lot for the ten modules included with the IBuySpy Portal download, but they share several common features:

❑   They all inherit from `PortalModuleControl`.

❑   Many of them use `DesktopModuleTitle.ascx` to render a title and edit link.

❑   Many of them use a separate data object for accessing database-stored data.

To illustrate all these features, let's look at a control that exhibits all three of the above: `Announcements.ascx`. The complete ASP.NET code for this control is as follows:

```
<%@ Control language="vb" Inherits="ASPNetPortal.Announcements"
           CodeBehind="Announcements.ascx.vb" AutoEventWireup="false" %>
<%@ Register TagPrefix="Portal" TagName="Title" Src="~/DesktopModuleTitle.ascx"%>
<portal:title EditText="Add New Announcement"
           EditUrl="~/DesktopModules/EditAnnouncements.aspx" runat="server" />
<asp:DataList id="myDataList" CellPadding="4" Width="98%" EnableViewState="false"
           runat="server">
    <ItemTemplate>
        <asp:HyperLink id="editLink" ImageUrl="~/images/edit.gif"
            NavigateUrl='<%# "~/DesktopModules/EditAnnouncements.aspx?ItemID=" &
            DataBinder.Eval(Container.DataItem,"ItemID") & "&mid=" & ModuleId %>'
            Visible="<%# IsEditable %>" runat="server" />
        <span class="ItemTitle">
          <%# DataBinder.Eval(Container.DataItem,"Title") %>
        </span>
        <br>
        <span class="Normal">
            <%# DataBinder.Eval(Container.DataItem,"Description") %>
             
            <asp:HyperLink id="moreLink"
                NavigateUrl='<%# DataBinder.Eval(Container.DataItem,"MoreLink") %>'
                Visible='<%# DataBinder.Eval(Container.DataItem,"MoreLink") <>
                String.Empty %>' runat="server">
                    read more...
            </asp:HyperLink>
        </span>
        <br>
    </ItemTemplate>
</asp:DataList>
```

Near the top of this code you can see the `<portal:title>` control that is used for the `DesktopModuleTitle.ascx` control detailed in the last section, with appropriate parameters used to provide a link to the edit page for the module. We won't look at `EditAnnouncements.aspx` here since the code is simple and makes use of data access objects in the same way as this user control, so we won't learn anything new there.

The main body of this module is a `DataList`, which is set to display the announcements obtained from the database. We'll come back to the specifics of this control shortly, once we've seen the data it is used to display.

The `DataList` control (`myDataList`) is initialized in the `Page_Load` event handler for the module (which constitutes 100% of the code for the user control):

```
Private Sub Page_Load(ByVal sender As System.Object, _
                     ByVal e As System.EventArgs) Handles MyBase.Load

    ' Obtain announcement information from Announcements table
    ' and bind to the datalist control
    Dim announcements As New ASPNetPortal.AnnouncementsDB()
```

```
          ' DataBind Announcements to DataList Control
          myDataList.DataSource = announcements.GetAnnouncements(ModuleId)
          myDataList.DataBind()

      End Sub
```

This code uses a data object, AnnouncementsDB, to obtain data for filling the DataList. The AnnouncementsDB.GetAnnouncements method gets a DataSet filled with the announcements that correspond with this particular module (as specified by the ID of the module). This DataSet is then databound to the DataList control.

Since we haven't looked in detail at one of the data objects in this application, this is a good opportunity to do so. The method used, GetAnnouncements, is as follows:

```
      Public Function GetAnnouncements(ByVal moduleId As Integer) As DataSet

          ' Create Instance of Connection and Command Object
          Dim myConnection As _
           New SqlConnection(ConfigurationSettings.AppSettings("connectionString"))
          Dim myCommand As New SqlDataAdapter("GetAnnouncements", myConnection)

          ' Mark the Command as a SPROC
          myCommand.SelectCommand.CommandType = CommandType.StoredProcedure

          ' Add Parameters to SPROC
          Dim parameterModuleId As New SqlParameter("@ModuleId", SqlDbType.Int, 4)
          parameterModuleId.Value = moduleId
          myCommand.SelectCommand.Parameters.Add(parameterModuleId)

          ' Create and Fill the DataSet
          Dim myDataSet As New DataSet()
          myCommand.Fill(myDataSet)

          ' Return the DataSet
          Return myDataSet

      End Function
```

The connection to the database is initialized using the connectionString value from the AppSettings of the application (stored in web.config). The moduleId parameter obtained from the module using this data object is then used as a parameter for the GetAnnouncements SQL stored procedure to obtain the required data.

The GetAnnouncements stored procedure is as follows:

```
CREATE PROCEDURE GetAnnouncements
(
    @ModuleID int
)
AS

SELECT
```

```
        ItemID,
        CreatedByUser,
        CreatedDate,
        Title,
        MoreLink,
        MobileMoreLink,
        ExpireDate,
        Description

FROM
        Announcements

WHERE
        ModuleID = @ModuleID
    AND
        ExpireDate > GetDate()

GO
```

This stored procedure wraps a simple SQL SELECT statement, returning all columns except ModuleId from the Announcements table for records with the selected ModuleId value.

The AnnouncementsDB data object also has methods for getting individual announcements, for deleting announcements, and for adding new announcements. These are used by the EditAnnouncements.aspx page.

Back in the ASP.NET code for the Announcements.ascx user control, we can see that the <ItemTemplate> starts with a link for editing the announcement item:

```
<asp:DataList id="myDataList" CellPadding="4" Width="98%" EnableViewState="false"
        runat="server">
   <ItemTemplate>
      <asp:HyperLink id="editLink" ImageUrl="~/images/edit.gif"
            NavigateUrl='<%# "~/DesktopModules/EditAnnouncements.aspx?ItemID=" &
            DataBinder.Eval(Container.DataItem,"ItemID") & "&mid=" & ModuleId %>'
            Visible="<%# IsEditable %>" runat="server" />
```

The URL of the page for editing the item is hardcoded here, and is combined with an ItemID querystring parameter taken from the ItemID field of the announcement being displayed and a mid querystring parameter taken from the PortalModuleControl.ModuleId property. This link is only displayed if the module is currently editable, making use of the IsEditable property of PortalModuleControl we saw earlier.

Next, we have the announcement title:

```
<span class="ItemTitle">
   <%# DataBinder.Eval(Container.DataItem,"Title") %>
</span>
```

This uses the `Title` field of the current announcement. Similarly, the `Description` field of the announcement is used to give the announcement summary, and `MoreLink` is used to display a link to more text if the field is present:

```
        <br>
        <span class="Normal">
            <%# DataBinder.Eval(Container.DataItem,"Description") %>
             
            <asp:HyperLink id="moreLink"
                NavigateUrl='<%# DataBinder.Eval(Container.DataItem,"MoreLink") %>'
                Visible='<%# DataBinder.Eval(Container.DataItem,"MoreLink") <>
                String.Empty %>' runat="server">
                    read more...
            </asp:HyperLink>
        </span>
        <br>
    </ItemTemplate>
</asp:DataList>
```

That is all that is required for a IBuySpy Portal module. In the next chapter we'll look at how we can make our own modules using the framework described here, recapping much of this information.

Security

As mentioned earlier in the chapter, the IBuySpy Portal works with both forms-based and Windows authentication.

Forms-based authentication is an independent authentication method that works equally well for local and remote users of the intranet, since login information is requested from the user as part of the web application, using the authentication module we looked at earlier.

Windows integrated authentication involves tying the intranet authentication in with existing network accounts. This is great for local network intranets, since users only need to log on once, when they log on to their Windows domain account. The account information is then passed on to the intranet code when they access the site, so that they don't need to enter additional information. This has the effect of streamlining things, and makes the intranet feel more like a corporate application. The main benefit is that all user account information is centralized.

There are, however, problems with Windows integrated authentication. For a start, we are assuming that all of our users are using Windows operating systems. If our organization uses other operating systems as well, such as Linux or Macintosh consoles, then it can be a bit tricky to configure the network users and groups correctly, resulting in many annoyed users being unable to connect to the intranet. I'm not saying that this is impossible - it's just more trouble than it's worth in most cases. In addition, remote users may find it difficult to log on to their network account, or might not even have such an account. There are also security concerns, since transmitting this information over the Internet is by definition less secure than doing so over a local network.

Security is covered in more depth in Chapter 4, where we will look at how the forms authentication system works and how we can configure IBuySpy Portal-based intranets for Windows authentication if desired.

Summary

In this chapter, we have taken a fairly in-depth tour of the IBuySpy Portal intranet architecture. We started out in general terms, looking at what is provided via the interface created for us. Once we got past the 'wow' stage, we proceeded to look at things in more depth, and at how things fit together. We covered the backend for the database structure, and the important user controls and types that encapsulate the intranet functionality. We saw how the framework works and how individual modules communicate with the framework as a whole.

The rest of this book is concerned with customizing this architecture, in both simple and advanced ways. Now we have a good understanding of how things work, we can start to do more interesting things with the code. In the next chapter, we'll look at the basic principles behind this.

Solutio
BM Referen
System
System.Data
System.Drawing
System.Web
System.XML
AssemblyInfo.vb
BM.vsdisco
Global.asax
Styles.css
Web.config
WebForm1.aspx

WebForm1.aspx* | WebForm1.aspx. \

ebForm1.aspx*

3

Customizing the Portal

In this chapter, we will begin to customize the IBuySpy Portal. There are three ways of doing this, listed in order of increasing complexity as follows:

❑ Stylesheet manipulation - the simplest way to manipulate the portal is to specify your own styles and color schemes for portal elements via the CSS stylesheet associated with it.

❑ Direct code manipulation - additional customization can be achieved with modifications to the existing code that makes up the application. This needn't be complex, minor modifications can result in dramatic changes.

❑ Additional modules and custom code - the greatest changes can be achieved by adding your own modules to the project, following the framework discussed in the last chapter. It is also possible to modify the framework and add your own custom logic, meaning that pretty much anything is possible.

Which route you take depends entirely on what you want to achieve. It's quite possible that the existing modules and intranet architecture meet your needs perfectly, in which case you might make only minor modifications; probably to the stylesheet to change the color schemes etc. to match your corporate look. This can easily be extended to modifying the ASP.NET code that the modules fit into to restructure things slightly.

For a more major overhaul, the portal makes an excellent starting point for adding your own functionality.

We'll look at each of these three subjects in turn, with the third making up most of the rest of the book, as we implement increasingly complex modifications.

Before we start though, there are some basic notes about customizing the site and versioning that we should discuss.

Portal Versioning

Many of the changes made to the portal in this chapter are general ones that you will probably apply before letting users run riot over your site. Of course, you will also want to fill the site with content before then.

Later though, you are quite likely to want to make modifications, add functionality, or just correct mistakes. In such cases, you are unlikely to want to alter the 'live' version of the portal. Instead, you should have a separate development server for trying things out and upgrading, only copying the results to the live version when you are sure they check out.

As an extension of this, it is often worth keeping multiple versions of the portal code, so you can revert quickly to an earlier version if something goes wrong.

In this chapter, we're not worried about this too much, as we are making basic 'pre-release' changes. Later in the book though, this subject will become more important, and will be discussed where necessary.

Customizing the Stylesheet

In the last chapter, you may well have noticed how CSS styles are applied to much of the ASP.NET code we looked at. For example, the `Announcements.ascx` file has the following reference to CSS:

```
<%@ Control language="vb" Inherits="ASPNetPortal.Announcements"
            CodeBehind="Announcements.ascx.vb" AutoEventWireup="false" %>
<%@ Register TagPrefix="Portal" TagName="Title" Src="~/DesktopModuleTitle.ascx"%>
<portal:title EditText="Add New Announcement"
            EditUrl="~/DesktopModules/EditAnnouncements.aspx" runat="server" />
<asp:DataList id="myDataList" CellPadding="4" Width="98%" EnableViewState="false"
            runat="server">
    <ItemTemplate>
        <asp:HyperLink id="editLink" ImageUrl="~/images/edit.gif"
            NavigateUrl='<%# "~/DesktopModules/EditAnnouncements.aspx?ItemID=" &
            DataBinder.Eval(Container.DataItem,"ItemID") & "&mid=" & ModuleId %>'
            Visible="<%# IsEditable %>" runat="server" />
        <span class="ItemTitle">
            <%# DataBinder.Eval(Container.DataItem,"Title") %>
        </span>
        <br>
        <span class="Normal">
            <%# DataBinder.Eval(Container.DataItem,"Description") %>
             
            <asp:HyperLink id="moreLink"
                NavigateUrl='<%# DataBinder.Eval(Container.DataItem,"MoreLink") %>'
                Visible='<%# DataBinder.Eval(Container.DataItem,"MoreLink") <>
```

```
                String.Empty %>' runat="server">
                  read more...
            </asp:HyperLink>
         </span>
         <br>
      </ItemTemplate>
   </asp:DataList>
```

These two classes, `ItemTitle` and `Normal`, are linked to a stylesheet via a `<link>` tag in the header of `DesktopDefault.aspx`:

```
<head>
   <title>ASP.NET Portal</title>
   <link href="portal.css" type="text/css" rel="stylesheet">
</head>
```

It is this file, `portal.css`, which contains the CSS style information for the whole portal. Making even just a few changes to this style information can take you a long way toward making the site feel like your own.

> *This `<link>` tag also appears in many of the module-specific `.aspx` pages, which aren't tied to the `DesktopDefault.aspx` page but use the same styles.*

Many of the styles found in `portal.css` share duplicate settings that work together to achieve a consistent look across the site. For example, the color `DarkRed` and the font family `Verdana` are specified several times in different classes and elements.

The following classes are contained in the stylesheet (listed in the order they appear in `portal.css`):

Class name	Usage
`.HeadBg`	Used as the class for the main `<table>` element in `DesktopPortalBanner.ascx` that contains all portal header content.
`.SiteTitle`	Used as the class for the name of the portal (that is, the text that reads **IBuySpy Portal** in the default installation), used in `DesktopPortalBanner.ascx`.
`.TabBg`	Used in `DesktopPortalBanner.ascx` as the class for the selected tab.
`.OtherTabsBg`	Used in `DesktopPortalBanner.ascx` as the class for non-selected tabs.
`.SelectedTab`	Used in `DesktopPortalBanner.ascx` as the class for text in the selected tab.
`.OtherTabs`	Used in `DesktopPortalBanner.ascx`, as the class for text in non-selected tabs. There are also four `A.OtherTabs:xxx` classes used to format the links shown in these tabs under different circumstances, including `A.OtherTabs:hover` used as the style for links to change to when the mouse passes over them.

Table continued on following page

Class name	Usage
.SiteLink	Used in DesktopPortalBanner.ascx for the links that appear in the top-right corner. This has four A.SiteLink:xxx styles associated with it, used in the same way as those for .OtherTabs.
.Accent	Used in DesktopPortalBanner.ascx for the separator between the links in the top right corner.
.Message	Used by the DiscussionDetails.aspx page for discussion message details.
.ItemTitle	Used by Announcements.ascx and Events.ascx for the title of individual items.
.Head	Used in DesktopModuleTitle.ascx for module titles, and in several other module specific and admin pages for general headings.
.SubHead	Used in several module-specific and admin pages for sub-headings.
.SubSubHead	Used in QuickLinks.ascx and SignIn.ascx for compact heading styles.
.Normal	Style used by most text in the portal.
.NormalTextBox	Style used by text boxes throughout the portal, including those on SignIn.ascx and module-specific pages.
.NormalRed	Used in SignIn.ascx and a couple of admin pages.
.NormalBold	Used in a few module-specific and admin pages.
.CommandButton	Used for buttons and link buttons in admin pages, also includes A.CommandButton:xxx styles for additional link styling.

In addition to these, several styles are defined for HTML elements, the following of which are especially useful:

Element name	Usage
Body	Used throughout the portal, handy for setting the background color throughout.
Hx	Used for HTML style headings wherever they appear (often in HTML content of modules).
A	General link formatting, includes A:xxx styles for link behavior styling.
HR	Style of horizontal rules used throughout the portal.

Modifying the Styles

We've taken a general look at the stylesheet and the key styles it contains, so let's walk through making modifications and see what effect the changes have. Since this is a Wrox book, we'll apply a more Wrox-like color scheme to things, and play with the text styles a little.

We'll work through `portal.css` from the top downwards, modifying styles as we go. First, we have the background color for the portal banner in `HeadBg`:

```
.HeadBg {
    background-color: DarkRed;
}
```

We'll change the background color to a brighter shade of red:

```
.HeadBg {
    background-color: crimson;
}
```

If you save `portal.css` with this change and view the portal in the browser, you should see a noticeable change. However, a single change such as this can look odd, since the colors and styles work together to create the overall look of the portal.

Next is the style specification for `<Body>` elements of the page, shared by all pages throughout the site:

```
/* background color for the content part of the pages */
Body {
    background-color: white;
}
```

We'll change this to a pastel pink color in keeping with the red color scheme:

```
/* background color for the content part of the pages */
Body {
    background-color: mistyrose;
}
```

The `<Body>` element style definition is a very versatile one, and can be used to place many default options for other content (including font styles if you wanted to provide a default for elements where no font information is specified). For now though, the background color change is enough.

The next style definition is `SiteTitle`, used for the title of the portal in the site banner:

```
.SiteTitle {
    font-family: Verdana, Helvetica, sans-serif;
    font-size: 20px;
    font-weight: bold;
    color:#cccc99;
}
```

A list of different fonts is used such that devices that don't have the first in the list will use the second or the third if they don't have that. We need to be careful here - if we choose a font that is only likely to exist on our development machine then things will look fine for us, but browsers using other platforms will see things completely differently. We've chosen a standard font family, Arial, as the first in the list, and left the rest the same. We've also increased the point size slightly and changed the color to white to make things look more in keeping with the rest of the site:

```
.SiteTitle {
    font-family: Arial, Helvetica, sans-serif;
    font-size: 28px;
    font-weight: bold;
    color: white;
}
```

There are several places where the original Verdana font appears in style definitions. One general stylistic rule of thumb is that sites tend to look more professional when they use as few different fonts as possible; in fact, a single font is often enough. If you use more than that then text often becomes harder to read, and can look inconsistent. Since we prefer Arial to Verdana, we ran a search and replace to change all references to Verdana to Arial. We'll sort out the point sizes (Arial looks smaller than Verdana for the same point size) as we come to them.

Next, we come to the definitions for tab styling:

```
.TabBg {
    background-color: white;
    border-color: white;
}

.OtherTabsBg {
    background-color: dimgray;
    border-color: black;
}

.SelectedTab {
    font-family: Verdana, Helvetica, sans-serif;
    font-size: 13px;
    color:DarkRed;
    font-weight: bold
}

.OtherTabs {
    font-family: Verdana, Helvetica, sans-serif;
    font-size: 13px;
    color:gainsboro;
    text-decoration:none;
    font-weight: bold
}

A.OtherTabs:link {
    text-decoration:     none;
    color:#eeeeee;
}
```

```
A.OtherTabs:visited {
    text-decoration:    none;
    color:#eeeeee;
}

A.OtherTabs:active {
    text-decoration:    none;
    color:#eeeeee;
}

A.OtherTabs:hover {
    text-decoration:    underline;
    color:white;
}
```

We've changed these so that the selected tab appears with a black border with red text on a yellow background, and the other tabs as black text on a dark red background, changing to yellow (not underlined) when the mouse passes over them:

```
.TabBg {
    border-color: black;
    background-color: yellow;
}

.OtherTabsBg {
    background-color: firebrick;
    border-color: black;
}

.SelectedTab {
    font-family: Arial, Helvetica, sans-serif;
    font-size: 13px;
    font-weight: bold;
    color: crimson;
}

.OtherTabs {
    font-family: Arial, Helvetica, sans-serif;
    font-size: 13px;
    font-weight: bold;
}

A.OtherTabs:link {
    text-decoration:    none;
    color: black;
}

A.OtherTabs:visited {
    text-decoration:    none;
    color: black;
}

A.OtherTabs:active {
```

```
    text-decoration:     none;
    color: black;
}

A.OtherTabs:hover {
    text-decoration:     none;
    color: yellow;
}
```

Next, we come to the styles for the site links in the upper right corner. Now, these links are placed directly on top of a background built up from an image called bars.gif, limiting what can be done to them without looking very odd, so we decided to cheat a bit: OK, so this section is about the stylesheets, but replacing this image with another one is basic enough to include here! The image we used is as follows:

The image is a 6x6 pixel .gif, with the shaded pixels above colored brick red, and the un-shaded pixels crimson - where these colors are the same as the ones used for the style changes so far.

To make this change you can simply change the bars.gif file found in the Images subdirectory of the portal root directory. Alternatively, you could create a new image file and modify the following line of code in DesktopPortalBanner.ascx, replacing bars.gif with your own filename:

```
<td colspan="3" class="SiteLink"
    background="<%= Request.ApplicationPath %>/images/bars.gif" align="right">
```

The next change to the CSS file was to alter the original site link code. The original code for this is as follows:

```
.SiteLink {
    font-family: Verdana, Helvetica, sans-serif;
    font-size: 11px;
    font-weight: bold
}

A.SiteLink:link {
    text-decoration:     none;
    color:white;
}

A.SiteLink:visited {
```

```
        text-decoration:      none;
        color:#eeeeee;
}


A.SiteLink:active {
        text-decoration:      none;
        color:#eeeeee;
}


A.SiteLink:hover {
        text-decoration:      underline;
        color:white;
}


.Accent {
        color: red;
        font-weight:      bold;
}
```

The changes we made were to make the font Arial, change the point sizes, make the text color black (changing to yellow without underlining when the mouse hovers over them, just like the tabs), and make the separator white:

```
.SiteLink {
        font-family: Arial, Helvetica, sans-serif;
        font-size: 13px;
        font-weight: bold
}


A.SiteLink:link {
        text-decoration:      none;
        color: black;
}


A.SiteLink:visited {
        text-decoration:      none;
        color: black;
}


A.SiteLink:active {
        text-decoration:      none;
        color: black;
}


A.SiteLink:hover {
        text-decoration:      none;
        color: yellow;
}


.Accent {
        color: white;
        font-weight:      bold;
}
```

The next section of the stylesheet deals with two module specific styles: Message for text in the discussions module, and ItemTitle for titles of discussion messages and announcements:

```
.Message {
    font-family: Verdana, Helvetica, sans-serif;
    font-size: 11px;
    font-weight: normal;
    font-size: 11px;
    background-color: #eeeeee
}

.ItemTitle {
    font-family: Verdana, Helvetica, sans-serif;
    font-size:  11px;
    font-weight:    bold;
    color: darkred;
}
```

We've changed the font, the size, the text color, and the background color:

```
.Message {
    font-family: Arial, Helvetica, sans-serif;
    font-size: 12px;
    font-weight: normal;
    background-color: white;
}

.ItemTitle {
    font-family: Arial, Helvetica, sans-serif;
    font-size:  14px;
    font-weight:    bold;
    color: crimson;
}
```

We've also removed the duplicate font-size specification in Message.

Next, we made some changes to general text and headings - we'll just show the changes from here on as we've covered most of the important modifications now:

```
.Head {
    font-family: Arial, Helvetica, sans-serif;
    font-size:  24px;
    font-weight:    bold;
    color: crimson;
}

.SubHead {
    font-family: Arial, Helvetica, sans-serif;
    font-size:  14px;
    font-weight:    bold;
    color: crimson;
}
```

```
.SubSubHead {
    font-family: Arial, Helvetica, sans-serif;
    font-size:  13px;
    font-weight:     bold;
    color: crimson;
}


.Normal {
    font-family: Arial, Helvetica, sans-serif;
    font-size: 12px;
    font-weight: normal;
    line-height: 13px;
}

.NormalTextBox {
    font-family: Arial, Helvetica, sans-serif;
    font-size: 12px;
    font-weight: normal;
}

.NormalRed {
    font-family: Arial, Helvetica, sans-serif;
    font-size: 12px;
    font-weight: bold;
    color: crimson
}

.NormalBold {
    font-family: Arial, Helvetica, sans-serif;
    font-size: 12px;
    font-weight: bold
}
```

Next, we have the `Admin` command styles:

```
.CommandButton {
    font-family: Arial, Helvetica, sans-serif;
    font-size: 12px;
    font-weight: normal;
}

A.CommandButton:link {
    text-decoration:     underline;
    color: crimson;
}

A.CommandButton:visited {
    text-decoration:     underline;
    color: crimson;
}

A.CommandButton:active {
    text-decoration:     underline;
    color: crimson;
```

```
    }

A.CommandButton:hover {
    text-decoration:      underline;
    color: salmon;
    }
```

Now we have the HTML element styles, most of which we'll omit for now to save some space. We changed most of the colors to crimson and the fonts to Arial, but there are not many elements that are worth showing. Some exceptions, though, are the hyperlink and horizontal rule styles, since they occur so often:

```
A:link {
    text-decoration:      none;
    color:  crimson;
    }

A:visited {
    text-decoration:      none;
    color:  crimson;
    }

A:active {
    text-decoration:      none;
    color:  crimson;
    }

A:hover {
    color: salmon;
    text-decoration: none;
    }

HR {
    color:  pink;
    height:2pt;
    text-align:left
    }
```

Now it's time to look at the results. Comparing the two styles, original and new, we see the following:

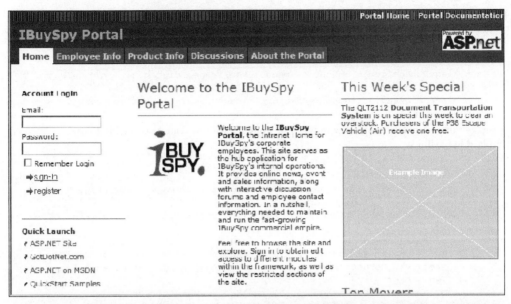

Even in black and white, you can see noticeable changes. It's surprising how much a site can become your own just by standardizing fonts, logos, and colors.

Correcting SignIn.ascx

There is one thing you might notice in the above screenshot though: the styles of the sign-in and register links have remained unchanged, and in the case of the register link the background color is wrong. This is because these links are actually images, added with the following ASP.NET code:

```
<asp:ImageButton id="SigninBtn" ImageUrl="~/images/signin.gif" runat="server" />
<br>
<a href="Admin/Register.aspx"><img src="images/register.gif" border="0"></a>
```

To make things more in keeping with the style changes we can change this code to use standard hyperlinks:

```
<span class="normal">
    <asp:ImageButton id="SigninBtnPic" ImageUrl="~/images/navlink.gif"
                    runat="server" />
    <asp:LinkButton id="SigninBtn" runat="server">Sign In</asp:LinkButton>
     
    <asp:HyperLink id="RegisterLink" ImageUrl="~/images/navlink.gif"
                    NavigateUrl="~/Admin/Register.aspx" runat="server" />
    <a href='<%= Request.ApplicationPath & "/Admin/Register.aspx" %>'>
        Register</a><br>
    <asp:label id="Message" class="NormalRed" runat="server" />
</span>
```

In order for this code to work, we also need to change the code for the form as follows:

```
    Private Sub SigninBtnPic_Click(ByVal sender As System.Object, _
        ByVal e As System.Web.UI.ImageClickEventArgs) _
        Handles SigninBtnPic.Click
        Signin()
    End Sub

    Private Sub SigninBtn_Click(ByVal sender As System.Object, _
        ByVal e As System.EventArgs) Handles SigninBtn.Click
        Signin()
    End Sub

    Private Sub Signin()
        ' Attempt to Validate User Credentials using UsersDB
        Dim accountSystem As New UsersDB()
        Dim userId As String = accountSystem.Login(email.Text, password.Text)

        If Not (userId Is Nothing) And userId <> "" Then

            ' Use security system to set the UserID within a client-side Cookie
            FormsAuthentication.SetAuthCookie(email.Text, _
                                            RememberCheckbox.Checked)

            ' Redirect browser back to originating page
            Response.Redirect(Request.ApplicationPath)
```

```
        Else

            Message.Text = "<" & "br" & ">Login Failed!" & "<" & "br" & ">"

        End If
    End Sub
```

Here the original logic has been placed in a new function called `SignIn`, called by the event handlers for the two new signing controls.

The result is as follows:

This is more in keeping with the rest of the site.

Customizing the Portal Code

The above modification is just one place where we can modify the code of the portal for our own devices. There are several other places where we can make modifications, without disrupting the framework that we dissected in the last chapter.

One obvious place to start is the `PortalBanner.ascx` control that appears at the top of the browser for most portal pages, and is responsible for showing the list of tabs in the portal among other things.

Customizing the PortalBanner.ascx Control

The ASP.NET code for this control consists largely of a table with three rows. The first row, which has the bars.gif background examined earlier, contains the sitelink links, along with a welcome message and logoff link if a user is logged in:

```
<table width="100%" cellspacing="0" class="HeadBg" border="0">
    <tr valign="top">
        <td colspan="3" class="SiteLink"
                background="<%= Request.ApplicationPath %>/images/bars.gif"
                align="right">
            <asp:label id="WelcomeMessage" forecolor="#eeeeee" runat="server" />
            <a href="<%= Request.ApplicationPath %>" class="SiteLink">
                Portal Home
            </a>
            <span class="Accent">|</span>
            <a href="<%= Request.ApplicationPath %>/Docs/Docs.htm" target="_blank"
                    class="SiteLink">
                Portal Documentation
            </a>
            <%= LogoffLink %>
        </td>
    </tr>
```

One thing to notice here is that the forecolor attribute for the welcome message is hardcoded - it doesn't follow a CSS style. We can change this straight away to something that fits in with out modified style:

```
<asp:label id="WelcomeMessage" forecolor="white" runat="server" />
```

Alternatively, and far better, we can create a new style for this for future compatibility (we should always consider such things to make our lives easier if we ever revisit our code to make changes). To do this we simply need to add the following class to portal.css:

```
/* text style for welcome message */
.WelcomeMessage {
    color: white;
}
```

In addition, modify the label again:

```
<asp:label id="WelcomeMessage" class="WelcomeMessage"
            runat="server" />
```

We only need the color style to be set here, the rest of the attributes are set on account of the message being inside a `<td>` element using the SiteLink CSS class.

The second row of the tables contains the portal title and a 'Powered by ASP.NET' image:

```
<tr>
    <td width="10" rowspan="2">

    </td>
    <td height="40">
        <asp:label id="siteName" CssClass="SiteTitle" EnableViewState="false"
                   runat="server" />
    </td>
    <td align="middle" rowspan="2">
        <a href="http://www.asp.net">
            <img id="logo"
                 src="<%=Request.ApplicationPath%>/images/poweredby_simple.gif"
                 border="0">
        </a>
    </td>
</tr>
```

The first cell here is one that spans this and the next row, aligning the title with the tabs. The third cell, which contains the 'Powered by ASP.NET' image, can be deleted. It could be said that ancillary content like this makes web pages look more cluttered, although it's understandable why this logo was included in the IBuySpy Portal installation. The users of a portal, however, are unlikely to be interested in this information.

The title itself is displayed with the `siteName` label, which is assigned text by the following code in the `Page_Load` event handler for the user control:

```
' Obtain PortalSettings from Current Context
Dim _portalSettings As PortalSettings = _
    CType(HttpContext.Current.Items("PortalSettings"), PortalSettings)

' Dynamically Populate the Portal Site Name
siteName.Text = _portalSettings.PortalName
```

This data comes from the `PortalName` column in the `Portals` table in the database. If you want to change the name of the site that is displayed here, you can change the data in this table either directly or via the Admin tab.

Next in the ASP.NET code for the control, we have the tab list:

```
<tr>
    <td>
        <asp:datalist id="tabs" cssclass="OtherTabsBg"
                repeatdirection="horizontal" ItemStyle-Height="25"
                SelectedItemStyle-CssClass="TabBg" ItemStyle-BorderWidth="1"
                EnableViewState="false" runat="server">
            <ItemTemplate>
                <a href='<%= Request.ApplicationPath %>
                        /DesktopDefault.aspx?tabindex=
                        <%# Container.ItemIndex %>
```

```
                        &tabid=
                        <%# Ctype(Container.DataItem, TabStripDetails).TabId %>'
                        class="OtherTabs">
                    <%# Ctype(Container.DataItem, TabStripDetails).TabName %>
                </a>
            </ItemTemplate>
            <SelectedItemTemplate>
                <span class="SelectedTab">
                    <%# Ctype(Container.DataItem, TabStripDetails).TabName %>
                </span>
            </SelectedItemTemplate>
        </asp:datalist>
    </td>
  </tr>
</table>
```

This list is a databound `DataList` control, using the `TabBg`, `OtherTabBg`, `SelectedTab`, and `OtherTabs` styles we looked at in the last section to format its styles.

There are all manner of modifications that we could do to this row. We could even remove the tabs from this control completely, perhaps reformatting them as a vertical list down the side of the portal pages. For this example though, we'll modify the tabs slightly to give a different appearance.

Specifically, we'll change the rectangular tabs shown below:

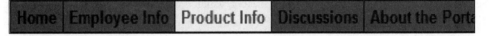

Into rounded tabs as follows:

In order to do this we need 16 small bitmaps with the correct colors for the corners and edges of the tabs. These are included with the downloadable code for this book.

The changes to achieve this are as follows:

```
<asp:datalist id="tabs" class="TabHolder" repeatdirection="horizontal"
            EnableViewState="false" runat="server">
    <ItemTemplate>
        <table border="0" cellpadding="0" cellspacing="0" height="28"
                class="OtherTabsBg">
            <tr>
                <td>
                    <img src='<%= Request.ApplicationPath %>/images/unselTL.gif'>
                </td>
                <td background='<%= Request.ApplicationPath %>/images/unselT.gif'>
                </td>
                <td>
```

```
                        <img src='<%= Request.ApplicationPath %>/images/unselTR.gif'>
                    </td>
                </tr>
                <tr>
                    <td>
                        <img src='<%= Request.ApplicationPath %>/images/unselL.gif'>
                    </td>
                    <td>
                        <a href='<%= Request.ApplicationPath %>/DesktopDefault.aspx
                        ?tabindex=<%# Container.ItemIndex %>
                        &tabid=<%# Ctype(Container.DataItem, TabStripDetails).TabId %>'
                        class="OtherTabs">
                            <%# Ctype(Container.DataItem, TabStripDetails).TabName %>
                        </a>
                    </td>
                    <td>
                        <img src='<%= Request.ApplicationPath %>/images/unselR.gif'>
                    </td>
                </tr>
                <tr>
                    <td>
                        <img src='<%= Request.ApplicationPath %>/images/unselBL.gif'>
                    </td>
                    <td background='<%= Request.ApplicationPath %>/images/unselB.gif'>
                    </td>
                    <td>
                        <img src='<%= Request.ApplicationPath %>/images/unselBR.gif'>
                    </td>
                </tr>
            </table>
        </ItemTemplate>
        <SelectedItemTemplate>
            <table border="0" cellpadding="0" cellspacing="0" height="28"
                class="TabBg">
                <tr>
                    <td>
                        <img src='<%= Request.ApplicationPath %>/images/selTL.gif'>
                    </td>
                    <td background='<%= Request.ApplicationPath %>/images/selT.gif'>
                    </td>
                    <td>
                        <img src='<%= Request.ApplicationPath %>/images/selTR.gif'>
                    </td>
                </tr>
                <tr>
                    <td>
                        <img src='<%= Request.ApplicationPath %>/images/selL.gif'>
                    </td>
                    <td>
                        <span class="SelectedTab">
                            <%# Ctype(Container.DataItem, TabStripDetails).TabName %>
                        </span>
                    </td>
```

```
                    <td>
                        <img src='<%= Request.ApplicationPath %>/images/selR.gif'>
                    </td>
                </tr>
                <tr>
                    <td>
                        <img src='<%= Request.ApplicationPath %>/images/selBL.gif'>
                    </td>
                    <td background='<%= Request.ApplicationPath %>/images/selB.gif'>
                    </td>
                    <td>
                        <img src='<%= Request.ApplicationPath %>/images/selBR.gif'>
                    </td>
                </tr>
            </table>
        </SelectedItemTemplate>
    </asp:datalist>
```

There is also a new CSS class, TabHolder, to make the display work properly:

```
/* Required for rounded tab display */
.TabHolder {
    border-width: 1;
    border-color: crimson;
}
```

Without this change, the background color of the tabs will bleed out around the edges of the bitmaps, making things look a bit odd. By forcing the tabs to have a border we prevent this from happening.

Of course, changes to the color scheme or font size may require modification of the bitmaps for the edges of the buttons, but this demonstrates how we can modify this control to change the look of the site more substantially.

Customizing the Layout of the Portal Pages

In the last chapter, we saw how the main body of DesktopDefault.aspx is made up of three columns called LeftPane, ContentPane, and RightPane:

```
<table width="100%" cellspacing="0" cellpadding="4" border="0">
    <tr height="*" valign="top">
        <td width="5">
             
        </td>
        <td id="LeftPane" Visible="false" Width="170" runat="server">
        </td>
        <td width="1">
        </td>
        <td id="ContentPane" Visible="false" Width="*" runat="server">
        </td>
        <td id="RightPane" Visible="false" Width="230" runat="server">
        </td>
```

```
        <td width="10">
             
        </td>
    </tr>
</table>
```

Note that the `ContentPane` column expands to fill the available space, so if modules are only placed on `LeftPane` and `ContentPane` then `ContentPane` will extend to the far right of the page.

When modules are added to the page at runtime they are added to one of these panes based on the value stored in the `PaneName` column in the `Modules` table. This column stores text values, and if you look at the existing data, you'll see that each module contains one of the values `LeftPane`, `ContentPane`, or `RightPane`.

In addition, the **Admin** page for tab design has three boxes on it showing the modules contained in each of these panes:

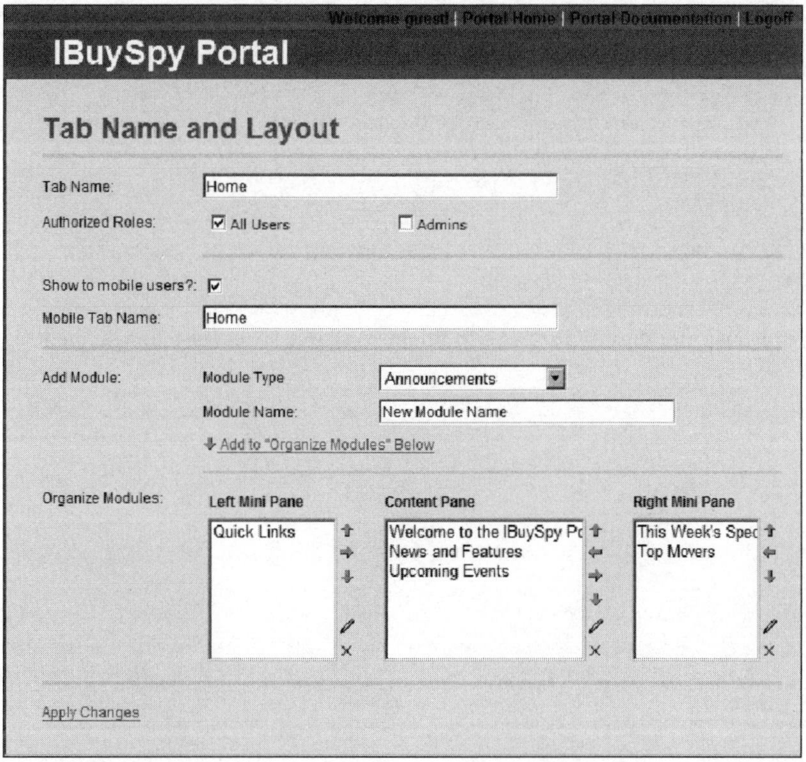

The upshot of all this is that if we change the layout of the form in `DesktopDefault.aspx` we need to make changes in other places to facilitate this. This isn't an insurmountable task, but requires quite a lot of work, as we will see shortly.

Alternatively, we could simply manipulate the three existing panes, requiring much less work. For example, we could place `ContentPane` underneath `LeftPane` and `RightPane`:

```
<table width="100%" cellspacing="0" cellpadding="4" border="0">
    <tr height="*" valign="top">
        <td width="5">
             
        </td>
        <td id="LeftPane" Visible="false" Width="170" runat="server">
        </td>
        <td width="1">
        </td>
        <td id="RightPane" Visible="false" Width="*" runat="server">
        </td>
        <td width="10">
             
        </td>
    </tr>
    <tr height="*" valign="top">
        <td width="5">
             
        </td>
        <td id="ContentPane" Visible="false" Width="*" runat="server" colspan="3">
        </td>
        <td width="10">
             
        </td>
    </tr>
</table>
```

The above code also modifies `RightPane` to fill the available space; else things might start looking very odd!

The result of this change is as follows:

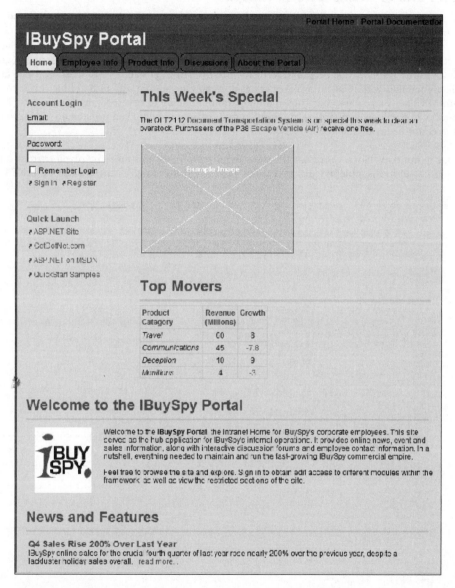

Admittedly, with the content as it is right now, this doesn't look too great, but it does illustrate what we can do without much effort, and this sort of layout may well be ideal for some applications.

O.K, let's look at adding a new pane and the steps we have to go through to achieve this.

Adding a Pane to DesktopDefault.aspx

Before getting started with modifications like this, it is worth sitting back and thinking carefully about what you are doing. The knock-on effects of making one small change in an application like this, where several sections are interlinked, are often more serious than you might expect. The change made in the last section turned out to be quite simple, but what if a specific module relied on the original code being exactly as it was? We must be prepared to deal with this sort of possibility - at least until you are completely familiar with the framework you are editing. One simple way of handling this is to make backups of whatever you are changing in anticipation of having to revert to an older version in case of disaster. Such problems may not be apparent at first; they may be picked up later so having safe code to revert to could be invaluable.

With this in mind, we'll walk through the steps required to make this more involved customization. The initial modification is simple; we just add a new place for things to go in the existing ASP.NET code:

```
<table width="100%" cellspacing="0" cellpadding="0" border="0">
    <tr valign="top">
        <td colspan="2">
            <portal:Banner id="Banner" SelectedTabIndex="0" runat="server" />
        </td>
    </tr>
    <tr>
        <td>
            <br>
            <table width="100%" cellspacing="0" cellpadding="4" border="0">
                <tr height="*" valign="top">
                    <td width="5">
                         
                    </td>
                    <td id="LeftPane" Visible="false" Width="170" runat="server">
                    </td>
                    <td width="1">
                    </td>
                    <td id="ContentPane" Visible="false" Width="*" runat="server">
                    </td>
                    <td id="RightPane" Visible="false" Width="230" runat="server">
                    </td>
                    <td width="10">
                         
                    </td>
                </tr>
            </table>
        </td>
    </tr>
    <tr valign="top">
        <td id="FooterPane" Visible="false" Width="*" runat="server">
        </td>
    </tr>
</table>
```

Since this pane currently has no content, nothing will change on the site.

```
<form runat="server">
    <table width="100%" cellspacing="0" cellpadding="0" border="0">
        <tr valign="top">
            ...Banner...
        </tr>
        <tr>
            <td>
                <br>
                <table width="98%" cellspacing="0" cellpadding="4">
                    <tr valign="top">
                        <td width="150">
                             
                        </td>
                        <td width="*">
                            <table border="0" cellpadding="2" cellspacing="1">
                                ...non-layout tab properties...
                                <tr valign="top">
                                    <td class="Normal">
                                        Organize Modules:
                                    </td>
                                    <td width="120">
                                        ...LeftPane content...
                                    </td>
                                    <td width="*">
                                        ...ContentPane content...
                                    </td>
                                    <td width="120">
                                        ...RightPane content...
                                    </td>
                                </tr>
                                ...padding and Apply Changes link...
                            </table>
                        </td>
                    </tr>
                </table>
            </td>
        </tr>
    </table>
</form>
```

The highlighted section is the code for the three panes containing module information for the three existing panes. What we need to do is to add another panel with a list of modules contained in our new pane, and hook it up to the rest of the page appropriately.

77

Taking the existing page content into account this is actually easier than it sounds. We can copy the code from one of the other `<td>` elements to a new one and modify the code to reflect the new content as follows (the changes from the code for the `RightPane` table are highlighted):

```
<td width="120">
    <table border="0" cellspacing="0" cellpadding="2" width="100%">
        <tr>
            <td class="NormalBold">
                 Footer Pane
            </td>
        </tr>
        <tr>
            <td>
                <table border="0" cellspacing="2" cellpadding="0">
                    <tr valign="top">
                        <td rowspan="2">
                            <asp:ListBox id="footerPane"
                                DataSource="<%# footerList %>"
                                DataTextField="ModuleTitle"
                                DataValueField="ModuleId" width="110"
                                rows="7" runat="server" />
                        </td>
                        <td valign="top" nowrap>
                            <asp:ImageButton ImageUrl="~/images/up.gif"
                                CommandName="up"
                                CommandArgument="footerPane"
                                AlternateText= "Move selected module up in list"
                                runat="server" id="FooterUpBtn" />
                            <br>
                            <asp:ImageButton ImageUrl="~/images/lt.gif"
                                sourcepane="footerPane"
                                targetpane="rightPane"
                                AlternateText=
                                    "Move selected module to the right pane"
                                runat="server" id="FooterLeftBtn" />
                            <br>
                            <asp:ImageButton ImageUrl="~/images/dn.gif"
                                CommandName="down"
                                CommandArgument="footerPane"
                                AlternateText="Move selected module down in list"
                                runat="server" id="FooterDownBtn" />
                        </td>
                    </tr>
                    <tr>
                        <td valign="bottom" nowrap>
                            <asp:ImageButton ImageUrl="~/images/edit.gif"
                                CommandName="edit"
                                CommandArgument="footerPane"
                                AlternateText="Edit this item"
                                runat="server" id="FooterEditBtn" />
                            <br>
                            <asp:ImageButton ImageUrl="~/images/delete.gif"
                                CommandName="delete"
                                CommandArgument="footerPane"
```

```
                                AlternateText="Delete this item"
                                runat="server" id="FooterDeleteBtn" />
                    </td>
                </tr>
            </table>
        </td>
    </tr>
</table>
</td>
```

There are also a few more changes to make. First, every `colspan` attribute of table cells above and below the module content panes must be increased by 1 to allow space for the new pane (we won't show this here as there are quite a few of them). Next, the width of the `ContentPane` table and `listbox` should be reduced to the same size as those for the other panes, since there is now an extra pane to fit in. Finally, we need to add a button to the `RightPane` code to allow modules to be moved into the new `FooterPane` window:

```
<asp:ImageButton ImageUrl="~/images/lt.gif" sourcepane="rightPane"
    targetpane="contentPane"
    AlternateText="Move selected module to the content pane" runat="server"
    id="RightLeftBtn" />
<br>
<asp:ImageButton ImageUrl="~/images/rt.gif" sourcepane="rightPane"
    targetpane="footerPane"
    AlternateText="Move selected module to the footer pane" runat="server"
    id="RightRightBtn" />
<br>
<asp:ImageButton ImageUrl="~/images/dn.gif" CommandName="down"
    CommandArgument="rightPane" AlternateText="Move selected module down in list"
    runat="server" id="RightDownBtn" />
```

This completes the changes for the ASP.NET code, now we have to make some modifications to the form code.

First, we need to make sure that when the page is loaded the list of modules for the new pane is populated. This occurs in `BindData` with the following code for the existing panes:

```
' Populate Right Hand Module Data
rightList = GetModules("RightPane")
rightPane.DataBind()

' Populate Content Pane Module Data
contentList = GetModules("ContentPane")
contentPane.DataBind()

' Populate Left Hand Pane Module Data
leftList = GetModules("LeftPane")
leftPane.DataBind()
```

The `GetModules` method simply checks the `PaneName` data for modules on the current tab, comparing the string with the data it is passed. This modification, then, is simple:

```
' Populate Left Hand Pane Module Data
leftList = GetModules("LeftPane")
leftPane.DataBind()

' Populate Footer Pane Module Data
footerList = GetModules("FooterPane")
footerPane.DataBind()
```

In order for this to work, we need to add a new protected member to the page class:

```
Protected leftList As ArrayList
Protected contentList As ArrayList
Protected rightList As ArrayList
Protected footerList As ArrayList
```

This is already hooked up to our list by the ASP.NET code added earlier, as shown below:

```
<asp:ListBox id="footerPane"
    DataSource="<%# footerList %>"
    DataTextField="ModuleTitle"
    DataValueField="ModuleId" width="110"
    rows="7" runat="server" />
```

Next, we need to make four of the event handlers in the code, `EditBtn_Click`, `Delete_Btn_Click`, `RightLeft_Click`, and `UpDown_Click`, respond to clicks on the new buttons we've added. This is simply a case of adding the `Click` events of the new controls to the list after the `Handles` keyword in the relevant code.

Specifically, we need to add `Click` events as follows:

Event Handler	Controls to Add Click Events for
EditBtn_Click()	FooterEditBtn
Delete_Btn_Click()	FooterDeleteBtn
RightLeft_Click()	FooterLeftBtn, FooterRightBtn
UpDown_Click()	FooterUpBtn, FooterDownBtn

Once this has been done you should find that you can move modules into the new pane we have added.

Of course, these changes aren't exactly the easiest in the world. Although you only have to do this once it may be worth completely redesigning the **Admin** page in question!

Building a Module

The last topic we'll cover in this chapter is adding a new module to the existing ten, integrating it with the framework. Again, this isn't as difficult as it might seem, and the results can be very satisfying.

The Books Module

The module we'll build in this chapter is called Books, and displays a list of books with various information and a link to buy them from Amazon as shown below:

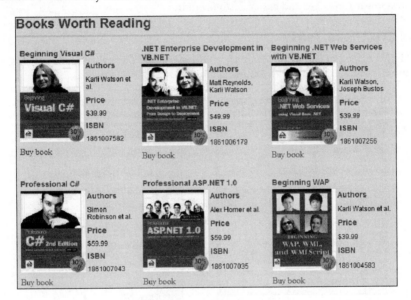

The content and number of columns to display will be fully editable from within the framework.

We will need to carry out the following tasks to implement this new Module:

❑ Add a database table to store the module data.

❑ Add stored procedures to query this data.

❑ Create a data access component to use these stored procedures to access data.

❑ Create a user control to display the data.

❑ Create an administration page for modifying data.

❑ Add the module to the list of modules recognized by the portal.

Only when we have done all this will we be able to add this new module to a portal tab and start inputting data. This task list makes things slightly awkward for module designers - you need to have a good idea of the result before you create a module. You may wish to experiment with various display schemes using dummy data on a separate page before you start, so you don't have to go back and change things. Of course, specific modules may require a lot more (or less) work than this, but that's down to the specifics of your end aim.

In adding this module, we will closely follow the scheme used by one of the other modules, Announcements. This will mean that we'll be able to get a better understanding of how these modules work. Later in the book, we'll take a slightly different approach, particularly in terms of data access, tailored more towards quicker and easier customization.

The Books Database Table

The new table we need to add to the database is called Books. This table contains fields similar to those for Announcements as shown in the following diagram:

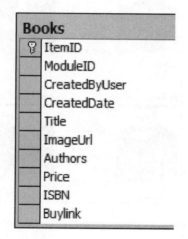

Each row of this table contains information about a single book, and links it to an instance of the Books module via ModuleID.

The columns are as follows:

Column	Data Type	Description
ItemID	int	ID of the book item. This column is the primary key of the table, and is set to Identity.
ModuleID	int	ID of the module containing the book item.
CreatedByUser	nvarchar (100)	The e-mail address of the user that created the book item.
CreatedDate	DateTime	The date the book item was added to the database.

Column	Data Type	Description
Title	nvarchar (150)	The title of the book item.
ImageUrl	nvarchar (150)	The URL of the book cover picture.
Authors	nvarchar (150)	A list of authors for the book.
Price	nvarchar (10)	The price of the book, omitting currency symbol.
ISBN	nvarchar (10)	The ISBN number of the book.
Buylink	nvarchar (150)	An optional URL link to a page where this book can be bought.

The SQL script to generate this table is included with the downloadable code for the chapter, in the file AddBooksTable.sql, which should be executed against the Portal database.

Stored Procedures

If you look in the Stored Procedures section of the Portal database, you'll see a long list of stored procedures, including the following that operate on data in the Announcements table:

Stored Procedure	Usage
AddAnouncement	Adds an announcement to the database, returns the new ItemID.
DeleteAnnouncement	Removes an announcement from the database, specified via ItemID.
GetAnnouncements	Obtains all data about all announcements in the database for a specified ModuleID.
GetSingleAnnouncement	Obtains all information about an ItemID-specified announcement.
UpdateAnnouncement	Modifies the data stored for an announcement with a given ItemID.

We need to add five similar stored procedures working with data in the Books table rather than the Announcements table. These stored procedures are shown below (and included in the AddBooksTable.sql script):

AddBook

This stored procedure adds a book item to the Books table, taking all the required parameters for a new book and returning the ItemID of the new record as an output parameter. It is worth noting that we don't specify a value for the CreatedDate field - the SQL GetDate function is used to add the date when the stored procedure is executed.

```
CREATE PROCEDURE AddBook
(
    @ModuleID        int,
    @UserName        nvarchar(100),
    @Title           nvarchar(150),
    @ImageUrl        nvarchar(150),
    @Authors         nvarchar(150),
    @Price           nvarchar(10),
    @ISBN            nvarchar(10),
    @BuyLink         nvarchar(150),
    @ItemID          int OUTPUT
)
AS

INSERT INTO Books
(
    ModuleID,
    CreatedByUser,
    CreatedDate,
    Title,
    ImageUrl,
    Authors,
    Price,
    ISBN,
    BuyLink
)

VALUES
(
    @ModuleID,
    @UserName,
    GetDate(),
    @Title,
    @ImageUrl,
    @Authors,
    @Price,
    @ISBN,
    @BuyLink
)

SELECT
    @ItemID = @@Identity
GO
DeleteBook
```

DeleteBook

This stored procedure deletes the book item with the specified ItemID:

```
CREATE PROCEDURE DeleteBook
(
    @ItemID int
)
AS
```

```
DELETE FROM
    Books

WHERE
    ItemID = @ItemID
GO
```

GetBooks

This stored procedure returns all the books associated with a specified module instance. The module to get books for is chosen using the `ModuleID` parameter:

```
CREATE PROCEDURE GetBooks
(
    @ModuleID int
)
AS

SELECT
    ItemID,
    CreatedByUser,
    CreatedDate,
    Title,
    ImageUrl,
    Authors,
    Price,
    ISBN,
    BuyLink

FROM
    Books

WHERE
    ModuleID = @ModuleID
GO
```

GetSingleBook

This stored procedure obtains a single book item by specifying its `ItemID`:

```
CREATE PROCEDURE GetSingleBook
(
    @ItemID int
)
AS

SELECT
    CreatedByUser,
    CreatedDate,
    Title,
    ImageUrl,
    Authors,
    Price,
```

```
        ISBN,
        BuyLink

    FROM
        Books

    WHERE
        ItemID = @ItemID
    GO
```

UpdateBook

This stored procedure modifies an existing book item by supplying new values for all its fields. Again, GetDate is used to get a new value for the CreatedDate field:

```
CREATE PROCEDURE UpdateBook
(
    @ItemID          int,
    @UserName        nvarchar(100),
    @Title           nvarchar(150),
    @ImageUrl        nvarchar(150),
    @Authors         nvarchar(150),
    @Price           nvarchar(10),
    @ISBN            nvarchar(10),
    @BuyLink         nvarchar(150)
)
AS

UPDATE
    Books

SET
    CreatedByUser   = @UserName,
    CreatedDate     = GetDate(),
    Title           = @Title,
    ImageUrl        = @ImageUrl,
    Authors         = @Authors,
    Price           = @Price,
    ISBN            = @ISBN,
    BuyLink         = @BuyLink

WHERE
    ItemID = @ItemID
GO
```

Data Access Component

The data access class for the Announcements module is called AnnouncementsDB, and is stored in a file called AnnouncementsDB.vb. This class has five methods with the same names as the five stored procedures for accessing announcement data, and the same parameters:

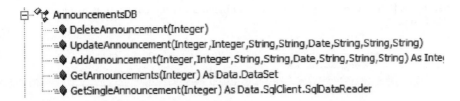

Each of these methods has three features in common:

- ❏ They start by initializing a connection using the connection string stored in the `AppSettings` section of `web.config`.

- ❏ Next they select a stored procedure to use with this connection:

- ❏ Then, they add parameters to this stored command using the method parameters and execute the command.

At this point, the methods differ, since some return data and some don't.

Again, we'll structure our data access class in the same way. The new class is called `BooksDB`, stored in `BooksDB.vb`. This file contains the same `Imports` statements as `AnnouncementsDB.vb`, and defines the `BooksDB` class in the `ASPNetPortal` namespace. This class has five methods, one for each of the stored procedures added earlier:

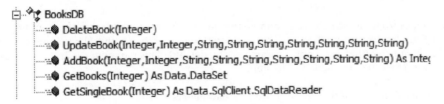

We'll walk through the code for `AddBook` then list the rest of the code, which is very similar.

AddBook

This method has parameters for each column in the database except `CreatedDate`, which is added automatically by the database:

```
Public Function AddBook(ByVal moduleId As Integer, _
                        ByVal itemId As Integer, ByVal userName As String, _
                        ByVal title As String, ByVal imageUrl As String, _
                        ByVal authors As String, ByVal price As String, _
                        ByVal isbn As String, ByVal buyLink As String) _
            As Integer
```

If no username is specified an `unknown` value is used:

```
If userName.Length < 1 Then
   userName = "unknown"
End If
```

The first step is to initialize a `SqlConnection` object, using the connection string stored in `web.config`:

```
' Create Instance of Connection and Command Object
Dim myConnection As _
  New SqlConnection(ConfigurationSettings.AppSettings("connectionString"))
```

We also need to initialize a `SqlCommand` object to access the stored procedure, in this case `AddBook`:

```
Dim myCommand As New SqlCommand("AddBook", myConnection)
```

`SqlCommand` objects contain SQL queries by default, so we need to specify that the text we have added is the name of a stored procedure (or SPROC):

```
' Mark the Command as a SPROC
myCommand.CommandType = CommandType.StoredProcedure
```

Next, we need to add parameters to the stored procedure, starting with `ItemID`:

```
' Add Parameters to SPROC
Dim parameterItemID As New SqlParameter("@ItemID", SqlDbType.Int, 4)
parameterItemID.Direction = ParameterDirection.Output
myCommand.Parameters.Add(parameterItemID)
```

We use types from the `SqlDbType` enumeration to specify types identical to those in the database, and a value from the `ParameterDirection` enumeration to specify whether the parameter is an `Input` or `Output` parameter (they are `Input` parameters by default). This parameter is an `Output` parameter - it returns the `ItemID` of the added book item.

Next, we have the rest of the stored procedure parameters:

```
Dim parameterModuleID As New SqlParameter("@ModuleID", SqlDbType.Int, 4)
parameterModuleID.Value = moduleId
myCommand.Parameters.Add(parameterModuleID)

Dim parameterUserName As New SqlParameter("@UserName", _
                                          SqlDbType.NVarChar, 100)
parameterUserName.Value = userName
myCommand.Parameters.Add(parameterUserName)

Dim parameterTitle As New SqlParameter("@Title", SqlDbType.NVarChar, 150)
parameterTitle.Value = title
myCommand.Parameters.Add(parameterTitle)

Dim parameterImageUrl As New SqlParameter("@ImageUrl", _
                                          SqlDbType.NVarChar, 150)
parameterImageUrl.Value = imageUrl
myCommand.Parameters.Add(parameterImageUrl)

Dim parameterAuthors As New SqlParameter("@Authors", _
```

```
                                                      SqlDbType.NVarChar, 150)
        parameterAuthors.Value = authors
        myCommand.Parameters.Add(parameterAuthors)

        Dim parameterPrice As New SqlParameter("@Price", SqlDbType.NVarChar, 10)
        parameterPrice.Value = price
        myCommand.Parameters.Add(parameterPrice)

        Dim parameterISBN As New SqlParameter("@ISBN", SqlDbType.NVarChar, 10)
        parameterISBN.Value = isbn
        myCommand.Parameters.Add(parameterISBN)

        Dim parameterBuyLink As New SqlParameter("@BuyLink", _
                                        SqlDbType.NVarChar, 150)
        parameterBuyLink.Value = buyLink
        myCommand.Parameters.Add(parameterBuyLink)
```

Once all parameters have been added, we can execute the stored procedure and close the connection:

```
        myConnection.Open()
        myCommand.ExecuteNonQuery()
        myConnection.Close()
```

Finally, we return the integer obtained from the ItemID parameter as the result of the method.

```
        Return CInt(parameterItemID.Value)

    End Function
```

The rest of the methods follow a very similar structure, although the return types are different.

DeleteBook

```
Public Sub DeleteBook(ByVal itemID As Integer)

        ' Create Instance of Connection and Command Object
        Dim myConnection As _
         New SqlConnection(ConfigurationSettings.AppSettings("connectionString"))
        Dim myCommand As New SqlCommand("DeleteBook", myConnection)

        ' Mark the Command as a SPROC
        myCommand.CommandType = CommandType.StoredProcedure

        ' Add Parameters to SPROC
        Dim parameterItemID As New SqlParameter("@ItemID", SqlDbType.Int, 4)
        parameterItemID.Value = itemID
        myCommand.Parameters.Add(parameterItemID)

        myConnection.Open()
        myCommand.ExecuteNonQuery()
        myConnection.Close()

    End Sub
```

GetBooks

```
Public Function GetBooks(ByVal moduleId As Integer) As DataSet

        ' Create Instance of Connection and Command Object
        Dim myConnection As _
         New SqlConnection(ConfigurationSettings.AppSettings("connectionString"))
        Dim myCommand As New SqlDataAdapter("GetBooks", myConnection)

        ' Mark the Command as a SPROC
        myCommand.SelectCommand.CommandType = CommandType.StoredProcedure

        ' Add Parameters to SPROC
        Dim parameterModuleId As New SqlParameter("@ModuleId", SqlDbType.Int, 4)
        parameterModuleId.Value = moduleId
        myCommand.SelectCommand.Parameters.Add(parameterModuleId)

        ' Create and Fill the DataSet
        Dim myDataSet As New DataSet()
        myCommand.Fill(myDataSet)

        ' Return the DataSet
        Return myDataSet

    End Function
```

GetSingleBook

```
Public Function GetSingleBook(ByVal itemId As Integer) As SqlDataReader

        ' Create Instance of Connection and Command Object
        Dim myConnection As _
         New SqlConnection(ConfigurationSettings.AppSettings("connectionString"))
        Dim myCommand As New SqlCommand("GetSingleBook", myConnection)

        ' Mark the Command as a SPROC
        myCommand.CommandType = CommandType.StoredProcedure

        ' Add Parameters to SPROC
        Dim parameterItemId As New SqlParameter("@ItemId", SqlDbType.Int, 4)
        parameterItemId.Value = itemId
        myCommand.Parameters.Add(parameterItemId)

        ' Execute the command
        myConnection.Open()
        Dim result As SqlDataReader = _
            myCommand.ExecuteReader(CommandBehavior.CloseConnection)

        ' Return the datareader
        Return result

    End Function
```

UpdateBook

```
Public Sub UpdateBook(ByVal moduleId As Integer, ByVal itemId As Integer, _
                      ByVal userName As String, ByVal title As String, _
                      ByVal imageUrl As String, ByVal authors As String, _
                      ByVal price As String, ByVal isbn As String, _
                      ByVal buyLink As String)

        If userName.Length < 1 Then
           userName = "unknown"
        End If
        ' Create Instance of Connection and Command Object
        Dim myConnection As _
         New SqlConnection(ConfigurationSettings.AppSettings("connectionString"))
        Dim myCommand As New SqlCommand("UpdateBook", myConnection)

        ' Mark the Command as a SPROC
        myCommand.CommandType = CommandType.StoredProcedure

        ' Add Parameters to SPROC
        Dim parameterItemID As New SqlParameter("@ItemID", SqlDbType.Int, 4)
        parameterItemID.Value = itemId
        myCommand.Parameters.Add(parameterItemID)

        Dim parameterUserName As New SqlParameter("@UserName", _
                                                    SqlDbType.NVarChar, 100)
        parameterUserName.Value = userName
        myCommand.Parameters.Add(parameterUserName)

        Dim parameterTitle As New SqlParameter("@Title", SqlDbType.NVarChar, 150)
        parameterTitle.Value = title
        myCommand.Parameters.Add(parameterTitle)

        Dim parameterImageUrl As New SqlParameter("@ImageUrl", _
                                                    SqlDbType.NVarChar, 150)
        parameterImageUrl.Value = imageUrl
        myCommand.Parameters.Add(parameterImageUrl)

        Dim parameterAuthors As New SqlParameter("@Authors", _
                                                    SqlDbType.NVarChar, 150)
        parameterAuthors.Value = authors
        myCommand.Parameters.Add(parameterAuthors)

        Dim parameterPrice As New SqlParameter("@Price", SqlDbType.NVarChar, 10)
        parameterPrice.Value = price
        myCommand.Parameters.Add(parameterPrice)

        Dim parameterISBN As New SqlParameter("@ISBN", SqlDbType.NVarChar, 10)
        parameterISBN.Value = isbn
        myCommand.Parameters.Add(parameterISBN)

        Dim parameterBuyLink As New SqlParameter("@BuyLink", _
```

```
                                                          SqlDbType.NVarChar, 150)
        parameterBuyLink.Value = buyLink
        myCommand.Parameters.Add(parameterBuyLink)

        myConnection.Open()
        myCommand.ExecuteNonQuery()
        myConnection.Close()

    End Sub
```

User Control

Next, we come to the .ascx file containing the new module, which is perhaps the most important part since it encapsulates the module's appearance and functionality.

The ASP.NET code for this module mirrors that for the Announcements module as follows:

- ❏ The class for the page inherits from PortalModuleControl.
- ❏ The ASP.NET code starts with a DesktopModuleTitle.ascx user control.
- ❏ The main body of the control consists of a DataList control called myDataList.

The layout of the <ItemTemplate> is slightly more complicated than that for Announcements, as more data needs to be displayed. The basic layout is a 2x8 cell table, containing the following text and column data for each cell:

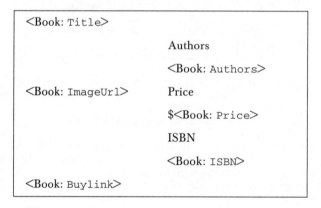

The code starts with the usual directives:

```
<%@ Register TagPrefix="Portal" TagName="Title" Src="~/DesktopModuleTitle.ascx"%>
<%@ Control Language="vb" Inherits="ASPNetPortal.Books" Codebehind="Books.ascx.vb"
          AutoEventWireup="false" %>
```

Next, we have the `title` control, which includes a link to `EditBooks.aspx` (the page we'll create in the next section used for editing the content of the module):

```
<portal:title id="Title1" runat="server" EditUrl="~/DesktopModules/EditBooks.aspx"
              EditText="Add New Book"></portal:title>
```

And then the `DataList` control itself:

```
<asp:datalist id="myDataList" runat="server" EnableViewState="false" Width="98%"
              CellPadding="4">
```

The `<ItemTemplate>` starts with a `<table>` element, and the first databound content, including an Edit link for the item to be displayed in **Admin** mode and the book title in `ItemTitle` format:

```
<ItemTemplate>
    <table>
        <tr>
            <td colspan="2">
                <asp:HyperLink id="editLink" ImageUrl="~/images/edit.gif"
                NavigateUrl='<%# "~/DesktopModules/EditBooks.aspx?ItemID=" &
                DataBinder.Eval(Container.DataItem,"ItemID") & "&mid=" &
                ModuleId %>' Visible="<%# IsEditable %>" runat="server" />
                <span class="ItemTitle">
                    <%# DataBinder.Eval(Container.DataItem,"Title") %>
                </span>
            </td>
        </tr>
```

The Edit link also references `EditBooks.aspx` (which we'll create shortly), including `ItemID` and `mid` querystring parameters used to choose which book item for which module will be edited by this form.

Next, we have the cell containing the cover picture, loaded via the `ImageUrl` field:

```
<tr>
    <td rowspan="6">
     <img src='<%# DataBinder.Eval(Container.DataItem,"ImageUrl") %>'>
    </td>
```

Next, we have the `Authors` data, including a plain HTML title in `ItemTitle` format and the bound data:

```
<td>
    <span class="ItemTitle">
        Authors
    </span>
</td>
    </tr>
    <tr>
```

```
        <td>
            <span class="Normal">
                <%# DataBinder.Eval(Container.DataItem,"Authors") %>
            </span>
        </td>
    </tr>
```

A similar scheme is used to display Price and ISBN data:

```
    <tr>
        <td>
            <span class="ItemTitle">
                Price
            </span>
        </td>
    </tr>
    <tr>
        <td>
            <span class="Normal">
                $<%# DataBinder.Eval(Container.DataItem,"Price") %>
            </span>
        </td>
    </tr>
    <tr>
        <td>
            <span class="ItemTitle">
                ISBN
            </span>
        </td>
    </tr>
    <tr>
        <td>
            <span class="Normal">
                <%# DataBinder.Eval(Container.DataItem,"ISBN") %>
            </span>
        </td>
    </tr>
```

Finally, we have the link to buy the book, which is only displayed if a URL is present in the database:

```
    <tr>
        <td colspan="2">
            <asp:HyperLink id="buyLink" NavigateUrl=
            '<%# DataBinder.Eval(Container.DataItem,"BuyLink") %>'
            Visible='<%# DataBinder.Eval(Container.DataItem,"BuyLink") <>
            String.Empty %>' runat="server">
                Buy book
            </asp:HyperLink>
        </td>
    </tr>
</table>
```

```
        <br>
    </ItemTemplate>
</asp:datalist>
```

The code for this control is very short indeed, since most of the hard work is carried out by the data access component. The only event handler used is Page_Load, which starts by instantiating a BooksDB object, extracting the relevant data, and binding it to the DataList:

```
Private Sub Page_Load(ByVal sender As System.Object, _
                      ByVal e As System.EventArgs) Handles MyBase.Load

    ' Obtain book information from Books table
    ' and bind to the datalist control
    Dim booksDB As New ASPNetPortal.BooksDB()

    ' DataBind Announcements to DataList Control
    myDataList.DataSource = booksDB.GetBooks(ModuleId)
    myDataList.DataBind()
```

This code uses the ModuleId property inherited from PortalModuleControl.

At the start of this section, we mentioned that the number of columns used to display books is customizable. This data is stored in the custom module settings database (ModuleSettings), in a setting called 'columns'. This data is accessible via the Settings property inherited from PortalModuleControl as discussed in the last chapter.

The remained of the code in Page_Load examines this setting to see if a value is present, and sets myDataList.RepeatColumns accordingly:

```
    Dim repeatColumns As Integer = CType(Settings("columns"), Integer)
    If repeatColumns = Nothing Then
        myDataList.RepeatColumns = 0
    Else
        myDataList.RepeatColumns = repeatColumns
    End If

End Sub
```

Note that the default value of 0 doesn't mean "zero columns", it just means that no value is suggested to the control. In practice, this means that 1 column will be used. Note also that the value specified is not an absolute value - the DataList control will often select a different value that leads to a more attractive arrangement, although the maximum amount of columns used is limited by this value.

Admin Page

At this point, the Books module is ready to display, but we are unable to add content or change the custom columns setting. To facilitate this we need an administration page, again based on the one for the Announcements module, EditAnnouncements.aspx.

`EditAnnouncements.aspx` consists of a single table, with the `DesktopPortalBanner.ascx` control at the top and various fields for editing announcement data in the remainder. The page for the `Books` modules, `EditBooks.aspx`, will contain a similar table, with `DesktopPortalBanner.ascx` at the top and book editing fields below. We'll also include a section for global module configuration, where we can edit the `columns` setting. The ASP.NET code for this page starts as follows:

```
<%@ Register TagPrefix="portal" TagName="Banner"
             Src="~/DesktopPortalBanner.ascx" %>
<%@ Page language="vb" CodeBehind="EditBooks.aspx.vb" AutoEventWireup="false"
         Inherits="ASPNetPortal.EditBooks" %>
<HTML>
  <HEAD>
    <link rel="stylesheet" href='<%= Request.ApplicationPath & "/Portal.css" %>'
          type="text/css" >
  </HEAD>
  <body leftmargin="0" bottommargin="0" rightmargin="0" topmargin="0"
        marginheight="0" marginwidth="0">
    <form runat="server">
      <table width="100%" cellspacing="0" cellpadding="0" border="0">
        <tr valign="top">
          <td colspan="2">
            <portal:Banner id="SiteHeader" runat="server" />
          </td>
        </tr>
```

From this point on, we have our book editing fields. This section starts with a heading in the CSS `Head` format:

```
        <tr>
          <td>
            <br>
            <table width="98%" cellspacing="0" cellpadding="4" border="0">
              <tr valign="top">
                <td width="150">
                   
                </td>
                <td width="*">
                  <table width="520" cellspacing="0" cellpadding="0">
                    <tr>
                      <td align="left" class="Head">
                        Book Details
                      </td>
                    </tr>
                    <tr>
                      <td colspan="2">
                        <hr noshade size="1">
                      </td>
                    </tr>
                  </table>
```

Next, we have the first field, `TitleField`, for setting the book title:

```
<table width="750" cellspacing="0" cellpadding="0">
  <tr valign="top">
    <td width="100" class="SubHead">
      Title:
    </td>
    <td rowspan="6">
       
    </td>
    <td>
      <asp:TextBox id="TitleField" cssclass="NormalTextBox"
        width="390" Columns="30" maxlength="100"
        runat="server" />
    </td>
    <td width="25" rowspan="6">
       
    </td>
```

We also include a `RequiredFieldValidator` validation control since a book needs a title:

```
    <td class="Normal" width="250">
      <asp:RequiredFieldValidator id="Req1" Display="Static"
        ErrorMessage="You Must Enter a Valid Title"
        ControlToValidate="TitleField" runat="server" />
    </td>
  </tr>
```

The code continues with fields for entering the `ImageUrl`, `Authors`, `ISBN`, `Price`, and `BuyLink` data:

```
  <tr valign="top">
    <td class="SubHead">
      Image URL:
    </td>
    <td>
      <asp:TextBox id="ImageUrlField" cssclass="NormalTextBox"
        width="390" Columns="30" maxlength="100"
        runat="server" />
    </td>
    <td class="Normal" width="250">
      <asp:RequiredFieldValidator id="Req2" Display="Static"
        ErrorMessage="You Must Enter a Valid URL"
        ControlToValidate="ImageURLField" runat="server" />
    </td>
  </tr>
  <tr valign="top">
    <td class="SubHead" nowrap>
      Authors:
    </td>
    <td>
      <asp:TextBox id="AuthorsField" cssclass="NormalTextBox"
```

```
          width="390" Columns="30" maxlength="100"
          runat="server" />
      </td>
      <td class="Normal" width="250">
        <asp:RequiredFieldValidator id="Req3" Display="Static"
        ErrorMessage="You Must Enter a Valid Author List"
        ControlToValidate="AuthorsField" runat="server" />
      </td>
    </tr>
    <tr valign="top">
      <td class="SubHead" nowrap>
        ISBN:
      </td>
      <td>
        <asp:TextBox id="ISBNField" cssclass="NormalTextBox"
          width="390" Columns="30" maxlength="100"
          runat="server" />
      </td>
      <td class="Normal" width="250">
        <asp:RequiredFieldValidator id="Req4" Display="Static"
        ErrorMessage="You Must Enter a Valid ISBN"
        ControlToValidate="ISBNField" runat="server" />
      </td>
    </tr>
    <tr valign="top">
      <td class="SubHead">
        Price:
      </td>
      <td>
        <asp:TextBox id="PriceField" runat="server"
          maxlength="100" Columns="30" width="390"
          cssclass="NormalTextBox"></asp:TextBox>
      </td>
      <td class="Normal">
        <asp:RequiredFieldValidator id="Req5" Display="Static"
        ErrorMessage="You Must Enter a Valid Price"
        ControlToValidate="PriceField" runat="server" />
      </td>
    </tr>
    <tr valign="top">
      <td class="SubHead">
        BuyLink:
      </td>
      <td>
        <asp:TextBox id="BuyLinkField" runat="server"
          maxlength="100" Columns="30" width="390"
          cssclass="NormalTextBox"></asp:TextBox>
      </td>
      <td class="Normal">
      </td>
    </tr>
</table>
```

Then, we have `LinkButton` controls allowing the user to update an existing book or add new book details, cancel the edit, or delete an existing book:

```
<p>
  <asp:LinkButton id="updateButton" Text="Update" runat="server"
    CssClass="CommandButton" BorderStyle="none" />
   
  <asp:LinkButton id="cancelButton" Text="Cancel"
    CausesValidation="False" runat="server"
    CssClass="CommandButton" BorderStyle="none" />
   
  <asp:LinkButton id="deleteButton" Text="Delete this item"
    CausesValidation="False" runat="server"
    CssClass="CommandButton" BorderStyle="none" />
  <hr noshade size="1" width="520">
```

Following on from this we have some read-only data about the book, specifically which user created the record and when:

```
<span class="Normal">Created by
  <asp:label id="CreatedBy" runat="server" />
  on
  <asp:label id="CreatedDate" runat="server" />
  <br>
</span>
<br>
<br>
```

Now we come to the global module settings section. We only have one of these, `columns`, so we include a heading, a field in a table structured just like the other fields above for consistency, and an `Update` button for applying changes to this field:

```
<span class="Head">Global Module Settings</span>
<hr noshade size="1" width="520">
<table width="750" cellspacing="0" cellpadding="0">
  <tr valign="top">
    <td width="100" class="SubHead">
      Columns:
    </td>
    <td>
       
    </td>
    <td>
      <asp:TextBox id="ColumnsField" cssclass="NormalTextBox"
        width="390" Columns="30" maxlength="100"
        runat="server" />
    </td>
    <td width="25">
       
    </td>
  </tr>
```

```
                    </table>
                    <br>
                    <asp:LinkButton id="updateGlobalButton" Text="Update"
                        runat="server" CssClass="CommandButton"
                        BorderStyle="none" />
                 <P></P>
              </td>
           </tr>
        </table>
      </td>
    </tr>
  </table>
</form>
</body>
</HTML>
```

The form looks as follows:

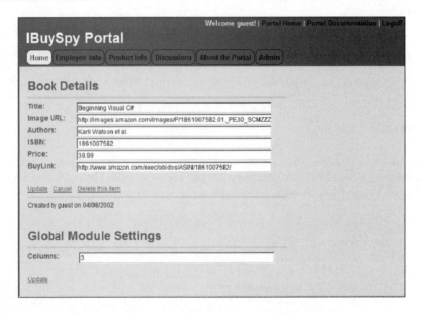

This layout is very similar to the EditAnnouncements.aspx page.

Now we need to look at the code for this page. First, Page_Load, which initializes the page. The first task here is to obtain the ID of the module that is being edited, check user permissions for editing, and see if a book item is requested for editing (that is, check to see if an ItemId querystring parameter is present):

```
Private Sub Page_Load(ByVal sender As System.Object, _
                     ByVal e As System.EventArgs) Handles MyBase.Load

  ' Determine ModuleId of Books Portal Module
  moduleId = Int32.Parse(Request.Params("Mid"))
```

```
' Verify that the current user has access to edit this module
If PortalSecurity.HasEditPermissions(moduleId) = False Then
    Response.Redirect("~/Admin/EditAccessDenied.aspx")
End If


' Determine ItemId of Book to Update
If Not (Request.Params("ItemId") Is Nothing) Then
    itemId = Int32.Parse(Request.Params("ItemId"))
End If
```

If an `itemId` parameter is present then we get details of the book using `BooksDB.GetSingleBook` and fill the fields on the page (remembering to close the `SqlDataReader` afterwards to close the associated connection):

```
' If the page is being requested for the first time, determine if an
' book itemId value is specified, and if so populate page
' contents with the book details
If Page.IsPostBack = False Then

    If itemId <> 0 Then

        ' Obtain a single row of announcement information
        Dim booksDB As New ASPNetPortal.BooksDB()
        Dim dr As SqlDataReader = booksDB.GetSingleBook(itemId)

        ' Load first row into DataReader
        dr.Read()

        TitleField.Text = CType(dr("Title"), String)
        ImageUrlField.Text = CType(dr("ImageUrl"), String)
        AuthorsField.Text = CType(dr("Authors"), String)
        ISBNField.Text = CType(dr("ISBN"), String)
        PriceField.Text = CType(dr("Price"), String)
        BuyLinkField.Text = CType(dr("BuyLink"), String)
        CreatedBy.Text = CType(dr("CreatedByUser"), String)
        CreatedDate.Text = CType(dr("CreatedDate"), _
                                DateTime).ToShortDateString()

        ' Close the datareader
        dr.Close()

    End If
```

Next, we get the custom settings from the shared `PortalSettings.GetModuleSettings` method (`settings` is a protected member of the class for the form, of type `HashTable`):

```
' Get global settings from the database
settings = PortalSettings.GetModuleSettings(moduleId)
```

Using the data returned, check for the presence of the `columns` setting. If no value appears then we set the associated field to the default value of 0, otherwise we set it to the stored value:

```
Dim repeatColumns As String = CType(settings("columns"), String)
If repeatColumns = Nothing Then
    ColumnsField.Text = "0"
Else
    ColumnsField.Text = repeatColumns
End If
```

Finally, we store a reference to the page used to navigate to the edit page, used in subsequent navigation:

```
        ' Store URL Referrer to return to portal
        ViewState("UrlReferrer") = Request.UrlReferrer.ToString()

    End If

End Sub
```

Next, we come to the event handler for the **Update** link for adding or updating book item details: `UpdateBtn_Click`. If the data entered is valid then the `BooksDB` data access component is used to either add a new book or update an existing book, using the appropriate method of the `BooksDB` class:

```
    Private Sub UpdateBtn_Click(ByVal sender As Object, ByVal e As EventArgs) _
            Handles updateButton.Click

        ' Only Update if the Entered Data is Valid
        If Page.IsValid = True Then

            ' Create an instance of the Books DB component
            Dim booksDB As New ASPNetPortal.BooksDB()

            If itemId = 0 Then

                ' Add the announcement within the Books table
                booksDB.AddBook(moduleId, itemId, Context.User.Identity.Name, _
                        TitleField.Text, ImageUrlField.Text, _
                        AuthorsField.Text, PriceField.Text, _
                        ISBNField.Text, BuyLinkField.Text)

            Else

                ' Update the announcement within the Books table
                booksDB.UpdateBook(moduleId, itemId, Context.User.Identity.Name, _
                        TitleField.Text, ImageUrlField.Text, _
                        AuthorsField.Text, PriceField.Text, _
                        ISBNField.Text, BuyLinkField.Text)

            End If
```

After making database changes the user is returned to the page from where they came:

```
        ' Redirect back to the portal home page
        Response.Redirect(CType(ViewState("UrlReferrer"), String))

    End If

End Sub
```

The handler for the **Delete** link, `DeleteBtn_Click`, is simpler since the required `BooksDB` method only has one parameter. Other than that, the code is very similar:

```
Private Sub DeleteBtn_Click(ByVal sender As Object, ByVal e As EventArgs) _
        Handles deleteButton.Click

    ' Only attempt to delete the item if it is an existing item
    ' (new items will have "ItemId" of 0)
    If itemId <> 0 Then

        Dim booksDB As New ASPNetPortal.BooksDB()
        booksDB.DeleteBook(itemId)

    End If

    ' Redirect back to the portal home page
    Response.Redirect(CType(ViewState("UrlReferrer"), String))

End Sub
```

The **Cancel** button handler, `CancelBtn_Click`, simply redirects the user to the referring page:

```
Private Sub CancelBtn_Click(ByVal sender As Object, ByVal e As EventArgs) _
        Handles cancelButton.Click

    ' Redirect back to the portal home page
    Response.Redirect(CType(ViewState("UrlReferrer"), String))

End Sub
```

Finally, we come to `updateGlobalButton_Click`, which handles updates of the custom `columns` data. This is the only method of this page that doesn't have a direct equivalent in the **Announcement** module edit page. Updating custom data is achieved using the `AdminDB.UpdateModuleSetting` method as follows:

```
Private Sub updateGlobalButton_Click(ByVal sender As System.Object, _
        ByVal e As System.EventArgs) Handles updateGlobalButton.Click

    ' Update settings in the database
    Dim admin As New AdminDB()

    ' Update columns setting
    admin.UpdateModuleSetting(moduleId, "columns", ColumnsField.Text)
End Sub
```

The AdminDB class (defined in AdminDB.vb) is one that we haven't yet looked at in this book. It contains various general purpose administration methods for performing tasks such as adding users, adding roles, associating users with roles, and so on. It is mainly used by the Admin tab tools, but as show above, it can also be useful for accessing other information from custom modules.

And that completes the code for this module!

Integrating with the Portal

The last thing to do is to make the portal recognize the new Books module. To do this we need to log in as a user in the Admin role (such as guest) and change a setting on the Admin tab. To the right of the page for this tab is a Module Definitions section showing available modules, and at the bottom of this is an Add New Module Type link. Click on this link and fill out the details as follows:

When you click on Update the module will be added to the list of those available.

Adding Data and Viewing Results

Now we can see the new module in action. From the Admin tab add a Books module called Books Worth Reading to the list of those available on the Product Info tab, moving it to the new FooterPane pane added earlier:

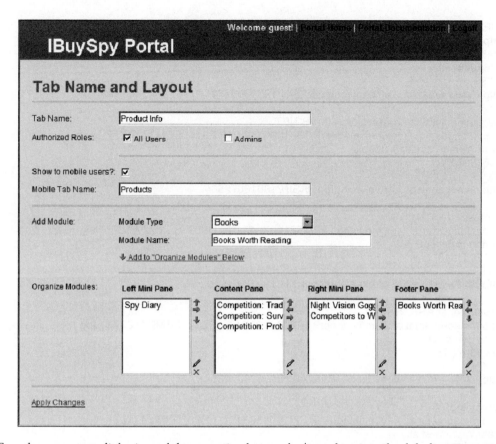

From here, we can edit basic module properties, but we don't need to since the default options are fine.

Next, navigate to the Product Info tab and you'll see the new module (currently empty) at the bottom of the screen. As you are still logged in as a member of the Admin group, you can proceed to add books to the module using the Add Book link. Feel free to add your own, or use the following records as sample data (fields listed in the order they appear on the book editing form):

Beginning Visual C#
http://images.amazon.com/images/P/1861007582.01._PE30_SCMZZZZZZZ_.jpg
Karli Watson et al.
1861007582
39.99
http://www.amazon.com/exec/obidos/ASIN/1861007582/

.NET Enterprise Development in VB.NET
http://images.amazon.com/images/P/1861006179.01._PE30_SCMZZZZZZZ_.jpg
Matt Reynolds, Karli Watson
1861006179
49.99
http://www.amazon.com/exec/obidos/ASIN/1861006179/

Beginning .NET Web Services with VB.NET
http://images.amazon.com/images/P/1861007256.01._PE30_SCMZZZZZZZ_.jpg
Karli Watson, Joseph Bustos
1861007256
39.99
http://www.amazon.com/exec/obidos/ASIN/1861007256/

Professional C#
http://images.amazon.com/images/P/1861007043.01._PE30_SCMZZZZZZZ_.jpg
Simon Robinson et al.
1861007043
59.99
http://www.amazon.com/exec/obidos/ASIN/1861007043/

Professional ASP.NET 1.0
http://images.amazon.com/images/P/1861007035.01._PE30_SCMZZZZZZZ_.jpg
Alex Homer et al.
1861007035
59.99
http://www.amazon.com/exec/obidos/ASIN/1861007035/

Beginning WAP
http://images.amazon.com/images/P/1861004583.01._PE30_SCMZZZZZZZ_.jpg
Karli Watson et al.
1861004583
39.99
http://www.amazon.com/exec/obidos/ASIN/1861004583/

Also, change the Columns field to a value such as 3 for better formatting. Lower values are useful for narrower panes, for example a single column works quite well if you add this module to the LeftPane or RightPane displays.

Along with editing links in place, the final display is as follows:

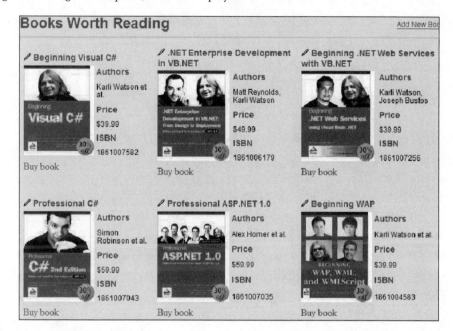

Summary

This chapter has laid the foundations for later chapters to build increasingly spectacular modifications to the IBuySpy Portal.

We started by covering the basics, such as changing the CSS stylesheet associated with the site and used to maintain consistency throughout. Minor changes here can have a dramatic impact on the look of the site.

Next, we looked at how modifications to the existing ASP.NET code can make even more of a difference, and corrected a problem with the SignIn.ascx control along the way. We saw how the DesktopPortalBanner.ascx can be changed, and how the layout of DesktopDefault.aspx can be modified.

Finally, we looked at how custom modules can be added, looking at all aspects of the existing module framework along the way and reinforcing the structural knowledge gained in the previous chapter. The specific module added here, for displaying a list of books, is useful in its own right, but the further insight into existing modules is invaluable when it comes to IBuySpy Portal customization.

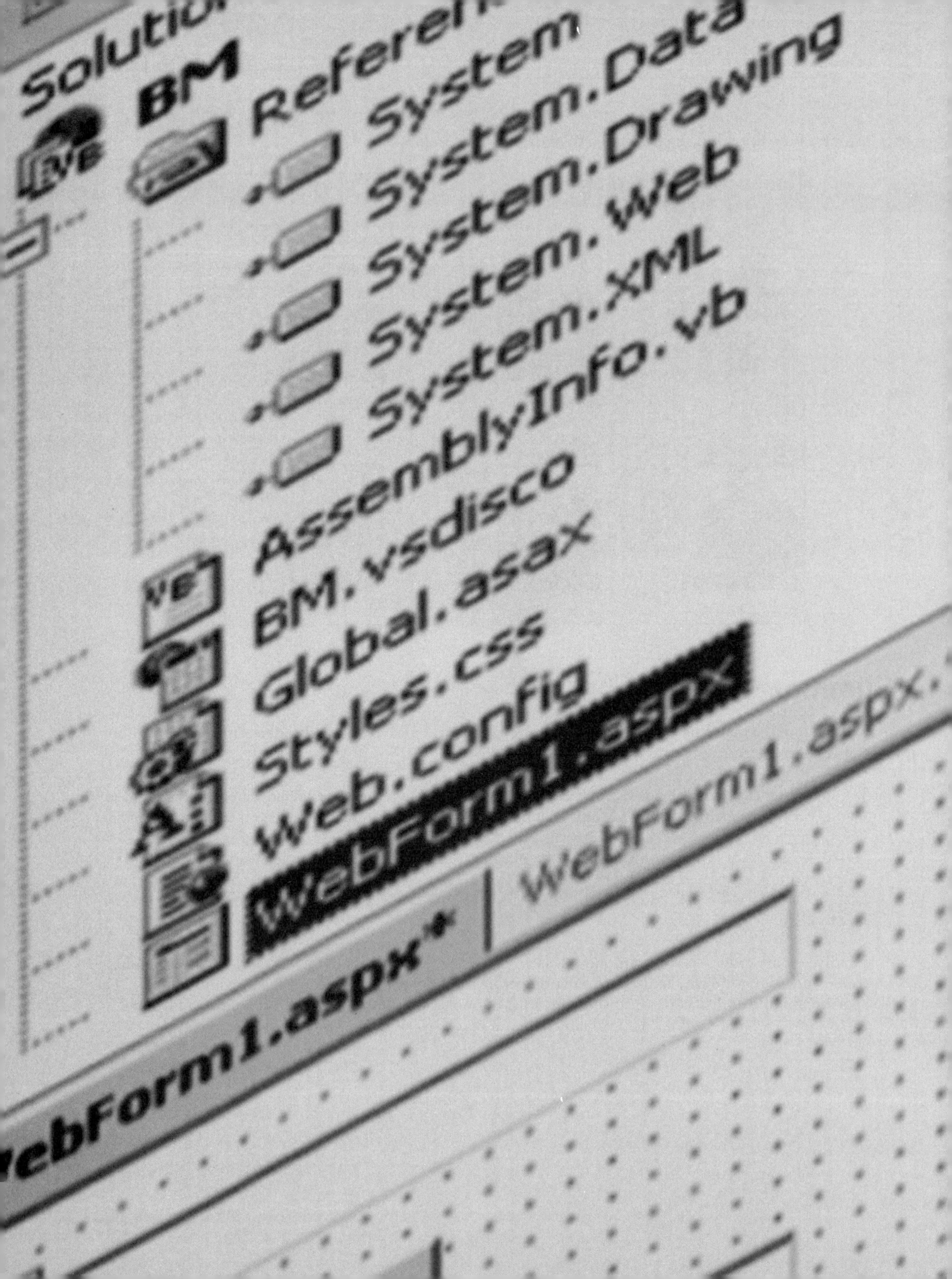

Solution
BM
References
System
System.Data
System.Drawing
System.Web
System.XML
AssemblyInfo.vb
Assembly
BM.vsdisco
Global.asax
Styles.css
Web.config
WebForm1.aspx
WebForm1.aspx* | WebForm1.aspx.

4

Security in the Intranet

Intrinsic support for security is an important feature of any intranet. It is often a requirement that parts of the portal can be accessed only by privileged users. Other parts may need to be personalized for individual users.

Fortunately, the IBuySpy Portal includes a framework for security. This can be used by all of the modules in the portal application. In this chapter we will take a look at the security features of the IBuySpy portal and examine some of the underlying ASP.NET technologies behind those features.

But first, let's start by having a word or two about the concept and importance of security itself in today's Intranet applications.

The Importance of Security

You don't have to look far these days to find a report about a recent security breach. As bad as the reports may seem, the reality is that there are thousands and thousands of similar cases that have happened to less prominent organizations whose report just has not found its way to the popular press. Furthermore, many more attacks go virtually unnoticed. The subject of Security has indeed taken center stage in the enterprise.

Most developers and architects realize that security is not just a last minute concern but rather an important consideration that needs to be embedded into the design of the web application from its very inception. Of course, one of the primary goals of implementing security in a web application is to provide some protection against malicious attacks or requests with ill intent to steal intellectual property.

Interestingly enough, research shows that most security breaches in an organization originate from inside the organization, either from inadvertent actions or ill intents on the part of employees.

An Intranet site can often contain crucial information about the company or employees. Employees need to trust the intranet and feel assured that their information is safe and secure. In addition to the obvious ethical obligations to protect the sensitive employee information, it is not uncommon for organizations to adhere to legal obligations pertaining to careful handling of employee data.

Imagine the chaos that would be created if, for example, the payroll information for all employees fell into the wrong hands. Therefore, it is imperative that the Intranet provides a secure and trustworthy infrastructure.

Certain areas of the intranet will need to be accessible only to specific users. One would not want to display the payroll information of an organization to all employees. Therefore, it is imperative that the identity of each user is verified and the set of privileges available to them is defined.

An Overview Of IBuySpy Security

Now that have we reinforced the importance of security in web applications, let's take a closer look at how security is implemented in the IBuySpy portal application. We'll see how some of the new security features in ASP.NET are leveraged to provide support for the various modules and components of our portal application.

There are really four themes that underlie the design of the IBuySpy security architecture:

- ❑   Viewing and editing Permissions
- ❑   Role Based Security
- ❑   Self-Sufficiency
- ❑   Reusability

Let's look at each of these and outline the features that they lead to.

Viewing And Editing Permissions

The IBuySpy portal architecture allows us to control access to information contained in our intranet in two different ways. We can control which users are allowed to view information, allowing us to set up restricted sections of the intranet for confidential information. We can also control which users are allowed to add and edit information. This allows us to put control of information in the hands of the people best able to keep that information up to date, without other users changing that information either accidentally or maliciously.

Control of viewing is done on a **per tab** basis. This means that a particular user will either be able to view all module instances placed on a tab or will not be able to view any of them.

Control of editing is done on a **per module instance** basis. This means that a user may be able to edit some modules on a particular tab while other modules cannot be edited.

We will be looking more at these two types of security check in the *Authorization* section later in this chapter.

Role Based Security

IBuySpy security revolves around groups of users, known as roles. Permissions for viewing and editing particular parts of the portal are granted on a role-by-role basis. Decisions about whether a user can view a tab or edit a module instance are made by checking which roles the user is a member of.

We will be looking at roles in more detail in the next section.

Self-Sufficiency

The IBuySpy portal is designed to be a complete, self-contained application that only requires the .NET Framework and a SQL Server database in order to operate. For this reason, IBuySpy stores it's own user and role data in the database and uses forms authentication to validate users. Forms authentication has no special requirements of the browser that is used and keeps security logic within our application. We will be looking at forms authentication in more detail later in this chapter.

Of course, we are able to make changes to IBuySpy in order to link it more closely with other systems. We will be looking at how we can use Windows authentication to provide seamless logins for users of Windows network later in this chapter.

By default, the IBuySpy portal takes advantage of the Forms Authentication along with other security classes in the .NET framework to provide an extensive and robust security framework for the portal.

Reusability

As we have seen in the previous chapters, the IBuySpy portal architecture allows additional modules to be plugged in. The security framework bears this in mind, aiming to provide reusable code for security checks that modules can call, rather than creating their own checks from scratch. This means that building new modules is easier, modules are consistent in the way that they handle security and we only have one set of security code to worry about.

Users And Roles In IBuySpy

Roles are simply organizational groupings of users that contain users with the same security privileges. They are used as a central mechanism to encapsulate user information and security settings in terms of various levels of permissions to the individual tabs and modules within the IBuySpy portal.

The `Admins` role that exists by default in the IBuySpy Portal contains users that have all administrative privileges, including editing modules, adding or deleting users and roles, assigning users to roles, along with full access to all other administration functions. The `Admins` role contains the highest level of security privilege whose members have the capability to make changes to the settings of the portal.

The guest user account that is also included with IBuySpy has the password 'guest' and is part of the Admins role, thereby having the highest level of security permissions. Given the generic nature of this account, it should be eliminated to prevent unauthorized access to the portal. If you still want to have a guest account for the portal, you should at least remove it from the Admins role and assign it minimum permissions required to access the desired resources in the portal.

> **Removing or altering the guest account is one of the first things that should be done after installing an IBuySpy application. Leaving it in place is a huge security hole.**

It is very easy to create your own role in IBuySpy portal as long as you are logged in as the user who belongs to the Admins role. Start by going to the Admins tab of the portal. The section called "Security Roles" displays all the roles that currently exist in IBuySpy as shown below:

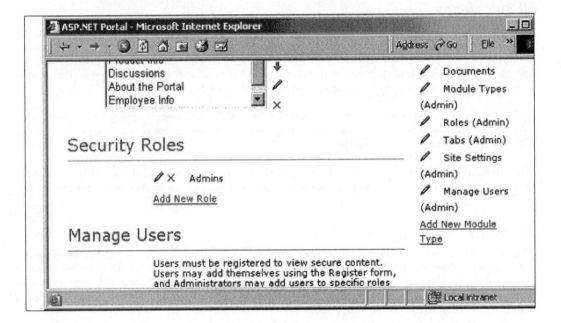

Each existing role is displayed along with the pencil icon and the X icon, which allow the user to modify or delete that particular role. There's also the 'Add New Role' link. To add a new role, you can simply click that link and you'd be taken to another page where you set the various settings for the new role, as shown below:

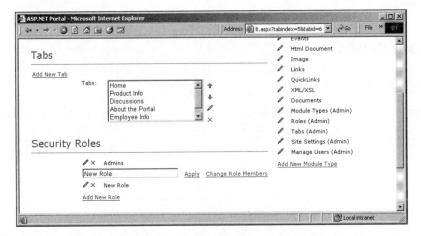

By default the role would be given a generic name, "New Role" which should be changed. To assign users to the new role, click on the "Change Role Members" which enables you to either add new or existing users to the role, as shown in the figure below:

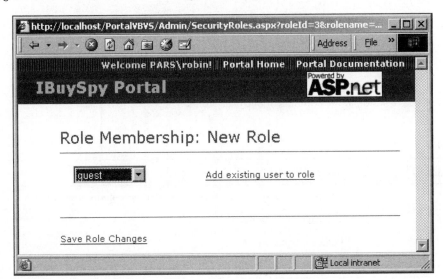

You can one-by-one add as many users as you would like to the new role. Just be sure to save the changes each time a user is added to the role or changes are made to other settings of the role. That's all there is to creating new roles in IBuySpy. As you can see, it's quite easy to create and manage roles in the IBuySpy portal. In the next section we will see how roles and user details are actually stored in the database.

Storing User Details

As mentioned earlier, all user information in the IBuySpy portal is saved in a few tables in the `Portal` database residing in SQL server.

Two tables are used to persist the user information, `Users` and `UserRoles`. `UserRoles` is used to define which roles each user is a member of The `Roles` table stores information about the roles themselves.

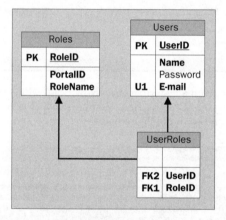

Let's briefly take a look at the columns of our user tables:

Users table

Field	Description
UserID	The primary key of the table. This is an auto generated column.
Name	The user's full name.
Password	The user's password.
Email	The user's e-mail address. (Also used as user name for login purposes).

UserRoles table

Field	Description
UserID	A key into the Users table
RoleID	A key into the Roles table

As you can see, the UserRoles table allows us to define each user as a member of as many roles as we like (by adding multiple entries for each user) and allows each role to have any number of members (by adding multiple entries for each role).

Roles table

Field	Description
RoleID	The primary key of the table. This is an auto generated column.
PortalID	ID of the current portal. This field was created for extensibility purposes (it allows more than one portal instance to share the same database).
RoleName	Actual name of the role

All interactions with the database are done through a set of stored procedures that are abstracted by the UsersDB class, which resides in the Security.vb component. There are a number of very important methods in UsersDB class and so it would be worthwhile to have a look at the various methods offered by it:

Method	Description
AddUser	Takes in the full name of the user along with the e-mail address as parameters and a password as entered by the user and adds it to the database. If the user is added successfully an integer is returned to indicate the newly created user ID for the user. If there are any errors, -1 is returned.
DeleteUser	Simply deletes a user from the Users table using a user's user ID, which it takes in as a parameter. This method is invoked when the user removes a user from the portal.
UpdateUser	Takes in the user ID, username/e-mail, and a password and updates the user information. This method is invoked when the user information is updated in the Manage Users of the Admin page.
GetRolesByUser	Returns all the roles in which the user belongs. This method takes in an e-mail/username and returns a SqlDataReader object with the IDs of the roles.
GetSingleUser	Returns a SqlDataReader object that contains the details of a specified user (note - these details do not include their roles)

Method	Description
GetRoles	Returns all the roles in which the user belongs. This method takes in an e-mail/username and returns a string array object with the roles. The only difference between this method and GetRolesByUser is the fact that this method's return type is a string array and not a SqlDataReader object.
Login	Validates an email address/password pair against credentials stored in the database. If the user's credentials are successfully verified, the e-mail address is sent back to the caller. If there are any errors, an empty string is returned. This method is used when users sign in.

Each method contains the code needed to make a connection to the database and invoke the appropriate stored procedures responsible for the actual interaction with the database. To better illustrate this, let's have a look at one of the shorter methods, DeleteUser:

```
Public Sub DeleteUser(ByVal userId As Integer)

    Dim myConnection As New
SqlConnection(ConfigurationSettings.AppSettings("connectionString"))
    Dim myCommand As New SqlCommand("DeleteUser", myConnection)

    myCommand.CommandType = CommandType.StoredProcedure

    Dim parameterUserId As New SqlParameter("@UserID", SqlDbType.Int)
    parameterUserId.Value = userId
    myCommand.Parameters.Add(parameterUserId)
    myConnection.Open()
    myCommand.ExecuteNonQuery()
    myConnection.Close()

End Sub
```

There really is nothing we haven't seen before in the above code. The connection string is fetched from the Web.config file and a connection is made to the database. After that a SqlCommand object is created to invoke the DeleteUser stored procedure from the database. The next few lines set up the command object with the right parameter and simply execute the command object. That's all there's to it. A user is deleted by his/her user ID.

Authentication

Authentication is the process of verifying the actual identity of the user. The user has to use credentials to prove who they are. In most cases, the credentials consist of a user name and password and are checked against some sort of authority for verification. Often, the source of authority simply happens to be a database in which user information resides. ASP.NET offers a few different approaches to authentication through authentication modules.

Authentication Type	Description
Forms Authentication	Although not a standard, forms authentication is quite popular since it's customizable. Unauthenticated user requests are redirected to an HTML/ASP.NET page in which user credentials are requested and upon verification the user gets redirected to the requested page. All subsequent requests by the same client in a single session are automatically authenticated by using a 'ticket' stored in a cookie.
Windows Authentication	The login information of a valid Windows account is used for authentication purposes. Three modes of Windows authentication are supported, basic, digest, and integrated. Windows authentication works closely with IIS and the operating system for authentication. This approach is more popular for intranet purposes.
Passport Authentication	An authentication service offered by Microsoft in which users can get authenticated through a single logon for a number of sites and services that support the .NET Passport services. Passport authentication is most suitable for large internet sites that target a wide audience and not really for intranet sites. In the case of intranets, it's best to be a self-contained entity and thus minimize reliance on external sites or services.

Since Passport authentication is not really suitable for our intranet, we will be looking at forms authentication (the default for the IBuySpy portal architecture) and Windows authentication.

Forms Authentication

Forms authentication is generally the preferred authentication scheme for use in the Internet, since Windows authentication's reliance on the user accounts in the operating system can get quite difficult to manage and maintain as the number of users grow. In the IBuySpy portal, forms authentication is the default authentication mechanism. User information is stored in a database, which allows for more granular and dynamic approach to user settings and alleviates extra reliance on the operating system for user accounts. This is very much in accordance with one of the design goals of the IBuySpy portal as mentioned earlier; to be a self-contained entity.

How Forms Authentication Works

Forms authentication works by collecting the credentials information from a user via a designated login page. All users that have not yet been authenticated and attempt to access a protected resource are redirected to the login page, where the user can attempt to get authenticated. The designated form page collects the user credentials such as a user name and password and validates the information against an authority. If validated, the user is authenticated and redirected to the initial page that was requested or a default page. All subsequent requests by the same user in a single browser session are automatically authenticated. This is made possible by the authentication ticket, which is usually stored in a cookie. The flow of forms based authentication is typically along the lines of the flowchart shown below:

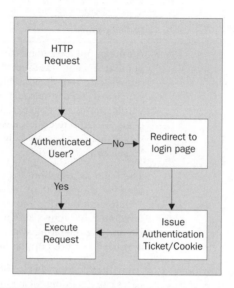

> If you choose to use forms authentication, be sure to select the `Anonymous Access` option in the IIS Authentication Methods dialog box.

In IBuySpy we actually allow all users to view the default page and then perform our own security checks within that page, to decide what to display to the user. This means that we never actually redirect the user to a login page. Instead, we provide a control that allows users to sign in. We'll be looking at this technique later in the chapter.

Limitations Of Forms Authentication

Much like all technologies, forms authentication is not perfect. Nor is it an authentication approach that applies to all scenarios. Although quite capable, forms authentication does have its shortcomings. First, keep in mind the fact that forms authentication can only protect `.ASPX` and other file types directly related to ASP.NET. It does not, by default, protect .html or other static pages. The only way other file types can be protected is to map them to ASP.NET, which in turn can result in performance hits since the static pages will now have to be sent to the ASP.NET worker process after having been parsed and compiled.

Another shortcoming of Forms authentication is that it does not do anything about protecting the user credentials that are send to it. In other words, by default, user name and password are accepted through clear text and more or less the only option to address that is to initiate an HTTPS/SSL session which would then create an end-to-end encryption, thereby protecting all communication between the client and the server.

Lastly, forms authentication very much relies on the use of cookies as a means of persisting the authentication ticket, which is used for subsequent requests after initial authentication. If any of your clients do not support cookies, you will have to do some extra work to support them.

Forms authentication is a great way of implementing security in ASP.NET pages, but like all other technologies, it should be used in situations to which it is suited.

Setting Up Forms Authentication

Forms authentication is the default authentication method for the IBuySpy portal architecture. It is, in any case, very simple to set up.

The <authentication> tab in the Web.config is responsible for setting the authentication mode. To enable forms authentication we simply set the mode attribute of the <authentication> element to Forms as shown below:

```
<authentication mode="Forms">
  <forms name=".ASPXAUTH" protection="All" timeout="60" />
</authentication>
```

Its that simple! There is a little extra work to do – as we shall see, the login control has to be set up correctly to issue authentication tickets but this is all the configuration that is required.

Forms Authentication in the IBuySpy Portal

As we have just seen, implementing forms authentication in ASP.NET at a basic level is quite easy to implement. Unfortunately that does not provide us with the level of flexibility that is required in a modular and extensible portal such as the IBuySpy portal. Therefore, some customization is added to the authentication process. In this section we will take a closer look at exactly what those customizations are all about.

Forms authentication in the IBuySpy portal starts with the login module, Signin.ascx. This user control contains the UI elements needed to get the required user information and authenticate the user as shown in the figure below:

Account Login

Email:

[   ]

Password:

[   ]

☐ Remember Login

➡ sign-in

➡ register

The user is asked to supply an e-mail address in place of a user name. The user can also check the "Remember Login" checkbox in order to be automatically authenticated in future visits (this works by setting a persistent cookie). If the user has not already created an account, he/she can easily do so by clicking on the register link. By default, the register link will send the user to a registration page through which a new account can be created with granted authentication for immediate use. We will be looking at whether the registration page is appropriate for our intranet later.

Let's see some of the code from the `Signin.ascx` module. There's only one main event in the signin page that has much implementation and that is the `LoginBtn_Click` which fires when the user clicks the "sign-in" link button.

```
Private Sub LoginBtn_Click(ByVal sender As Object, ByVal e As ImageClickEventArgs)
Handles SigninBtn.Click

    Dim accountSystem As New UsersDB()
    Dim userId As String = accountSystem.Login(email.Text, password.Text)

    If Not (userId Is Nothing) And userId <> "" Then

        FormsAuthentication.SetAuthCookie(email.Text, _
                                        RememberCheckbox.Checked)
    Response.Redirect(Request.ApplicationPath)

    Else
        Message.Text = "<" & "br" & ">Login Failed!" & "<" & "br" & ">"

    End If

End Sub
```

The core funtionality of the `LoginBtn_Click` method occurs in these couple of lines:

```
Dim userId As String = accountSystem.Login(email.Text, password.Text)

If Not (userId Is Nothing) And userId <> "" Then
    FormsAuthentication.SetAuthCookie(email.Text, RememberCheckbox.Checked)
    Response.Redirect(Request.ApplicationPath)
Else
```

Upon setting the `UserId` variable to the result of the method call to the Login method, the conditional statement checks to ensure that a user ID was returned and that it is a value other than an empty string. If so, the `SetAuthCookie` method of the `FormsAuthentication` object is called to store the authentication cookie in the client machine.

After that, the user is sent back to the originating page. If an appropriate user ID is not returned, the user is presented with an error message and a chance for another login attempt. You might be wondering where the `FormsAuthentication` object came from and what role it plays in forms authentication. The class is from the `System.Web.Security` namespace and is basically a helper/utility class with a few handy methods for authentication tickets as issued in forms authentication.

The SetAuthCookie method has two parameters. The first is a string variable holding the user name and/or information and the second parameter being a Boolean value indicating whether or not a persistent cookie is issued. A persistent cookie is one that spans across many sessions and is not just limited to a single session. Therefore, if the user checks the "Remember Login" checkbox, the cookie will be persisted and remain alive for more than just the active session.

Lastly, we have to manually redirect the user back to the originating page by using a simple Response.Redirect statement.

The Registration Page

By default, if the user does not have a valid e-mail/user name and password, he/she can register for one by clicking on the "register" link button which forwards the user to the registration page, Register.aspx as shown below:

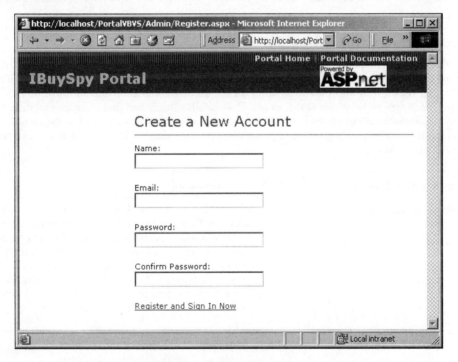

Since it is normal to want to control which people have access to an intranet site, you may well want to remove the registration page from the application – it is really designed for using the portal in a more public context.

Windows Authentication

An alternative to forms authentication is Windows authentication. Windows authentication is ideal for situations where there is an intranet and users have existing Windows.

Let's start our discussion on Windows authentication by taking a look at how Windows authentication actually works.

How Windows Authentication Works

When Windows authentication is active, the responsibility for authenticating the user is handed off to IIS. IIS will use one of its methods to authenticate the user (see the next section for more details on the methods it uses) and will pass the identity to ASP.NET along with the request. We can then make use of the identity of the user in the same way as if they were authenticated with forms authentication.

Types of Windows Authentication

There are three different types of Windows authentication that, although similar to one another, differ in the way they collect credential information from the users. The one technical attribute that they all have in common is their reliance on the operating system for the user authentication and authorization. Furthermore, each type of Windows authentication has its advantages and disadvantages relative to the other Windows authentication schemes. You must assess your security goals as well as the technical setup of the target platform before deciding which approach is ideal for your use. The table below shows the various Windows authentication options:

Authentication Type	Description
Basic Authentication	The user ID and password and/or other credentials are transferred from the client to the server in clear text. The user information must correspond to a valid Windows account. This type of authentication will only suffice if the possibility of intrusion with malicious intent is not a concern since the user information is not encrypted over the wire. At times SSL (Secure Socket Layer) is used along with basic authentication to provide a greater level of security.
Digest Authentication	Similar to basic authentication. The main difference is that user credentials are not transferred in clear text and instead are encrypted using a hashing algorithm.
Integrated Windows Authentication	The current logon credentials of the user are used as opposed to asking for user credentials again. The user is only prompted for credentials if he/she does not have access to the requested resource(s).

Let's have a close look at the three different kinds of authentication available within Windows authentication. We'll start the discussion by talking about basic authentication.

Basic Authentication

Even though it sounds like it is a Microsoft technology, basic authentication is actually supported by the World Wide Web Consortium(W3C) since it is very much a part of the HTTP protocol itself. User credentials such as a user name and a password are embedded into the HTTP headers. Upon receiving the user credentials IIS tries to map the user to an existing user in the domain to which it belongs.

The great thing about basic authentication is the fact that it has widespread support in both browsers and web servers. Unfortunately, however, the draw back of basic authentication is the lack of security in its mechanism. The user credentials are not encrypted and thus can become an easy target for those with malicious intent. Therefore, it is recommended that if you wish to implement basic authentication, do so over an SSL (Secured Sockets Layer) channel. In this way, the entire communication link is encrypted.

Having said all that, let's see how easy it is to implement basic authentication in IIS. Go ahead and open up the IIS management console. Right-click any virtual directory in there and go to the `Directory Security` tab. Under the `Anonymous access` and `Authentication` sections, click the `Edit` button.

When you select the check box for basic authentication, IIS displays a message box to remind you that user credentials are not encrypted and that you should consider using SSL in conjunction with basic authentication. In any case, when a user attempts to access a page in the site or virtual directory protected with basic authentication, they will be presented with the following dialog box asking the user for credentials:

Digest Authentication

In a lot of ways, digest authentication is very much like basic authentication. In fact, for most part the user can hardly even notice the difference between two authentication methods. When attempting to access a protected site/resource, the user is prompted with a dialog box to enter credential information in exactly the same way. However, digest authentication does not transfer the user credentials over the wire in clear text as basic authentication does. The user name and password are encrypted before transfer.

The reason digest authentication is not more widespread is that not all browsers and servers have support for it. In fact, it wasn't until version 5.0 of IE that support for digest authentication became available.

Like basic authentication, the digest scheme is based on a simple challenge-response paradigm. The Digest scheme challenges the client, providing a generated nonce value to be used by the client for this request. A valid response contains a checksum of the username, the password, the given nonce value, the HTTP method, and the requested UR. In this way, the password is never sent in clear text. An optional header allows the server to specify the algorithm used to create the checksum or digest. By default the MD5 algorithm is used.

Integrated Windows Authentication

This is the most integrated and robust solution for web security if the target web application is in an intranet environment in which the number of users is limited. Integrated Windows authentication simply uses the logon information of the current user to authenticate and authorize the user. This way, the user does not have to deal with any new dialog boxes or have to give any more information. All the work is done under the hood by the operating system.

The important point to remember about integrated Windows authentication is that it is not really suitable for Internet purposes. The web server needs to be within the domain in which all the user accounts reside. With the use of VPNs (Virtual Private Networks), it is technically possible to have integrated Windows authentication over the Internet, but other issues such as user management soon take center stage.

Integrated Windows authentication is not by any means an industry standard and its use is completely out of the question when dealing with anything other than a Microsoft-based operating system. Integrated Windows authentication relies on proprietary ports for its communication, which means that firewalls have next to no tolerance for it.

By the same token, integrated Windows authentication is very well suited within the realm of the network behind the firewall since it is tightly integrated into the operating system and the user accounts management infrastructure already in place.

Setting up the IBuySpy Architecture for Windows Authentication

In this section we will see how easy it is to switch from forms authentication to integrated Windows authentication. Let's assume that we're modifying the IBuySpy portal for intranet use in a small office with a relatively low number of users. The very first thing that we need to do is to switch the authentication mode from `Forms` to `Windows` in the `Web.config` file. As a matter of fact, the code is already there and just has to be uncommented. You can comment out the code for forms authentication and instead uncomment the following lines of code:

```
<authentication mode="Windows" />
<authorization>
    <deny users="?" />
</authorization>
```

Notice that `<authorization>` tag in the above denies access to all anonymous users. This way any user that does not have a valid user account in the server is unable to view the site. Switching modes to windows authentication is that easy, but there are a few other steps before we can have our IBuySpy portal up and running with windows authentication. Another simple step is to go to the `Properties` view of the virtual directory for our intranet site in IIS and enable integrated windows authentication.

We also need to eliminate the sign-in module from the main page since we are no longer going to rely on forms authentication. For that we go to the `DefaultDesktop.aspx` page where the sign-in module is dynamically loaded and displayed. You can just go ahead and comment out the few lines responsible for loading the module as shown below:

```
'If Request.IsAuthenticated = False And _portalSettings.ActiveTab.TabIndex
                                                    _ = 0 Then
'    LeftPane.Controls.Add(Page.LoadControl("~/DesktopModules/SignIn.ascx"))
'    LeftPane.Visible = True
'End If
```

The final step is to ensure that the Windows logon name exists in the database table. It's really important to remember that although we are switching our initial authentication mechanism from forms to integrated Windows, our authorization scheme still very much depends on the data in the database. We are not using ACL based authorization; our custom roles-based authorization scheme is going to remain very much intact.

If you recall, there are three tables that we need to make additions to, the Users table, UserRoles, and the Roles table. Let's say that we have a user named Robin with the Windows account name set to robin in Windows domain called PARS. We want to add that user to the Admins role to ensure that he has administrative privileges. Let's start with the Users table. We can use the following T-SQL statement to insert a new record into the table:

```
INSERT INTO Users(Name, Password, Email)
VALUES('Robin','dummyPassword','PARS\robin')
```

Keep in mind that the password in the Users table for a particular user does not necessarily have to match the actual password of the user held in the Windows account. The password field in the Users table is only used for the purposes of forms authentication and we have deactivated that. Since the Email field represents the user name we have to provide it with the full user name in the Domain/User format.

Next, we need to add a new addition to the UserRoles table to include the new user ID and the role to which that user is assigned. Since we want the user to be assigned to the Admins role, we'll use 0 for the RoleID field, as shown by the following T-SQL statement:

```
INSERT INTO UserRoles(UserID, RoleID)
VALUES(2, 0)
```

And that's all! Since we did not define any new roles, we do not have to make any changes to the Roles table. Of course, this is just for proof of concept purposes. In the real world, we would have to have numerous roles with a lot more users.

Let's launch the IBuySpy portal and see what happens:

As expected, the portal recognized the user as one belonging to the Admins role and thus granted the user administrative privileges to have edit permissions and access to the Admin module. Also notice, the welcome message on top of the page, which further indicates that the user was indeed recognized and properly authenticated.

Now that we have one administrative user, we can use that login to access the IBuySpy admin tool and add more users and roles as we wish. The important thing here is to set up one administrative login to get us started.

Storing Roles and Creating Authentication Tickets

An important part of the IBuySpy authentication process is the linking of roles to users - these roles will be used later to decide what the user can do.

The problem is that, since HTTP is a stateless protocol, we have to map the users to a role at every request. An ideal place to implement the association between a role and a user is the Application_AuthenticateRequest event which gets invoked at the beginning of every request. This event is located in the Global.asax file.

We will be using the Application_AuthenticateRequest event to write or read a custom authentication ticket that will be stored in a cookie. This ticket will contain the roles that the user belongs to and will be used to populate the Context.User objects with the roles that the security check code will use to make decisions about what the user is allowed to do.

> One thing that commonly confuses people about this code is that the authentication ticket created here is not the same one that is used for forms authentication. If we are using forms authentication, then this code actually creates a second authentication cookie. This means that the users identity and the users roles are stored in separate tickets and cookies.
>
> This is done in order that we can change the authentication method without having to recode this system for persisting roles between requests. Even if we switch to using Windows authentication to identify users, a forms authentication ticket will still be used to persist roles, unless we replace this code.

Lets have a look at the code:

```
Sub Application_AuthenticateRequest(ByVal sender As Object, ByVal e As _
                                EventArgs)

    If Request.IsAuthenticated = True Then

        Dim roles() As String

        If Request.Cookies("portalroles") Is Nothing Then
```

```
            Dim _user As New UsersDB()
            roles = _user.GetRoles(User.Identity.Name)

            Dim roleStr As String = ""
            Dim role As String

            For Each role In roles

                roleStr += role
                roleStr += ";"

            Next role

            Dim ticket As New FormsAuthenticationTicket(1, _
                Context.User.Identity.Name, _
                DateTime.Now, _
                DateTime.Now.AddHours(1), _
                False, _
                roleStr)

            Dim cookieStr As String = FormsAuthentication.Encrypt( _
                                ticket)

            Response.Cookies("portalroles").Value = cookieStr
            Response.Cookies("portalroles").Path = "/"
            Response.Cookies("portalroles").Expires = _
                                DateTime.Now.AddMinutes(1)

        Else

            Dim ticket As FormsAuthenticationTicket =
            FormsAuthentication.Decrypt(Context.Request.Cookies _
                                ("portalroles").Value)

            Dim userRoles As New ArrayList()

            Dim role As String

            For Each role In ticket.UserData.Split(New Char() {";"c})
                userRoles.Add(role)
            Next role

            roles = CType(userRoles.ToArray(GetType(String)), _
                    String())

        End If

    Context.User = New GenericPrincipal(Context.User.Identity, roles)

    End If

End Sub
```

128

The very first thing that we need to do inside the method is to make sure the user has already been authenticated because if for any reason that's not the case yet, we can't continue. All the code of this method resides within a conditional block ensuring execution if, and only if, the user has already been authenticated:

```
If Request.IsAuthenticated = True Then
    ...
End If
```

After that, we have to check to see if the authentication cookie containing the roles information has already been assigned to the client as shown below:

```
If Request.Cookies("portalroles") Is Nothing Then
```

If the cookie has not already been created it we need to create one. We do so by creating a new instance of the `UsersDB` class and call the `GetRoles` method to get a string array containing all of the roles to which the user belongs.

```
Dim roles() As String
Dim _user As New UsersDB()

roles = _user.GetRoles(User.Identity.Name)
Dim roleStr As String = ""
Dim role As String

For Each role In roles
    roleStr += role
    roleStr += ";"
Next role
```

You can see that we are going through the array and reading the individual values into a new string variable such that all the roles are separated by semicolons. The reason for this is that we want to store the roles in a `FormsAuthenticationTicket` object, so we need them in string form.

The `FormsAuthenticationTicket` class is designed to facilitate storage of authentication tickets in cookies. It has a number of methods and properties that add more support and include some utilities for dealing with authentication tickets in the case of forms authentication.

We need to instantiate a new object and to create our cookie-based authentication ticket. The following fields are going to be required for the ticket:

❑ **Version** – This property is for future extensions. We should use the value 1.

❑ **User Name** – The user name we wish to persist in the authentication cookie.

❑ **Time of Issue** – The time at when the cookie was issued.

❑ **Expiration** – Expiration date for the cookie.

❑ **IsPersistent** – Boolean value indicating whether or not it is a persistent cookie.

❑ **UserData** – This is a custom field. This is where we're going to place the roles information.

With that in mind, we can go ahead and at last create the authentication ticket as shown below:

```
Dim ticket As New FormsAuthenticationTicket(1, _
                        Context.User.Identity.Name, _
                        DateTime.Now, _
                        DateTime.Now.AddHours(1), _
                        False, _
                        roleStr)
```

Before sending the authentication ticket to the client, it is imperative that the ticket is encrypted; otherwise the security of the user can very easily be compromised. Fortunately, the FormsAuthentication class contains methods for encryption and decryption as we saw earlier and it's quite easy to implement. Upon encrypting the authentication ticket, we simply create a cookie by the name of portalRoles and save the encrypted version of the authentication ticket in it as shown in the code segment below:

```
Dim cookieStr As String = FormsAuthentication.Encrypt(ticket)

Response.Cookies("portalroles").Value = cookieStr
Response.Cookies("portalroles").Path = "/"
Response.Cookies("portalroles").Expires = DateTime.Now.AddMinutes(1)
```

At this point we create a new instance of the GenericPrincipal object with the roles variable, which contains a string array of all the user roles. We want to store this object in the Context.User object so that it will be available for other code during the current page request:

```
Context.User = New GenericPrincipal(Context.User.Identity, roles)
```

Remeber back to the beginning of the event handler where we checked for the existence of the portalRoles cookie? If the cookie exists then, instead of creating a new one, we have to just read in its values before instantiating a new GenericPrincipal object. Nothing special is required, we just need to do more or less the exact opposite of what we did when we created the authentication ticket. Let's have a look at the code below:

```
Dim ticket As FormsAuthenticationTicket = FormsAuthentication.Decrypt( _
                    Context.Request.Cookies("portalroles").Value)

Dim userRoles As New ArrayList()
Dim role As String

For Each role In ticket.UserData.Split(New Char() {";"c})
        userRoles.Add(role)
Next role

roles = CType(userRoles.ToArray(GetType(String)), String())
```

A new FormsAuthenticationTicket variable is instantiated and set equal to the decrypted result of the portalRoles cookie. The next few lines of code traverse through the semicolon delimited string and insert the individual roles in an ArrayList object which is then used to create the roles array containing all the roles for the user. After we have the roles array, we can create the object exactly like we did before.

Authorization

Once we have authenticated a user, we have to also know what resources that particular user has access to. Authorization is basically a mechanism through which a user is granted access to the requested resources.

In the IBuySpy architecture, all authorization is based on the roles that a user belongs to. It is possible for modules that are added to the architecture to use authorization based on the users themselves (for example, if we want to allow users to edit only their own postings on a forum) but none of the default modules do this.

Configured Authorization

At the basic level, the Authorization> element within the Web.Config file is a very quick and easy approach for configuring authorization for an ASP.NET web application. You can allow or deny a particular, user, group of users, or roles to have access to your web application as shown below:

```
<authorization>
      <allow users="[user(s)]"
             roles="[role(s)]"/>
      <deny users="[user(s)]"
             roles="[role(s)"/>
</authorization>
```

The <authorization> element has two different sub-elements. These elements are <allow> and <deny>. The <allow> tag allows you to explicitly identify a comma separated list of users and/or roles that can access the requested URL. The allow> tag supports users, roles, anonymous and all access. The deny> tag specifies a comma separated list of users and/or roles that are denied access to the requested resource. For instance, to allow a user by the name of John to access your web application and deny everyone else access to your site you can easily do so by use of the following code:

```
<authorization>
     <allow users="John" />
     <deny users="*" />
</authorization>
```

There is certainly a lot more to what can be done with the authorization> element as mentioned here but you get the basic idea. Much like using the credentials tag in the case of authentication, this approach is not very pragmatic in the case of large sites because it will create one huge web.config file but more importantly lacks the dynamic support needed for modular sites that require a higher level of customized authorization scheme.

> In the IBuySpy architecture, we only use <authorization> to control access to the whole system. More finely grained authorization is done in custom security checks, which we will look at in the next section.

Custom Security Checks

The security features of the IBuySpy portal manifest themselves in two forms as far as the user is concerned: 'Tab View Security' and 'Module Editing Security'. The user must be a member of the Admins role in order to have the appropriate rights to make any security setting changes to any tab or module.

As we mentioned earlier in this chapter, the IBuySpy portal comes with one built-in user account, guest. The guest account does in fact belong to the Admins role and thus can be used to make desired changes to the various components of the portal. It is obviously a good idea to delete the guest account as soon as the actual user data information has been loaded and used in the portal.

Let's go ahead and login the portal using the guest account so that we see the Admin tab and can also edit the various modules in the page. As you can see in the figure below, the Admin tab has been added to the end of the tabs bar on top of the page and additional edit link buttons have been added to the various components in the page:

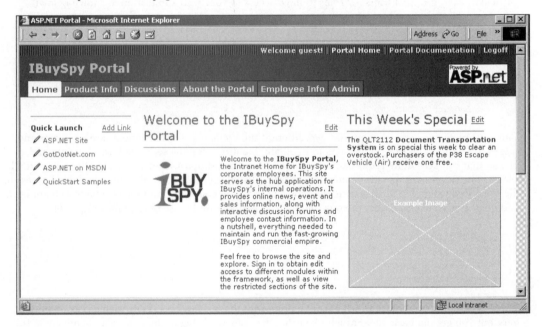

Now that we have seen the automatic nature of how tabs and edit links are enabled, we're going to take a lower level view of how to set view permissions for tabs and enable editing privileges for a module. We'll examine these from both an operational/visual standpoint as well as code/implementation standpoint.

Foundations For The Security Checks

In order for any of the methods of authorization that we will be looking at to work, we need to have a means of checking whether a user is in one or more roles.

We saw earlier in the chapter that the `Context.User` object is populated with the correct roles during authentication. What we need is a way of checking a specified user against these roles.

This functionality is provided by the `PortalSecurity` class. This can be found in the `Security.VB` source file.

Let's have a look at the methods that this class provides. All of these methods are `shared`, so we do not need an instance of `PortalSecurity` to use them.

The first method is very simple. `IsInRole` checks whether the user is in a named role

```
Public Shared Function IsInRole(ByVal role As String) As Boolean
   Return HttpContext.Current.User.IsInRole(role)
End Function
```

As you can see, `IsInRole` simply uses the `IsInRole` method of the `Context.User` object to do the check.

The next method is a little more involved. `IsInRoles` checks whether the user is in any one of a set of named roles (provided as a semicolon delimited string) by iterating through the provided roles and checking each of them in turn.

```
Public Shared Function IsInRoles(ByVal roles As String) As Boolean

  Dim context As HttpContext = HttpContext.Current

  Dim role As String
  For Each role In roles.Split(New Char() {";"c})

    If role <> "" And Not role Is Nothing And _
       (role = "All Users" Or context.User.IsInRole(role)) Then
      Return True
    End If

  Next role

  Return False

End Function
```

First, we get the current `HttpContext` and set up a string variable to hold each role as we check it.

```
Dim context As HttpContext = HttpContext.Current

Dim role As String
```

Next, we use the `String.Split` method to create an array of role names. We use a `For Each` statement to interate over these strings.

```
For Each role In roles.Split(New Char() {";"c})
```

For each role, we run a check somewhat like the one we did in `IsInRole`, returning `True` if the user is in the role.

```
If role <> "" And Not role Is Nothing And _
    (role = "All Users" Or context.User.IsInRole(role)) Then
  Return True
End If
```

Note that we also check that the role is not empty. If we did not do this, an empty role name would short-circuit this check.

Finally, if we get all the way through the roles without any of them matching, we return `False`.

```
Next role

Return False
```

The final method in `PortalSecurity` is the longest. `HasEditPermissions` checks whether the current user is allowed to edit a specified module instance:

```
Public Shared Function HasEditPermissions(ByVal moduleId As Integer)_
    As Boolean

  ' Obtain PortalSettings from Current Context
  Dim _portalSettings As PortalSettings = _
      CType(HttpContext.Current.Items("PortalSettings"), PortalSettings)

  ' Create Instance of Connection and Command Object
  Dim myConnection As New _
      SqlConnection(ConfigurationSettings.AppSettings("connectionString"))
  Dim myCommand As New SqlCommand("GetAuthRoles", myConnection)

  ' Mark the Command as a SPROC
  myCommand.CommandType = CommandType.StoredProcedure

  ' Add Parameters to SPROC
  Dim parameterModuleID As New SqlParameter("@ModuleID", SqlDbType.Int, 4)
  parameterModuleID.Value = moduleId
  myCommand.Parameters.Add(parameterModuleID)

  Dim parameterPortalID As New SqlParameter("@PortalID", SqlDbType.Int, 4)
  parameterPortalID.Value = _portalSettings.PortalId
  myCommand.Parameters.Add(parameterPortalID)

  ' Add out parameters to Sproc
```

```
    Dim parameterAccessRoles As New SqlParameter("@AccessRoles", _
        SqlDbType.NVarChar, 256)
    parameterAccessRoles.Direction = ParameterDirection.Output
    myCommand.Parameters.Add(parameterAccessRoles)

    Dim parameterEditRoles As New SqlParameter("@EditRoles", _
        SqlDbType.NVarChar, 256)
    parameterEditRoles.Direction = ParameterDirection.Output
    myCommand.Parameters.Add(parameterEditRoles)

    ' Open the database connection and execute the command
    myConnection.Open()
    myCommand.ExecuteNonQuery()
    myConnection.Close()

    If PortalSecurity.IsInRoles(CStr(parameterAccessRoles.Value)) = _
        False Or PortalSecurity.IsInRoles(CStr(parameterEditRoles.Value)) = _
        False Then
      Return False
    Else
      Return True
    End If

  End Function
```

Most of the method consists of data access code that calls the `GetAuthRoles` stored procedure. This procedure returns a semicolon delimited string of roles that are authorized to view the specified module and a semicolon delimited string of roles that are authorized to edit the module.

The interesting part is after this procedure has been called:

```
    If PortalSecurity.IsInRoles(CStr(parameterAccessRoles.Value)) = _
        False Or PortalSecurity.IsInRoles(CStr(parameterEditRoles.Value)) = _
        False Then
      Return False
    Else
      Return True
    End If
```

We use the `PotalSecurity.IsInRoles` method that we discussed earlier to check whether the current user has permission to view and to edit the module by passing it the output parameters from the stored procedure call. If either of these checks is negative, we return `False`.

Only if the user has both view and edit permissions do we return `True`.

Tab View Security

In order to see how tab view security is implemented and integrated into the portal application we need to take a close look at the code in `DesktopPortalBanner.ascx` user control. This control is responsible for generating the tab bar on the very top of every page within the IBuySpy portal application.

Most of the functionality is within the `Page_Load` event of the user control as shown below:

```
Private Sub Page_Load(ByVal sender As System.Object, _
     ByVal e As System.EventArgs) Handles MyBase.Load

  Dim _portalSettings As PortalSettings = _
    CType(HttpContext.Current.Items("PortalSettings"),_
    PortalSettings)

  siteName.Text = _portalSettings.PortalName

  If Request.IsAuthenticated = True Then

    WelcomeMessage.Text = "Welcome " & _
      Context.User.Identity.Name & _
      "! <" & "span class=Accent" & _
      ">|<" & "/span" & ">"

    If Context.User.Identity.AuthenticationType = "Forms" Then
      LogoffLink = "<" & "span class=""Accent"">|</span>" & _
        ControlChars.Cr & "<" & "a href=" & _
        Request.ApplicationPath & _
        "/Admin/Logoff.aspx class=SiteLink> Logoff" & "<" & "/a>"
    End If

  End If

  If ShowTabs = True Then

    tabIndex = _portalSettings.ActiveTab.TabIndex

    Dim authorizedTabs As New ArrayList()
    Dim addedTabs As Integer = 0

    Dim i As Integer

    For i = 0 To _portalSettings.DesktopTabs.Count - 1

      Dim tab As TabStripDetails = _
        CType(_portalSettings.DesktopTabs(i), TabStripDetails)

      If PortalSecurity.IsInRoles(tab.AuthorizedRoles) Then
        authorizedTabs.Add(tab)
      End If

      If addedTabs = tabIndex Then
        tabs.SelectedIndex = addedTabs
```

```
      End If

      addedTabs += 1

   Next i

   tabs.DataSource = authorizedTabs
   tabs.DataBind()

  End If
End Sub
```

First, an instance of the `PortalSettings` class is created to store the `PortalSettings` object contained in the `HttpContext` object:

```
Dim _portalSettings As PortalSettings = _
  CType(HttpContext.Current.Items("PortalSettings"), _
  PortalSettings)
```

The `PortalSettings` object contains information about the individual tabs as well as information pertaining to the security settings of each of those tabs in terms of which roles may view them.

The next few lines check to see whether or not a user has already logged in. If so, it will go ahead and implement a little personalization by displaying a welcome message with the user's user name.

```
If Request.IsAuthenticated = True Then

  WelcomeMessage.Text = "Welcome " & _
    Context.User.Identity.Name & _
    "! <" & "span class=Accent" & _
    ">|<" & "/span" & ">"

  If Context.User.Identity.AuthenticationType = "Forms" Then
    LogoffLink = "<" & "span class=""Accent"">|</span>" & _
      ControlChars.Cr & "<" & "a href=" & _
      Request.ApplicationPath & _
      "/Admin/Logoff.aspx class=SiteLink> Logoff" & "<" & "/a>"
  End If

End If
```

After that, there's a for/next loop to iterate over each tab object and if the user privileges permit, the tab is displayed on the tab bar.

```
For i = 0 To _portalSettings.DesktopTabs.Count - 1
```

The `TabStripDetails` class is used to hold each tab object.

```
Dim tab As TabStripDetails = _
  CType(_portalSettings.DesktopTabs(i), TabStripDetails)
```

A call is made to the PortalSecurity class to check to make sure that the authorized roles within each tab object are within the roles as defined by the user information in the HttpContext object. If the result is positive, the tab is added to the tab bar.

```
If PortalSecurity.IsInRoles(tab.AuthorizedRoles) Then
  authorizedTabs.Add(tab)
End If
```

As you can see, the focal point of the code segment above was the call made to the PortalSecurity class to determine whether or not the current user belongs to the appropriate roles that have access to an individual tab. The PortalSecurity class along with a few other critical classes that we will see later, reside in the Security.vb source file. This, along with the rest of the business objects, is located in the Components directory.

Notice the fact that we did not have to instantiate a copy of the class and instead made a direct call to the IsInRoles function itself. As we saw earlier, all methods within the PortalSecurity class are shared in nature and thus don't require a new instance of their class to run.

Well, now that we have seen how tab views are actually implemented, we can move on and see how we can go about changing view permissions of a tab from the UI.

Changing the view permissions for tab can come in handy when we have a tab that we don't want all users to have access to. The Admin tab, which is available only to users who belong to the Admins role, is a perfect example of that.

Modifying View Permissions of a Tab

To make any modifications to an existing or a new tab, one needs to be logged in with a user name that belongs to the Admins role and thus has administrative privileges. Upon login, click on the Admin tab on top of the page, as shown below:

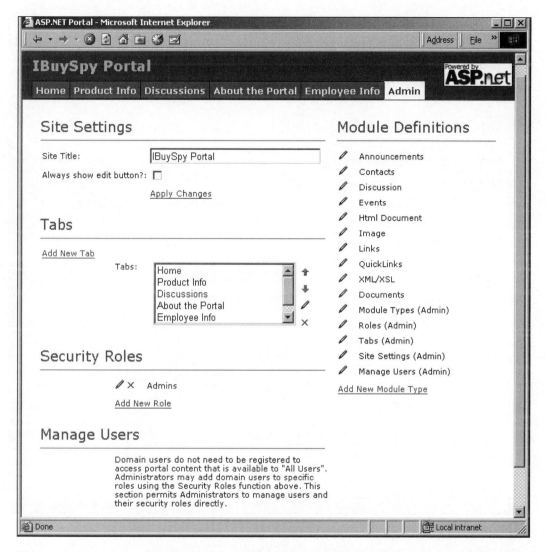

The Admin page contains functionality for managing various aspects of the portal. In the Tabs sections you can see a list of tabs that have already been defined. There is also a link to create new tabs. You can change the display order of the tabs by clicking on any one of them and using the up and down arrows on the right of the combo box to move them around. You can also delete a tab by clicking the 'X' link or edit the properties of a tab by clicking on the pencil link. Let's go ahead and edit the Discussions tab:

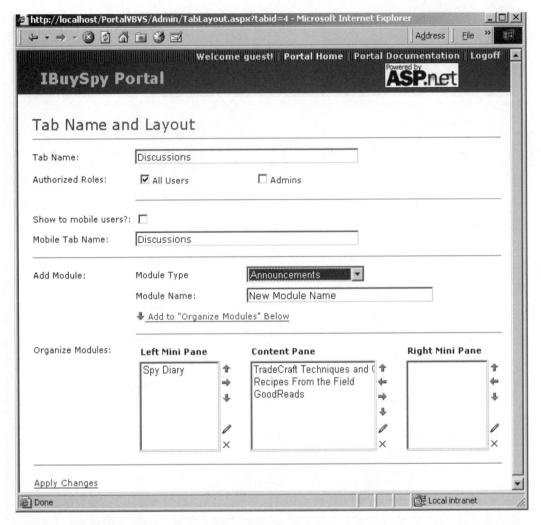

This page contains all information pertaining to a tab including security, layout, and related module information. For now, we're interested in the first section of the page.

In the 'Authorized Roles' line, there are check boxes for all the different roles available in the database as well as the 'All Users' checkbox, which provides open access for everyone. In this case, since we only have the Admins role in the database, that's all we see. Therefore, enabling or disabling a group of individuals from having access permissions to an individual tab is as easy as checking or unchecking a role checkbox.

Upon clicking the 'Apply Changes' link on the bottom of the page, all changes are persisted in the database and the portalSettings object.

Module Editing Security

As mentioned in the previous chapters, the modules are the main components of the IBuySpy portal since they are the ones that contain the content for each section of the portal. A little earlier in this chapter, when we logged on with the guest account which has administrative privileges, we noticed that there were 'Edit' or 'Add New..' links next to a few of the modules within the main page of the portal, in addition to the Admin tab on top of the page. Let's take a look under the hood and see what actually takes place when the modules are loaded.

We'll use the events module for our example. Notice that there are little pencil links next to each event in the Events section meaning that each event can be edited.

When we look in the `Events.ascx` page, we notice the declaration of another user control at the top of the page:

```
<%@ Register TagPrefix="Portal" TagName="Title" src="~/DesktopModuleTitle.ascx" %>
```

`DesktopModuleTitle` is the control responsible for displaying the Edit or in the case of the Events user control, **Add New Event** link. All UI modules in the IBuySpy portal utilize this to enable the editing features of the module at runtime. `DesktopModuleTitle` control is instantiated with a string for `EditText` and another for `EditUrl`. The `EditText` variable simply holds the text value that is going to be presented to the users as the link while the `EditUrl` contains the target URL for the edit page, as shown below:

```
<portal:title EditText="Add New Event" EditUrl="~/DesktopModules/EditEvents.aspx"
runat="server" id=Title1 />
```

Notice that we did not have to mention anything about security permissions of the module. The `DesktopModuleTitle` control takes care of that internally. We can see that in the `Page_Load` event of the `DesktopModuleTitle` control.

```
Private Sub Page_Load(ByVal sender As System.Object, ByVal e As_ System.EventArgs)
Handles MyBase.Load

  Dim _portalSettings As PortalSettings = _
    CType(HttpContext.Current.Items("PortalSettings"), _
```

```
        PortalSettings)

    Dim portalModule As PortalModuleControl = _
      CType(Me.Parent, PortalModuleControl)

    ModuleTitle.Text = portalModule.ModuleConfiguration.ModuleTitle

    If _portalSettings.AlwaysShowEditButton = _
      True Or (PortalSecurity.IsInRoles _
        (portalModule.ModuleConfiguration.AuthorizedEditRoles) _
      And Not (EditText Is Nothing)) Then

      EditButton.Text = EditText
      EditButton.NavigateUrl = EditUrl + "?mid=" + _
      portalModule.ModuleId.ToString()
      EditButton.Target = EditTarget
    End If

  End Sub
```

As expected, the very first thing the code does is getting hold of the current instance of the `PortalSettings` object sitting in the current context of the `HttpContext` object which contains all the necessary information pertaining to the calling module.

```
    Dim _portalSettings As PortalSettings = _
      CType(HttpContext.Current.Items("PortalSettings"), _
      PortalSettings)
```

A security check is then performed:

```
    If _portalSettings.AlwaysShowEditButton = _
      True Or (PortalSecurity.IsInRoles _
        (portalModule.ModuleConfiguration.AuthorizedEditRoles) _
      And Not (EditText Is Nothing)) Then
```

Here we check for:

❑   The 'Always show edit button' setting

❑   The user being in at least one role that has permission to edit the module instance

❑   The Edit text being empty (i.e. there is no edit option)

If the 'Always show edit button' setting is active, the security check is overridden to show the edit button. If the text for the edit button is empty then the security check is overridden to not show the edit button. Otherwise, the decision is based on users roles.

If the edit button is to be shown, the values of the edit button are set.

```
EditButton.Text = EditText
EditButton.NavigateUrl = EditUrl + "?mid=" + _
portalModule.ModuleId.ToString()
EditButton.Target = EditTarget
```

Notice that extra `mid` variable is appended to the URL in the form of a query string to signify the ID of the module.

As for the rest of the edit links for individual events, they are created a little differently. The data is retrieved from the database using the `EventsDB` component and is bound to a `DataList` control for display as we can see in the `Page_Load` event of the `Events` user control:

```
Private Sub Page_Load(ByVal sender As System.Object, ByVal e As _
    System.EventArgs) Handles MyBase.Load

    Dim events As New ASPNetPortal.EventsDB()

    myDataList.DataSource = events.GetEvents(ModuleId)
    myDataList.DataBind()

End Sub
```

From that point on, edit links are created and their actual visibility to the user is dependent on the Boolean value stored in the `IsEditable` property. Keep in mind that the `IsEditable` property has been originally defined in the `PortalModuleControl` class and since the modules in the IBuySpy portal including the `Events.ascx` inherit the `PortalModuleControl` class, they have access to that property as well.

Let's look at a code segment from the `Events.ascx`:

```
<asp:DataList id="myDataList" CellPadding="4" Width="98%" EnableViewState="false"
runat="server">
    <ItemTemplate>
        <span class="ItemTitle">
            <asp:HyperLink id="editLink" ImageUrl="~/images/edit.gif"
NavigateUrl='<%# "~/DesktopModules/EditEvents.aspx?ItemID=" &
DataBinder.Eval(Container.DataItem,"ItemID") & "&mid=" & ModuleId %>' Visible="<%#
IsEditable %>" runat="server" />
            ....
    </ItemTemplate>
</asp:DataList>
```

When a user clicks on the pencil link next to a particular event, the `ItemID` variable containing the ID of the specified event, along with the aforementioned `mid` variable, are passed on to the `EditEvents.aspx` page for editing.

You might think that security will be compromised if the user just remembers the path of the edit page for a particular module and tries to manually launch the page without proper authentication. Well, manual navigation to an edit page in the IBuySpy portal does not guarantee access if the right level of authentication does not exist, as shown in the figure below:

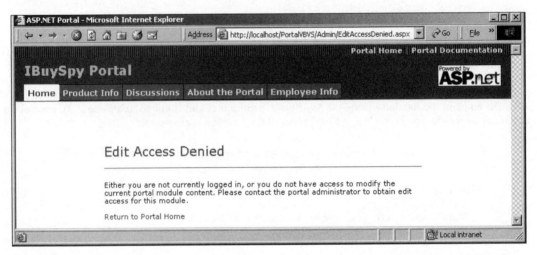

The reason for that is the fact that a security check is made in every edit page to ensure that only users with the correct permissions can access it. The HasEditPermissions method of the PortalSecurity object is used along with module ID of the current module to check to see whether or not the current user has sufficient permissions to edit this module.

A simple If statement is used to do the job in the Page_Load event of the EditEvents.aspx page:

```
If PortalSecurity.HasEditPermissions(moduleId) = False Then
    Response.Redirect("~/Admin/EditAccessDenied.aspx")
End If
```

Modifying Edit Permissions of a Module

As usual, the user must belong to the Admins role in order to be able to make any changes to the roles that have Edit access to a particular module.

To modify an existing module's Edit access, choose a module in the Tabs section of the Admin page, let's say the Discussions tab, and click the pencil link on the right of the modules combo box as shown in the previous section.

The 'Tab Name and Layout' page contains general information about the tab and allows the user to modify the position of individual modules in the page within the preformatted template of the page. Go ahead and choose the Spy Diary module. Keep in mind that Spy Diary is merely the name of the module instance and not a physical module name. Spy Diary among many other modules used in the IBuySpy portal are actually instances of the HtmlModule.ascx user control.

Finally, we can get to the Module Settings page by clicking the pencil link in the right of the combo box in the Spy Diary.

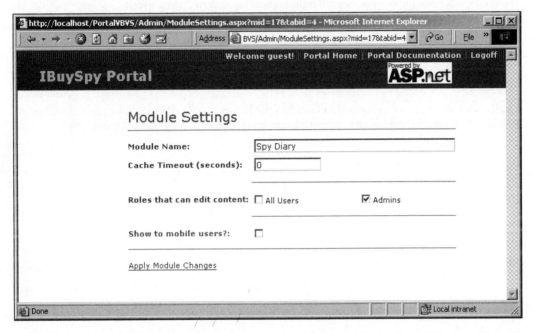

We can check the roles that we want to have edit access to in this particular module in the "Roles that can edit content" section. At the moment there are only two choices (the Admins role and All users) since we only have the Admins role that came built-in along with the portal. If we had added more roles, we would see more checkboxes there.

Upon making any modifications, we must click the 'Apply Module Changes' link in order for changes to be saved otherwise all changes will be discarded.

Summary

In this chapter, we have looked at why security is important when we are developing an intranet.

We discussed the four principals that underpin the security implementation provided by IBuySpy:

❑   Viewing and editing permissions

❑   Role based security

❑   Self-sufficiency

❑   Reusability

We then went on to examine the security infrastructure provided by the IBuySpy architecture.

We saw how we can implement two different options for authenticating users:

- ❏ Forms authentication
- ❏ Windows authentication

We discussed the relative pros and cons of using these options.

Finally, we looked at how security is enforced in the IBuySpy code. We saw how the authorization checks are performed and how we should administer this functionality using the IBuySpy administration interface.

Soluti...

BM

Referen...

System

System.Data

System.Drawing

System.Web

System.XML

AssemblyInfo.vb

Assembly

BM.vsdisco

Global.asax

Styles.css

Web.config

WebForm1.aspx

ebForm1.aspx*   WebForm1.aspx,

5

The Discussions Module

So far, we have been looking at the core IBuySpy architecture – the glue that holds together the modules that actually provide the functionality of our intranet. In Chapter 3, we looked at how to build a simple module but the discussion was mainly centered on how the module interacts with the architecture. In this chapter, the module will now take center stage, as we dissect one of the IBuySpy modules.

We will be looking at the IBuySpy Discussion module – IBuySpy's forum. We will see what it does, how it does it, and why it does it that way. We will also look at ways that we can improve on the module, solving some security issues and increasing efficiency where we can.

What Is The Purpose Of Forums?

Forums can be the "life" of any intranet. They offer a living, breathing document that invites participation, encourages feedback, and nurtures discussion. They can also create a dynamic interest in the site as users check in to read the latest entries and add their own thoughts or ideas. A well-designed forum can add tremendous value to the end-user's experience of an intranet; a poorly designed forum… well, let's just say that it can really detract from the overall impression and leave it at that!

Forums are an incredibly useful tool for promoting collaboration and the sharing of knowledge. As each new message is posted it forms part of a permanent record of the discussion of an idea or a problem. In this regard, forums are an excellent alternative to e-mail list servers where messages are typically read and then disposed of.

This is not to say that forums are a better solution in all cases. List servers have the advantage of being a "push" technology; when new information, such as a product launch or a bulletin, needs to be disseminated quickly, a list server provides a method of notification that requires little or no effort on the part of the recipient. A forum, on the other hand, requires a user to actively choose to review new posts.

Forums also have their dark side, as an un-moderated discussion can frequently degenerate to name-calling, insults, and generally unproductive commentary. Often, the costs associated with moderating a forum will cause a company to think twice before implementing one on their site. This is more typically a problem on Internet sites though, as their somewhat anonymous nature lends itself more easily to socially unacceptable behavior.

As conscientious developers, it is our responsibility to inform our customers of the pros and cons of including a forum on their site. Ultimately though, the decision on whether to include a forum on their site or not should be left up to the customer. For our part we are more concerned with providing an efficient and effective design should they choose to use it.

The IBuySpy Discussion Module

The IBuySpy Discussion module is a complete, functional forum and can be used as is, without any modifications (although we would need to tighten its current security routines before we could comfortably roll out a private forum). It provides all of the basic features that our users would expect, including a summary display of the available threads in the forum:

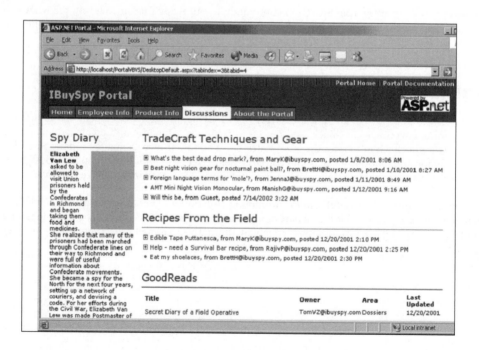

The ability to navigate and display the messages (or posts) within a thread:

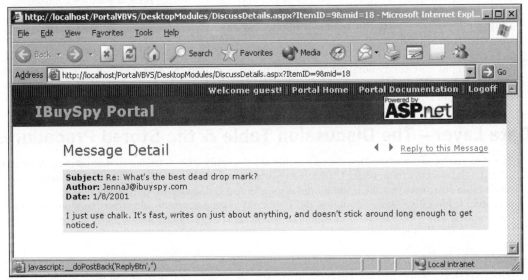

And, of course, the ability to add new threads or reply to existing ones.

What the Module Comprises

The Discussion module is built around the same n-tier principles as the other modules: it has specific presentation layer, business layer, and data layer components. The Discussion module is comprised of the following:

Data Layer	Data Table	Discussion
	Stored Procedures	AddMessage
		GetNextMessageId
		GetPrevMessageId
		GetSingleMessage
		GetThreadMessages
		GetTopLevelMessages
Business Layer	Business Component	DiscussionDB.vb
Presentation Layer	Edit/Display Page	DiscussDetails.aspx
	User Control	Discussion.ascx

It's a bit different from the other modules in that it doesn't display the detail level (the actual messages) in the user control displayed on the tabs of `DesktopDefault.aspx`. Instead the user control provides a summary of the different discussion threads. It's also unique among the modules supplied with IBuySpy in that it combines the module's editing and display components into a single page, `DiscussDetails.aspx`.

We're going to start our exploration of the module by looking at the data layer – where the messages are stored, how the reply hierarchy is maintained. We will also examine the stored procedures that manipulate the Discussion module data.

Data Layer – The Discussion Table & the Stored Procedures

The data components of the Discussion module are probably a bit more fun to discuss than those of the other modules in the framework. Unlike the typical parent/child relationships and non-hierarchical, single table structures that the other modules use, threaded discussions involve maintaining unnatural sort orders. They also require complex and frequently changing relationships between messages and their replies. The way that the discussion data is stored in the database involves the use of some very interesting data design techniques!

The first thing to note is that all of the data for this module is stored in a single table, which for obvious reasons is called `Discussion`. The structure of the discussion table is, in and of itself, relatively simple:

Column Name	Data Type	Size	Allows Nulls	Description
ItemID	int	4	No	Primary Key – Uniquely identifies each message in the portal
ModuleID	Int	4	No	Associates an individual message with a particular module
Title	nvarchar	100	Yes	Title for the thread or the thread replies
CreatedDate	datetime	8	Yes	Date that the message was created
Body	nvarchar	3000	Yes	The message text

Column Name	Data Type	Size	Allows Nulls	Description
DisplayOrder	nvarchar	750	Yes	A text field that determines the sort order of the messages. It is designed to display the threads in date order and the replies in hierarchical order by date below each thread
CreatedByUser	nvarchar	100	Yes	Identifies the user that created the thread.

The real challenge in the design of the Discussion table is in maintaining two kinds of message relationships; the relationship between a thread and all of its messages, as well as the relationship between any given message and the replies made to it.

In the design that was implemented in IBuySpy, both of these relationships are managed through the DisplayOrder field. This 750 character, variable-length, Unicode character field contains a concatenation of one or more date/time values representing each level of a given message's reply hierarchy. A little confusing at first read through, isn't it?

It might clarify things a bit if we walked through what happens as a thread gets started and as replies get added to it. Let's start with the thread titled "What's the best dead drop mark?" from the "TradeCraft Techniques and Gear" module on the Discussions tab. When Mary creates the first message in the new thread the new record looks like this:

ItemID	ModuleID	CreatedDate	CreatedByUser
8	18	2001-01-08 08:06:52.000	MaryK@ibuyspy.com
Title:		What's the best dead drop mark?	
Body:		I know this is a total newbie question, but how do I mark a dead drop? What's the best mark?	
Display Order:		2001-01-08 08:06:51.607	

As we can see from the above, the DisplayOrder field is initialized to a 23 character string representation of the current date and time. So is the CreatedDate field but the two won't necessarily match. That's because the GETDATE() function is called twice to populate them and there may be some processing overhead between the calls. The next message to get posted is Jenna's reply to Mary's original post.

ItemID	ModuleID	CreatedDate		CreatedByUser
9	18	2001-01-08 08:07:59.000		JennaJ@ibuyspy.com
Title:		Re: What's the best dead drop mark?		
Body:		I just use chalk. It's fast, writes on just about anything, and doesn't stick around long enough to get noticed.		
Display Order:		**2001-01-08 08:06:51.607**2001-01-08 08:07:59.177		

This time the `DisplayOrder` is the value of the `DisplayOrder` field from Mary's original message (in bold) plus the date and time that Jenna's message was posted.

The next person to respond is Tom and, since Tom is replying to Mary's original message, he also gets the value of the `DisplayOrder` field from Mary's message (along with the date and time of his message of course):

ItemID	ModuleID	CreatedDate		CreatedByUser
11	18	2001-01-09 08:14:57.000		TomVZ@ibuyspy.com
Title:		Re: What's the best dead drop mark?		
Body:		There are several things to consider in making your mark: it has to be made (and later erased) quickly and discreetly, durable enough to stick around until it's read, easily ignored by passers by, and not missed when it's gone. Lots of folks like chalk, but I find it washes away too easily in rainy weather. Chewing gum (already chewed) works great, but you'll want to place it well below eye level lest some zealous maintenance worker cleans it off before it has done the job.		
Display Order:		**2001-01-08 08:06:51.607**2001-01-09 08:14:57.357		

Now Brett responds to Jenna's message directly (as opposed to replying to Mary's message). In the new record for Brett's message the `DisplayOrder` field contains the <u>full value</u> of Jenna's `DisplayOrder` field, which is itself a concatenation of the date and time of Mary's post and the date and time of Jenna's post, plus the date and time of Brett's post:

ItemID	ModuleID	CreatedDate		CreatedByUser
10	18	2001-01-09 08:15:33.000		BrettH@ibuyspy.com
Title:		Re: What's the best dead drop mark?		
Body:		I use chalk too -- it's really easy to erase.		
Display Order:		**2001-01-08 08:06:51.607**2001-01-08 08:07:59.177**2001-01-09 08:15:32.970		

Because Tom replied to Mary's message his message shouldn't be indented as deeply when we display the messages hierarchically. Because there are only two dates in Tom's `DisplayOrder` field as opposed to the three in Brett's we can actually calculate the indentation level for each of their messages from the length of their respective `DisplayOrder` field values. In fact that's how `GetThreadMessages` (the stored procedure that is responsible for retrieving the replies in a thread) actually figures out the indentation!

Here's the `SELECT` statement from `GetThreadMessages` with the calculation highlighted:

```
SELECT
  ItemID,
  DisplayOrder,
  REPLICATE(' ', ((LEN(DisplayOrder)/23) - 1) * 5) AS Indent,
  Title,
  CreatedByUser,
  CreatedDate,
  Body
FROM
  Discussion
WHERE
  LEFT(DisplayOrder, 23) = @Parent
 AND
  (LEN( DisplayOrder ) / 23 ) > 1
ORDER BY
  DisplayOrder
```

Back in our user control this translates to the following listing:

TradeCraft Techniques and Gear

⊟ What's the best dead drop mark? , from MaryK@ibuyspy.com , posted 1/8/2001 8:06 AM
　　Re: What's the best dead drop mark? , from JennaJ@ibuyspy.com , posted 1/8/2001 8:07 AM
　　　Re: What's the best dead drop mark? , from BrettH@ibuyspy.com , posted 1/9/2001 8:15 AM
　　Re: What's the best dead drop mark? , from TomVZ@ibuyspy.com , posted 1/9/2001 8:14 AM

So we can see now how the indentation portion of the message listing is accomplished, but to be honest, this seems like a rather complicated way to go about it! Why not just store the indent level as a numerical value and maintain it by simply storing the value from the parent record plus one whenever we create a reply? We wouldn't even need to calculate the indent level when we selected the messages – we could use the indent level value directly! If all we were concerned about were the indent level, this would be a much simpler alternative – but displaying the hierarchy is more complicated than that.

Take another look at the listing in the previous screenshot. Brett's message is actually listed <u>before</u> Tom's even though Brett's message was created <u>after</u> Tom's! That's because the messages are sorted according to the `DisplayOrder` field instead of by the `CreationDate`. Take a look at the same set of records with corresponding `DisplayOrder` values:

CreatedByUser	DisplayOrder
MaryK@ibuyspy.com	2001-01-08 08:06:51.607
JennaJ@ibuyspy.com	2001-01-08 08:06:51.6072001-01-08 08:07:59.177
BrettH@ibuyspy.com	**2001-01-08 08:06:51.6072001-01-08 08:07:59.177**2001-01-09 08:15:32.970
TomVZ@ibuyspy.com	2001-01-08 08:06:51.6072001-01-09 08:14:57.357

It's the `DisplayOrder` of the message that Brett responded to that's responsible for moving his message ahead of Tom's. Jenna responded to Mary's message before Tom did, and since Brett responded to Jenna's message he gets to piggyback on her priority in the message order.

It's a pretty ingenuous solution to an otherwise vexing problem! After that, the rest of the data manipulations are pretty routine. The only other parts of the data layer that are really interesting are the way that we select the top level thread messages and the method for selecting messages that belong to a single thread.

Selecting Top Level Thread Messages

The interesting thing here is that nowhere in the `Discussion` table is a top-level thread message explicitly identified. Take a look at the body of the `GetTopLevelMessages` stored procedure, which is responsible for selecting these records:

```
SELECT
  ItemID,
  DisplayOrder,
  LEFT(DisplayOrder, 23) AS Parent,
  (SELECT COUNT(*) -1  FROM Discussion Disc2
     WHERE LEFT(Disc2.DisplayOrder,LEN(RTRIM(Disc.DisplayOrder)))
           = Disc.DisplayOrder)
     AS ChildCount,
  Title,
  CreatedByUser,
  CreatedDate
FROM
  Discussion Disc
WHERE
  ModuleID=@ModuleID
    AND
  (LEN( DisplayOrder ) / 23 ) = 1
ORDER BY
    DisplayOrder
```

Look at the highlighted portion of the where clause and we'll see that the top level messages are identified by calculating the length of the `DisplayOrder` field and eliminating any entries that aren't exactly 23 characters. You can bet we'll be discussing this when we look at increasing the efficiency of the data layer!

GetTopLevelMessages actually contains a few redundant calculations too. If we look at the body of the SELECT statement again, we'll notice that there are several items we can improve on:

❑ The first is that the entire Parent column is completely unnecessary – the WHERE clause limits the results to records with DisplayOrder values that are exactly 23 characters long, so the expression LEFT(DisplayOrder, 23) will always be identical to the full value of the DisplayOrder field. Parent will always be a duplicate of the DisplayOrder field, so we can simply remove it from the SELECT statement.

❑ Second is the LEN(RTRIM(Disc.DisplayOrder)) sub-expression within the inner SELECT statement. This sub-expression calculates the length of the DisplayOrder field from the outer SELECT statement. The LEN function in SQL Server automatically ignores white space at the end of an expression, so the RTRIM is redundant.

What's worse is that the whole LEN statement is unnecessary! As was mentioned in the previous bullet we know we are limited to records where the DisplayOrder values are exactly 23 characters long; so why bother <u>calculating</u> the length of a field when we already know the answer? We can replace the whole LEN(RTRIM(Disc.DisplayOrder)) sub-expression with the literal value 23.

❑ Finally, the criteria expression (LEN(DisplayOrder) / 23) = 1 in the WHERE clause, which limits the records to messages with 23 character DisplayOrder fields, performs an extra calculation. We know that we want 23 character long values, so why divide by 23 and then check to see if it divides evenly a single time? Why not just simplify this to LEN(DisplayOrder) = 23?

We won't implement any change to this procedure just yet – we'll be proposing a couple of changes to the structure of the Discussion table in the *Squeezing a Little More out of the Data Layer* section that will eliminate them for us anyway.

Selecting Thread Replies

We've already looked at part of the GetThreadMessages stored procedure that selects thread replies for a given thread. GetThreadMessages is responsible for grabbing all of the messages in a particular thread, excluding the top-level message. It takes a single input parameter, @ParentID, which is the 23 character DisplayOrder value for the first message in the thread:

```
SELECT
  ItemID,
  DisplayOrder,
  REPLICATE(' ', ((LEN(DisplayOrder)/23) - 1) * 5) AS Indent,
  Title,
  CreatedByUser,
  CreatedDate,
  Body
FROM
  Discussion
WHERE
  LEFT(DisplayOrder, 23) = @Parent
AND
  (LEN( DisplayOrder ) / 23 ) > 1
ORDER BY
  DisplayOrder
```

It selects all of the messages in a particular thread by comparing the first 23 characters of their `DisplayOrder` value to the value in `@ParentID`. Because we're only interested in the reply messages here, it filters out the original message by selecting `DisplayOrder` values that are greater than 23 characters. The remaining records are returned sorted by `DisplayOrder`.

Selecting Individual Messages

Individual messages are returned by the `GetSingleMessage` stored procedure. `GetSingleMessage` takes a single parameter, `@ItemID` and returns the corresponding message. The body of the procedure looks like this:

```
DECLARE @nextMessageID int
EXECUTE GetNextMessageID @ItemID, @nextMessageID OUTPUT
DECLARE @prevMessageID int
EXECUTE GetPrevMessageID @ItemID, @prevMessageID OUTPUT

SELECT
    ItemID,
    Title,
    CreatedByUser,
    CreatedDate,
    Body,
    DisplayOrder,
    NextMessageID = @nextMessageID,
    PrevMessageID = @prevMessageID
FROM
    Discussion
WHERE
    ItemID = @ItemID
```

The first four lines call out to two helper stored procedures and set up variables to store results from their output parameters:

```
DECLARE @nextMessageID int
EXECUTE GetNextMessageID @ItemID, @nextMessageID OUTPUT
DECLARE @prevMessageID int
EXECUTE GetPrevMessageID @ItemID, @prevMessageID OUTPUT
```

`GetNextMessageID` and `GetPrevMessageID` look up the `ItemID`s for the messages that are before and after the current message in the reply hierarchy. They both operate in the same fashion: by looking up the current item's `DisplayOrder` value and then selecting the first record with either a higher or lower `DisplayOrder` value. Here's the listing for `GetNextMessageID`:

```
DECLARE @CurrentDisplayOrder as nvarchar(750)
DECLARE @CurrentModule as int

/* Find DisplayOrder of current item */
SELECT
    @CurrentDisplayOrder = DisplayOrder,
    @CurrentModule = ModuleID
FROM
    Discussion
```

```
WHERE
    ItemID = @ItemID

/* Get the next message in the same module */
SELECT Top 1
    @NextID = ItemID
FROM
    Discussion
WHERE
    DisplayOrder > @CurrentDisplayOrder
    AND
    ModuleID = @CurrentModule
ORDER BY
    DisplayOrder ASC

/* end of this thread? */
IF @@Rowcount < 1
    SET @NextID = null
```

The first SELECT statement is the one that finds the DisplayOrder value for the @ItemID parameter that was passed in (it also finds the associated ModuleID so that we can properly filter the values in the SELECT statement that comes afterward). The second SELECT statement retrieves the next record with a higher display order and places its ItemId in the output parameter. The IF block at the end of the procedure checks to see if this message is the last message for the module – not the thread, even though its comment says differently – and returns a NULL value if it is.

The only real difference between GetNextMessageID and GetPrevMessageID (aside from the names of their parameters and the code comments) is the sort order for the second SELECT statement. GetNextMessageID sorts in ascending order to get the next highest DisplayOrder value; GetPrevMessageID sorts in descending order to get the next lowest (i.e. previous) DisplayOrder value. Other than that the two stored procedures operate identically.

Getting back to the GetSingleMessage stored procedure; its SELECT statement simply pulls the field values for the given ItemId and adds the next and previous message IDs:

```
SELECT
    ItemID,
    Title,
    CreatedByUser,
    CreatedDate,
    Body,
    DisplayOrder,
    NextMessageID = @nextMessageID,
    PrevMessageID = @prevMessageID
FROM
    Discussion
WHERE
    ItemID = @ItemID
```

Posting a New Message

New posts to a thread are handled through the AddMessage stored procedure. AddMessage takes a whopping six parameters:

❑ @ItemID – An output parameter used to return the ItemID for the new message.

❑ @Title – The title of the message or thread.

❑ @Body – The message text.

❑ @ParentID – The ItemID of the message that this is a reply to.

❑ @UserName – The name of the user posting the message.

❑ @ModuleID – The ID for the module that the message is supposed to be displayed in.

The body of the stored procedure can be broken down into three parts. The first is the section that looks up the DisplayOrder of the message we are replying to so that we can add our new message into the right spot in the reply hierarchy:

```
/* Find DisplayOrder of parent item */
DECLARE @ParentDisplayOrder as nvarchar(750)

SET @ParentDisplayOrder = ""

SELECT
    @ParentDisplayOrder = DisplayOrder
FROM
    Discussion
WHERE
    ItemID = @ParentID
```

The first two lines declare the variable @ParentDisplayOrder to hold the value of the parent record's DisplayOrder field and then initialize it to an empty string. The SELECT statement looks up the value of the DisplayOrder field for the message that we are posting a reply to. If the new message is the start of a new thread it won't have a parent record, meaning the SELECT statement won't have any effect and the value of @ParentDisplayOrder will still be an empty string.

The line that initializes the variable might seem like an unnecessary step, but it is needed to circumvent SQL Server's behavior when it comes to dealing with a NULL value, which is the default value for variables declared in a stored procedure. Whenever any value is concatenated with a NULL, SQL Server returns a NULL.

Later in the stored procedure we'll want to append a date string to the value in @ParentDisplayOrder. If we weren't able to look up a value for @ParentDisplayOrder we'll just want to get back the date string value. If the value in @ParentDisplayOrder is NULL what we'll get back is NULL, which we really don't want – we'd never get a value in the DisplayOrder field since we'd always be concatenating to NULL values!

The line that initializes @ParentDisplayOrder to an empty string prevents this from happening.

The next section takes care of inserting the message into the `Discussion` table:

```
INSERT INTO Discussion
(
    Title,
    Body,
    DisplayOrder,
    CreatedDate,
    CreatedByUser,
    ModuleID
)
VALUES
(
    @Title,
    @Body,
    @ParentDisplayOrder + CONVERT( nvarchar(24), GetDate(), 21 ),
    GetDate(),
    @UserName,
    @ModuleID
)
```

The highlighted line above is where the date string is concatenated to form the new `DisplayOrder` value – simultaneously maintaining both the display order and the indentation level.

The last part of `AddMessage` is the line that stores the `ItemID` of the newly created message in the output parameter `@InputID`:

```
SELECT
    @ItemID = @@Identity
```

While this line works and is not necessarily incorrect, the SQL Server documentation recommends using the SET statement to update the value of a single variable. It never hurts to see an alternate technique but SET @ItemID = @@Identity would be preferable.

That wraps up our examination of the `Discussion` table and the Discussion module stored procedures. In the next section we're going to look at a few suggestions to improve and optimize the performance of the data objects that we've just taken a look at.

Squeezing a Little More Out of the Data Layer

What should be readily apparent from the sections above is that the techniques for identifying top-level messages and for determining which messages belong to a particular thread are a little cumbersome. The fact that we have to calculate field lengths and compare portions of text fields every time we want to read a thread should already be speaking loudly for a round of optimization. Consider that the bulk of the activity in the discussions module centers on reading messages and it positively screams out!

Optimizing the Data Layer for Reads

The simplest solution to the problem is to add another `int` field called `ThreadID` to the `Discussion` table. It will increase the size of each record a bit, but considering that the table currently holds duplicates of all the titles and uses a relatively large value in `DisplayOrder` to track the record hierarchy, the increase is fairly minor.

To modify the table from within Visual Studio .NET:

1. Expand the Server Explorer pane.

2. Navigate to the Tables node of the Portal database and right-click on the Discussion table:

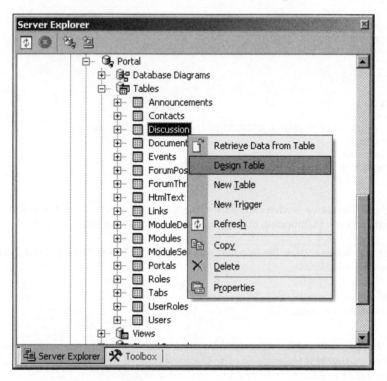

3. Choose Design Table from the shortcut menu and the Table Designer window will open.

4. Right-click on the row selector for the **Title** field and choose **Insert Column** from the shortcut menu. Set the **Column Name** to `ThreadID` and the rest of the column properties as shown below:

	Column Name	Data Type	Length	Allow Nulls
🔑	ItemID	int	4	
	ModuleID	int	4	
▶	ThreadID	int	4	✓
	Title	nvarchar	100	✓
	CreatedDate	datetime	8	✓
	Body	nvarchar	3000	✓
	DisplayOrder	nvarchar	750	✓
	CreatedByUser	nvarchar	100	✓

dbo.Discussion...EBOOK.Portal)*

5. Click the Save button to have Visual Studio .NET update the table definition in the database.

You can apply all of the modifications to the Discussion table, whether they are done here or in later sections, by executing the change script DiscussionTableUpdates.sql, which you can find in the downloadable code for this book.

Now that we have a `ThreadID` column, we'll need to modify the `AddMessage` stored procedure so that a message that starts a thread has its `ItemID` value copied into its `ThreadID`. It will be a simple matter to look up the `ThreadID` from the parent record whenever we add a new reply message.

To edit the `AddMessage` stored procedure:

6. Expand the **Stored Procedures** node in the **Server Explorer** pane.

7. Right-click on the **AddMessage** node and select **Edit Stored Procedure** option from the shortcut menu to open the stored procedure in the **Transact-SQL Code Editor**.

Make the following changes to the first part of `AddMessage` to look up the `ThreadID` from the parent record:

```
/* Find DisplayOrder of parent item */
DECLARE @ParentDisplayOrder as nvarchar(750)

SET @ParentDisplayOrder =

-- Also look up the ThreadID of the parent item
DECLARE @ThreadID as int

SELECT
    @ThreadID = ThreadID,
    @ParentDisplayOrder = DisplayOrder
```

```
FROM
     Discussion
WHERE
     ItemID = @ParentID
     AND ModuleID = @ModuleID
```

We've added the `ModuleID` = `@ModuleID` criteria for two reasons. The first is that the `Discussion` table comes pre-populated with a dummy record which has an `ItemId` of 0. Since the user interface passes in a `@ParentID` parameter of 0 whenever it creates a new thread we want to be sure that we don't match the dummy record.

The second reason is that the `ItemID` field in the `Discussion` table has a seed value of 0, so even if we've dropped and re-created it to get a clean table we might now have a legitimate record with an `ItemID` of 0. This ensures that we will only match it if we <u>intend</u> to match it.

This doesn't really cost us anything since we were looking up the parent item's display order anyway. Now let's change the UPDATE statement so that it includes the ThreadID field and the value we just looked up:

```
INSERT INTO Discussion
(
     ThreadID,
     Title,
     Body,
     DisplayOrder,
     CreatedDate,
     CreatedByUser,
     ModuleID
)
VALUES
(
     @ThreadID,
     @Title,
     @Body,
     @ParentDisplayOrder + CONVERT( nvarchar(24), GetDate(), 21 ),
     GetDate(),
     @UserName,
     @ModuleID
)
```

Don't worry if the value we've looked up and inserted for @ThreadID is NULL – we can use that to perform a check to see if this is a new thread. If @ThreadID is NULL we'll know that this is a new thread, so we'll perform an UPDATE that changes the value in the new record's ThreadID field to match the newly added ItemID. Add the following to the bottom of the stored procedure:

```
SELECT
    @ItemID = @@Identity

-- Check to see if this is a new thread
IF @ThreadID IS NULL
    BEGIN
    -- It is, so update the ThreadID to match the new ItemID
    UPDATE
        Discussion
    SET
        ThreadID = @ItemID
    WHERE
        ItemID = @ItemID

    END
```

That's it! Click the Save button and Visual Studio .NET will update the stored procedure for us.

If you get the clear and informative error message below when you try to save the stored procedure:

Switch the quotation marks in the line below from double-quotes:

```
SET @ParentDisplayOrder = ""
```

To single-quotes:

```
SET @ParentDisplayOrder = ''
```

> *Unless we set certain compatibility options first, SQL Server won't understand double quotes as text delimiters.*

AddMessage now implements explicit thread tracking for us. We've added a little overhead to the process of inserting new messages, but again, the discussions module should really be optimized for reading data rather than writing it.

While we're editing AddMessage let's take the opportunity to change:

```
SELECT
    @ItemID = @@Identity
```

To the preferred syntax:

```
SET @ItemID = @@Identity
```

Ah, that's better! Click the **Save** button one more time to save this last little change. We can also run the following pair of UPDATE statements against the existing data in the Discussion table to populate the ThreadID column with values:

```
-- Set the ThreadId values for the top level messages
UPDATE
    Discussion
SET
    ThreadID = ItemID
WHERE
    Len(DisplayOrder) <= 23


-- Set the ThreadID values for the replies
UPDATE
    Discussion
SET
    ThreadID = (SELECT
                    Threads.ThreadID
                FROM
                    Discussion Threads
                WHERE
                    LEFT(Discussion.DisplayOrder, 23) = Threads.DisplayOrder
                    AND Threads.ThreadID IS NOT NULL)
WHERE
    LEN(Discussion.DisplayOrder) > 23
```

> *You'll find these statements in a file called* `PopulateThreadID.sql` *in the downloaded code. To run them you can either open the file in Query Analyzer and run it there, or copy the statements into the open* **SQL Editor** *window, highlight them, right-click and then choose the* **Run Selection** *menu item. Don't forget to delete the lines once they've run though!*

Once we have a ThreadID to work with, selecting the top level messages is a matter of selecting for messages where the ItemID value matches the value of the ThreadID field. Open GetTopLevelMessages from the **Server Explorer** and make the following three changes:

```
SELECT
    ItemID,
    DisplayOrder,
    ThreadID,
    (SELECT COUNT(*) -1  FROM Discussion Disc2
        WHERE Disc2.ThreadID = Disc.ThreadID)
      AS ChildCount,
    Title,
    CreatedByUser,
    CreatedDate
```

```
FROM
    Discussion Disc
WHERE
    ModuleID=@ModuleID
    AND ItemID = ThreadID
ORDER BY
    DisplayOrder
```

Save it and `GetTopLevelMessages` will now use a much more efficient numerical comparison to count the replies and to identify the top-level messages. It also returns the `ThreadID` with the other fields (instead of the leftmost 23 characters of the `DisplayOrder` field) so that we will be able to use it when we search for the reply messages in a thread.

The last procedure that we need to update to take advantage of the new `ThreadID` field is `GetThreadMessages`. We'll need to change two things in `GetThreadMessages` so open it up in the **SQL Editor**. The first is the input parameter that it takes:

```
ALTER PROCEDURE GetThreadMessages
(
    @Parent nvarchar(750)
)
AS
```

We only need the `ThreadID` to look up the messages now, so change it to:

```
ALTER PROCEDURE GetThreadMessages
(
    @ThreadID int
)
AS
```

The second change is a quick update of its `WHERE` clause to make use of the `@ThreadID`:

```
WHERE
    ThreadID = @ThreadID
    AND ItemID <> ThreadID
ORDER BY
    DisplayOrder
```

The first criterion finds all of the messages in the thread, but the second eliminates the top-level message (since we only want replies, not the original message).

> The changes we've made here will require updates to the business layer and to the presentation layer. To keep discussions of the original design separate from the changes we make, we'll look at the original code for each layer first and save the revisions for the *Squeezing a Little More Out of...* sections.

We've made a relatively simple change to the structure of the `Discussion` table, but some quick testing in the Wrox Testing Labs' Vancouver Office (a.k.a. the author's apartment) showed performance increases of anywhere up to 30% in the test environment.

> If we wanted to embark on a more radical revision of the existing structures we could split the `Discussion` table into separate tables for threads and messages. We could also bias the design more heavily towards reading records rather than writing them by pre-calculating most of the expressions embedded in `GetTopLevelMessages` and `GetThreadMessages` – calculations like indent levels and the child counts could easily be determined and updated during message inserts.
>
> This would eliminate the storage of the essentially redundant title information for the replies, speed up the selection of top level message even further, and allow for an efficient place to store statistics about the thread (e.g. reply counts, last updated values, etc.).

Minor Tweaks

We can still make a few minor changes to the data structures to get a little bit more out of the data layer, but these changes would mostly be in the area of reducing the storage requirements for our table.

One idea would be to alter the way that the message hierarchy is stored in `DisplayOrder`. As it stands, the field uses a 23-character representation of the current date and time to create a (hopefully) unique sorting value. Since the `ItemID` is a sequentially assigned integer value that is guaranteed to be unique we could use it to set the sort order instead. Knowing that an integer data type value can never be larger than ten digits we can pad the value to the left with zeros (e.g. "0000000123") and use that in place of the date string, saving 13 characters per level of reply hierarchy, per message.

The original `DisplayOrder` implementation allowed for up to 32.61 levels of message reply indents (750 characters per field divided by 23 characters per level of indentation). We're really not sure why the developer who originally designed the table didn't choose a field size that was an even multiple of 23 characters! With our shorter version of the `DisplayOrder` contents, we can reduce the field size to 320 characters and still support 32 levels of indentation.

We can also change the data type of `DisplayOrder` to a plain `varchar` rather than the Unicode version, `nvarchar`. This isn't because of our enhancement – even with the original implementation the contents of DisplayOrder were never intended for display and they never contained Unicode values. Because `varchar` fields use half the storage space of `nvarchar`s for the same number of characters, we can sizably reduce the storage requirements for our table.

Let's go ahead and make these changes. Switch back to the **Table Designer** window for the `Discussion` table and change the properties for the `DisplayOrder` field so that they look like this:

Body	nvarchar	3000	✓
DisplayOrder	varchar	320	✓
CreatedByUser	nvarchar	100	✓

When we save the changes to the table we will receive a warning that "Data might be lost converting column 'DisplayOrder' from 'nvarchar(750)'". The current values of `DisplayOrder` will fit within the new size and data type, so just click the **Yes** button to continue the save attempt.

Now that we've changed the table structure, let's update the `AddMessage` stored procedure so that it uses our new `DisplayOrder` technique. Open `AddMessage` in the **SQL Editor** and change declaration of the `@ParentDisplayOrder` variable to match the new data type and field size for `DisplayOrder`:

```
/* Find DisplayOrder of parent item */
DECLARE @ParentDisplayOrder as varchar(320)
```

Because we won't know the value of the `ItemID` until after the new record is added, we're going to have to set the value of the `DisplayOrder` field after the `INSERT` statement. Removing the lines that set the value of the `DisplayOrder` field from the INSERT statement we get:

```
INSERT INTO Discussion
(
    ThreadID,
    Title,
    Body,
    CreatedDate,
    CreatedByUser,
    ModuleID
)
VALUES
(
    @ThreadID,
    @Title,
    @Body,
    GetDate(),
    @UserName,
    @ModuleID
)
```

Now we'll change the last section of the stored procedure. We'll pre-calculate the new `DisplayOrder` value:

```
SET @ItemID = @@Identity

-- Determine the new display order
DECLARE @NewDisplayOrder varchar(320)
SET @NewDisplayOrder = @ParentDisplayOrder +
                       REPLICATE('0', 10 - LEN(@ItemID)) +
                       CONVERT(varchar(10), @ItemID)
```

Then we'll make it so that the `IF` block that updates the `ThreadID` for new top level messages also sets the `DisplayOrder` field and we'll add an UPDATE statement in an `ELSE` block so that reply messages will get their `DisplayOrder` set as well:

```
-- Check to see if this is a new thread
IF @ThreadID IS NULL
    BEGIN
    -- It is, so update the ThreadID to match the new ItemID
    -- as well as updating the display order
    UPDATE
        Discussion
    SET
        DisplayOrder = @NewDisplayOrder,
        ThreadID = @ItemID
    WHERE
        ItemID = @ItemID

    END
ELSE
    BEGIN
    -- Just update the display order
    UPDATE
        Discussion
    SET
        DisplayOrder = @NewDisplayOrder
    WHERE
        ItemID = @ItemID

    END
```

Save the changes and we can go on to update the GetThreadMessages stored procedure. Remember that in GetThreadMessages there is a calculation to set up the message indentation. That calculation, which looks like this:

```
REPLICATE(' ', ((LEN(DisplayOrder)/23) - 1) * 5) AS Indent,
```

It uses the old 23 character length so open up GetThreadMessages in the **SQL Editor** and change it to:

```
REPLICATE(' ', ((LEN(DisplayOrder)/10) - 1) * 5) AS Indent,
```

Save the stored procedure and we're done!

With this fairly minor tweak we have managed to reduce the maximum storage requirements of the DisplayOrder field by over 75%, from an upper limit of 1,500 bytes to an upper limit of 320 bytes. We aren't likely to see a drop in record size of the full 1180 bytes as that would only happen for messages that are at the maximum indentation level. We will see a proportional drop in size though for the values that are stored in DisplayOrder field.

The only bad news in this section is that there is no easy way to change the existing DisplayOrder values for the sample data! We'll either have to delete the sample data and create our own, or manually update the values. To save the reader the trouble of having to figure out the values, the nice editors at Wrox have prepared the following table for us:

ItemID	ModuleID	ThreadID	CreatedByUser	DisplayOrder
1	19	1	MaryK@ibuyspy.com	0000000001
2	19	1	JennaJ@ibuyspy.com	00000000010000000002
3	19	3	RajivP@ibuyspy.com	0000000003
4	19	3	ManishG@ibuyspy.com	00000000030000000004
5	19	3	TomVZ@ibuyspy.com	00000000030000000005
6	19	3	BrettH@ibuyspy.com	000000000300000000050000000006
7	19	7	BrettH@ibuyspy.com	0000000007
8	18	8	MaryK@ibuyspy.com	0000000008
9	18	8	JennaJ@ibuyspy.com	00000000080000000009
10	18	8	BrettH@ibuyspy.com	000000000800000000090000000010
11	18	8	TomVZ@ibuyspy.com	00000000080000000011
12	18	12	BrettH@ibuyspy.com	0000000012
13	18	12	TomVZ@ibuyspy.com	00000000120000000013
14	18	14	JennaJ@ibuyspy.com	0000000014
15	18	14	TomVZ@ibuyspy.com	00000000140000000015
16	18	16	ManishG@ibuyspy.com	0000000016

For an alternate solution to maintaining the reply hierarchies take a look at the implementation used in the ASP.NET Forums sample code. The ASP.NET Forums approach uses a sequential, integer-based sort order but uses an algorithm when inserting a new message that renumbers all of the following on posts in the thread. This is a write-intensive technique when inserting new messages, but it is far faster than the IBuySpy technique when it comes to reading the messages back out.

The bulk of the code which implements this in the ASP.NET Forums can be found in the sp_AddPost stored procedure in the ASP.NET Forums sample code.

Removing Unused Data from Returned Results

As long as we are discussing the `DisplayOrder` field, it's worth noting that `DisplayOrder` is only used within the data layer to set the sort order for the thread messages. Now that we have implemented a `ThreadID` field to link messages in a thread together, it isn't even used to look up reply messages anymore.

Even before we added the `ThreadID` field, sending the `DisplayOrder` back in the message result sets was unnecessary. It is never displayed anywhere in the presentation layer, nor is it ever used by the business layer. The only time that even a part of it was used was to look up thread messages and that was through the calculated value of the Parent field from `GetTopLevelMessages`.

Let's eliminate the transmission of all that unused data when we retrieve messages. Open up the `GetTopLevelMessages`, `GetThreadMessages`, and `GetSingleMessage` stored procedures in the SQL Editor. Remove `DisplayOrder` from the fields returned by each of the SELECT statements and then save the changes.

> Remember, these changes will require changes to the business and presentation layers.

Indexing

The most significant performance enhancement that we can make to the Discussion module's data layer is the addition of indexes in the `Discussion` table. No other single change would have anywhere near the impact, especially as the table grows!

The existing table structures in IBuySpy are woefully under-indexed! The only index currently in use in the `Discussion` table, for instance, is the one that SQL Server created automatically when the table's designer marked `ItemID` as the primary key.

We'll want to add any indexes that will aid in the evaluation of the criteria in the WHERE clauses of our stored procedures or in returning results in a particular sort order. Since we are primarily interested in read-access performance we can afford to add multiple indexes even though we'll pay the cost of the additional overhead of maintaining them when we add new messages to the table.

The three most important indexes to add in the `Discussion` table are indexes for the `ModuleID` field, the `ThreadID` field and for the `DisplayOrder` field. To create the indexes from within Visual Studio .NET switch back to the **Table Designer** for the `Discussion` table and do the following:

1. Look for the Manage Indexes and Keys button on the Table toolbar:

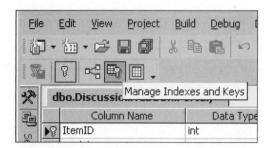

2. Click it to open up the table's property pages to the Indexes/Keys tab:

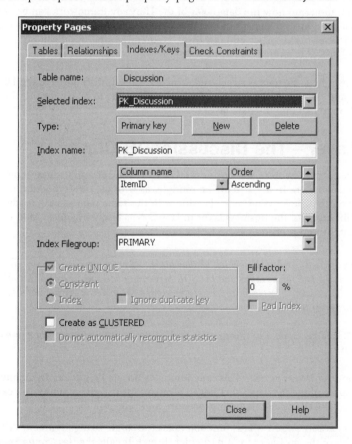

3. Now we're ready to create our new indexes. Click the New button and a new index will be created called IX_Discussion. Rename it to IX_Discussion_ModuleID.

4. In the Column Name drop-down list pick the `ModuleID` field as the source for the indexed values. Leave the Order as Ascending.

5. Repeat the last two steps to create the separate indexes for each of the `ThreadID` and `DisplayOrder` fields.

6. Close the `Property Page` dialog box.

7. Click the Save button to submit our changes to the database.

That's it for the first *Squeezing More Out of...* section in this chapter. Hopefully we've opened some avenues of exploration into how the data layer of the IBuySpy framework can be extended and optimized. It's a good idea to keep the ideas that we covered here in mind as we work with other modules in the framework or as we add our own. Remember that optimization is an ongoing process and even a good design can often be improved upon!

So, now we've seen how the data is structured, how the stored procedures of the Discussion module act upon that data, and the data layer could be optimized. It's time to take a look at the business class used by our application to call into the data layer.

Business Layer – The DiscussionDB Class

As we saw in the earlier chapters, the business layer is where our application implements business rules and calls to the data layer. In the Discussion module, as with the other modules in the IBuySpy framework, the business layer is a single class file with the same name as the module and a 'DB' suffix. As the 'DB' suffix suggests, the business layer in IBuySpy is frequently just a thin wrapper around calls to the appropriate stored procedures.

> *In fact, n-tier purists would probably tell us that the stored procedures in IBuySpy <u>are</u> the business layer and that the individual tables and the SQL Server database engine are the actual data layer. A... umm... fascinating... topic for conversations around the water cooler but not a big distinction in day-to-day programming!*

`DiscussionDB` is fairly typical in this respect and contains only four methods (meaning this will be a pretty short section):

❑ `GetTopLevelMessages` – This function takes the single integer argument, `ModuleId`, and looks up all of the messages that began a thread for the given module. It calls the `GetTopLevelMessages` stored procedure and returns a data reader.

❑ `GetThreadMessages` – This function takes the single string argument `Parent` and uses it to return all of the messages for a particular thread. It calls the `GetThreadMessages` stored procedure and returns a data reader.

- ❑ GetSingleMessage – This function takes the single integer argument ItemId and uses it to return a single message. It calls the GetSingleMessage stored procedure and returns a data reader.

- ❑ AddMessage – This function takes the following arguments: the integer moduleId, the integer parentId, the string userName, the string title, and the string body. It calls the AddMessage stored procedure and returns the value of the @ItemId output parameter as an integer.

The only one of the methods listed above that does anything in addition to calling its associated stored procedure is AddMessage. AddMessage pre-checks the userName argument to see if it is an empty string. If it is then AddMessage resets it to 'Unknown' – thus creating a business rule that all threads must have a user name associated with them and if one isn't supplied then that user name should be 'Unknown'. (Of course, there could be some confusion if one of the users on the site has the username 'Unknown'...)

Each function creates and executes its own set of ADO.NET objects. Since we've already seen how this is done in previous chapters, we won't bother going through each of the functions.

Squeezing a Little More Out of DiscussionDB

There are a couple of areas where we can squeeze a little extra efficiency out of the functions in DiscussionDB.

Converting to Shared Members

If we take a look at the code in each of the methods in the DiscussionDB class we'll notice that each one is completely self-contained. They don't rely on any properties (instance or otherwise) of the class and they don't call any other methods (again instance or otherwise) in the class. In other words they are perfect candidates to become shared members instead of instance members!

To convert each method just add the keyword Shared between the Public scope statement and the procedural declaration, like so:

```
Public Shared Function GetTopLevelMessages( _
                ByVal moduleId As Integer) _
                As SqlDataReader
```

If we convert all of them to shared members we can eliminate the extra step of creating an instance of the class in order to use the functions. This would also eliminate the overhead of declaring, instantiating, and then garbage collecting one or more DiscussionDB instances on each of our pages.

Now we can remove all of the lines that declare and create an instance of the DiscussionDB class from methods like BindData (found in the Page_Load method of the Discussion.ascx control):

```
Sub BindList()
   ' Obtain a list of discussion messages for the module
   ' and bind to datalist
   Dim discuss As New ASPNetPortal.DiscussionDB()
   TopLevelList.DataSource = discuss.GetTopLevelMessages(ModuleId)
   TopLevelList.DataBind()
End Sub
```

And re-write them to refer to the shared members by prefacing the method name with the name of the class:

```
Sub BindList()
    ' Obtain a list of discussion messages for the module
    ' and bind to datalist
    TopLevelList.DataSource = DiscussionDB.GetTopLevelMessages(ModuleId)
    TopLevelList.DataBind()
End Sub
```

Fewer variables to declare, lower overhead, and shorter, simpler code listings – not bad!

Heightening the Security of our Business Layer

One more step to take would be to change the declaration of our business classes from having `Public` scope to having `Friend` scope. This would help to secure our application by making the methods in our business classes unavailable to code outside our project. Our application will run the same way but an unsecured application on the same server would be prevented from creating an instance of a business object and calling its methods.

The updated class declaration would be:

```
Friend Class DiscussionDB
```

Tweaking GetSingleMessage

There is a very minor oversight in the `GetSingleMessage` function. The function only returns a single row, but the call to `ExecuteReader` doesn't take advantage of the optimization offered by using the `CommandBehavior.SingleRow` enumeration value.

We can re-write the last part of the function to fix this by changing this:

```
myConnection.Open()
Dim result As SqlDataReader = myCommand.ExecuteReader( _
                CommandBehavior.CloseConnection)


' Return the datareader
Return result
```

To this:

```
myConnection.Open()
Dim result As SqlDataReader = myCommand.ExecuteReader( _
                CommandBehavior.CloseConnection _
                Or CommandBehavior.SingleRow)


' Return the datareader
Return result
```

As long as we're talking about minor oversights though, we could write this even more efficiently as:

```
myConnection.Open()

' Return the datareader
Return myCommand.ExecuteReader(CommandBehavior.CloseConnection _
                    Or CommandBehavior.SingleRow)
```

According to the Intermediate Language Disassembler (ILDASM) tool provided with the .NET framework, we can eliminate allocating space for an additional object reference, as well as a few instructions, by returning the data reader directly. When we declare a function the CLR automatically creates a reference variable with the same name and data type as the function. If we declare the `result` variable we add yet another object reference. When we return the `result` variable, the framework actually uses a few additional instructions to update the object reference in the `GetSingleMessage` variable that it created and then returns that instead of `result`. If we want to take this to extremes, the CLR actually has optimized commands for manipulating the first four local variables in a function. In the case of the `GetSingleMessage` function, `result` would actually be the fifth local variable and so working with it would be less optimized than working with the `GetSingleMessage` variable directly.

> When working within a function, always try to make use of the local variable of the same name and data type instead of creating an additional "result" variable.

Updating DiscussionDB to use the Database Class

Remember the Database class that we discussed back in Chapter 3? The idea was to abstract all of the database code into a single utility class, so that our business layer would be insulated from the mechanics of creating the connection to our database, of creating command objects, data readers, parameters, and the like. The best way to reduce problems with the data access code is to centralize it into a single class so that any corrections, updates, and enhancements can be made in one place and all of the code in our site will benefit.

Let's change the methods of the `DiscussionDB` so that they call on our `Database` class to do all of the tedious data access work. Three of the four methods – `GetTopLevelMessages`, `GetThreadMessages`, and `GetSingleMessage` – call a stored procedure, pass it a single parameter, and return a data reader.

Since these three methods are virtually identical we should only need to take a look at how the `Database` class is implemented in one of them to understand how it will work in the others. Let's work with `GetTopLevelMessages` – here's the original listing:

```
Public Shared Function GetTopLevelMessages( _
                    ByVal moduleId As Integer) _
                    As SqlDataReader
    ' Create Instance of Connection and Command Object
    Dim myConnection As New SqlConnection( _
            ConfigurationSettings.AppSettings("connectionString"))
    Dim myCommand As New SqlCommand("GetTopLevelMessages", myConnection)
```

```
        ' Mark the Command as a SPROC
        myCommand.CommandType = CommandType.StoredProcedure
        ' Add Parameters to SPROC
        Dim parameterModuleId As _
                New SqlParameter("@ModuleId", SqlDbType.Int, 4)
        parameterModuleId.Value = moduleId
        myCommand.Parameters.Add(parameterModuleId)


        ' Execute the command
        myConnection.Open()
        Dim result As SqlDataReader _
                = myCommand.ExecuteReader(CommandBehavior.CloseConnection)


        ' Return the datareader
        Return result
    End Function
```

When we update it to use the `Database` class the listing becomes much shorter:

```
        Public Shared Function GetTopLevelMessages( _
                            ByVal moduleId As Integer) _
                            As SqlDataReader
```

```
        ' Create an instance of our database class
        Dim db As New Wrox.Intranet.Database()

        ' Get the results (passing in the default procedure variable)
        db.RunProcedure("GetTopLevelMessages", _
                    New SqlParameter() _
                    {db.MakeParameter("@ModuleId", moduleId)}, _
                    GetTopLevelMessages)

        ' When the function ends it will automatically return the data reader
        ' in the default procedure variable
    End Function
```

There are really only two functional lines of code in this method:

❑   The first creates an instance of our `Database` class

❑   The second calls the freshly created `db` object's `RunProcedure` method to get back a
    `SqlDataReader` object. It also happens to take the `moduleId` argument and passes it
    wrapped up as the only element in a new `SqlParameter` array. It uses the default variable
    that the runtime creates for the function to return the data reader.

Finally, when the method completes, the data reader referenced in the `GetTopLevelMessages`
variable gets passed back to the calling procedure.

The functionality in `GetThreadMessages` and in `GetSingleMessage` is identical to what's in
`GetTopLevelMessages`. The only real difference is in the arguments that they take and in the stored
procedures that they call.

We'll still need to review `GetThreadMessages` though. Remember that in the *Squeezing a Little More Out of the Data Layer* section we added the `ThreadID` field to the `Discussion` table and subsequently we altered the `GetThreadMessages` to take `@ThreadID` as an integer input parameter? Well, now we need to alter the `GetThreadMessages` method so that it takes an integer `threadID` argument and creates the appropriate parameter to pass to `RunProcedure`:

```
Public Shared Function GetThreadMessages(ByVal threadId As Integer) _
                                          As SqlDataReader
   Dim db As New Wrox.Intranet.Database()

   db.RunProcedure("GetThreadMessages", _
                   New SqlParameter() _
                   {db.MakeParameter("@ThreadID", threadId)}, _
                   GetThreadMessages)
End Function
```

There is one more piece to this, which is updating the user interface to call the `GetThreadMessages` method with the right data. We'll get to that in the *Squeezing a Little More Out of Discussion.ascx* section. Since we'll also be tweaking `GetSingleMessage` a little in the *Squeezing a Little More Out of DiscussDetails.aspx* section later in the chapter, we'll hold off on looking at it until then.

The fourth method, `AddMessage`, calls a stored procedure, passes it multiple parameters, and returns an integer representing the identity field of the inserted record:

```
Public Shared Function AddMessage(ByVal moduleId As Integer, _
                   ByVal parentId As Integer, _
                   ByVal userName As String, _
                   ByVal title As String, _
                   ByVal body As String) As Integer

   If userName.Length < 1 Then
      userName = "unknown"
   End If

   ' Create an instance of our database class
   Dim db As New Wrox.Intranet.Database()

   'Create the parameter array
   Dim parameters() As SqlParameter = { _
         db.MakeParameter("@ItemID", ParameterDirection.Output, 0), _
         db.MakeParameter("@Title", title), _
         db.MakeParameter("@Body", body), _
         db.MakeParameter("@ParentID", parentId), _
         db.MakeParameter("@UserName", userName), _
         db.MakeParameter("@ModuleID", moduleId) _
         }

   ' Run the stored procedure
   db.RunProcedure("AddMessage", parameters)

   'Now get back the itemId
   AddMessage = CInt(parameters(0).Value)

   'Close everything up
   db.Close()
End Function
```

In the original procedure, the SqlConnection, SqlCommand, and SqlParameter objects were all created as explicit variables with each parameter object being added to the command object's Parameters collection. Here we have replaced the explicit data objects with an array of parameter objects and a call to one of the Database class' RunProcedure method overloads. Where the original code used six separate variables to reference the parameters we use a single array and we access the value returned by the @ItemID parameter through its index in the array.

Most of the changes we've suggested to the DiscussionDB class are more or less optimizations, with the exception of changing the class declaration, which improves the security of our application. We've touched on three major areas for improving an existing design:

❑ Reduce Resource Use – in converting to Shared members we reduced the overhead of creating and then garbage collecting unnecessary instance variables;

❑ Look for Efficiency – we've cut down on extra processing instructions where we could by examining programming practices and looking for unnecessary steps in the code;

❑ Increase Maintainability – and, finally, we've improved our ability to maintain our code by abstracting common functionality into a separate class.

These concepts are not specific to the business layer, of course. Each one can be applied to any component in our application and it's a good practice to regularly review our code to see if we can improve it in any of these three areas.

We're going to move on to examine the presentation layer components next.

Presentation Layer – The Discussion.ascx User Control

The discussion user control is the entry point to the Discussions module. Its main function is to display threads and thread messages as links to the display page for individual posts – making it the primary navigation tool for the Discussions module. It also allows authorized users to start new discussions by optionally displaying an "Add New Thread" link. Like our other modules, it is dynamically added to the DesktopDefault.aspx page based on the portal settings for the active tab.

The design of the interface is to allow users to view a hierarchical display of threads, aesthetically similar to a TreeView control. The user control accomplishes this through the use of a pair of nested DataList controls; one to display the thread level messages and another to display the replies to the currently selected thread. One of the goals here is to graphically reflect the relationship of individual messages to one another – that is, to show that Brett was replying to Jenna's message and that Tom was replying to Mary's original post.

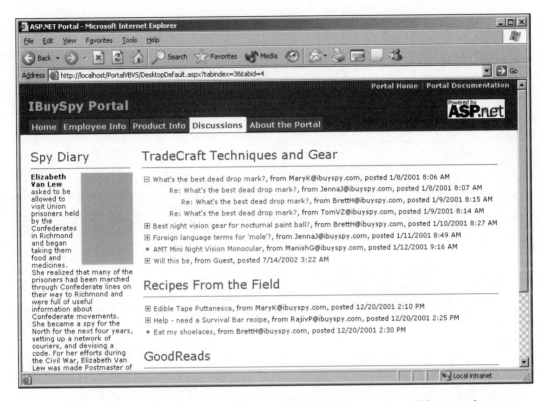

Let's take a look at how the user control implements this. The design canvas of the control is pretty simple – take a look at `Discussion.ascx` in the designer and all we'll see on the page is the `DesktopModuleTitle` control and a `DataList`. If no thread has been selected, or if the user collapses the current thread, those two controls are all that would be displayed (the data list control has been selected in the figure below):

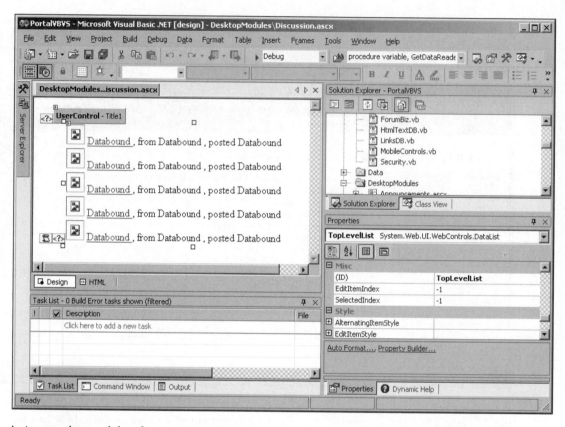

As in our other modules, the `DesktopModuleTitle` controls access to the add/edit functionality of the module. It checks to see whether the user belongs to a role with editing permission and, if they do it displays a link to the editing page for the module. If we were logged in with an account with editing permissions for the module we'd see the edit link beside the title. The editing page for the discussions module is stored in the `DesktopModules` folder and it's called `DiscussDetails.aspx`. Since it isn't a part of the tab display, the link has been set to launch the editing page in a new browser window.

The `DataList` that shows up on the design canvas, called `TopLevelList`, displays the first message for each thread in the module. It spits out the title of the message (which is also the title of the thread) as a hyperlink, as well as the e-mail address of the user who created the message and the date that the message was created as plain text. It also displays an image button beside each message that is either a plus symbol or a dot depending on whether there have been replies to the message or not. When the user clicks on the image button for a thread with replies the plus sign toggles to become a minus sign. Then the user control displays the replies for the selected thread in the nested `DataList`, called `DetailList`.

In order to see the `DetailList` control we'll need to take a look at the HTML source. Switch to the **HTML View** and we should see the following listing:

```
<%@ Control
      language="vb"
      AutoEventWireup="false"
      Inherits="ASPNetPortal.Discussion"
      CodeBehind="Discussion.ascx.vb" %>
<%@ Register
      TagPrefix="Portal"
      TagName="Title"
      Src="~/DesktopModuleTitle.ascx"%>
<portal:title
  id="Title1" runat="server"
  EditTarget="_new"
  EditUrl="~/DesktopModules/DiscussDetails.aspx"
  EditText="Add New Thread">
</portal:title>
<%-- discussion list --%>
<asp:DataList
  id="TopLevelList" width="98%"
  ItemStyle-Cssclass="Normal"
  DataKeyField="Parent" runat="server">
 <ItemTemplate>
  <asp:ImageButton
    id="btnSelect"
    ImageUrl='<%# NodeImage(Cint(DataBinder.Eval( _
                  Container.DataItem, "ChildCount"))) %>'
    CommandName="select" runat="server" />
  <asp:hyperlink
    Text='<%# DataBinder.Eval(Container.DataItem, "Title") %>'
    NavigateUrl='<%#
      FormatUrl(CInt(DataBinder.Eval( _
              Container.DataItem, "ItemID"))) %>'
    Target="_new" runat="server" />,
  from
  <%# DataBinder.Eval(Container.DataItem,"CreatedByUser") %>
  , posted
  <%# DataBinder.Eval(Container.DataItem,"CreatedDate", "{0:g}") %>
 </ItemTemplate>
 <SelectedItemTemplate>
  <asp:ImageButton
    id="btnCollapse"
    ImageUrl="~/images/minus.gif"
    CommandName="collapse"
    runat="server" />
  <asp:hyperlink
    Text='<%# DataBinder.Eval(Container.DataItem, "Title") %>'
    NavigateUrl='<%# FormatUrl(CInt(DataBinder.Eval( _
                  Container.DataItem, "ItemID"))) %>'
    Target="_new" runat="server" />,
  from
  <%# DataBinder.Eval(Container.DataItem,"CreatedByUser") %>
  , posted
```

```
<%# DataBinder.Eval(Container.DataItem,"CreatedDate", "{0:g}") %>
<asp:DataList
  id="DetailList"
  ItemStyle-Cssclass="Normal"
  datasource="<%# GetThreadMessages() %>"
  runat="server">
 <ItemTemplate>
 <%# DataBinder.Eval(Container.DataItem, "Indent") %>
 <img src="<%=Request.ApplicationPath%>/images/1x1.gif" height="15">
 <asp:hyperlink
    Text='<%# DataBinder.Eval(Container.DataItem, "Title") %>'
    NavigateUrl='<%# FormatUrl(CInt(DataBinder.Eval( _
                   Container.DataItem, "ItemID"))) %>'
    Target="_new" runat="server" />,
 from
 <%# DataBinder.Eval(Container.DataItem,"CreatedByUser") %>
 , posted
 <%# DataBinder.Eval(Container.DataItem,"CreatedDate", "{0:g}") %>
 </ItemTemplate>
 </asp:DataList>
 </SelectedItemTemplate>
 </asp:DataList>
```

The `DetailList` server control is highlighted above. It may not be obvious at first, but it is actually contained within the `SelectedItemTemplate` tags of the `TopLevelView`. This makes expanding and collapsing the listing of a thread's replies really easy, because all that's required to toggle the display is to mark a thread as selected.

Let's take a look at the server controls that are being displayed in `TopLevelList`. We have two controls that are responsible for expanding or collapsing the listings – the two `ImageButton` controls. Each button triggers the `ItemCommand` event on the `TopLevelList` control and the only functional difference between the two is the `CommandName` argument that gets passed in the `DataListCommandEventArgs` parameter. For `btnSelect` in the `ItemTemplate` section the `CommandName` argument is `"select"`.

```
<ItemTemplate>
 <asp:ImageButton
   id="btnSelect"
   ImageUrl='<%# NodeImage(Cint(DataBinder.Eval( _
               Container.DataItem, "ChildCount"))) %>'
   CommandName="select" runat="server" />
 <asp:hyperlink
   Text='<%# DataBinder.Eval(Container.DataItem, "Title") %>'
   NavigateUrl='<%#
     FormatUrl(CInt(DataBinder.Eval( _
            Container.DataItem, "ItemID"))) %>'
   Target="_new" runat="server" />,
```

Note the call to `NodeImage()` in the databinding expression for the `ImageUrl` property. `NodeImage()` determines which graphic to display beside each thread item. We'll take a look at `NodeImage()` in the section on `Discussion.ascx`'s codebehind class.

For btnCollapse in the SelectedItemTemplate section the CommandName argument is "collapse":

```
<SelectedItemTemplate>
 <asp:ImageButton
   id="btnCollapse"
   ImageUrl="~/images/minus.gif"
   CommandName="collapse"
   runat="server" />
 <asp:hyperlink
   Text='<%# DataBinder.Eval(Container.DataItem, "Title") %>'
   NavigateUrl='<%# FormatUrl(CInt(DataBinder.Eval( _
                  Container.DataItem, "ItemID"))) %>'
   Target="_new" runat="server" />,
```

The only other server controls in the user control are the three Hyperlink controls in each of the templates (the TopLevelList's ItemTemplate and SelectedItemTemplate sections, as well as the DetailList's ItemTemplate section) that display the links to the actual posts. Each of them calls on a helper function, FormatUrl(), in the codebehind to build the URL to the DiscussDetails.aspx page:

```
<ItemTemplate>
 <asp:ImageButton
   id="btnSelect"
   ImageUrl='<%# NodeImage(Cint(DataBinder.Eval( _
                  Container.DataItem, "ChildCount"))) %>'
   CommandName="select" runat="server" />
 <asp:hyperlink
   Text='<%# DataBinder.Eval(Container.DataItem, "Title") %>'
   NavigateUrl='<%#
     FormatUrl(CInt(DataBinder.Eval( _
            Container.DataItem, "ItemID"))) %>'
   Target="_new" runat="server" />,
```

The remainder of the ASPX page is a series of simple databinding expressions to display the rest of the data from the data sources.

Creating the Display Hierarchy – The Indent Field

There is one databinding expression that we might want to single out for special attention. In the ItemTemplate section of the DetailList data list control, the first databinding expression binds to the content of the Indent field in the data source:

```
<asp:DataList
  id="DetailList"
  ItemStyle-Cssclass="Normal"
  datasource="<%# GetThreadMessages() %>"
  runat="server">
 <ItemTemplate>
  <%# DataBinder.Eval(Container.DataItem, "Indent") %>
```

It's this databinding expression that gives us the hierarchical, newsreader-type appearance of `DetailList`. More to the point, it is the `Indent` field that is output here that creates the hierarchical display of message responses.

`Indent` is a text-based field containing a varying number of non-breaking spaces. The number of non-breaking spaces is determined for us by the stored procedure that retrieves the data; it replicates five non-breaking spaces for every level of indentation. There is a problem with using the stored procedure directly to generate the non-breaking spaces for us – it forces us into using a single technique to display the indent.

If we decide that we want to, say, switch to using three spaces per indent we'd have to edit the stored procedure to do it. Even worse, if we wanted to make it so that the indent width was a property of the user control that could be customized for each module we wouldn't be able to without some complicated and messy manipulation of the contents of `Indent`. Now imagine that we decide we want to switch to displaying the records in a table – instead of being able to set the indent through things like style properties (like a table cell's width) we're stuck with dumping in non-breaking spaces and hoping that it doesn't cause the message title to wrap in some ugly way.

The real problem here is that we've got a presentation element being determined in the Data layer. We're going to look at a way to fix this in the *Squeezing a Little More Out of Discussion.ascx* section.

However we arrive at it, the final output looks like this:

TradeCraft Techniques and Gear

⊟ What's the best dead drop mark? , from MaryK@ibuyspy.com , posted 1/8/2001 8:06 AM
  Re: What's the best dead drop mark? , from JennaJ@ibuyspy.com , posted 1/8/2001 8:07 AM
    Re: What's the best dead drop mark? , from BrettH@ibuyspy.com , posted 1/9/2001 8:15 AM
      Re: What's the best dead drop mark? , from guest , posted 7/27/2002 4:13 AM
    Re: What's the best dead drop mark? , from guest , posted 7/29/2002 4:15 AM
    Re: What's the best dead drop mark? , from guest , posted 7/29/2002 4:34 AM
  Re: What's the best dead drop mark? , from TomVZ@ibuyspy.com , posted 1/9/2001 8:14 AM
⊞ Best night vision gear for nocturnal paint ball? , from BrettH@ibuyspy.com , posted 1/10/2001 8:27 AM

That's it for `Discussion.ascx`! Now that we've reviewed the UI portion of the user control, it's time to look at the code that glues it all together.

Discussion.ascx.vb – The Codebehind Class

One of the best practices that IBuySpy follows is that the code in the ASPX pages really only serves as a conduit between the user interface and the business objects. `Discussion.ascx` is a perfect example of this; the longest method in the whole class is only seven lines long! Each function or sub-procedure is solely dedicated to either display or to calling a business object to perform the actual work.

Lets walk through the codebehind class in the order that the code gets called, starting with the
`Page_Load`. (In this section and the rest that deal with codebehind classes, we'll skip over any standard
or web designer generated code). The first time the control is displayed it needs to populate the
`TopLevelList` with data so it calls a helper method called `BindList`:

```
Private Sub Page_Load(ByVal sender As System.Object, _
          ByVal e As System.EventArgs) Handles MyBase.Load
 If Page.IsPostBack = False Then
  BindList()
 End If
End Sub
```

`Bindlist` is in turn a simple wrapper around a call to the `GetTopLevelMessages` method of the
`DiscussionDB` business object. It passes in the `ModuleId` and gets back a data reader containing the
first message of each thread. Remember that the user controls in each module of IBuySpy inherit from
`PortalModuleControl` so we also inherit the base class' `ModuleId` property.

```
Sub BindList()
 ' Obtain a list of discussion messages for the module
 ' and bind to datalist
 Dim discuss As New ASPNetPortal.DiscussionDB()
 TopLevelList.DataSource = discuss.GetTopLevelMessages(ModuleId)
 TopLevelList.DataBind()
End Sub
```

Once it has retrieved the data reader, it calls `TopLevelList`'s `DataBind` method to display the
records. Control passes back to the `Page_Load` event procedure and that's it for the custom code in the
first call to `Discussion.ascx`!

TradeCraft Techniques and Gear

⊞ What's the best dead drop mark?, from MaryK@ibuyspy.com, posted 1/8/2001 8:06 AM

⊞ Best night vision gear for nocturnal paint ball?, from BrettH@ibuyspy.com, posted 1/10/2001 8:27 AM

⊞ Foreign language terms for 'mole'?, from JennaJ@ibuyspy.com, posted 1/11/2001 8:49 AM

• AMT Mini Night Vision Monocular, from ManishG@ibuyspy.com, posted 1/12/2001 9:16 AM

Let's take a look at what happens when we click on `btnSelect` (the `ImageButton` in `TopLevelList`'s
`ItemTemplate` section that displays the plus symbol or the dot for each top level message title).
Because it is a child control of the `DataList`, clicking it will cause it to trigger the
`TopLevelList.ItemCommand` event, which is handled by the `TopLevelList_Select` sub-
procedure:

```
Private Sub TopLevelList_Select(ByVal Sender As Object, _
          ByVal e As DataListCommandEventArgs) _
          Handles TopLevelList.ItemCommand

 ' Determine the command of the button (either "select" or "collapse")
 Dim command As String _
```

```
                = CType(e.CommandSource, ImageButton).CommandName

      ' Update asp:datalist selection index depending upon the type
      ' of(command)and then rebind the asp:datalist with content
      If command = "collapse" Then
       TopLevelList.SelectedIndex = -1
      Else
       TopLevelList.SelectedIndex = e.Item.ItemIndex
      End If

      BindList()
    End Sub
```

This is the longest method in the class! Although reformatting the listing above to fit the page makes it appear longer, it's still just seven logical lines long. One of the true joys of ASP.NET is how little code we need to write to get a functional page!

The code here either sets or clears the `SelectedIndex` based on the value of the `CommandName` received from the triggering control. Since we clicked on `btnSelect` the `CommandName` is `"select"`, which causes the associated data row to display using the `SelectedItemTemplate`. This sets up all of the UI for us as the row now displays `btnCollapse` instead of `btnSelect`, the minus sign graphic instead of the plus, and the `DetailList` control completely populated with all of the thread message replies.

Wait a minute… at no point have we seen any code to bind data to the `DetailList` control! This is actually taken care of for us by the databinding expression in the `DataSource` property of the `<asp:datalist>` tag back in the ASPX page:

```
    <asp:DataList id="DetailList"
      ItemStyle-Cssclass="Normal"
      datasource="<%# GetThreadMessages() %>"
      runat="server">
```

The databinding expression calls on the `GetThreadMessages` function in the codebehind page to retrieve a data reader containing just the replies to the selected thread. This happens when we call the `TopLevelList`'s `DataBind` method – during the parent control's databinding process, as it creates the child controls for each data row, it calls the `DataBind` method on each of the child controls. So the `TopLevelList` actually calls the `DetailList.DataBind` method for us, but it will only happen for the selected item in the `TopLevelList` control and then only if there is a selected item. Even though the control is never explicitly data bound through code, it gets data bound none-the-less!

We mentioned above that the `GetThreadMessages` function retrieves a data reader containing the replies to the selected thread. Just like the `BindList` function, this `GetThreadMessages` is a thin wrapper around a call to the discussions module business class method of the same name:

```
    Function GetThreadMessages() As SqlDataReader
      ' Obtain a list of discussion messages for the module
      Dim discuss As New ASPNetPortal.DiscussionDB()
      Dim dr As SqlDataReader = _
          discuss.GetThreadMessages( _
          TopLevelList.DataKeys(TopLevelList.SelectedIndex).ToString())
```

```
        ' Return the filtered DataView
        Return dr
    End Function
```

The only really interesting part of this is that it uses the `TopLevelList.DataKeys` collection. The `DataKeys` collection is a complete list of key field values from the `TopLevelList`'s data source. It gets populated during databinding from the field specified in the `DataKeyField` property:

```
<asp:DataList
    id="TopLevelList"
    width="98%"
    ItemStyle-Cssclass="Normal"
    DataKeyField="Parent"
    runat="server">
```

We're only looking for the key field value for the selected item, so we use the `TopLevelList.SelectedIndex` to retrieve it from the collection. This gets passed into the business class' `GetThreadMessages` function, which returns all of the replies in the thread. As we saw earlier, some <u>very</u> funky things happen to link the messages in a thread together in the original data layer components! We're going to see how to implement the changes we made to the data layer shortly, but we haven't quite gotten there yet!

The only methods that we haven't looked at so far are the `NodeImage` function and the `FormatUrl` function. As we mentioned earlier, `NodeImage` determines whether we should display an expansion leaf graphic or a node graphic depending on whether there have been replies to the first message in the thread or not. It is able to determine whether the message has replies because the data that we've bound to includes a `ChildCount` field that has pre-calculated this for us. So, if the count is anything greater than zero, `NodeImage` passes back the URL to the `plus.gif` otherwise it returns the URL of the `node.gif`:

```
    Function NodeImage(ByVal count As Integer) As String
     If count > 0 Then
      Return "~/images/plus.gif"
     Else
      Return "~/images/node.gif"
     End If
    End Function
```

If you haven't come across it before, the tilde (the "~" character) is a shortcut for the application path of our web site. When we're working with server controls the control automatically expands it for us.

The `FormatUrl` function simply builds a string containing a URL that will open the discussion display page for a given message:

```
    Function FormatUrl(ByVal item As Integer) As String
     Return "~/DesktopModules/DiscussDetails.aspx?ItemID=" _
         & item & "&mid=" & ModuleId
    End Function
```

It takes the ItemId from the current row in the data source of whichever data list is calling it and it combines it into a URL along with the ModuleId for the current instance of the Discussion.ascx control.

That's it for the Discussion.ascx.vb codebehind class!

Squeezing a Little More Out of Discussion.ascx

Now that we've looked at all of the functionality in the discussion user control, it's time to see how we can improve on the existing code a bit. We're going to start by updating Discussion.ascx to take advantage of the enhancements that we made to the data layer.

Updating Discussion.ascx to Incorporate Data Layer Changes

Because IBuySpy typically does such a good job of separating the presentation layer from the data layer, we won't need to make a lot of changes to make it work with the ThreadID that we added to the Discussion table and the GetThreadMessages stored procedure. Start by changing the DataKeyField attribute of the TopLevelList control to use the ThreadID instead of the Parent field:

```
<asp:DataList
    id="TopLevelList"
    width="98%"
    ItemStyle-Cssclass="Normal"
    DataKeyField="ThreadID"
    runat="server">
```

Now in the code behind file, open up the GetThreadMessages method and remove the ToString conversion of the data key value:

```
Function GetThreadMessages() As SqlDataReader
    ' Obtain a list of discussion messages for the module
    Dim discuss As New ASPNetPortal.DiscussionDB()
    Dim dr As SqlDataReader = _
            discuss.GetThreadMessages( _
            TopLevelList.DataKeys(TopLevelList.SelectedIndex))

    ' Return the filtered DataView
    Return dr
End Function
```

That's it. Those are the only changes we need to make in Discussion.ascx to make it work with the enhancements we made in the data layer!

Rewrite Calls to DiscussionDB to Use the Shared Members

Remember back in the *Squeezing a Little More Out of DiscussionDB* section we converted all of the methods to be Shared? As an example of the usage of a Shared member we revised the BindData expression. The only other method in Discussion.ascx.vb that calls out to the DiscussionDB is GetThreadMessages, which we saw above. Change it to:

```
Function GetThreadMessages() As SqlDataReader
    ' Obtain a list of discussion messages for the module
    Dim dr As SqlDataReader = _
            DiscussionDB.GetThreadMessages( _
        TopLevelList.DataKeys(TopLevelList.SelectedIndex))

    ' Return the filtered DataView
    Return dr
End Function
```

As long as we're editing it anyway let's get rid of the superfluous `dr` variable and return the data reader directly:

```
Function GetThreadMessages() As SqlDataReader
    ' Obtain a list of discussion messages for the module
    Return DiscussionDB.GetThreadMessages( _
        TopLevelList.DataKeys(TopLevelList.SelectedIndex))

End Function
```

Separate the Presentation Layer from the Data Layer

We mentioned earlier that the databinding expression that creates the hierarchical display of the thread replies needed a little work. Remember that we get back a string of non-breaking spaces from the data layer that creates our indent levels for the thread replies. To properly separate the presentation from the data layer we'll update the `GetThreadMessages` stored procedure so that it returns a numeric value to indicate the indent level.

Open up `GetThreadMessages` in the **SQL Editor** and locate the line that calculates the `Indent` field:

```
SELECT
    ItemID,
    REPLICATE( ' ', ( ( LEN( DisplayOrder ) / 10 ) - 1 ) * 5 ) AS Indent,
    Title,
```

The indent level is already being calculated to figure out how many non-breaking spaces ('s) to return. All we need to do is remove the REPLICATE statement and the multiplier at the end. Change the procedure so that it reads:

```
SELECT
    ItemID,
    ((LEN( DisplayOrder ) / 10 ) - 1 ) AS Indent,
    Title,
```

Save the changes and we'll go on to editing the `Discussion.ascx` page. In `Discussion.ascx` find the databinding expression for the indent field (it's the first line in the `DetailList`'s `ItemTemplate`):

```
<%# DataBinder.Eval(Container.DataItem, "Indent") %>
```

Change it to:

```
<%# FormatIndent(CInt(DataBinder.Eval(Container.DataItem, "Indent")), _
                 5, _
                 " ") %>
```

`FormatIndent` is a helper method that we're going to create in the codebehind class. It will take three arguments: the indent level as an `Integer`, an indent multiplier as an `Integer`, and the replacement string as a `String`:

```
Function FormatIndent(ByVal IndentLevel As Integer, _
                      ByVal IndentMultiplier As Integer, _
                      ByVal ReplaceWith As String) As String
  ' Create a string made up of the number of spaces we want to
  ' use for the indent and then replace the spaces with the
  ' non-breaking space character entity
  Dim CharacterCount As Integer = IndentLevel * IndentMultiplier
  Return New String(" ", CharacterCount).Replace(" ", ReplaceWith)
End Function
```

Now it's a simple matter to change the depth of the indent or even the characters used to create the indent. We simply change the call to FormatIndent in the **Html View** of `Discussion.ascx`:

```
<%# FormatIndent(CInt(DataBinder.Eval(Container.DataItem, "Indent")), _
                 3, _
                 ".") %>
```

And now we'll see:

TradeCraft Techniques and Gear

⊟ What's the best dead drop mark? , from MaryK@ibuyspy.com , posted 1/8/2001 8:06 AM
...   Re: What's the best dead drop mark? , from JennaJ@ibuyspy.com , posted 1/8/2001 8:07 AM
......   Re: What's the best dead drop mark? , from BrettH@ibuyspy.com , posted 1/9/2001 8:15 AM
...   Re: What's the best dead drop mark? , from TomVZ@ibuyspy.com , posted 1/9/2001 8:14 AM
⊞ Best night vision gear for nocturnal paint ball? , from BrettH@ibuyspy.com , posted 1/10/2001 8:27 AM
⊞ Foreign language terms for 'mole'? , from JennaJ@ibuyspy.com , posted 1/11/2001 8:49 AM
● AMT Mini Night Vision Monocular , from ManishG@ibuyspy.com , posted 1/12/2001 9:16 AM

Eliminating Unnecessary Server Controls

One of the things that you may have noticed is that the three hyperlink server controls in `Discussion.ascx` don't have any code associated with them. Their sole purpose is to display the titles and link each post to the detail display page. Since we aren't manipulating any of the hyperlink properties through code, we can make the page just a touch more efficient by changing each of these to pure HTML instead of server controls, with simple databinding expressions like these:

```
<a title='Click to read the post'
href='<%# FormatUrl(CInt(DataBinder.Eval(Container.DataItem, "ItemID"))) %>'
target='_new'>
```

The title attribute is there just to add a bit to the UI by providing a tooltip when the user hovers over the link in a modern browser.

> Now the additional overhead of creating a couple of extra server controls isn't that big a deal. Remember though, that those **Hyperlink** server controls were inside of the data lists. Because of the repeating nature of the data list they weren't just being created once – a new instance was being created for every single message on the page!
>
> That could definitely have a noticeable effect on scalability of our intranet site as the number of messages and the number of users increases!

We'll also need to tweak the `FormatUrl` function just a bit. Since we are no longer using server controls we need to expand the application path ourselves, so we'll re-write the `FormatUrl` function like this:

```
Function FormatUrl(ByVal item As Integer) As String
  Return String.Format( _
   "{0}/DesktopModules/DiscussDetails.aspx?ItemID={1}&mid={2}", _
   Request.ApplicationPath, _
   item, _
   ModuleId)
End Function
```

We're using the `String.Format()` method to skip having to do all of that messy concatenation. It will also be easier to maintain as we don't have to mentally filter out the ampersands that perform the concatenation from the ones that are supposed to be part of the output string!

Now we've recreated the functionality of the original, but we've done it without the use of the `Hyperlink` server controls!

Fixing the Behavior of an Empty Node

Remember how the `NodeImage` function uses the child count for a top-level message to determine whether to display a plus sign or a node image beside the thread? We want to let the user know that clicking on a node image doesn't do anything. Or does it?

If we click on a node image the `ImageButton` control still fires the `ItemCommand` event, which means that it still selects the empty thread, it still triggers the database calls, and it still causes the data lists to rebind. It also has the unfortunate effect of changing the displayed image as we go from:

- AMT Mini Night Vision Monocular , from ManishG@ibuyspy.com , posted 1/12/2001 9:16 AM

To

⊟ AMT Mini Night Vision Monocular , from ManishG@ibuyspy.com , posted 1/12/2001 9:16 AM

This isn't a big deal in the grand scheme of things – it is unlikely that a user will click on a node image in the first place. Even if they do, it won't cause the code to break – it just creates an inconsistent display state and a superfluous call to the database when we try to retrieve the non-existent reply messages. Still, it's irksome to know that a user can cause the code to produce unexpected results. Fortunately, the fix for this is very simple!

In the ASPX page, find the `ImageButton` tags for `btnSelect` and add the `Enabled` attribute to it:

```
<asp:ImageButton
  id="btnSelect"
  ImageUrl='<%# NodeImage(Cint(DataBinder.Eval( _
           Container.DataItem, "ChildCount"))) %>'
  Enabled='<%# CBool(DataBinder.Eval( _
          Container.DataItem, "ChildCount")).ToString %>'
  runat="server" />
```

We use the same `ChildCount` value that we send to `NodeImage` to determine whether to enable `btnSelect` or not. Since the Boolean equivalent of zero is `False` and any non-zero value is equivalent to `True`, we've effectively created a switch that disables the button on empty threads. Now if a user clicks on an empty node, it won't even cause a server postback!

The implementation of the discussion user control is pretty solid, so we've probably tweaked it about as much as we need to. There are a few areas where we could still improve on it a bit, like adding caching, but we'll cover that when we build our own modules. Let's go on and take a look at the `DiscussDetails.aspx` page.

DiscussDetails.aspx – The Display and Edit Page

Unlike similar modules in the IBuySpy framework, for example the documents module, the display and edit pages for discussions have been combined into a single page. It still provides the same set of functionality as two separate pages, but it takes advantage of a few efficiencies that can be gained by combining the pages.

The layout for this control is more complicated in than that of `Discussion.ascx`. We have more controls, a panel that toggles the display of the editing controls, another that toggles the display of the navigation buttons, and all of this is contained in multiple tables. The good news is that the actual functionality is much simpler!

The ASPX page itself really doesn't do a lot. There are no databinding expressions in it and most of the controls are there purely for display or editing purposes. In fact, the only thing that actually happens within the page itself is the setting of a few paths with inline expressions (`<%= %>` blocks).

In the screen shot below I've highlighted the two panels that actually provide most of the functional content of the page:

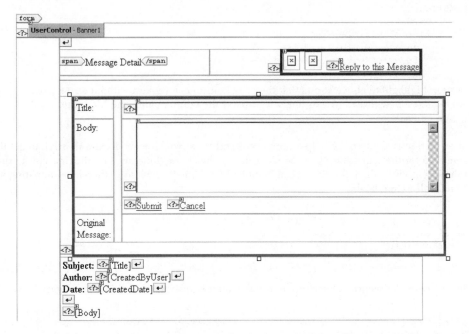

The ButtonPanel (In the upper right hand corner) is responsible for providing navigation and allowing authorized users to reply to the current message. The selected panel in the center is the EditPanel, which is responsible for hiding or showing the editing controls. EditPanel has its Visible property set to False by default and it is only made visible in response to an authorized user's request in the click event of the 'Reply to this Message' link button.

Since there's nothing much happening here, let's go straight to the codebehind page!

DiscussDetails.aspx.vb – The Codebehind Class

As we did in the previous codebehind section, we are going to walk through the class in the order that the code gets called. Again, in the interests of brevity, we'll ignore any standard or web designer generated code.

Starting with the code in the Page_Load event, we'll see some familiar snippets from other modules. The procedure starts out by pulling the ModuleId and the ItemId from the query string:

```
Private Sub Page_Load(ByVal sender As System.Object, _
        ByVal e As System.EventArgs) _
        Handles MyBase.Load
  ' Obtain moduleId and ItemId from QueryString
  moduleId = Int32.Parse(Request.Params("Mid"))
```

```
If Not (Request.Params("ItemId") Is Nothing) Then
 itemId = Int32.Parse(Request.Params("ItemId"))
Else
 itemId = 0
 EditPanel.Visible = True
 ButtonPanel.Visible = False
End If
```

The section highlighted above shows that the page considers a request without an `ItemId` to be a request to start a new thread. Accordingly it displays the editing panel and hides the navigation controls.

The next section is a call to the helper function, `BindData` (which we'll discuss shortly), to get the message data for the requested `ItemId`. The call only has to be done once on the first visit to the page. For subsequent visits, the information can be pulled from the `Viewstate`, thereby eliminating an additional call to the database:

```
' Populate message contents if this is the first visit to the page
If Page.IsPostBack = False Then
 BindData()
End If
```

Finally, we have the security check to see if they have permission to post new messages:

```
If PortalSecurity.HasEditPermissions(moduleId) = False Then
 If itemId = 0 Then
  Response.Redirect("~/Admin/EditAccessDenied.aspx")
 Else
  ReplyBtn.Visible = False
 End If
End If
End Sub
```

The call to the shared member of the `PortalSecurity` class, `HasEditPermissions`, checks to see if the user is authorized to edit the current module (we'll look at `HasEditPermissions` in detail in the *Squeezing a Little More Out of DiscussDetails.aspx* section). The response to a failed authorization check varies depending on whether this is a request to view a message or to start a new thread. If it's a request to view a message (`itemId <> 0`) then the reply button is hidden; if it's a request to start a new thread (`itemId = 0`) then they are redirected to an "Access Denied" page.

As we saw above, the `Page_Load` procedure only calls out to one other function and that is `BindData`. `BindData`'s main job is to get and display the data for a single message. It follows the standard practice of using the `DiscussionDB` business class to get the data, rather than pulling it directly from the database:

```
Sub BindData()
 ' Obtain the selected item from the Discussion table
 Dim discuss As New ASPNetPortal.DiscussionDB()
 Dim dr As SqlDataReader = discuss.GetSingleMessage(itemId)
```

```
' Load first row from database
dr.Read()

' Update labels with message contents
Title.Text = CType(dr("Title"), String)
Body.Text = CType(dr("Body"), String)
CreatedByUser.Text = CType(dr("CreatedByUser"), String)
CreatedDate.Text = String.Format("{0:d}", dr("CreatedDate"))
```

There is one additional step here, in that BindData also populates one of the editing control values as well:

```
TitleField.Text = ReTitle(Title.Text)
```

The ReTitle function used here is a helper method that adds the prefix 'Re: ' to the message title unless it's already present.

It also has to update the navigational controls though! Fortunately, the data reader that was returned from GetSingleMessage was populated with information necessary to do this, so all that needs to happen is to read the data and update the appropriate user interface elements:

```
Dim prevId As Integer = 0
Dim nextId As Integer = 0

' Update next and preview links
Dim id1 As Object = dr("PrevMessageID")

If Not id1 Is DBNull.Value Then
 prevId = CInt(id1)
 prevItem.HRef = Request.Path & "?ItemId=" _
                 & prevId & "&mid=" & moduleId
End If

Dim id2 As Object = dr("NextMessageID")

If Not id2 Is DBNull.Value Then

 nextId = CInt(id2)
 nextItem.HRef = Request.Path & "?ItemId=" _
                 & nextId & "&mid=" & moduleId

End If

' close the datareader
dr.Close()

' Show/Hide Next/Prev Button depending on whether there is a
' next/prev message
If prevId <= 0 Then
 prevItem.Visible = False
End If
```

```
   If nextId <= 0 Then
    nextItem.Visible = False
   End If
 End Sub
```

That's it for the initial page display! If the user has editing permission they'll see a page that looks like this:

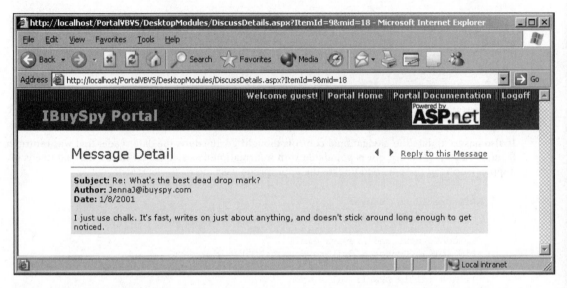

The next and previous hyperlinks would trigger the display of another message, repeating the code that we've just gone through above. If, instead, the user clicks on the "Reply to this Message" link button they'll trigger a postback to the server.

On postback, everything in the Page_Load will run again, except that it skips the call to BindData. The next piece of code to fire will be ReplyBtn_Click:

```
 Private Sub ReplyBtn_Click(ByVal Sender As Object, _
            ByVal e As EventArgs) _
            Handles ReplyBtn.Click
  EditPanel.Visible = True
  ButtonPanel.Visible = False
 End Sub
```

This just flips the panel displays, hiding the navigation buttons and showing the editing controls. Now the user can write their new message:

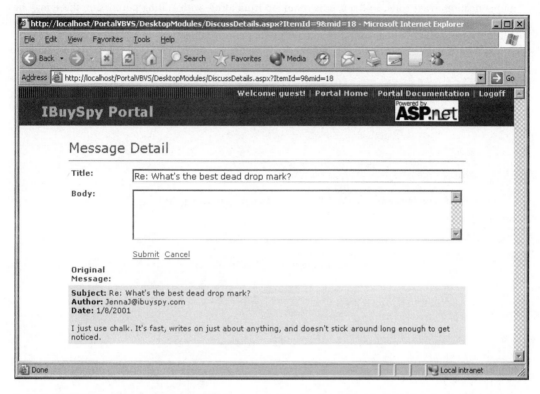

In a nice little bit of UI design, the editing controls show up just ahead of the details for the message that they are replying to! No need to open multiple browser windows just to be able to see the item that they are responding to, just a quick scroll downward.

Some other forum designs accomplish the same goal by copying the original message into the body of the new message. This works but it has the drawback that unless the user is conscientious about message size and deletes the portions of the original message that they don't need, it quickly increases the storage requirements of the forum table. If you've ever visited a forum like this you'll also notice very quickly that it makes reading the thread very cumbersome – you continually have to scroll past the original message body that has been repeated in every reply!

So, once our user has carefully crafted their detailed reply, and clicks the "Submit" link we go back to the server to process their message.

If they click the "Cancel" link instead all that happens is that the button's click event code flips the visibility properties of the panels so that we're back to viewing the original message without the editing controls.

Once again, the `Page_Load` runs to make sure that the user still has permission to edit in the current module. The information about a user's roles is only refreshed periodically by the `Global.asax` authentication event code, so if a user is removed from a role with editing permission there may be a time delay before the changes come into effect. However if a <u>module</u> is updated so that the roles with editing permissions are changed, the changes go into effect immediately.

We skip the call to `BindData` again, so the next procedure to run is the `updateButton`'s click event handler:

```
Private Sub UpdateBtn_Click(ByVal sender As Object, _
            ByVal e As EventArgs) _
            Handles updateButton.Click

    ' Create new discussion database component
    Dim discuss As New DiscussionDB()

    ' Add new message (updating the "itemId" on the page)
    itemId = discuss.AddMessage(moduleId, _
            itemId, _
            User.Identity.Name, _
            Server.HtmlEncode(TitleField.Text), _
            Server.HtmlEncode(BodyField.Text))

    ' Update visibility of page elements
    EditPanel.Visible = False
    ButtonPanel.Visible = True

    ' Repopulate page contents with new message
    BindData()

End Sub
```

There are three steps in this procedure. First is to create an instance of the `DiscussionDB` business class and to call the `AddMessage` method on it with data from the editing controls. Second is to switch the panel visibility so that we are out of editing mode. Third is to re-bind the data by pulling across the record for the newly returned `itemId`.

We've seen the last two steps already and we're going to discuss what happens when we call `AddMessage` in a later section, but the one thing to note is the use of the `Server.HtmlEncode` method. This is to prevent the user from inserting their own mark-up into their message. Not only will it keep the appearance of our messages consistent, but, as we will see, it also eliminates a potential security risk.

Without this extra step a user could create a message with something like:

```
<script>alert('Is this irritating or what?')</script>
```

And then every time the message is displayed the user will be confronted by a dialog box like this:

The example is really only mildly irritating but forgetting to encode user responses before displaying them can open the site up to a whole range of cross-site scripting (XSS) attacks.

> *For more information on cross site scripting, along with other attacks on ASP.NET applications and ways of preventing them, see Professional ASP.Net Security (ISBN 1861006209).*

And that's it for code in `DiscussDetails.aspx.vb`! The call to `BindData` will retrieve the new data record, update the now visible navigation elements, and display the message:

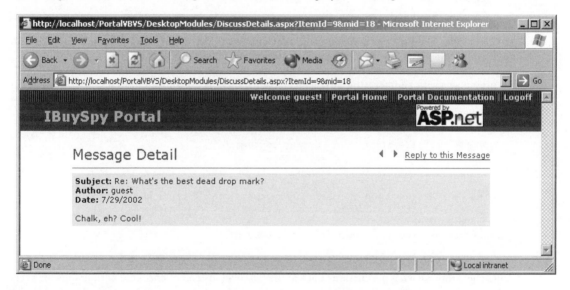

Squeezing a Little More Out of DiscussDetails.aspx

As was the case with `Discussion.ascx` there are a couple of things we can do to improve on `DiscussDetails.aspx`.

Rewrite Calls to DiscussionDB to Use the Shared Members

Remember that we need to convert all of the code that calls out to the `DiscussionDB` class so that it uses the shared members! The only two procedures that need to be edited are `BindData` and `UpdateBtn_Click` and, since we've already seen how to do this, we won't bother showing the revised versions here.

> *The updated code is in the download if you wish to review it.*

Closing a Security Loophole

Remember that in `Page_Load` we have the following snippet of code to ensure that the user is authorized to edit the current module:

```
If PortalSecurity.HasEditPermissions(moduleId) = False Then
  If itemId = 0 Then
   Response.Redirect("~/Admin/EditAccessDenied.aspx")
  Else
   ReplyBtn.Visible = False
  End If
End If
```

The problem with this is that it never checks to see if the user is authorized to <u>view</u> messages in the current module! The user can manually enter any existing `itemId` and `moduleId` into the address bar and this code will still allow the message to be displayed.

This presents us with an interesting predicament, since there is no equivalent to `HasEditPermissions` for checking viewing permissions! In `DesktopDisplay.aspx` the framework takes advantage of the fact that viewing permissions are granted at the tab level:

```
' Obtain PortalSettings from Current Context
Dim _portalSettings As PortalSettings = _
   CType(HttpContext.Current.Items("PortalSettings"), PortalSettings)

' Ensure that the visiting user has access to the current page
If PortalSecurity.IsInRoles(_portalSettings.ActiveTab.AuthorizedRoles) _
   = False Then
 Response.Redirect("~/Admin/AccessDenied.aspx")
End If
```

It only checks for viewing permissions once at the tab level instead of checking permissions for every module on the page. This makes perfect sense in `DesktopDisplay.aspx` since it is designed to show multiple modules within the tab framework. If we examine `HasEditPermissions` we'll see that it works perfectly for edit pages since it checks to be sure that the user has both viewing and editing permissions for a given module.

Our problem is that, in our combined viewing and editing scenario, we don't want to bounce a user just because they don't have editing rights. We need a way to check the viewing and editing permissions individually. To do this we are going to add a new method to the `PortalSecurity` class, which is physically located in the `Security.vb` class file. Let's start by reminding ourselves about the functionality in `HasEditPermissions`:

```
Public Shared Function HasEditPermissions(ByVal moduleId As Integer) _
                    As Boolean
  ' Obtain PortalSettings from Current Context
  Dim _portalSettings As PortalSettings = CType( _
          HttpContext.Current.Items("PortalSettings"), _
          PortalSettings)

  ' Create Instance of Connection and Command Object
  Dim myConnection As New SqlConnection( _
        ConfigurationSettings.AppSettings("connectionString"))
  Dim myCommand As New SqlCommand("GetAuthRoles", myConnection)

  ' Mark the Command as a SPROC
  myCommand.CommandType = CommandType.StoredProcedure

  ' Add Parameters to SPROC
  Dim parameterModuleID As New _
          SqlParameter("@ModuleID", SqlDbType.Int, 4)
  parameterModuleID.Value = moduleId
  myCommand.Parameters.Add(parameterModuleID)

  Dim parameterPortalID As New _
          SqlParameter("@PortalID", SqlDbType.Int, 4)
  parameterPortalID.Value = _portalSettings.PortalId
  myCommand.Parameters.Add(parameterPortalID)

  ' Add out parameters to Sproc
  Dim parameterAccessRoles As New _
        SqlParameter("@AccessRoles", SqlDbType.NVarChar, 256)
  parameterAccessRoles.Direction = ParameterDirection.Output
  myCommand.Parameters.Add(parameterAccessRoles)

  Dim parameterEditRoles As New _
        SqlParameter("@EditRoles", SqlDbType.NVarChar, 256)
  parameterEditRoles.Direction = ParameterDirection.Output
  myCommand.Parameters.Add(parameterEditRoles)

  ' Open the database connection and execute the command
  myConnection.Open()
  myCommand.ExecuteNonQuery()
  myConnection.Close()

  If PortalSecurity.IsInRoles(CStr(parameterAccessRoles.Value)) _
     = False _
    Or PortalSecurity.IsInRoles(CStr(parameterEditRoles.Value)) _
     = False Then
   Return False
  Else
   Return True
  End If
End Function
```

The bulk of this function is taken up in setting up the call to the `GetAuthRoles` stored procedure. `GetAuthRoles` looks like this:

```
SELECT
  @AccessRoles = Tabs.AuthorizedRoles,
  @EditRoles  = Modules.AuthorizedEditRoles

FROM
  Modules
 INNER JOIN
  Tabs ON Modules.TabID = Tabs.TabID

WHERE
  Modules.ModuleID = @ModuleID
 AND
  Tabs.PortalID = @PortalID
```

`GetAuthRoles` takes two input parameters, `@ModuleID` and `@PortalID`, and returns two output parameters, `@AccessRoles` and `@EditRoles`, which define the viewing and editing permissions for the module respectively. It does this using a `SELECT` statement that joins the `Modules` table with the `Tabs` table, effectively performing a lookup of the viewing permissions from the tab that the module is displayed on.

If we take a look at the last part of `HasEditPermissions`:

```
If PortalSecurity.IsInRoles(CStr(parameterAccessRoles.Value)) _
  = False _
 Or PortalSecurity.IsInRoles(CStr(parameterEditRoles.Value)) _
  = False Then
 Return False
Else
 Return True
End If
End Function
```

We can see that `HasEditPermissions` actually performs a check on both viewing and editing permissions with the helper method `IsInRoles`. `IsInRoles` compares the roles that are passed in through the argument with the roles stored in the `context.User` object supplied by the framework.

We could create a new method to check just the viewing permissions by copying the entire method, renaming it, and then changing the `If` statement to:

```
Public Shared Function HasViewPermissions(ByVal moduleId As Integer) _
                As Boolean
 ' Obtain PortalSettings from Current Context
 Dim _portalSettings As PortalSettings = CType( _
          HttpContext.Current.Items("PortalSettings"), _
          PortalSettings)
 ' Create Instance of Connection and Command Object
 .
 .
 .
```

```
If PortalSecurity.IsInRoles(CStr(parameterAccessRoles.Value)) Then
 Return False
Else
 Return True
End If
End Function
```

That's not quite optimal though because in our case we are going to check for edit permissions first and then, if that fails and the request is to view a message, we'll have to check for viewing permissions as well. With two separate calls we'd actually end up hitting the database twice.

Instead, let's break up the task a little bit differently. Let's create a new method, one that takes three arguments: the moduleId and two new Boolean arguments, EditPermission and ViewPermission. We'll pass the Boolean arguments by reference so that we can return both values. We'll call our new method CheckPermissions and its declaration will look like this:

```
Public Shared Sub CheckPermissions( _
         ByVal moduleId As Integer, _
         ByRef EditPermission As Boolean, _
         ByRef ViewPermission As Boolean)
```

Copy the code from HasEditPermissions. The only part we'll need to modify is the last If statement block:

```
' Obtain PortalSettings from Current Context
Dim _portalSettings As PortalSettings = CType( _
        HttpContext.Current.Items("PortalSettings"), _
        PortalSettings)
' Create Instance of Connection and Command Object
 .
 .
 .


' Check to see whether they have viewing permission
ViewPermission = IsInRoles(CStr(parameterAccessRoles.Value))

If ViewPermission Then
 EditPermission = IsInRoles(CStr(parameterEditRoles.Value))
Else
 EditPermission = False
End If
End Sub
```

We start by checking for viewing permissions and storing that in the ViewPermission argument variable. We then make the method a little more efficient by doing a little logical short-circuiting of our own. We know from the original code that our business rule says that they can't have editing permission unless they also have viewing permission – they can't edit something that they can't see!

So we'll only call IsInRoles to check for editing permission if they already have viewing permission. If they don't have viewing permission, we can automatically deny them editing permission.

The original HasEditPermissions function could have benefited from this as well, it just would have required switching from the standard Or keyword to the logical short-circuiting version of it, OrAlso.

Earlier in the book we introduced the Database class to encapsulate all of our calls to the data layer. If we change the calls to the data layer in our new method to use the Database class, the new listing becomes much less complex:

```
Public Shared Sub CheckPermissions( _
                            ByVal moduleId As Integer, _
                            ByRef EditPermission As Boolean, _
                            ByRef ViewPermission As Boolean)

    ' Obtain PortalSettings from Current Context
    Dim _portalSettings As PortalSettings = CType( _
                        HttpContext.Current.Items("PortalSettings"), _
                        PortalSettings)

    ' Create the database class object
    Dim db As New Database()

    ' Create the parameter array for the stored procedure we want to call
    Dim params As SqlParameter() = { _
        db.MakeParameter("@ModuleID", moduleId), _
        db.MakeParameter("@PortalID", _portalSettings.PortalId), _
        db.MakeParameter("@AccessRoles", ParameterDirection.Output, Nothing), _
        db.MakeParameter("@EditRoles", ParameterDirection.Output, Nothing)}

    'Set the type & size of the output parameters
    With params(2)
      .SqlDbType = SqlDbType.NVarChar
      .Size = 256
    End With
    With params(3)
      .SqlDbType = SqlDbType.NVarChar
      .Size = 256
    End With

    ' Call the stored procedure
    db.RunProcedure("GetAuthRoles", params)

    ' Clean up any resources associated with the Database class
    db.Dispose()

    ' Check to see whether they have viewing permission
    ViewPermission = IsInRoles(CStr(params(2).Value))

    If ViewPermission Then
      ' They may also have edit permission, so let's check
```

```
      EditPermission = IsInRoles(CStr(params(3).Value))
    Else
      ' If they can't see it then by default they can't edit it,
      ' so we can skip the call to PortalSecurity.IsInRoles and
      ' set the value of EditPermission directly
      EditPermission = False
    End If
  End Sub
```

Note, though, that since we are using a parameter array instead of creating individual parameter objects we need to change the references to the output parameter variables to point to the appropriate array elements instead. We'll also need to add an Imports statement at the top of the class file for the Wrox.Intranet namespace if we want to get away without fully qualifying our references to the Database class.

We're done with writing CheckPermissions, so now we can re-write the HasEditPermissions function as a wrapper around a call to CheckPermissions:

```
Public Shared Function HasEditPermissions(ByVal moduleId As Integer) _
                    As Boolean
  Call CheckPermissions(moduleId, HasEditPermissions, False)
End Function
```

For the sake of completeness, we'll also create a new method called HasViewPermissions for times when we only need to check for viewing permission:

```
Public Shared Function HasViewPermissions(ByVal moduleId As Integer) _
                    As Boolean
  Call CheckPermissions(moduleId, False, HasViewPermissions)
End Function
```

Finally we are back to DiscussDetails.aspx.vb where we can update our Page_Load procedure to use the new CheckPermissions method in PortalSecurity:

```
  ' Check for both permissions in a single call
  PortalSecurity.CheckPermissions(moduleId, CanEdit, CanView)

  If CanEdit = False Then
    If itemId = 0 Then
      Response.Redirect("~/Admin/EditAccessDenied.aspx")
    ElseIf CanView Then
      ReplyBtn.Visible = False
    Else
      ' CanView must be False (it's the least likely situation so
      ' so we want to make sure it's the last thing we check for)
      Response.Redirect("~/Admin/AccessDenied.aspx", True)
    End If
  End If
```

This is much better! Now we have a single call that checks both types of permission for the requested module and the user is no longer able to circumvent the module security check. We've even customized the response so that we can display a more targeted message to the unauthorized user – either an "Access Denied" or an "Edit Access Denied" message depending on the kind of access they requested.

Moving the Security Check Code Block

Now that we've corrected the security check, let's take a look at where it's called in the procedure:

```
' Populate message contents if this is the first visit to the page
If Page.IsPostBack = False Then
  BindData()
End If

' Check for both permissions in a single call
PortalSecurity.CheckPermissions(moduleId, CanEdit, CanView)

If CanEdit = False Then
  .
  .
  .
End If
```

Suppose that an unauthorized user hits our page. Because of the order that these statements are in we'll actually incur the overhead of hitting the database and updating the server controls, even though they'll never get to see the page!

Let's move the security check code block so that it comes before the `If` block that populates the page with the message contents:

```
' Check for both permissions in a single call
PortalSecurity.CheckPermissions(moduleId, CanEdit, CanView)

If CanEdit = False Then
  .
  .
  .
End If

' Populate message contents if this is the first visit to the page
If Page.IsPostBack = False Then
  BindData()
End If
```

Now we'll only hit the database when we can actually show the page to the user!

Closing another Security Loophole

We fixed the loophole that allows a user to view any message in any module by adding a new shared function to the `PortalSecurity` class; unfortunately, it is still possible for a user to read messages from modules that they aren't authorized to view. This doesn't have anything to do with our solution to the original security problem though. Instead it's because of an oversight in the business object, `DiscussionDB`.

We made it so that a user can no longer open the `DiscussDetails.ascx` page without having access to the `moduleID` in the query string. That solves the initial problem, but once a malicious user has view access to one module, they can manually enter any `itemId` into the address bar including ones for messages in other modules.

> `DiscussDetails.ascx` verifies that the user has access to the `moduleId` passed in through the querystring before it calls out to the `GetSingleMessage` function in the `DiscussionDB` class. However, since the `GetSingleMessage` function doesn't actually verify that the message belongs to the current module, the user can now view any message in any module.

Since authorization to view a module is granted at the tab level of the IBuySpy framework, this bug would require us to have at least two tabs with discussion modules displayed on them. The only way that a user could exploit this loophole is if they had viewing access to at least one of the tabs but not to one or more of the others.

This isn't an unlikely scenario, as we could very easily have a forum tab that is open to the public and another that is only available to employees... or perhaps a tab for managers and another for general employees... or even tabs specific to each department in a company. In fact, it's probably more likely to be the norm than not!

To fix this we need to update the `GetSingleMessage` function to take a `moduleId` argument and to pass that argument in as a parameter to the stored procedure:

```
Public Shared Function GetSingleMessage(ByVal moduleId As Integer, _
                                        ByVal itemId As Integer) _
                                        As SqlDataReader
    ' Create an instance of our database class
    Dim db As New Wrox.Intranet.Database()

    ' Get the results (passing in the default procedure variable)
    db.RunProcedure("GetSingleMessage", _
            New SqlParameter() _
            {db.MakeParameter("@ModuleId", moduleId), _
            db.MakeParameter("@ItemId", itemId)}, _
            GetSingleMessage)

    ' When the function ends it will automatically return the data reader
    ' in the default procedure variable
End Function
```

We'll also need to alter the `GetSingleMessage` stored procedure to take a `@ModuleId` parameter and modify the `WHERE` clause of its `SELECT` statement to match both the `@ItemId` and the `@ModuleId` parameters. Open the `GetSingleMessage` stored procedure up in the **SQL Editor** and make the following changes:

```
ALTER Procedure GetSingleMessage
(
    @ModuleID int,
    @ItemID int
)
AS

DECLARE @nextMessageID int
EXECUTE GetNextMessageID @ItemID, @nextMessageID OUTPUT
DECLARE @prevMessageID int
EXECUTE GetPrevMessageID @ItemID, @prevMessageID OUTPUT

SELECT
    ItemID,
    Title,
    CreatedByUser,
    CreatedDate,
    Body,
    NextMessageID = @nextMessageID,
    PrevMessageID = @prevMessageID
FROM
    Discussion
WHERE
    ItemID = @ItemID
    AND ModuleID = @ModuleID
```

We now need to change the line in `DiscussDetails.aspx.vb` where `BindData` calls the `GetSingleMessage` method so that it passes in the `moduleId` as well:

```
Sub BindData()
    ' Obtain the selected item from the Discussion table
    Dim dr As SqlDataReader = DiscussionDB.GetSingleMessage(moduleId, itemId)

    ' Load first row from database
    dr.Read()
```

We should make one more change so that those pesky "malicious users" know that we are on to them. Change the line that reads in the first record from the data reader:

```
Sub BindData()
    ' Obtain the selected item from the Discussion table
    Dim dr As SqlDataReader = DiscussionDB.GetSingleMessage(moduleId, itemId)

    ' Load first row from database
    If dr.Read() = False Then
        ' Either the item doesn't exist (unlikely) or they tried to
        ' read a message from another module. Either way redirect
```

```
        ' them to the "Access Denied" page
        Response.Redirect("~/Admin/AccessDenied.aspx", True)
    End If
```

Now the method will attempt to read in the row but if it doesn't find a record it will redirect them to the "Access Denied" page. Save the files that we've been working on and we've officially closed the security loophole.

> It's worth noting that this loophole only applies to unauthorized viewing of messages, not to unauthorized posting of messages. Because messages can only be created during the server postback for the **btnReply** click event there is no way for a user to change the **moduleID** once they are into the editing mode of **DiscussDetails.aspx**. So, while they can post a reply to a message from another thread, the reply will always get saved in the current module. They can never create content in another module.

Knowing that we've fixed this and prevented unauthorized users from accessing important messages like "Best night vision gear for nocturnal paint ball?" we should be able to sleep easier at night!

Eliminating the call to BindData when Starting a New Thread

There's another case where we might hit the database when we don't need to. If the user clicks on the "Add New Thread" link from the `Discussion.ascx` control, the link includes a `moduleID` but no item ID. In fact, that's how we can tell that we are starting a new thread!

Now when we're starting a new thread, we don't actually have an original message to display. Yet, if we look at the code, we'll see that we still end up calling `BindData` anyway. There is a quick fix for this one! Just amend the `If` statement to add a check to make sure that this isn't a new thread:

```
    ' Populate message contents if this is the first visit to the page
    ' and we actually have an itemId to display
    If Page.IsPostBack = False AndAlso itemId <> 0 Then
      BindData()
    End If
```

Disabling the TitleField for Replies

Because the `TitleField` control is always enabled, a user can change the title of their message reply if they want to. Depending on how we look at it this is either a useful piece of functionality or an "Unintended Product Feature" (read "bug"). If we find ourselves in the second camp we can fix this by adding the following line in the `btnReply_Click` procedure:

```
    Private Sub ReplyBtn_Click(ByVal Sender As Object, _
              ByVal e As EventArgs) _
              Handles ReplyBtn.Click
      EditPanel.Visible = True
      ButtonPanel.Visible = False
      TitleField.Enabled = False
    End Sub
```

Preventing a Blank Title or a Blank Body

It would also be nice to make sure that users don't accidentally submit new threads without titles and replies without bodies! We'll add a pair of RequiredFieldValidator controls and a ValidationSummary control to the page. Whether we add them through the designer or manually through code we'll want to end up with something like this if we look at the HTML View:

```
<TR vAlign="top">
 <TD class="SubHead" width="150">
  <asp:RequiredFieldValidator
    id="TitleRequired"
    runat="server"
    ErrorMessage="The title can't be blank"
    ControlToValidate="TitleField"
    Display="Dynamic">*</asp:RequiredFieldValidator>
  Title:
 </TD>
  .
  .
  .
</TR>
<TR vAlign="top">
 <TD class="SubHead">
  <asp:RequiredFieldValidator
    id="BodyRequired"
    runat="server"
    ErrorMessage="The message body can't be blank"
    ControlToValidate="BodyField"
    Display="Dynamic">*</asp:RequiredFieldValidator>
  Body:
 </TD>
  .
  .
  .
</TR>
<TR vAlign="top">
  .
  .
  .
  <asp:ValidationSummary
    id="ValidationSummary1"
    runat="server"
    ShowMessageBox="True"
    ShowSummary="False"
    HeaderText="Please correct the following items
      (marked with a red '*' in the page):" />
 </TD>
</TR>
```

The end result should be:

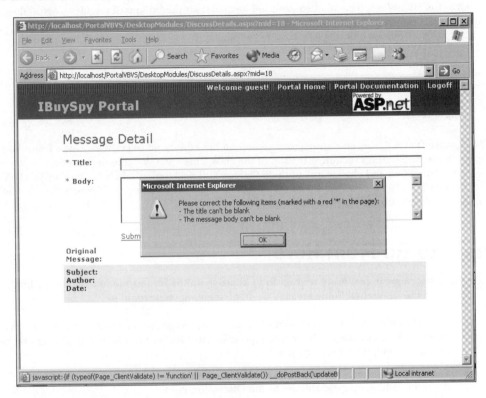

Why Use a Label Control When a Literal Will Do?

Okay, this is really getting down to the most minor of details! Literal controls have been provided in the framework for those times when we need to put in an unformatted piece of text. They are the most lightweight server control that we can create in ASP.NET. Because they don't have any built-in support for formatting, positioning, embedded controls, or any of the other features that server controls typically support they don't have the same overhead when they are instantiated or when they are rendered.

Why do we care though? What does it matter if a page uses a couple of label controls where they could be using literals? It's not as though most of us are building sites like Amazon.com where scalability is the driving factor in our design. That's true, but many of us <u>will</u> be using shared servers to host our application! The contention for resources between applications on a shared server can easily create the same kind of need for scalability, at the single server level, as many high traffic internet sites face.

So in the case of choosing whether to use the most lightweight controls that we can, this should really be a no-brainer. This is especially true for choosing between a literal and a label when we don't need to provide formatting or support for nested controls. We get the same functionality, any code we've written to work with the control text will still work, we use less memory, and we've reduced the overhead of processing our page!

To convert the label controls in `DiscussDetails.aspx` open the page up in Visual Studio.NET and switch to the **Html View**. The label controls are located near the bottom of the file so scroll down and wherever we see:

```
<asp:label ... />
```

Replace it with

```
<asp:literal ... />
```

When we've finished, we can right-click anywhere in the editor and select **View Code** from the context menu. In the declarations section at the top of the class, check the variable declarations for the controls we've just converted and change any of them that are still declared as labels to literals. We should also check the task list to be sure that our new changes have not created any build errors (which would happen if we were using label-specific properties).

Where to Go From Here

There is, of course, a great deal more we can do to improve on the forums module that we've built so far. This is really just the beginning! Some areas to try implementing next would be:

❑ Thread ratings – Let the users rank threads by their usefulness or interest. We could even build another module to display the top-ranked threads as a summary list (perhaps by using the Links module as a starting point).

❑ Paging – Over time we'll hopefully see tremendous activity in our forums, so it will only be natural to add paging capabilities to the Discussion module.

Adding paging capabilities to the thread display page would be pretty simple. Since we have a numbering system in place for the thread replies we really only need to add page number and page size parameters to the stored procedure that retrieves thread posts. With those two pieces of information we can calculate the range of thread post `ReplyIndex` values for each page and can alter the `SELECT` statement so that it retrieves just those values.

Once we have set up our database routines to retrieve a page of messages at a time, implementing custom paging on the display page is fairly straightforward.

Setting up paging on the thread summary page is a little more complex. We don't have a field that would provide us with sequential numbering for the threads when they are in most recently updated order, so we can't simply calculate a range of values for a given page. Check out Chapter 8 for a discussion of some paging techniques that we could use for the thread summary page.

❑ Forum Administration – There are a host of forum administration features we could add to take this from beyond being a simple un-moderated forum. Features like message vetting, objectionable content filters, administrative editing and deletion capabilities, etc.

❑ Thread Archiving – Currently there is no way to archive threads, but as our forum grows this may become vital. As it stands the only way to archive messages at all would be to remove a module from a "main forums" tab and move it to an "archived forums" tab. This really isn't powerful enough for most scenarios where forums play a part.

❑ Finally, it should also be possible to report a post to the administrator or moderator so that objectionable content can be detected and reported to the webmaster/moderator/administrator/thread-owner.

Summary

This chapter has introduced you in detail to the architecture and implementation of an existing IBuySpy module. The aim has been to familiarize you with the inner workings of the Discussions module as a way of preparing you for implementing your own modules or extending an existing one.

We also took the opportunity to identify some of the best practices used in the IBuySpy framework – and in the *Squeezing a Little More Out of...* sections we saw how even a well written framework like IBuySpy can benefit from a little code review!

Solutio...
BM
References
System
System.Data
System.Drawing
System.Web
System.XML
AssemblyInfo.vb
BM.vsdisco
Global.asax
Styles.css
Web.config
WebForm1.aspx

WebForm1.aspx* | WebForm1.aspx.

ebForm1.aspx*

Extending The Events Module

In this chapter we will be taking one of the original IBuySpy modules (the events module) and extending it by adding new functionality. We will be using the existing code as a starting point for building a module that provides the functionality that we want.

The changes we will be making in this chapter are bigger in scope than those we made to the discussions module in the last chapter. In that chapter, we made changes that improved the efficiency and security of the existing functionality – we did not add any additional features. In this chapter, we will be taking the events module apart; reusing the parts that do not need to change and making alterations to the parts that do not do what we want.

You might find it useful to have a look at the IBuySpy events module before reading this chapter, in order that you can see where we make changes and improvements to customize the module for our purposes.

Features

Before we dive into the code, it would be a good idea to list out the features we are planning to implement so that there is a clear picture of what's going to come ahead.

The highlights of the module we will be building in this chapter are as follows:

- ❑ A calendar that highlights the event dates.
- ❑ The ability for an administrator to add, update and delete events.
- ❑ The ability to define events for particular roles and restrict viewers.
- ❑ The ability to view events based on different criteria.

The Database

Before we start coding our application we need to create a new `Events` table in our `WroxIntranet` database, which will be used to store our events. The following figure shows the schema for the `Events` table.

Column Name	Data Type	Length	Allow Nulls
ItemID	int	4	
ModuleID	int	4	
CreatedByUser	nvarchar	100	
CreatedDate	datetime	8	
EventDate	datetime	8	
Title	nvarchar	150	
WhereWhen	nvarchar	150	
Description	nvarchar	2000	
AuthorizedViewRoles	nvarchar	256	

This table is very similar to the original `Events` table used by the events module. We have changed the `ExpiresDate` column into `EventDate`, as our module will be using this column as the date of the event itself. We have also added the `AuthorizedViewRoles` column to store the roles that are allowed to view the event.

Here are details of all the columns.

Column Name	Description
ItemID	The primary key field for the database.
ModuleID	The `ModuleID` of the module to which the particular event row belongs. The portal architecture allows multiple instances of the same control to be used, hence the `ModuleID` column is used to keep track of events related to a single module.
CreatedByUser	The username of the user that created the event.
CreatedDate	The date when the event was created.
EventDate	The date of the event. The module automatically expires events after their `EventDate` has elapsed.
Title	The title of the event.
WhereWhen	The time and the location of the event.
Description	The full details for the event.
AuthorizedViewRoles	The semicolon separated list of roles that are authorized to view this event. This column is used to restrict the display of certain events based on the roles a user belongs to. A generic value of *All User* makes the event viewable to all users.

One point to note is that in the `EventDate` column we will be just storing date of the events and not the time. It is possible to store the date and time in a single column but our module is only concerned with the date of events – the precise time of each event can be communicated through the `WhereWhen` column.

Stored Procedures

Our Events module needs 6 Stored Procedures as listed below:

Stored Procedure	Description
up_Events_AddEvent	Add an new event for a particular module.
up_Events_UpdateEvent	Update an existing event.
up_Events_DeleteEvent	Delete an existing event.
up_Events_GetSingleEvent	Get details of a single event based on its `ItemID`.
up_Events_GetAllEvents	Get all the events for a particular module.
up_Events_GetMonthlyEvents	Get all the events for a particular month and module.

Most of these are very similar to the stored procedures in the original events module. We have renamed them to fit the naming convention we are using in our project.

The `up_Events_GetMonthlyEvents` procedure is new and has been added in order to support the functionality we will be adding for displaying events month by month.

up_Events_AddEvent

This stored procedure takes the appropriate parameters for the event and adds a new event entry into the database:

```
CREATE PROCEDURE up_Events_AddEvent
(
    @ModuleID     int,
    @UserName     nvarchar(100),
    @Title        nvarchar(100),
    @EventDate    DateTime,
    @Description  nvarchar(2000),
    @WhereWhen    nvarchar(100),
    @ViewRoles    nvarchar(256)
)
AS

INSERT INTO Events
(
    ModuleID,
    CreatedByUser,
    Title,
```

```
        CreatedDate,
        EventDate,
        Description,
        WhereWhen,
        AuthorizedViewRoles
    )

VALUES
(
        @ModuleID,
        @UserName,
        @Title,
        GetDate(),
        @EventDate,
        @Description,
        @WhereWhen,
        @ViewRoles
    )

GO
```

We have added a parameter (@ViewRoles) to the original IBuySpy version of this procedure to set the authorized roles for the new event.

up_Events_UpdateEvent

This stored procedure updates an existing event entry based upon the ItemID of the event. This stored procedure is called from the events administration module to make changes to the event fields.

```
CREATE PROCEDURE up_Events_UpdateEvent
(
    @ItemID         int,
    @UserName       nvarchar(100),
    @Title          nvarchar(100),
    @EventDate      datetime,
    @Description    nvarchar(2000),
    @WhereWhen      nvarchar(100),
    @ViewRoles      nvarchar(256)
)

AS

UPDATE
    Events

SET
    CreatedByUser = @UserName,
    CreatedDate   = GetDate(),
    Title         = @Title,
    EventDate     = @EventDate,
    Description   = @Description,
    WhereWhen     = @WhereWhen,
    AuthorizedViewRoles = @ViewRoles
```

```
WHERE
    ItemID = @ItemID
GO
```

As with the previous procedure, we have added a parameter to set the authorized roles.

up_Events_DeleteEvent

This stored procedure takes the ItemID value of an Event and deletes it from the database. This stored procedure is also called from the events administration page.

```
CREATE PROCEDURE up_Events_DeleteEvent
(
    @ItemID int
)
AS

DELETE FROM
    Events

WHERE
    ItemID = @ItemID

GO
```

up_Events_GetSingleEvent

This stored procedure retrieves details of a single event based on the ItemID provided.

```
CREATE PROCEDURE up_Events_GetSingleEvent
(
    @ItemID int,
    @ModuleID int
)
AS

SELECT
    CreatedByUser,
    CreatedDate,
    EventDate,
    Title,
    Description,
    WhereWhen,
    AuthorizedViewRoles

FROM
    Events

WHERE
    ItemID = @ItemID
    AND
    ModuleID = @ModuleID
GO
```

up_Events_GetAllEvents

This stored procedure retrieves all the future events for a particular module. One interesting point you will note here is that we are passing the CurrentDate parameter along with the ModuleID parameter. The CurrentDate parameter consists of just today's date (not time) i.e. If today is 18th July 2002, the parameter will default to the value 07/18/2002 12:00 AM. The CurrentDate parameter is used to retrieve only those events that occur at the *current date or in the future*. As we have mentioned before we are storing only the date of the event in the EventDate field, hence the time defaults to 12:00 AM for each event. Generally we use the GetDate function of the MS SQL Server to check for the current date, but the GetDate function returns the current date as well as the current time. So, if you use the GetDate SQL function to check the event dates, the events for the current date will not be returned since the time of GetDate will usually be higher than the default time (12:00 AM) in the EventDate column. We therefore need to pass the current date separately.

```
CREATE PROCEDURE up_Events_GetAllEvents
(
    @ModuleID int,
    @CurrentDate datetime
)
AS

SELECT
    ItemID,
    Title,
    WhereWhen,
    EventDate,
    Title,
    Description,
    AuthorizedViewRoles

FROM
    Events

WHERE
    ModuleID = @ModuleID
  AND
    EventDate >= @CurrentDate
ORDER BY EventDate
GO
```

up_Events_GetMonthlyEvents

This stored procedure is used to retrieve the events for the provided month and module. As with the previous procedure, we pass a CurrentDate parameter to check for the validity of events. We also compare the month and year of the ShowDate parameter, which contains the date for whose month we want to retrieve the events. It is essential to check the month as well as the year, since if you have your application running for multiple years, then wrong values will be returned if we just check the month.

The MONTH and YEAR SQL functions are used to extract the month and year values from the date respectively.

```
CREATE PROCEDURE up_Events_GetMonthlyEvents
(
    @ModuleID int,
    @ShowDate datetime,
    @CurrentDate datetime
)
AS

SELECT
    ItemID,
    Title,
    WhereWhen,
    EventDate,
    Title,
    Description,
    AuthorizedViewRoles

FROM
    Events

WHERE
    ModuleID = @ModuleID
    AND
    (YEAR(EventDate) = YEAR(@ShowDate))
    AND
    (MONTH(EventDate) = MONTH(@ShowDate))
    AND
    EventDate >= @CurrentDate
ORDER BY EventDate

GO
```

These six stored procedures form a data access layer for our Shared Calendar module; all communication with the database takes places through them. We also use the Database class defined in earlier chapters to populate and call the Stored Procedures. The Database class manages all the database connection and command execution functions.

The Business Class

The second layer in your module is the business logic tier. This layer takes care of all communication with the Database class and in turn invokes the stored procedures.

Our Business tier is provided by the EventsDB class. It is defined in the EventsDB.vb file placed in the Components folder.

This class is based on the original `EventsDB` class from the IBuySpy events module but we will be making several changes in order to accommodate the functional changes we require. We will also be changing the data access code in the class to use the common database access class that we are using for our intranet project (You can read more about the database access class in Appendix A).

The `EventsDB` class provides six methods:

Method	Description
AddEvent	Calls the up_Events_AddEvent stored procedure to add a new event to the Events table.
UpdateEvent	Calls the up_Events_UpdateEvent stored procedure to update an existing event.
DeleteEvent	Calls the up_Events_DeleteEvent stored procedure to delete an existing event.
GetSingleEvent	Takes the ItemID of the event and returns a SqlDataReader object with the details of that event.
GetAllEvents	Takes the ModuleID to call the up_Events_GetAllEvents stored procedure and returns a DataSet containing all the events that particular user is authorized to view.
GetMonthlyEvents	Takes the ModuleID and ShowDate to call the up_Events_GetMonthlyEvents stored procedure and returns a DataSet containing all the events that particular user is authorized to view for the supplied month.

We will be describing two of these six methods here. The others are very similar. You can see their implementations in the download source code.

The `AddEvent` Method

The `AddEvent` method is very similar to the original IBuySpy events module `AddEvent` method. It takes the appropriate parameters and calls the up_Events_AddEvent stored procedure to add a new event to the `Events` table.

The only changes we have made to this method are to use the `Database` class for data access.

```
Public Sub AddEvent(ByVal moduleId As Integer, _
                    ByVal itemId As Integer, _
                    ByVal userName As String, _
                    ByVal title As String, _
                    ByVal eventDate As DateTime, _
                    ByVal description As String, _
                    ByVal wherewhen As String, _
                    ByVal viewRoles As String)
```

```
    ' Check if the user exists
   If userName.Length < 1 Then
     userName = "unknown"
   End If

    ' Create Instance of Database object
   Dim dataCon As New Database()

   Dim params(6) As SqlParameter

   params(0) = dataCon.MakeParameter("@ModuleID", SqlDbType.Int, 4, moduleId)

   params(1) = dataCon.MakeParameter("@UserName", SqlDbType.NVarChar, _
                 100, userName)

   params(2) = dataCon.MakeParameter("@Title", SqlDbType.NVarChar, _
                 100, title)

   params(3) = dataCon.MakeParameter("@WhereWhen", SqlDbType.NVarChar, _
                 100, wherewhen)

   params(4) = dataCon.MakeParameter("@ViewRoles", SqlDbType.NVarChar, _
                 256, viewRoles)

   params(5) = dataCon.MakeParameter("@EventDate", SqlDbType.DateTime, _
                 8, eventDate)

   params(6) = dataCon.MakeParameter("@Description", SqlDbType.NVarChar, _
                 2000, description)

   Try
     dataCon.RunProcedure("up_Events_AddEvent", params)
   Finally
     dataCon.Close()
     dataCon.Dispose()
   End Try

End Function
```

First, we check whether a username was supplied. If none was, we make the username 'unknown'.

```
If userName.Length < 1 Then
  userName = "unknown"
End If
```

We then create an instance of the Database class that we will use to communicate with the database.

```
Dim dataCon As New Database()
```

Next, we create the parameters that our stored procedure requires.

Once we have the procedures, we use the `Database` object we created to execute the procedure:

```
Try
  dataCon.RunProcedure("up_Events_AddEvent", params)
Finally
  dataCon.Close()
  dataCon.Dispose()
End Try
```

Note that we use the `Finally` part of the `Try` block to clean up after ourselves by calling the `Close` and `Dispose` methods of the `Database` class.

The `GetMonthlyEvents` Method

The `GetMonthlyEvents` method is not present in the original IBuySpy events module – we need to add it to support the view-by-months functionality that we want to add to the module.

The method takes the `ModuleID` and the `DateTime` for which month we want to view the events and returns a `DataSet` containing all events for that month. It filters out events that the current user is not allowed to view.

```
Public Function GetMonthlyEvents(ByVal moduleId As Integer, _
                                 ByVal showDate As DateTime) _
                                 As DataSet

  ' Create Instance of Database object
  Dim dataCon As New Database()
  ' Create an Array of SqlParameters
  Dim params(2) As SqlParameter

  ' Load the Parameters
  params(0) = dataCon.MakeParameter("@ModuleID", SqlDbType.Int, _
                      4, moduleId)

  params(1) = dataCon.MakeParameter("@ShowDate", SqlDbType.DateTime, _
                      8, showDate)

  params(2) = dataCon.MakeParameter("@CurrentDate", SqlDbType.DateTime, _
                      8, DateTime.Today)

  Dim myDataSet As New DataSet()

  Try
    ' Fill the DataSet
    dataCon.RunProcedure("up_Events_GetMonthlyEvents", params, myDataSet)
  Finally
    dataCon.Close()
    dataCon.Dispose()
  End Try

  ' Check if the Module Admin's Role
  If Not PortalSecurity.HasEditPermissions(moduleId) Then
```

```
      ' Code to filter out the events based on the user roles
      Dim dr As DataRow
      Dim roleStr As String
      ' Loop through the DataSet
      For Each dr In myDataSet.Tables(0).Rows
        roleStr = CType(dr("AuthorizedViewRoles"), String)
        ' Check if the user role is present in the event's
        ' AuthorizedViewRoles value
        If (Not PortalSecurity.IsInRoles(roleStr)) Then
          ' If the user is not allowed to view the event
          ' delete it from the DataSet
          dr.Delete()
        End If
      Next
      ' Make the changes to the DataSet permanent
      myDataSet.AcceptChanges()
    End If

    ' Return the DataSet
    Return myDataSet

  End Function
```

As with the `AddEvent` method that we looked at previously, this method starts by creating an instance of the `Database` class and setting up parameters to call a stored procedure. In this case, the stored procedure we are calling is `up_Events_GetMonthlyEvents`.

Things get interesting after we have run the procedure and retrieved the events for the specified month. We now need to ensure that we remove events that the current user is not authorized to view from the `DataSet`.

If the user has edit permissions for the module, they should be able to see all events, so we check for that first:

```
If Not PortalSecurity.HasEditPermissions(moduleId) Then
```

If they do not have edit permissions, we iterate through each event:

```
For Each dr In myDataSet.Tables(0).Rows
```

We want to check whether the user is in any of the roles that are authorized to view the event, (the `AuthorizedViewRoles` column in the table) so we extract the roles from the `DataSet`:

```
roleStr = CType(dr("AuthorizedViewRoles"), String)
```

We then use the `IsInRoles` method of the `PortalSecurity` class that we looked at in Chapter 4 to determine if the current user is in any of the roles in the list:

```
If (Not PortalSecurity.IsInRoles(roleStr)) Then
```

227

If the user is not in any of the roles, we remove the event from the `DataSet`:

```
    dr.Delete()
```

Once we have iterated over all of the events, we accept the changes to the `DataSet` and return it:

```
  Next
  ' Make the changes to the DataSet permanent
  myDataSet.AcceptChanges()
End If

' Return the DataSet
Return myDataSet
```

User Interface

In the previous sections we have completed the database design and access layer and the business logic layer. We now turn our attention to the presentation layer. The user interface for the Shared Calendar is divided into a web form that supports the administration of the module and a user control that contains the module itself. These user interface objects call on the business layer `EventsDB` class to perform communication with the database.

Editing Events

The functionality to `add`, `update` and `delete` events is provided by the edit page for the events module, `EditEvents.aspx`

Because of the extra functionality we are adding, this page needs to be a little different from the edit page included in the original IBuySpy events module.

Here is what the page looks like:

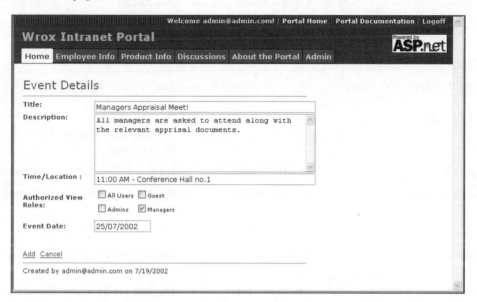

We will not be looking at the code for the .aspx file in detail as it is composed of standard controls. Here is a list of the controls used on the page:

Control	Control Name	Description
DesktopPortalBanner.ascx	SiteHeader	This user control is used to display the title on the page and setup the tabs.
TextBox	TitleField	Used to add the title for the event.
RequiredFieldValidator	RequiredFieldValidator1	This validates the TitleField textbox.
TextBox (Multi-line)	DescriptionField	Used to add the description for the event.
RequiredFieldValidator	RequiredFieldValidator2	This validates the DescriptionField textbox.
TextBox	WhereWhenField	Used to add the time and location for the event.
RequiredFieldValidator	RequiredFieldValidator3	This validates the WhereWhenField textbox.

Table continued on following page

Control	Control Name	Description
CheckBoxList	AuthViewRoles	Used to add the roles authorized to view the event.
TextBox	EventDateField	Used to add the date of the event.
RequiredFieldValidator	RequiredField Validator4	This validates the EventDate textbox.
CompareValidator	VerifyEventDate	This checks if the value in the EventDate textbox if of type DateTime.
LinkButton	updateButton	Used to add or update the event data.
LinkButton	cancelButton	Used to cancel the form and return to the home page.
LinkButton	deleteButton	Used to delete a particular event.
Label	CreatedBy	Displays the username of the user who created the event.
Label	CreatedDate	Displays the date when the event was created.

The interesting part of this page for us is in the methods of the codebehind for the page.

The Page_Load Event Handler

In this event handler, we use the query string to determine the module that is being edited and check that the current user has permission to edit the module.

The code for this method is shown below:

```
Private Sub Page_Load(ByVal sender As System.Object, _
                ByVal e As System.EventArgs) _
                Handles MyBase.Load

  ' Determine ModuleId of Events Portal Module
  If Not (Request.Params("Mid") Is Nothing) Then
    moduleId = Int32.Parse(Request.Params("Mid"))
  Else
    ' If mid is not present then return the user back
    Response.Redirect("~/Default.aspx")
  End If

  If Not (Request.Params("ItemID") Is Nothing) Then
    itemId = Int32.Parse(Request.Params("ItemID"))
  End If

    ' Verify that the current user has access to edit this module
```

```
   If PortalSecurity.HasEditPermissions(moduleId) = False Then
     Response.Redirect("~/Admin/EditAccessDenied.aspx")
   End If

   If Page.IsPostBack = False Then
     ' Call method to bind the controls
     Bind()
     ' Store URL Referrer to return to portal
     If IsNothing(Request.UrlReferrer) Then
       ViewState("UrlReferrer") = "~/Default.aspx"
     Else
       ViewState("UrlReferrer") = Request.UrlReferrer.ToString()
     End If

   End If

 End Sub
```

The first thing we do is to retrieve the module ID from the query string. If no module ID is supplied, we return the user to the default portal page.

```
If Not (Request.Params("Mid") Is Nothing) Then
  moduleId = Int32.Parse(Request.Params("Mid"))
Else
  ' If mid is not present then return the user back
  Response.Redirect("~/Default.aspx")
End If
```

We then parse the item ID from the query string into an integer, if an item ID exists in the query string.

```
If Not (Request.Params("ItemID") Is Nothing) Then
  itemId = Int32.Parse(Request.Params("ItemID"))
End If
```

Then, a security check is made by calling the `HasEditPermissions` method of the `PortalSecurity` class. This method takes the module ID and checks if the current user belongs to the appropriate role to access this page. In case the user is not from an appropriate role they are redirected to the `EditAccessDenied.aspx` page.

```
If PortalSecurity.HasEditPermissions(moduleId) = False Then
  Response.Redirect("~/Admin/EditAccessDenied.aspx")
End If
```

Next, we check the `IsPostBack` property of the page to determine if the page is being loaded for the first time, if so we call the `Bind` method to bind our controls. We will be looking at the `Bind` method in the next section.

```
If Page.IsPostBack = False Then
  ' Call method to bind the controls
  Bind()
```

Finally, we store the value of the `UrlReferrer` property. This value is used when we want to return to the actual page that called this page, even if some postbacks occur while the user is using this page.

```
If IsNothing(Request.UrlReferrer) Then
   ViewState("UrlReferrer") = "~/Default.aspx"
Else
   ViewState("UrlReferrer") = Request.UrlReferrer.ToString()
End If
```

The Bind Method

The `Bind` method binds the page controls to the events data. The complete listing of the `Bind` method is shown below.

```
Private Sub Bind()

   ' Obtain PortalSettings from Current Context
   Dim _portalSettings As PortalSettings = _
CType(Context.Items("PortalSettings"), PortalSettings)

   ' Populate checkbox list with all security roles for this portal
   ' and "check" the ones already configured for this tab
   Dim admin As New AdminDB()
   Dim roles As SqlDataReader = admin.GetPortalRoles(_portalSettings.PortalId)

   ' Databind the checkboxlist
   AuthViewRoles.DataSource = roles
   AuthViewRoles.DataTextField = "RoleName"
   AuthViewRoles.DataValueField = "RoleID"
   AuthViewRoles.DataBind()
   roles.Close()

   ' Add a generic item to the checkboxlist
   Dim allItem As New ListItem()
   allItem.Text = "All Users"
   AuthViewRoles.Items.Add(allItem)

   If itemId <> 0 Then

      ' Obtain a single row of event information
      Dim events As New ASPNetPortal.EventsDB()
      Dim dr As SqlDataReader = events.GetSingleEvent(moduleId, itemId)

      ' Read first row from database
      dr.Read()
      ' Restore the values from the database to the controls
      TitleField.Text = CType(dr("Title"), String)
      DescriptionField.Text = CType(dr("Description"), String)
      CreatedBy.Text = CType(dr("CreatedByUser"), String)
      WhereWhenField.Text = CType(dr("WhereWhen"), String)
      EventDateField.Text = CType(dr("EventDate"), _
                   DateTime).ToShortDateString()
```

```
        CreatedDate.Text = CType(dr("CreatedDate"), _
                    DateTime).ToShortDateString()

        ' Code to select the appropriate checkboxes
        ' after reading the roles from the database
        Dim rolesStr As String()
        ' Split the roles into an array
        rolesStr = CType(dr("AuthorizedViewRoles"), String).Split(";"c)
        Dim singleRole As String
        Dim roleItem As ListItem
        ' loop over the array
        For Each singleRole In rolesStr
          ' Try to find a CheckBox with similar Text
          roleItem = AuthViewRoles.Items.FindByText(singleRole)
          If Not IsNothing(roleItem) Then
            ' Select the CheckBox
            roleItem.Selected = True
          End If
        Next

        dr.Close()
      Else
        AuthViewRoles.Items.FindByText("All Users").Selected = True
        ' Change the Text property of the Update Button
        updateButton.Text = "Add"
        ' Hide the Delete button for a new event
        deleteButton.Visible = False
        ' Set the Username label
        CreatedBy.Text = Context.User.Identity.Name
        ' Set the creation date label
        CreatedDate.Text = DateTime.Now.ToShortDateString()

      End If

    End If

End Sub
```

The first thing we do in this method is populate the CheckBoxList with the roles defined in the portal. We get a reference to the PortalSettings class from the Context object. The PortalSettings class is used to get the PortalId of the currently running portal.

```
Dim _portalSettings As PortalSettings = _
CType(Context.Items("PortalSettings"), PortalSettings)
```

Then we create an instance of AdminDB. This class, provided with IBuySpy, allows you to access the various portal-related administration options. We use the GetPortalRoles method of the AdminDB object to get all of the roles defined for the portal.

```
Dim admin As New AdminDB()
Dim roles As SqlDataReader = admin.GetPortalRoles(_portalSettings.PortalId)
```

The `SqlDataAdapter` is databound to the `CheckBoxList` and a generic 'All Users' item is then added:

```
Dim allItem As New ListItem()
allItem.Text = "All Users"
AuthViewRoles.Items.Add(allItem)
```

This item is used to allow access to be granted to all users.

The `itemId` variable is now checked, if its value is zero then it indicates we are adding a new event, else we are updating an existing record. In the case we are updating an existing event, an object of our business layer class `EventsDB` is created and its `GetSingleEvent` method is called.

```
If itemId <> 0 Then

    ' Obtain a single row of event information
    Dim events As New ASPNetPortal.EventsDB()
    Dim dr As SqlDataReader = events.GetSingleEvent(moduleId, itemId)
```

The values returned by the method call are used to populate the textboxes. To select the appropriate `CheckBoxes`, based upon the value of the `AuthorisedViewRoles` column, the following code is used.

```
Dim rolesStr As String()
' Split the roles into an array
rolesStr = CType(dr("AuthorizedViewRoles"), String).Split(";"c)
    Dim singleRole As String
    Dim roleItem As ListItem
    ' loop over the array
    For Each singleRole In rolesStr
       ' Try to find a CheckBox with similar Text
       roleItem = AuthViewRoles.Items.FindByText(singleRole)
     If Not IsNothing(roleItem) Then
        ' Select the CheckBox
       roleItem.Selected = True
     End If
    Next
```

We first split the value of the `AuthorizedViewRoles` column into a string array and then loop over the array. If our role matches a `CheckBox` text then we select it.

If the `itemId` is 'zero' indicating we are adding a new record, then we set up the controls appropriately to indicate a new event is being added.

The `UpdateBtn_Click` Event Handler

This method is called whenever the update button is clicked. Remember, we use the same `LinkButton` to add or update an event, so this method serves a dual purpose. The full code for the method is below.

```
Private Sub UpdateBtn_Click(ByVal sender As Object, ByVal e As EventArgs)_
                 Handles updateButton.Click

   ' Only Update if the Entered Data is Valid
```

```
If Page.IsValid = True Then

  Dim viewRoles As String = ""
  'Prepare the roles string
  If IsNothing(AuthViewRoles.SelectedItem) Or _
    AuthViewRoles.Items.FindByText("All Users").Selected = True _
      Then
    ' Set the default to all users
    viewRoles = "All Users"
  Else
    Dim roleItem As ListItem
    ' loop through the CheckBoxList
    For Each roleItem In AuthViewRoles.Items
      If roleItem.Selected = True Then
        viewRoles = viewRoles & roleItem.Text & ";"
      End If
    Next
  End If

  ' Create an instance of the Event DB component
  Dim events As New ASPNetPortal.EventsDB()

  If itemId = 0 Then

    ' Add the event within the Events table
    events.AddEvent(moduleId, itemId, _
        Context.User.Identity.Name, TitleField.Text, _
        DateTime.Parse(EventDateField.Text), DescriptionField.Text, _
        WhereWhenField.Text, viewRoles)

  Else

    ' Update the event within the Events table
    events.UpdateEvent(moduleId, itemId, _
        Context.User.Identity.Name, TitleField.Text, _
        DateTime.Parse(EventDateField.Text), DescriptionField.Text, _
        WhereWhenField.Text, viewRoles)

  End If

  ' Redirect back to the portal home page
  Response.Redirect(CType(ViewState("UrlReferrer"), String))

  End If

End Sub
```

This method is pretty straightforward. It collects the values from the appropriate controls, and then calls the AddEvent or UpdateEvent method of the EventsDB object to add or update an event respectively. Once done, it redirects the user back to the original URL, which referred to this page. The only slightly complex part in the method is shown below:

```
Dim viewRoles As String = ""
    'Prepare the roles string
    If IsNothing(AuthViewRoles.SelectedItem) Or _
       AuthViewRoles.Items.FindByText("All Users").Selected = True _
          Then
       ' Set the default to all users
       viewRoles = "All Users"
    Else
       Dim roleItem As ListItem
       ' loop through the CheckBoxList
       For Each roleItem In AuthViewRoles.Items
          If roleItem.Selected = True Then
             viewRoles = viewRoles & roleItem.Text & ";"
          End If
       Next
    End If
```

The `AuthorizedViewRoles` field in the database stores a semicolon separated list of roles, so we need to loop over the `CheckBoxList`, check if the `CheckBox` is selected, and append its text to our roles list. Although, in case the user does not select any `CheckBoxes` in the list then we default to adding the value of `All Users` indicating all users can view the event. Also if `All Users CheckBox` is selected then we only add that single role to the database, since it does not make sense to filter particular roles when all users are given access to view the event.

The `DeleteBtn_Click` Event Handler

This method is called when the **delete** button is clicked. It simply creates a new `EventsDB` object and calls it's `DeleteEvent` method passing the `itemId` of the current event. The user is redirected back to the page that they came from (the referrer).

```
Private Sub DeleteBtn_Click(ByVal sender As Object, ByVal e As EventArgs) _
       Handles deleteButton.Click

   ' Only attempt to delete the item if it is an existing item
   ' (new items will have "ItemId" of 0)
   If itemId <> 0 Then

      Dim events As New ASPNetPortal.EventsDB()
      events.DeleteEvent(itemId)

   End If

   ' Redirect back to the portal home page
   Response.Redirect(CType(ViewState("UrlReferrer"), String))

End Sub
```

The *CancelBtn_Click* Event Handler

This method simply redirects the user back to the page they were on before they came to
EditEvent.aspx.

```
Private Sub CancelBtn_Click(ByVal sender As Object, ByVal e As EventArgs) _
    Handles cancelButton.Click

    ' Redirect back to the portal home page
    Response.Redirect(CType(ViewState("UrlReferrer"), String))

End Sub
```

Displaying Events

The Events.ascx user control takes care of displaying the events to the user. This control allows the
user to see events depending upon different criteria that they specify. A user with administration access
is shown links to edit a particular event or add a new event.

Here is what the control will look like:

The functionality we want from our calendar is that only the dates that have events should appear as selectable (hyperlinked). And when the user clicks on a particular day, events for that date should be displayed in the `DataList` control below. Also, to increase the efficiency of our application, we only load the data for a single month at a time and as the user selects a new month in the calendar control, data for that month is loaded.

Using the `Calendar` Control

Our user control uses the `Calendar` control to provide users with an easy to understand interface. The `Calendar` control is one of the new rich web controls that ships with ASP.NET. Following the pattern of other web controls, the `Calendar` control is able to generate UI (user interface) appropriate to the browser viewing the control. So, if your browser supports DHTML then a rich interface will be generated, and if your browser supports just HTML then an appropriate downgraded version of the `Calendar` will be displayed.

The `Calendar` control supports templates so it's very easy to modify the style of rendering the control. In this module we will be using some of the important events of the `Calendar` control.

We won't look at all of the HTML for the `Events.ascx` control but here is a rundown of the controls that it includes:

Control	Control Name	Description
DesktopModuleTitle	Title1	Used to display the title for the module.
Calendar	myCalendar	Used to highlight the dates of events.
DropDownList	ViewByList	Used to select different criteria to view the events.
DataList	myDataList	Used to display event details.

Defining Custom Templates

One part of the HTML for the control that is worth looking at is the custom templates for our `DataList` control that we define so that we can format them how we want them:

```
<asp:datalist id="myDataList" runat="server" Width="98%" CellPadding="4">
  <HeaderTemplate>
    <asp:label id="eventsMessage" runat="server"
    Text="<%# dataListTitle %>" CssClass="ItemTitle">
    </asp:label>
  </HeaderTemplate>
  <ItemTemplate>
    <SPAN class="ItemTitle">
```

```
        <asp:HyperLink id="editLink" runat="server"
        Visible="<%# IsEditable %>"
        NavigateUrl='<%# "~/DesktopModules/EditEvents.aspx?ItemID="
        &amp; DataBinder.Eval(Container.DataItem,"ItemID") &amp;
        "&amp;mid=" &amp; ModuleId %>'
        ImageUrl="~/images/edit.gif">
        </asp:HyperLink>
        <asp:Label id="Label1" runat="server"
        Text='<%# DataBinder.Eval(Container.DataItem,"Title") %>'>
        </asp:Label>
        </SPAN><BR>
        <SPAN class="Normal">
        <I>
        <%# DataBinder.Eval(Container.DataItem,"EventDate","{0:D}") %>
        -
        <%# DataBinder.Eval(Container.DataItem,"WhereWhen") %>
        </I>
        </SPAN><BR>
        <SPAN class="Normal">
        <%# DataBinder.Eval(Container.DataItem,"Description") %>
        </SPAN><BR>
    </ItemTemplate>
</asp:datalist>
```

In the above `DataList`, we define a `HeaderTemplate` and place a `Label` control there; this `Label` will be used to display the heading for the `DataList`. Then we define an `ItemTemplate`. The first control in the `ItemTemplate` is a HyperLink control. This control's `Visible` property is set by checking the `IsEditable` property that is exposed by the `PortalModuleControl`. This helps us control the visibility of the edit button for only those users who have the appropriate authorizations to edit the controls. The other items in the `ItemTemplate` define the layout of each item.

The *Page_Load* Event Handler

In the `Page_Load` method we check the `IsPostBack` property of the `Page` and, if the page is being loaded for the first time, we call two methods `FillCalendar` and `BuildList`. The `FillCalendar` method populates our calendar control by marking up the event dates using the date passed to it, while the `BuildList` method builds our `DropDownList` control, which is used to display various view categories.

```
Private Sub Page_Load(ByVal sender As System.Object, _
    ByVal e As System.EventArgs) Handles MyBase.Load

  ' Check if page is loaded for first time
  If Not Page.IsPostBack Then
    ' Call a method to fill the calendar
    FillCalendar(myCalendar.TodaysDate)
    BuildList()
  End If

End Sub
```

The FillCalendar Method

This method is used to mark the dates that have events in the calendar, so that users can select them.

This method takes care of loading the calendar control as well as showing the relevant events in the DataList.

```
Private Sub FillCalendar(ByVal showDate As System.DateTime)

    Dim events As New ASPNetPortal.EventsDB()
    Dim monthlyEvents As New DataSet()

    ' Get events for the month
    monthlyEvents = events.GetMonthlyEvents(ModuleId, showDate)

    If monthlyEvents.Tables(0).Rows.Count <> 0 Then

        ' Create a DataView out of the DataSet
        Dim dayView As New DataView(monthlyEvents.Tables(0))

        If Me.myCalendar.SelectedDate = Nothing Then

            ' Filter the events for the current date
            dayView.RowFilter = "EventDate = #" & _
                Me.myCalendar.TodaysDate.ToString() & "#"
            dataListTitle = "Events for Today!"
        Else

            ' Filter the events for the selected date
            dayView.RowFilter = "EventDate = #" & _
                myCalendar.SelectedDate.ToString() & "#"
            dataListTitle = "Events for the date :" & _
                myCalendar.SelectedDate.ToShortDateString()
            ViewByList.ClearSelection()

        End If
        If dayView.Count > 0 Then

            ' Databind the DataList
            myDataList.DataSource = dayView
            myDataList.DataBind()

        End If

    End If

    If (monthlyEvents.Tables(0).Rows.Count) Then

        ' Populate an Array with the Dates for Events
        ReDim dateDR(monthlyEvents.Tables(0).Rows.Count)
        Dim i As Integer

        For i = 0 To (monthlyEvents.Tables(0).Rows.Count - 1)
```

```
        dateDR(i) = monthlyEvents.Tables(0).Rows(i)("EventDate")

    Next i

  End If

End Sub
```

In the code above we first create an `EventDB` object and then call its `GetMonthlyEvents` method by passing the date from input parameter. Recall that the `GetMonthlyEvents` method returns a `DataSet` containing the details of all events for that particular month.

We then check the `SelectedDate` property of the calendar control, if this property is `Nothing` it indicates we are loading the control for the first time, so we create a `DataView` object from the `DataSet` and use its `RowFilter` property to filter all the events for the current date. Therefore, when the page first loads, if there are any events for the current day, they are displayed in the `DataList`.

```
If Me.myCalendar.SelectedDate = Nothing Then

    ' Filter the events for the current date
    dayView.RowFilter = "EventDate = #" & _
        Me.myCalendar.TodaysDate.ToString() & "#"
    dataListTitle = "Events for Today!"
```

In the case that `SelectedDate` property is not `Nothing`, it contains the date the user has clicked in the calendar control, so we use the `RowFilter` property of the `DataView` object to filter events for the selected date.

```
    dayView.RowFilter = "EventDate = #" & _
        myCalendar.SelectedDate.ToString() & "#"
    dataListTitle = "Events for the date :" & _
        myCalendar.SelectedDate.ToShortDateString()
    ViewByList.ClearSelection()
```

Also note that we have to wrap the data parameter in # (hash) while constructing a query for the `RowFilter` property since `RowFiler` property requires the `DateTime` type to be bound within hashes (#).

Then, the `DataView` is bound to the `DataList`.

```
If dayView.Count > 0 Then

  ' Databind the DataList
  myDataList.DataSource = dayView
  myDataList.DataBind()

End If
```

In the second part of this method we populate a page level variable array `dateDR` with the event dates. We need to do this since, in the `DayRender` event handler of the calendar control, we need to determine if the particular date has an event and then appropriately change its rendering. Since we already have the `DataSet` filled with monthly event details, it's a good idea to fill the array in this method itself. We iterate over the `DataRowCollection` of the table and fill up the `dateDR` array:

```
If (monthlyEvents.Tables(0).Rows.Count) Then

    ' Populate an Array with the Dates for Events
    ReDim dateDR(monthlyEvents.Tables(0).Rows.Count)
    Dim i As Integer

    For i = 0 To (monthlyEvents.Tables(0).Rows.Count - 1)

      dateDR(i) = monthlyEvents.Tables(0).Rows(i)("EventDate")

    Next i
End If
```

The BuildList Method

The `BuildList` method is used to build the `DropDownList`, which will be used to display various criteria that a user can select to display events. These criteria are:

❑   View All Events

❑   View Current Month's Events

❑   View Events meant for All Users

❑   View Event for particular roles the user belongs to

Here is the method:

```
Private Sub BuildList ()
  Dim viewOptions As New ArrayList()
  ' Add Custom options
  viewOptions.Add("Select Option")
  viewOptions.Add("All Events")
  viewOptions.Add("Current Month's Events")
  viewOptions.Add("Events for All Users")

  ' Get all roles for the current user
  Dim userRoles As New UsersDB()
  Dim roles As SqlDataReader = _
      userRoles.GetRolesByUser(Context.User.Identity.Name)
  ' Add the roles
  While roles.Read
    viewOptions.Add("Events for " & CType(roles("RoleName"), String))
  End While
  roles.Close()

  ' Databind the DropDownList
  ViewByList.DataSource = viewOptions
  ViewByList.DataBind()

End Sub
```

The method above is pretty simple; we create an `ArrayList` and add all the view options we need. Then we loop over the roles the current user belongs to, to build additional view filters. Finally, we databind the `DropDownList` to the `ArrayList`.

Event Handlers for Calendar Control

The `Calendar` control exposes a rich set of events that can be used to gain customized functionality out of the control. In order for our `Calendar` control to work we need to handle the three events described below.

The DayRender Event

This event is raised before each day of the `Calendar` control is rendered to the browser. The purpose of this event is to fine tune the display of each date in the control. The `DayRenderEventArgs` parameter available in this method exposes two important properties `Cell` and `Day`. The `Cell` property allows you to set the styling of table cell that displays the date. So you can set things like `BorderColor`, `BackColor`, `ForeColor` etc. for each cell generated. The `Day` property gives you information of the day that's currently being rendered. You can use the `Day` property to compare and select dates as per your criteria.

There are a lot of things you could do here, like add some text next to selected days, add custom colouring for different cells which can be used to easily identify different kinds of days etc.

We just want to ensure that only days with events can be selected and that the days that have events are clearly shown.

Here is our event handler:

```
Private Sub myCalendar_DayRender(ByVal sender As System.Object, _
        ByVal e As System.Web.UI.WebControls.DayRenderEventArgs) _
        Handles myCalendar.DayRender

    ' Check for dates array
    If Not IsNothing(dateDR) Then

        ' Search for the current date in the Array
        If Array.BinarySearch(dateDR, e.Day.Date) < 0 Then

            ' If not found then make the Cell un-selectable
            e.Day.IsSelectable = False

        Else

            ' Setup some Cell properties
            e.Cell.BorderColor = Color.Maroon
            e.Cell.BorderWidth = Unit.Pixel(2)

        End If

    End If

    ' Set special background for Today's date
    If e.Day.IsToday Then
```

```
         e.Cell.BackColor = Color.LightGray

      End If

   End Sub
```

We use the `BinarySearch` method of the `Array` object to search for the occurrence of the particular day been rendered within the `dateDR` array populated in the `FillCalendar` method.

```
      If Array.BinarySearch(dateDR, e.Day.Date) < 0 Then
```

If the day was not in the array, we set its `IsSelectable` property to false

```
         e.Day.IsSelectable = False
```

Otherwise, we color the day with a maroon border.

```
         e.Cell.BorderColor = Color.Maroon
         e.Cell.BorderWidth = Unit.Pixel(2)
```

The VisibleMonthChanged Event

This event is raised when the user navigates to a different month in the calendar control. The `MonthChangedEventArgs` parameter passed in this method contains information of previous month's date and the new month's date. As we've mentioned before, for efficiency we will just load the current month's events. Therefore, for every month change we need to call the `FillCalendar` method to load events for that month.

```
   Private Sub myCalender_VisibleMonthChanged(ByVal sender As System.Object, _
      ByVal e As MonthChangedEventArgs) _
      Handles myCalendar.VisibleMonthChanged

   FillCalendar(e.NewDate)
   End Sub
```

The SelectionChanged Event

This event is raised whenever the user clicks on a new day in the calendar. This event is useful when you want to display particular information depending upon the date selected. An important point to note is that if you programmatically select a day and if the user clicks on the same day then this event will not be raised, since the day has already been selected. Also in case you have made multiple date selections programmatically and if the user clicks on any of the days, all your multiple selection dates are lost upon postback and you can only reference the date the user clicked.

In our implementation we just pass the selected date to the `FillCalendar` method, which will appropriately display the selected day's events in the `DataList`.

```
Private Sub myCalender_SelectionChanged(ByVal sender As System.Object, _
    ByVal e As EventArgs) Handles myCalendar.SelectionChanged

        FillCalendar(myCalendar.SelectedDate)

End Sub
```

Changing Viewing Options

We set the `AutoPostBack` property of the `ViewByList DropDownList` to True. Therefore as soon as the user selects a new item, the page is posted back and the `SelectedIndexChanged` event is raised. In this method we check the value of the `SelectedItem` and then display the events in the `DataList` accordingly.

```
Private Sub ViewByList_SelectedIndexChanged(ByVal sender As System.Object, _
    ByVal e As System.EventArgs) _
    Handles ViewByList.SelectedIndexChanged

  Dim events As New ASPNetPortal.EventsDB()
  ' Select a case
  Select Case ViewByList.SelectedItem.Text
    Case "Select Option"
      ' Default option
      Exit Select
    Case "All Events"
      ' Show all Events
      dataListTitle = "All Events"
      myDataList.DataSource = events.GetEvents(ModuleId)
      myDataList.DataBind()
    Case "Current Month's Events"
      ' Show current month's events
      dataListTitle = "Current Month's Events"
      myDataList.DataSource = events.GetMonthlyEvents(ModuleId, _
          Me.myCalendar.TodaysDate)
      myDataList.DataBind()
    Case "Events for All Users"
      ' Filter the events based on role
      dataListTitle = "Events for All Users"
      Dim userView As New DataView(events.GetEvents(ModuleId).Tables(0))
      userView.RowFilter = "AuthorizedViewRoles LIKE '%All Users%'"
      myDataList.DataSource = userView
      myDataList.DataBind()
    Case Else
      ' Filter the events based on role selected
      dataListTitle = ViewByList.SelectedItem.Text
      ' Extract the Role name from the item
      Dim userView As New DataView(events.GetEvents(ModuleId).Tables(0))
      userView.RowFilter = "AuthorizedViewRoles LIKE '%" & _
```

```
            ViewByList.SelectedItem.Text.Substring(11) & "%'"
        myDataList.DataSource = userView
        myDataList.DataBind()
    End Select

End Sub
```

In the above code, we use the `Select Case` statement to filter the different values from the `dropdownlist`. In any case, we create an `EventsDB` object and call the appropriate method to retrieve the events and `databind` it to the `DataList`. In the last two cases we need to filter the events based upon the role. Recall that we store the values in the `AuthorizedViewRoles` column in a semicolon separated list, so we have used the SQL `LIKE` operator to filter out the events as shown below:

```
userView.RowFilter = "AuthorizedViewRoles LIKE '%All Users%'"
```

A limitation of the above approach is that if there are roles with clashing names like `'Administrators'` and `'System Administrators'` then incorrect data will be selected. In that case you will have to split the value from the `AuthorizedViewRoles` column and then check each `DataRow` (we have adopted a similar method in the `EventsDB` class). Using the above filtering technique you can build multiple different kinds of search criteria; like allowing the user to view events for two or more roles together or, the user could enter their search criteria in a textbox and the appropriately filtered records are delivered to him.

Configuration

In order to use this module you will have to configure the module in the portal. Sign in to the portal as **administrator** and switch to the **Admin** tab.

In the **Admin Tab** under the **Module Definitions** header **Add New Module** go to the **Add Module Type Definition** page. Enter the **Friendly Name** as 'Shared Calendar' and the `Desktop Source` as "DesktopModules/Events.ascx" then click on **Update** to add the new module to your portal. Now you can easily add the new module to any of your pages using the **Tabs** module from the **Admin** page.

Looking Ahead

We have added some additional functionality to our events module but there is still plenty more that could be done. Here are some suggestions:

❑ **Paging** – Currently the `DataList` control in the module shows all the events together. If your company has a very busy events schedule you might want to use paging on the list of events. The `DataList` control by itself does not support pagination but you can write this custom functionality yourself. Of course, you will have to modify the business tier to meet your requirements. You might also think of switching to a `DataGrid` control which supports automatic pagination.

❏ **Event Reminders** – There are cases where your company would like to send out reminders before each event, or allow users to selectively pick events they want to receive notification about. Notifications could be in any form like e-mails or instant messenger alerts or maybe mobile SMS messages.

❏ **Event Registrations** – There are many times a company needs to reserve seats for their employees at some third party event. In such cases, they need to first find out the list of users willing to participate in the external event and then book seats accordingly. Instead of the event manager running from user to user asking for his preference, an event registration module can be set up, where the users wishing to attend a event can register. Accordingly the event manager can make bookings.

❏ **Time Details** – If you plan to use this module as a shared time planner, you could write a control that details the hours of the particular day and lists events and announcements on a per-hour basis. The `SelectionChanged` event of the `Calendar` control could be utilized to pass the day information to your time control.

Summary

In this chapter, we built a module that is heavily based on the original events module supplied with IBuySpy.

We extended the module in a few ways:

❏ We converted the data access to use a common database access class

❏ We added code to support viewing events by months

❏ We added functionality to restrict which users see which events

❏ We enhanced the user interface by adding a calendar control and the ability to filter events in different ways

Solution
BM
Reference
System
System.Data
System.Drawing
System.Web
System.XML
AssemblyInfo.vb
Assembly
BM.vsdisco
Global.asax
Styles.css
Web.config
WebForm1.aspx
WebForm1.aspx* | WebForm1.aspx

ebForm1.aspx*

Content Management

An important feature of an intranet is the ability for users to share information with each other. We have already seen some methods for enabling users to share information, such as the discussions module that we looked at in Chapter 5, or the shared calendar that we extended in Chapter 6, but what about more general information? It would be good to allow users to share information that is slightly less structured than that allowed by the discussions or events modules; giving them more freedom in how they present it.

In our intranet, we refer to this ability for users to share less structured information as *content management*. The term 'content management' is used with different meanings in a variety of contexts. Here, we are specifically referring to content that is shared between users of the intranet.

In this chapter, we will be building a content management module that will allow users to easily format information in the way that they want to and share it with other users.

We will look at:

❑   What features we think a good content management system should have

❑   Creating reusable controls to support our development

❑   Displaying content to users of the intranet

❑   Allowing authorized users to format and publish content through an easy to use interface

Features of a Content Management System

Let's start with a discussion of the features that we think our content management module will need to have in order to be a valuable part of our intranet.

Content Authoring

An important feature of our module will be the ability for users to create content – without that, there will be no content for the system to manage!

We want to make the process of authoring content as easy as possible for users, as our intranet will have some non-technical users. This means that we will not be able to rely on users being able to add HTML tags to their content to create formatting. We will need to provide an interface that allows them to format content in the way they would in a word processor – by selecting text and clicking a button.

We will refer to this ability for users to apply formatting without HTML knowledge as *rich text editing*.

Content Administration

Business information has a tendency to change from time to time. The information that is published in a company's intranet is no exception. If the information on the intranet becomes out of date, its value will be depreciated.

Our content management module needs to allow users to update the content they share. It also needs to allow users to remove content that is no longer appropriate.

Content Scheduling

Sometimes information could be time sensitive. In these situations, it is important that the content is scheduled to appear at the right time.

Let's assume that the company has decided to be generous with its employees and wants to announce a sale on every item in its store for the holiday season. This announcement (content) should appear to the employees of the company on the Content Management System only during the holiday season and should automatically disappear (expire) when the holiday season is over.

Our module will need to allow each item of content to be scheduled to appear over a particular date range.

Related Content

Content is never an isolated piece of information. Sometimes it makes sense to relate content with some other content to explain it better.

A good example of related content is the MSDN .NET Framework SDK documentation. For example, when you look at the content for the Delegate class in the .NET Framework Class Library, at the end of the document you will see the **See Also** section that points you to several documents related to the Delegate class. By following the links in the **See Also** section, you realize that these documents are related to Delegate class. Seeing the related content makes it easier to understand the concepts.

Our module will need to allow content items to be linked to other content items in an easy to use manner.

Targeted Content

Sometimes content items should not be shown to every user of the intranet. This may be because the information is confidential and should not be shared with everyone. Alternatively, it may simply be that the content is only of interest to some users and we do not want to waste the time of other users.

Targeting content means that we can decide which users should see which content items. Our module should allow content items to be targeted at specific groups of intranet users.

Search

Once there is a reasonable amount of content in our intranet, finding specific content items may become an issue. A keyword based search system can provide a good solution to this problem, helping users to locate the content that they need.

Our module should provide a search interface that will search content items based on keywords.

A Summary Of Features

Here is a summary of the features we require from our module:

- ❑ Content authoring with rich text editing
- ❑ Scheduling of content to appear in a specified date range
- ❑ The ability to relate content items
- ❑ Targeting of content at specific groups of users
- ❑ Keyword search of content items

Module Design

Our content management module will use the same architecture that we have seen for other modules in our intranet:

- ❑ A database with stored procedures that provide access to the data
- ❑ A business component that uses the stored procedures
- ❑ A presentation layer consisting of controls and pages

The rest of this chapter will look at these layers and show how they are implemented in our module.

The Database

The database design is fairly simple, consisting of two tables. The following image shows how the Content Management System's database tables are designed and related.

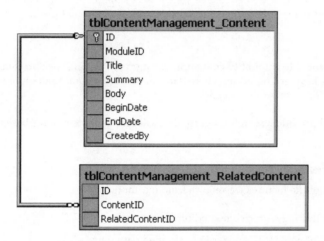

The table `tblContentManagement_Content` is used to store the main content. Each content item will have title, summary and body sections. The content table also saves a begin date and an end date for each content item. The begin date and end dates in this table are going to be used in **content scheduling**.

The column `ModuleID` identifies the module instance that each content item belongs to. As we saw in Chapter 2, this module ID will allow multiple instances of our module to exist independently in the intranet, by separating their data.

We use the table `tblContentManagement_RelatedContent` to store the related content details. Each entry in the related content table points to another content item in the content table as a related content item.

Stored Procedures

A set of stored procedures is used to manipulate the data in the database tables. The stored procedures can be found in the support material with a prefix `upContentManagement`.

Most of the procedures deal with content items themselves:

- ❏ `upContentManagement_DeleteContent` deletes a specified content item
- ❏ `upContentManagement_EditContent` makes changes to a content item
- ❏ `upContentManagement_GetContent` retrieves the details of a specific content item

- ❑ `upContentManagement_SaveContent` creates a new content item
- ❑ `upContentManagement_SearchContent` returns content items that have specified keywords in their title or summary
- ❑ `upContentManagement_ViewContent` returns all content items for an instance of the content management module that should be displayed (i.e. we are inside their scheduled date range)
- ❑ `upContentManagement_ViewMyContent` returns all content created by a specified user

We also have three procedures that deal with the relationship between content items:

- ❑ `upContentManagement_ClearRelatedContent` removes the content item relationships for a specified content item
- ❑ `upContentManagement_SaveRelatedContent` adds a new content item relationship
- ❑ `upContentManagement_ViewRelatedContent` returns details of the content items that are related to a particular item

We won't look at all of these procedures in detail here, as many of them are very simple but we will examine some of the more interesting ones. You can find the complete code for all the stored procedures in the code download for this book.

It is worth noting that the `upContentManagement_GetContent` procedure checks whether content items should be displayed today by comparing the `BeginDate` and `EndDate` columns to the SQL `GETDATE()` function:

```
CREATE PROCEDURE upContentManagement_GetContent
(
@ContentID As Int
)
AS
    SELECT c.ID, c.Title, c.Summary, c.Body, c.BeginDate, c.EndDate, c.ModuleID
    FROM tblContentManagement_Content c
    WHERE (c.ID = @ContentID AND GETDATE() <= c.EndDate
        AND GETDATE() >= c.BeginDate)
GO
```

The `upContentManagement_ViewRelatedContent` procedure uses a join to return the details of the content items that are related to a content item in the `tblContentManagement_RelatedContent` table.

```
CREATE PROCEDURE upContentManagement_ViewRelatedContent
(
@ContentID As int
)
AS
    SELECT DISTINCT(c.ID), c.Title, c.Summary, c.BeginDate, c.ModuleID
    FROM tblContentManagement_Content c
    INNER JOIN tblContentManagement_RelatedContent RelCon
        ON (RelatedContentID = c.ID)
    WHERE (RelCon.ContentID = @ContentID  AND GETDATE() <= c.EndDate AND GETDATE()
>= c.BeginDate)
    ORDER BY c.BeginDate DESC
GO
```

Note also that `SELECT DISTINCT` is used in order to avoid returning duplicate items.

The procedure, `upContentManagement_DeleteContent`, implements the access rights check before deleting the content. If the logged-in user is the owner of the content, then the procedure clears all related content entries in the related content table and then deletes the main content itself. If the logged-in user is not the owner of the content, an error will be thrown:

```
CREATE PROCEDURE upContentManagement_DeleteContent
(
     @ContentID As int,
     @CreatedBy As varchar(200)
)

AS

     DECLARE @Owner varchar(200)

     SET @Owner = ( SELECT CreatedBy
                    FROM tblContentManagement_Content
                    WHERE ID = @ContentID
                  )

IF ( @Owner = @CreatedBy )

     BEGIN

     --First Delete Related Content
     DELETE tblContentManagement_RelatedContent
     WHERE ContentID = @ContentID OR
          RelatedContentID = @ContentID
     --Then Delete the actual Content itself
     DELETE tblContentManagement_Content
     WHERE ID = @ContentID

     END

ELSE
     BEGIN
        RAISERROR ('Not Authorized to delete this content', 16,1)
     END
GO
```

The `upContentManagement_SearchContent` procedure uses the SQL `LIKE` keyword to find items that have a keyword in their title or summary:

```
CREATE PROCEDURE upContentManagement_SearchContent
(
@KeyWord as varchar(50),
@ModuleID As int
)
AS
     SELECT DISTINCT(c.ID), c.Title, c.Summary, c.BeginDate, c.ModuleID
```

```
       FROM tblContentManagement_Content c
       WHERE (c.ModuleID = @ModuleID AND GETDATE() <= c.EndDate AND
             GETDATE() >= c.BeginDate)   AND
             (c.Title LIKE '%' + @KeyWord + '%'
             OR c.Summary LIKE '%' + @KeyWord + '%')
       ORDER BY c.BeginDate DESC
   GO
```

The Business Component

We are going to encapsulate the Content Management functionality into a component called
ContentManagement (you can find this class in the Components folder by the name
ContentManagementDB.vb). This class can be found in the namespace
Wrox.Intranet.ContentManagement.Components and the class definition is shown below:

```
Namespace Wrox.Intranet.ContentManagement.Components
    Public Class ContentManagement
```

The ContentManagement class contains a set of public methods that are exposed to presentation layer.
They, in turn, make use of the stored procedures we saw in the last section.

The class has the following methods:

- ❏ ViewContent – calls upContentManagement_ViewContent to return all content items for
  a particular instance of the content management module

- ❏ ViewMyContent – calls upContentManagement_ViewMyContent to return all content
  created by a specified user

- ❏ GetContent – calls upContentManagement_GetContent to return details of a particular
  content item

- ❏ AddContent – calls upContentManagement_SaveContent to add a new content item to
  the database

- ❏ EditContent – calls upContentManagement_EditContent to make changes to a
  content item

- ❏ DeleteContent – calls upContentManagement_DeleteContent to remove a content item

- ❏ SearchContent – calls upContentManagement_SearchContent to perform a search

- ❏ AddRelatedContent – calls upContentManagement_ClearRelatedContent and
  upContentManagement_SaveRelatedContent to update the related content for an item

- ❏ ViewRelatedContent – calls upContentManagement_ViewRelatedContent to return
  all content items related to a specified item

255

As you can see, most of these methods have a one-to-one relationship with one of the stored procedures that we discussed in the previous section.

Handling Errors

This class also exposes a public property, ErrorMessage, as a string to return the error message to the presentation layer if an error occurs.

```
Private _errorMessage As String
Public ReadOnly Property ErrorMessage() As String
    Get
        Return _errorMessage
    End Get
End Property
```

As with the stored procedures, we will not be looking at all of the methods of ContentManagement in detail. Most of them simply use our common Database class (detailed in Appendix A) to call the relevant stored procedure. You can see the full code for the class in the code download.

The ViewContent Method

As an example, let's have a look at the ViewContent method. This method returns all the content items from an instance of the content management module that should be displayed today. It does this by calling the upContentManagement_ViewContent stored procedure:

```
Public Function ViewContent(ByVal ModuleID As Integer) As SqlDataReader

    Dim db As New Wrox.Intranet.DataTools.Database()
    Dim dr As SqlDataReader
    Dim params(0) As SqlParameter

    Try
       params(0) = db.MakeParameter("@ModuleID", ModuleID)
       db.RunProcedure("upContentManagement_ViewContent", params, dr)
       If dr Is Nothing Then
          _errorMessage = db.ErrorMessage
       End If
    Catch e As Exception
       _errorMessage = "Unable to view content [" & e.Message & "]"
       dr = Nothing
    End Try

    Return dr
End Function
```

First, we create a new instance of our `Database` class. (Remember, there are full details of this class in Appendix A). We also create a `SqlDataReader` to contain the results and a `SqlParameter` array to contain the parameter we will send to the stored procedure:

```
Dim db As New Wrox.Intranet.DataTools.Database()
Dim dr As SqlDataReader
Dim params(0) As SqlParameter
```

We then start a `Try` statement so that we can catch any errors that occur, create the `SqlParameter` that we require and run the procedure:

```
Try
    params(0) = db.MakeParameter("@ModuleID", ModuleID)
    db.RunProcedure("upContentManagement_ViewContent", params, dr)
```

We need to check at this stage whether `SqlDataReader` was successfully filled. If it was not, we store the error message from the `Database` class so that the code that calls the method can access it:

```
If dr Is Nothing Then
    _errorMessage = db.ErrorMessage
End If
```

If an exception occurs, we store the exception details in the error message:

```
Catch e As Exception
    _errorMessage = "Unable to view content [" & e.Message & "]"
    dr = Nothing
End Try
```

The *AddRelatedContent* Method

The `AddRelatedContent` method is interesting because it uses two stored procedures.

Here is the complete method:

```
Public Function AddRelatedContent(ByVal ContentID As Integer, _
                            ByVal RelatedContent() As Object) As Integer

    Dim result As Integer
    Dim db As New Wrox.Intranet.DataTools.Database()
    Dim params_Clear(0) As SqlParameter
    Dim params(1) As SqlParameter
    Dim Counter As Integer = 0

    Try
        params_Clear(0) = db.MakeParameter("@ContentID", ContentID)
        'Clear the existing items
        db.RunProcedure("upContentManagement_ClearRelatedContent", _
                                                    params_Clear)
```

```
            Do While (Counter < RelatedContent.Length)
                params(0) = db.MakeParameter("@ContentID", ContentID)
                params(1) = db.MakeParameter("@RelatedContentID", _
                                     CType(RelatedContent(Counter), Integer))
            result = db.RunProcedure("upContentManagement_SaveRelatedContent", _
                                                                        params)

                Counter += 1
            Loop
        Catch e As Exception
            _errorMessage = "Unable to edit the content [" & e.Message & "]"
            result = -1
        Finally
            db = Nothing
        End Try

        Return result

    End Function
```

The first procedure call is to `upContentManagement_ClearRelatedContent`, to remove the current related content for the item.

```
        db.RunProcedure("upContentManagement_ClearRelatedContent", _
                                                         params_Clear)
```

We then loop over all of the related content items passed to the method, calling `upContentManagement_SaveRelatedContent` to add each relationship to the database.

```
        Do While (Counter < RelatedContent.Length)
            params(0) = db.MakeParameter("@ContentID", ContentID)
            params(1) = db.MakeParameter("@RelatedContentID", _
                                 CType(RelatedContent(Counter), Integer))
        result = db.RunProcedure("upContentManagement_SaveRelatedContent", _
                                                                    params)

            Counter += 1
        Loop
```

We remove all relationships before adding the specified relationships because, this way, the method can be used to make all changes to the related content on an item. Whether the user needs to remove related content or add related content, the method will do the job. Our user interface will work by retrieving the relationships, allowing users to make changes and then sending the updated list to this method.

The Presentation Layer

We now come to the final layer of our module – the presentation layer that will provide the user interface. This has several parts:

❑   Two controls for interface elements

❑   A control for displaying summaries of content items

❑   A page that allows content items to be added or edited

❑   A page that displays related content for a content item

❑   A page that displays all of the content authored by the current user

❑   A page that enables users to search content items by keyword

Reusable User Controls

There are some user interface elements that we will need to use more than once in the code that implements our module. It makes sense to create these elements as controls that we can reuse. This means that we only have to develop them once and, if we want to make changes to them, we only have to do so in one place.

Content Module Title User Control

The `ContentModuleTitle.ascx` user control encapsulates the functionality to display the title of the module. It also displays hyperlinks to add the content, search the content, and view all content that is published by a logged-in user. This sounds simple, but don't forget that we need to implement security checks for the access rights to see if a logged-in user has access to these hyperlinks when we display the module header.

Here is an example of the control in action:

Developer News   Add Content Search My Content

XML Web Services Overview
7/1/2002
An XML Web service is a programmable entity that provides a particular element of functionality, such as application logic, and is accessible to any number of potentially disparate systems using ubiquitous Internet standards, such as XML and HTTP. XML Web services depend heavily upon the broad acceptance of XML and other Internet standards to create an infrastructure that supports application interoperability at a level that solves many of the problems that previously hindered such attempts.

As you can see from the above picture, the header portion of the module displays the necessary hyperlinks to manage the content (such as `Add Content`, `Search` and `My Content`).

Now let's see how to implement the above user control to display a module's name and the hyperlinks to manage the content, based on the user's roles.

ContentModuleTitle.ascx

This user control's codebehind class (ContentModuleTitle) is inherited from the user control base class System.Web.UI.UserControl as shown below:

```
Namespace Wrox.Intranet.ContentManagement.Controls

    Public MustInherit Class ContentModuleTitle
        Inherits System.Web.UI.UserControl
```

This class has the following Protected fields declared:

```
Protected ModuleTitle As System.Web.UI.WebControls.Label
Protected EditBLink As System.Web.UI.WebControls.HyperLink
Protected SearchLink As System.Web.UI.WebControls.HyperLink
Protected MyContentLink As System.Web.UI.WebControls.HyperLink
```

The ModuleTitle is a Label control and is used to display the name of the module. The three HyperLink controls are used to display the hyperlinks **Add Content**, **Search** and **My Content**. To set properties for the above Hyperlink controls, the ContentModuleTitle class exposes the following Public members:

```
'Edit Text
Public EditText As [String] = Nothing
Public EditUrl As [String] = Nothing
Public EditTarget As [String] = Nothing

'Search Text
Public SearchText As [String] = Nothing
Public SearchUrl As [String] = Nothing
Public SearchTarget As [String] = Nothing

'My Content Text
Public MyContentText As [String] = Nothing
Public MyContentUrl As [String] = Nothing
Public MyContentTarget As [String] = Nothing
```

The permission checks to display the hyperlinks for the logged-in user are in the Page_Load method of the user control class. As you would imagine, the permissions are driven by the role that the user belongs to:

```
Private Sub Page_Load(ByVal sender As System.Object, _
        ByVal e As System.EventArgs) Handles MyBase.Load

    ' Obtain PortalSettings from Current Context
    Dim portalSettings As portalSettings = _
                CType(HttpContext.Current.Items("PortalSettings"), _
                                            portalSettings)
```

```
        ' Obtain reference to parent portal module
        Dim portalModule As PortalModuleControl = _
                            CType(Me.Parent, PortalModuleControl)
    'Display Module Title Text
    ModuleTitle.Text = portalModule.ModuleConfiguration.ModuleTitle

    ' Check the permissions to display "add" and "my content" links
    If portalSettings.AlwaysShowEditButton = True Or _
        (PortalSecurity.IsInRoles( _
        portalModule.ModuleConfiguration.AuthorizedEditRoles)) Then

        If Not (EditText Is Nothing) Then
            EditButton.Text = EditText
            EditButton.NavigateUrl = EditUrl + "?mid=" + _
                            portalModule.ModuleId.ToString()
            EditButton.Target = EditTarget
        End If

        'Set the My Content Button
        If Not IsNothing(MyContentText) Then
            MyContentButton.Text = MyContentText
            MyContentButton.NavigateUrl = MyContentUrl + "?mid=" _
                    + portalModule.ModuleId.ToString()
            MyContentButton.Target = MyContentTarget
        End If

    End If

    'Set the Search Button
    If Not IsNothing(SearchText) Then
        SearchButton.Text = SearchText
        SearchButton.NavigateUrl = SearchUrl + "?mid=" + _
        portalModule.ModuleId.ToString()
        SearchButton.Target = SearchTarget
    End If
End Sub
```

The first thing we do is to get a `PortalSettings` object that contains the current settings for the portal.

```
Dim portalSettings As portalSettings = _
            CType(HttpContext.Current.Items("PortalSettings"), _
                                            portalSettings)
```

We then need to get a reference to the module control that this header control belongs to:

```
Dim portalModule As PortalModuleControl = _
                        CType(Me.Parent, PortalModuleControl)
```

This allows us to access the title of the module:

```
ModuleTitle.Text = portalModule.ModuleConfiguration.ModuleTitle
```

Next, we check whether we should display the **Add Content** and **My Content** links. To do this, we check whether the module is set up to always allow editing or whether the user is in a role that allows them to edit this module. (See Chapter 4 for more details of roles and role checking)

```
If portalSettings.AlwaysShowEditButton = True Or _
    (PortalSecurity.IsInRoles( _
    portalModule.ModuleConfiguration.AuthorizedEditRoles)) Then
```

If the test is successful, we display the **Add Content** link:

```
If Not (EditText Is Nothing) Then
    EditButton.Text = EditText
    EditButton.NavigateUrl = EditUrl + "?mid=" + _
                        portalModule.ModuleId.ToString()
    EditButton.Target = EditTarget
End If
```

Similar code is used to display the **My Content** link.

The final thing that the `Page_Load` event handler does is to display the search link:

```
If Not IsNothing(SearchText) Then
    SearchButton.Text = SearchText
    SearchButton.NavigateUrl = SearchUrl + "?mid=" + _
    portalModule.ModuleId.ToString()
    SearchButton.Target = SearchTarget
End If
```

Using The `ContentModuleTitle` Control

To use this user control to display a module header, we need to include the `Register` directive at the beginning of the .aspx/.ascx page and set the values for the properties as shown below:

```
<%@ Register TagPrefix="Wrox" TagName="Title" Src="ContentModuleTitle.ascx"%>

. . .

<Wrox:Title Runat="server" ID="ModuleTitle"
EditText="Add Content" EditUrl="EditContent.aspx"
SearchText="Search" SearchUrl="ContentSearch.aspx"
MyContentText="My Content" MyContentUrl="MyContent.aspx" />
```

Now, let's take a look another user control that is used in displaying content action tabs (hyperlinks).

Content Action Tabs User Control

Each content item will be associated with a set of actions based on the logged-in user's access rights. These actions usually include Read, Edit, and Read Related Content in the context of a Content Management System. Take a look at the following picture for a better understanding:

XML Web Services Overview
7/1/2002
An XML Web service is a programmable entity that provides a particular element of functionality, such as application logic, and is accessible to any number of potentially disparate systems using ubiquitous Internet standards, such as XML and HTTP. XML Web services depend heavily upon the broad acceptance of XML and other Internet standards to create an infrastructure that supports application interoperability at a level that solves many of the problems that previously hindered such attempts.

Read Related Content Edit

These actions should be present with each and every content item on the intranet's Content Management System and we are going to encapsulate this functionality into a user control, `ContentActionTabs.ascx`.

ContentActionTabs.ascx

Like the previous control we looked at, `ContentActionTabs` derives from `System.Web.UI.UserControl`:

```
Public MustInherit Class ContentActionTabs
    Inherits System.Web.UI.UserControl
```

This control defines three hyperlink controls and exposes public members so that calling code can set values.

```
Protected ReadButton As System.Web.UI.WebControls.HyperLink
Protected EditButton As System.Web.UI.WebControls.HyperLink
Protected RelatedContentButton As System.Web.UI.WebControls.HyperLink

Public EditText As [String] = Nothing
Public EditUrl As [String] = Nothing
Public EditVisible As [Boolean] = False

Public ReadText As [String] = Nothing
Public ReadUrl As [String] = Nothing

Public RelatedContentText As [String] = Nothing
Public RelatedContentUrl As [String] = Nothing
```

The `Page_Load` method does the processing to set the values for the ReadButton, EditButton and RelatedContentButton hyperlink server controls.

```
Private Sub Page_Load(ByVal sender As System.Object, _
            ByVal e As System.EventArgs) Handles MyBase.Load
    'Check the read text and display the read button
    If Not Me.Page.IsPostBack Then
        If Not (ReadText Is Nothing) Then
            ReadButton.Text = ReadText
            ReadButton.NavigateUrl = ReadUrl
        End If

        'Check the permissions and display the related content
        If Not (RelatedContentText Is Nothing) Then
            RelatedContentButton.Text = RelatedContentText
            RelatedContentButton.NavigateUrl = RelatedContentUrl
        End If

        'Check the permissions and display the edit button
        If EditVisible And (Not IsNothing(EditText)) Then
            EditButton.Text = EditText
            EditButton.NavigateUrl = EditUrl
        End If
    End If
End Sub
```

As we can see, the **Read** button and the **Related Content** button do not check for any access rights, because the access rights for the logged-in user are already verified at the module (category) level. However, to edit the content item, we are checking the `EditVisible` flag, which takes the value from the module `IsEditable` property from the module control (to understand the module control, please refer to Chapter 3).

Using The `ContentActionTabs` Control

Using this user control will be as simple as shown in the code below:

```
<%@ Register TagPrefix="Wrox" TagName="Actions" Src="ContentActionTabs.ascx"%>
. . .
<Wrox:Actions ID="Actions" Runat=server
EditVisible=<%# IsEditable %> EditText="Edit" EditUrl="EditContent.aspx"
ReadText="Read" ReadUrl="GetContent.aspx"
RelatedContentText="Related Content" RelatedContentUrl="RelContent.aspx" />
```

Let's move on to the next section where we actually build the functional features for a Content Management System.

Displaying Content Summaries

We will display the content summary for each module. A logged in user will then click on the read button to read the content or related content button to browse through the related content and so on.

We are going to use a user control to display the content summaries. This control is named `DisplayContentSummary.ascx`. It uses the two user controls that we have discussed earlier in the chapter.

Here is an example that shows two instances of the content management module displaying content summaries:

Developer News

Add Content Search My Content

XML Web Services Overview
7/1/2002
An XML Web service is a programmable entity that provides a particular element of functionality, such as application logic, and is accessible to any number of potentially disparate systems using ubiquitous Internet standards, such as XML and HTTP. XML Web services depend heavily upon the broad acceptance of XML and other Internet standards to create an infrastructure that supports application interoperability at a level that solves many of the problems that previously hindered such attempts.

Read Related Content Edit

Coding Tips

Add Content Search My Content

Using 'using'
1/1/2001
The using statement defines a scope at the end of which an object will be disposed. Read on...

Read Related Content Edit

DisplayContentSummary.ascx

This control belongs to the namespace `Wrox.Intranet.ContentManagement.Controls` namespace, and is inherited from the `PortalModuleControl`. To read more about the `PortalModuleControl` class please refer to Chapter 3.

Here is the HTML part of the control:

```
<%@ Control language="vb"
Inherits="Wrox.Intranet.ContentManagement.Controls.DisplayContentSummary"
CodeBehind="DisplayContentSummary.ascx.vb" AutoEventWireup="false" %>

<%@ Register TagPrefix="Wrox" TagName="Title" Src="ContentModuleTitle.ascx"%>
```

```
<%@ Register TagPrefix="Wrox" TagName="Actions" Src="ContentActionTabs.ascx"%>

<Wrox:Title EditText="Add Content"
            EditUrl="~/DesktopModules/EditContent.aspx"
            SearchText="Search"
            SearchUrl="~/DesktopModules/ContentSearch.aspx"
            MyContentText="My Content"
            MyContentUrl="~/DesktopModules/MyContent.aspx"
            runat="server"
            id="Title1" />

<br>
<asp:Label ID="ErrorMessage" Runat="server" CssClass="NormalRed"></asp:Label>
<asp:DataList id="myDataList" CellPadding="4" Width="98%"
            EnableViewState="false" runat="server">
  <ItemTemplate>
    <span class="ItemTitle">
      <asp:Label Text='<%# DataBinder.Eval(Container.DataItem,"Title") %>'
                 runat="server" ID="Label1"/>
    </span>
    <br>
    <span class="Normal">
      <i>
        <%# DataBinder.Eval(Container.DataItem,"BeginDate", "{0:d}") %>
      </i>
    </span>
    <br>
    <span class="Normal">
      <%# DataBinder.Eval(Container.DataItem,"Summary") %>
    </span>
    <br>
    <p align="right">

      <Wrox:Actions Id="Actions2"
                    Runat=server
                    EditVisible=<%# IsEditable %>
                    EditText="Edit"
                    EditUrl='<%# "EditContent.aspx?ItemID="
                            & DataBinder.Eval(Container.DataItem,"ID")
                            & "&mid=" & ModuleID %>'
                    ReadText="Read"
                    ReadUrl='<%# "GetContent.aspx?ItemID=" &
                    DataBinder.Eval(Container.DataItem,"ID") & "&mid="
                            & ModuleID %>'
                    RelatedContentText="Related Content"
                    RelatedContentUrl='<%# "RelatedContent.aspx?ItemID="
                            & DataBinder.Eval(Container.DataItem,"ID")
                            & "&mid=" & ModuleId %>' />
    </p>
  </ItemTemplate>
  <AlternatingItemStyle BackColor="lightGray"></AlternatingItemStyle>
  <AlternatingItemTemplate>
    <span class="ItemTitle">
```

```
        <asp:Label Text='<%# DataBinder.Eval(Container.DataItem,"Title") %>'
                runat="server" ID="Label2"/>
    </span>
    <br>
    <span class="Normal">
      <i>
        <%# DataBinder.Eval(Container.DataItem,"BeginDate", "{0:d}") %>
      </i>
    </span>
    <br>
    <span class="Normal">
      <%# DataBinder.Eval(Container.DataItem,"Summary") %>
    </span>
    <br>
    <p align="right">

    <Wrox:Actions Id="Actions1" runat=server
                EditVisible=<%# IsEditable %>
                EditText="Edit" EditUrl='<%# "EditContent.aspx?ItemID="
                    & DataBinder.Eval(Container.DataItem,"ID")
                    & "&mid=" & ModuleID %>'
                ReadText="Read" ReadUrl='<%# "GetContent.aspx?ItemID="
                    & DataBinder.Eval(Container.DataItem,"ID") & "&mid="
                    & ModuleID %>'
                RelatedContentText="Related Content"
                RelatedContentUrl='<%# "RelatedContent.aspx?ItemID="
                    & DataBinder.Eval(Container.DataItem,"ID")
                    & "&mid=" & ModuleId %>' />
    </p>
  </AlternatingItemTemplate>
</asp:DataList>
```

As you can see from the code above, we are using the Content Module Title control and the Content Action Tabs control. Along with these two user controls, this control is also using a DataList server control and a Label server control. The Label control is used to display the error message if there is one and the DataList control is used to display the content items.

Let's move to the codebehind for the control, where we have to declare the Label and DataList controls:

```
  Protected WithEvents ErrorMessage As System.Web.UI.WebControls.Label
  Protected WithEvents myDataList As System.Web.UI.WebControls.DataList
```

The Page_Load method is implemented to retrieve the content items and bind them to the DataList control.

```
    Private Sub Page_Load(ByVal sender As System.Object, _
       ByVal e As System.EventArgs) Handles MyBase.Load

       'Get the contents and bind to the DataList Control
```

```
     Dim cm As New _
         Wrox.Intranet.ContentManagement.Components.ContentManagement()
     Dim datareader As SqlDataReader
     datareader = cm.ViewContent(ModuleId)
     myDataList.DataSource = datareader
     If IsNothing(datareader) Then
       ErrorMessage.Text = cm.ErrorMessage
     Else
       myDataList.DataBind()
       datareader.Close()
     End If

   End Sub
```

The method implementation is pretty simple: the module calls the ViewContent function of the ContentManagement class that we discussed earlier.

Now the content summary is available for the logged-in intranet user. The options available with each of the content items are **Read**, **Related Content** and **Edit**. Each one of these options are presented to the user as hyperlinks and each hyperlink exposes a feature of the Content Management System; they are:

❑   Displaying a selected Content Item

❑   Editing an existing Content Item (also adding new content)

❑   Browsing Related Content Items

Let's take a look at the functionality of each of the above in detail.

Displaying a Selected Content Item

The .aspx page for this functionality is GetContent.aspx. The codebehind class for this .aspx page is in the GetContent.aspx.vb file.

The Page_Load method implements the actual process of retrieving the content item and displaying it:

```
     Private Sub Page_Load(ByVal sender As System.Object, _
         ByVal e As System.EventArgs) Handles MyBase.Load

       ' Determine ModuleId
       moduleId = Int32.Parse(Request.Params("Mid"))

       ' Determine ItemId to Update
       If Not (Request.Params("ItemId") Is Nothing) Then
         itemId = Int32.Parse(Request.Params("ItemId"))
       End If

       If Page.IsPostBack = False Then
         If itemId <> 0 Then
           Dim cm As New _
```

```
            Wrox.Intranet.ContentManagement.Components.ContentManagement()
        Dim dr As SqlDataReader = cm.GetContent(itemId)

            ' Read first row from database
            If IsNothing(dr) Then
                ErrorMessage.Text = cm.ErrorMessage
            Else
                dr.Read()
                Title.Text = CType(dr("Title"), String)
                Summary.Text = CType(dr("Summary"), String)
                body.InnerHtml = CType(dr("Body"), String)
                dr.Close()

                ' Verify that the current user has access to edit this module
                If PortalSecurity.HasEditPermissions(moduleId) Then
                    Actions.EditVisible = True
                    Actions.EditText = "Edit"
                    Actions.EditUrl = "EditContent.aspx?ItemID=" & itemId _
                        & "&mid=" & moduleId
                End If

                Actions.RelatedContentText = "Related Content"
                Actions.RelatedContentUrl = "RelatedContent.aspx?ItemID=" _
                    & itemId & "&mid=" & moduleId
            End If
        End If
    End If

End Sub
```

The first thing we do is to extract the module ID and the item ID from the query string sent to the page:

```
moduleId = Int32.Parse(Request.Params("Mid"))

' Determine ItemId to Update
If Not (Request.Params("ItemId") Is Nothing) Then
    itemId = Int32.Parse(Request.Params("ItemId"))
End If
```

Then, if we are not processing a postback, we need to populate the controls on the page. We therefore check whether we are dealing with a postback and also that an item ID has been received, before using our business component to get the details of the requested content item:

```
If Page.IsPostBack = False Then
        If itemId <> 0 Then
            Dim cm As New _
                Wrox.Intranet.ContentManagement.Components.ContentManagement()
            Dim dr As SqlDataReader = cm.GetContent(itemId)
```

If the `SqlDataReader` is not returned, we populate the error message on the page:

```
If IsNothing(dr) Then
   ErrorMessage.Text = cm.ErrorMessage
```

Otherwise, we populate the details of the content item:

```
Else
   dr.Read()
   Title.Text = CType(dr("Title"), String)
   Summary.Text = CType(dr("Summary"), String)
   body.InnerHtml = CType(dr("Body"), String)
   dr.Close()
```

The last thing we need to do is to set up the `ContentActionTabs` control that we use on the page (see the earlier section for details of this control). We check whether the user has edit permissions for this module; if they do, we set up the edit link.

```
If PortalSecurity.HasEditPermissions(moduleId) Then
   Actions.EditVisible = True
   Actions.EditText = "Edit"
   Actions.EditUrl = "EditContent.aspx?ItemID=" & itemId _
         & "&mid=" & moduleId
End If
```

We also set up the related content link:

```
Actions.RelatedContentText = "Related Content"
Actions.RelatedContentUrl = "RelatedContent.aspx?ItemID="  _
         & itemId & "&mid=" & moduleId
```

We now have the ability to display content but this will be a bit pointless if there is no way to get content into the system in the first place – let's move on to talk about how we will enable users to author content.

Content Authoring

We want to make the creation of content very easy for our users, even those who do not have technical knowledge of HTML. We therefore need to provide them with an interface that will allow them to format text without adding their own tags.

We will achieve an easy to use authoring interface by creating a control that will provide Internet Explorer users with WYSIWYG (What You See Is What You Get) editing of content. Once we have created this control, we will use it to provide the edit page for this module.

Rich Text Editor Design

Our goal in this section is to design a Rich Text Editor Server Control that will enable the intranet users to publish and edit rich content with no knowledge of HTML. To achieve this functionality, we will need to provide the following:

❑   Ability to edit/enter the content (could be plain text or some rich content)

❑   Ability to format the content

❑   Ability to extract the HTML from the rich content.

When used on a web form, the server control should look like this:

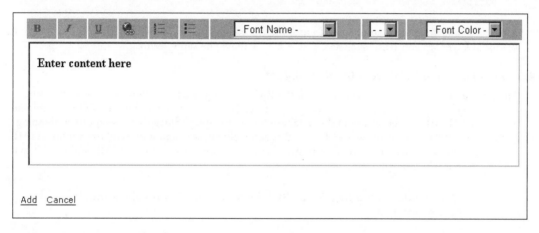

Before we jump into the specifics of the server control, here is an outline of how we are going to achieve the above-mentioned design requirements:

Ability to Edit/Enter the Content

We are going to use the `<Iframe>` element from DHTML to enable to the control's users to be able to edit the rich text. An `<Iframe>` element creates inline-floating frames within an HTML document. But the real cool thing about `Iframes` is that you can programmatically set the HTML Document contained in the `<Iframe>` element to design mode, which means you can edit the HTML document sitting inside the `<Iframe>` element! This will enable the user to edit and enter the rich content.

> **The design mode trick will only work with Internet Explorer and only with versions 5.0 or higher.**

As this technique will only work with Internet Explorer version 5.0 and above, our server control will not work for the Netscape browsers and IE browsers with versions less than 5.0. We therefore need to provide a mechanism to determine the browser version when the control is loaded and then decide to render the control or not. We will see how to handle this problem later on.

Ability to Format the Content

Formatting content is also implemented easily using DHTML and JavaScript on the client side. The rich formatting can be done by calling the execCommand function on the inner HTML document of the <Iframe> element contained in the server control. So, for example, if you select some content in the Rich Text Editor and if you want to make it look bold, the command to do that would be:

```
varIframe.document.execCommand('bold');
```

We will be attaching these commands to user interface elements in our control. The user can also use the usual keyboard shortcuts, such as CTRL + B to achieve the same result.

Ability to extract the HTML from the rich content

Finally, we need to extract the HTML from the Rich Text document contained in the <Iframe> element so that we can process it according to our needs. For example, in our content management system, the HTML will be stored in the database for later display. Since there is no direct mapping between a .NET web control type and an <Iframe> element, we cannot directly extract the HTML from the <Iframe> element – we have to use client-side code to extract the HTML and send it to the server. Here is what we will do:

1. Declare a hidden form field in the Rich Editor Server Control along with the <Iframe> element.

2. Add an OnBlur event to the <Iframe> element that copies the <Iframe> inner HTML document's HTML to the hidden field. This event will fire whenever the user finishes using the rich text box.

3. Since the HTML string is available in the hidden field, we can access it on the server side (in the Rich Edit Control) to extract the HTML.

Now let's move on to the next section where we will dig into some coding specifics.

Developing the Rich Text Editor Server Control

The Server control is inherited from the System.Web.UI.Control base class and also implements InamingContainer and IPostBackDataHandler interfaces.

The `InamingContainer` interface identifies a container control that creates a new ID namespace within a `Page` object's control hierarchy. This is a marker interface only, which means there are no methods to implement when you implement this interface.

The `IpostBackDataHandler` defines methods that an ASP.NET server control must implement to automatically load postback data. We need this interface as we need to extract the HTML string from the Rich Text formatted content.

So the definition of our `Server Control` class will look like this:

```
Public Class RTFEditor
    Inherits System.Web.UI.Control
    Implements INamingContainer, IPostBackDataHandler
```

We're going to discuss only the most important functions of this class but you can download the class from the support material (the class is named `ContentManagementEditor.vb`) to take a look at the full class.

This class defines several public properties such as `Width`, `Height` etc. But the properties that are important in this context are `RichHTML` and `RichText`.

The `RichHTML` property is a `ReadOnly` public property that returns a string. This property returns the HTML string for the Rich Text format entered. If you want to extract the HTML string from the Rich content that you have entered, this is the property that you should use. The property is defined as shown below:

```
Public ReadOnly Property RichHtml() As String
    Get
        Return CType(ViewState.Item("_text2html"), String)
    End Get
End Property
```

The `RichText` property is a public property that takes in an HTML string and sets the Rich Text content to the control. So if you want to set some Rich Text to the server control to display, this is the property that you should use. The property definition is shown below:

```
Public Property RichText() As String
    Get
        Dim text As String = CType(ViewState.Item("_Html2Text"), String)
        If IsNothing(text) Then
            text = String.Empty
        End If
        Return text
    End Get

    Set(ByVal Value As String)
        ViewState.Item("_Html2Text") = Value
    End Set
End Property
```

The next method that you should take a look at is `CreateChildControls`. We are going to override this method to provide the child controls that are required for the Rich Text server control such as the buttons that can be used for formatting the text, the `<Iframe>` element and the hidden input element to hold the HTML string. Here is part of the (very long) method:

```
Protected Overrides Sub CreateChildControls()

    Dim t As New Table()
    Dim tr As New TableRow()
    Dim tc As New TableCell()

    'Add a table entry with Bold link
    tc.Attributes.Add("align", "center")
    tc.Width = Unit.Pixel(10)
    tc.Attributes.Add("align", "center")
    tc.HorizontalAlign = HorizontalAlign.Center

    tc.Controls.Add(PrepareLinkControl _
    (HttpContext.Current.Server.MapPath("~/images/circle_b.gif"), _
                                         "Bold", "Bold"))
    tr.Cells.Add(tc)
```

The `PrepareLinkControl` method actually creates the image buttons and adds the `OnClick` attribute to call the JavaScript function to format the text.

Here is another extract from `CreateChildControls`:

```
    'Add the IFrame element
    Dim hg As New HtmlGenericControl()

    hg.TagName = "iframe"
    hg.ID = Me.ClientID + "eSynaps_RTE"
    hg.Attributes.Add("width", "100%")
    hg.Attributes.Add("Height", "100%")
    hg.Attributes.Add("OnBlur", String.Concat("PostIt", Me.ClientID, "();"))
    tc.Controls.Add(hg)
    tc.Width = Unit.Percentage(100)
    tr.Cells.Add(tc)
    t.Rows.Add(tr)
```

Here you can see the `<Iframe>` element being added, along with the `OnBlur` event that will call the `PostIt` Javascript function to extract the content.

The `PostIt` function is added to the page with the `PreparePostItJs` method:

```
    Private Function PreparePostItJs() As String
        Dim sb As New StringBuilder()
        sb.Append(ControlChars.CrLf & "function PostIt" + Me.ClientID _
            + "()" & ControlChars.CrLf)
        sb.Append("{" & ControlChars.CrLf)
        sb.Append("document.getElementById('" + Me.ClientID _
```

```
            + "_hidden').value = ")
        sb.Append(Me.ClientID + "_WROX_TB.document.body.innerHTML;" _
            & ControlChars.CrLf)
        sb.Append("}")
        Return sb.ToString()
    End Function
```

This looks quite complex but actually just adds something of this form:

```
function PostIt[ID]
{
document.getElementByID('[ID]_hidden').value =
    [ID]_WROX_TB.document.body.innerHTML;
}
```

Where [ID] is the element ID of the control we insert it into the function name so that more than one of these controls can be used on the same page if necessary.

The executeCommand JavaScript function is constructed in a similar way, this time by the PrepareCmdExecJs method:

```
    Private Function PrepareCmdExecJs() As String

    Dim stringBuilder As New stringBuilder()
    stringBuilder.Append("function ExecThisCmd" + Me.ClientID _
        + "(command, arg)" & ControlChars.CrLf)
    stringBuilder.Append("{" & ControlChars.CrLf)
    stringBuilder.Append("if (arg == null)" & ControlChars.CrLf)
    stringBuilder.Append("{")
    stringBuilder.Append(Me.ClientID _
        + "_WROX_TB.document.execCommand(command);" & ControlChars.CrLf)
    stringBuilder.Append("}")
    stringBuilder.Append("else")
    stringBuilder.Append("{")
    stringBuilder.Append(Me.ClientID _
        + "_WROX_TB.document.execCommand(command, '', arg);" _
            & ControlChars.CrLf)
    stringBuilder.Append("}")
    stringBuilder.Append(Me.ClientID _
        + "_WROX_TB.focus();" & ControlChars.CrLf & "}" & ControlChars.CrLf)
    Return stringBuilder.ToString()

    End Function
```

This creates JavaScript in this form:

```
function ExecThisCmd[ID](command,arg)
{
if (arg == null)
{
[ID]_WROX_TB.document.execCommand(command);
```

```
  }
  else
  {
  [ID]_WROX_TB.document.execCommand(command, '', arq);
  }
  [ID]_WROX_TB.focus();
  }
```

You can see that we simply pass on the commands to the execCommand method of the document in the <Iframe>.

The next method that we are going to take a look at is PrepareBrowserMsgJs. This function actually checks the browser version to see if this Rich Text control is going to work or not. The browser details are obtained from the HTTP Request context as shown below:

```
Dim hbc As New HttpBrowserCapabilities()
hbc = HttpContext.Current.Request.Browser
```

Then we need to check for the version of the browser to see if this Rich Text control is going to work. Here is how we do it:

```
If ((hbc.MajorVersion < 5) Or (hbc.Browser <> "IE") Or _
    ((hbc.Platform <> "Win95" And hbc.Platform <> "Win98" And _
                    hbc.Platform <> "WinNT"))) Then
    'Display a message that this Rich Text Box does not work with this
    'Browser
ELSE
    'Do the processing to register the JavaScript that we have generated
    in this control to copy the IFRame's HTML to the hidden field.
END IF
```

A worthwhile improvement to this control might be to have it detect browser capabilities and use a standard textbox on browsers that do not support <Iframe>.

Finally, let's take a look at the method, LoadPostData, which is responsible for capturing the HTML that is copied from the <Iframe> element to the hidden field upon submitting the web form. The LoadPostData method is one of the methods that you have to implement when you implement the interface IpostBackDataHandler. The method's implementation is shown below:

```
Public Function LoadPostData(ByVal postDataKey As String, _
                    ByVal values As NameValueCollection) _
            As Boolean Implements IPostBackDataHandler.LoadPostData

    Dim htmlstring As String = values(MyBase.ClientID & "_hidden")

    If htmlstring <> String.Empty Then
        ViewState.Add("_text2html", htmlstring)
        Return True
    End If

    Return False

End Function
```

As you can see in the above code, the hidden field is accessed in the control to extract the HTML string.

This completes the development of the Rich Text editor control. Now, let's move to the next section where we actually use this control in publishing/editing the content.

Content Publishing and Editing

Both of these two functions are handled in the `EditContent.aspx` page. The codebehind page for this .aspx page is `EditContent.aspx.vb`. You can find this .aspx page in the `ContentManagement` folder from the support material.

The `EditContent.aspx` web form defines the server controls that are required to publish a content item and to edit an existing content item. The web form is shown in the picture below:

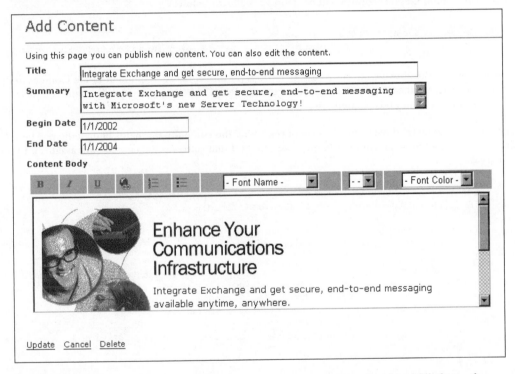

When editing an existing content item using this page, content is retrieved and filled into the corresponding text areas in the web form. Also, as you can see we are using a Rich Text editor control for the Content body section.

The following steps are required in order to use the Rich Text editor control in our .aspx pages:

First, we add the Register directive at the beginning of the page:

```
<%@ Register TagPrefix="ContentEditor"
Namespace="Wrox.Intranet.ContentManagement.Components" Assembly="Portal"%>
```

Then, we add the Rich Text editor control tag to our HTML:

```
<ContentEditor:RTFEditor id="ContentBody" RichText="<B>Enter content here</B>"
Runat="server" Width="656px" Height="198px"></ContentEditor:RTFEditor>
```

In the codebehind file, this control will be defined as shown below:

```
Protected WithEvents ContentBody As
                    Wrox.Intranet.ContentManagement.Components.RTFEditor
```

Now we can use the above control's RichText property to display Rich Content in the Content body section. We can use the RichHTML property to extract the HTML from the Rich Content you have entered in the Content body section.

The Page_Load method performs the task of retrieving the content item that is being edited. The code shown below is an excerpt from the Page_Load method that retrieves the content and assigns it to the text areas.

```
Dim cm As New ContentManagement.Components.ContentManagement()
Dim dr As SqlDataReader = cm.GetContent(itemId)

If IsNothing(dr) Then
    ErrorMessage.Text = cm.ErrorMessage
Else
    dr.Read()
    Title.Text = CType(dr("Title"), String)
    Summary.Text = CType(dr("Summary"), String)
    ContentBody.RichText = CType(dr("Body"), String)
    BeginDate.Text = CType(dr("BeginDate"), DateTime).ToShortDateString()
    EndDate.Text = CType(dr("EndDate"), DateTime).ToShortDateString()
    dr.Close()
End If
```

Upon editing the content item, when the user clicks on the **Update** button, the function updateButton_Click is invoked to save the changes back to the database. The code for the updatebutton_Click method is shown below:

```
Dim result As Integer
If Page.IsValid = True Then
    Dim cm As New ContentManagement.Components.ContentManagement()
    . . .
```

```
        result = cm.EditContent(itemId, moduleId, Title.Text, Summary.Text,_
                        ContentBody.RichHtml, BeginDate.Text, EndDate.Text, _
                                        Context.User.Identity.Name)
    . . .
    If result > 0 Then
        Response.Redirect("AddRelatedContent.aspx?ItemID=" _
            & result.ToString() & "&Mid=" & moduleId.ToString())
    Else
        ErrorMessage.Text = cm.ErrorMessage
    End If
    cm = Nothing
End If
```

The important part of this function is the call to the `EditContent` function of the `ContentManagement` class. This class takes the content item ID and all other content item details along with the logged-in user name from the current `HttpContext` object as arguments to save them back to the database.

Publishing a new content item works along similar lines, except the fact that when you publish a new content item using the `EditContent` web form, the function `UpdateButton_Click` calls the `AddContent` function on the `ContentManagement` class instance, as shown below:

```
Private Sub updateButton_Click(ByVal sender As System.Object, _
                ByVal e As System.EventArgs) Handles updateButton.Click


    Dim result As Integer

    Dim cm As New ContentManagement.Components.ContentManagement()

        If itemId = 0 Then
            result = cm.AddContent(moduleId, Title.Text, Summary.Text,_
                            Body.Text, BeginDate.Text, EndDate.Text, _
                            Context.User.Identity.Name)
```

Now we know how to publish and edit the content. Upon publishing/editing the content, you will be automatically redirected to the page where you can assign related content to the content you have just published. So, the next step is assigning related content to the published content. Let's see how we can implement this.

Assigning the Related Content

The `AddRelatedContent.aspx` page handles assigning related content functionality. The codebehind file is the `AddRelatedContent.aspx.vb`.

The functionality of the `AddRelatedContent.aspx` is pretty straightforward. It retrieves all the content items that belongs to the same module as the newly published content and displays the list so that the logged-in user can select the related content. See the picture below:

Add Related Content

Using this page you can assign related content to the content that you have published.

☐ Simple Web Services

☐ Using Web Services for Application Integration

☑ XML Web Services Overview

Save

Upon selecting the related content, the user can save the related content back to the database into the tblContentManagement_RelatedContent table. A click on the **save** button invokes the method relCon_Click which in turn calls the AddRelatedContent function of the ContentManagement class to save the related content. The following code is an excerpt from the relCon_Click method.

```
Dim cm As New ContentManagement.Components.ContentManagement()
Dim aL As New ArrayList()
Dim objListItem As ListItem
Dim result As Integer
Try
    For Each objListItem In relContent.Items
        If objListItem.Selected Then
            aL.Add(objListItem.Value)
        End If
    Next

    result = cm.AddRelatedContent(itemId, aL.ToArray())

Catch
    ErrorMessage.Text = "Unable to Add related content at this time."
End Try

cm = Nothing
```

The AddRelatedContent method from the ContentManagement class takes the content item id and an array of related content item ids as arguments.

Publishing related content to an existing content item completes the process of publishing a content item in the content management system. Now let's revisit the 'Related Content' feature by showing how we will display related content to users.

Viewing the Related Content

The RelatedContent.aspx page implements the process to view the related content for a selected content item. This page can be found in the ContentManagement folder from the support material. The Page_Load method of this page class implements the process to load the content related to a selected content item. The following code excerpt is from the Page_Load method of the RelatedContent.aspx page:

```
Dim cm As New ContentManagement.Components.ContentManagement()
Dim datareader As SqlDataReader
datareader = cm.ViewRelatedContent(itemId)
If IsNothing(datareader) Then
    ErrorMessage.Text = cm.ErrorMessage
Else
    myDataList.DataSource = datareader
    myDataList.DataBind()
    datareader.Close()
End If
```

And, the `DataList` template on the .aspx page is shown below:

```
<asp:DataList id="myDataList" CellPadding="4" Width="98%"
                                    EnableViewState="false" runat="server">
  <ItemTemplate>
    <span class="ItemTitle">
     <asp:Label Text='<%# DataBinder.Eval(Container.DataItem,"Title") %>'
                                        runat="server" ID="Label1"/>
    </span>
    <br>
    <span class="Normal">
     <i>
     <%# DataBinder.Eval(Container.DataItem,"BeginDate", "{0:d}") %>
     </i>
    </span>
    <br>
    <span class="Normal">
      <%# DataBinder.Eval(Container.DataItem,"Summary") %>
    </span>
    <br>
     <p align="right">
     <Wrox:Actions Id="Actions2" runat=server ReadText="Read"
        ReadUrl='<%# "GetContent.aspx?ItemID=" &
        DataBinder.Eval(Container.DataItem,"ID") & "&mid=" &
        DataBinder.Eval(Container.DataItem,"ModuleID")  %>'
        RelatedContentText="Related Content"
        RelatedContentUrl='<%# "RelatedContent.aspx?ItemID=" &
        DataBinder.Eval(Container.DataItem,"ID") & "&mid=" &
        DataBinder.Eval(Container.DataItem,"ModuleID")  %>' />
     </p>
  </ItemTemplate>
</asp:DataList>
```

281

As you can see, the `ViewRelatedContent` function of the `ContentManagement` class is called to retrieve the related content. The following picture displays related content related to a content `id` in the **Developer News** module.

Related Content

Using this page you can view all related content for a selected content item.

XML Web Services Infrastructure
7/5/2002
XML Web services must be agnostic regarding the choice of operating system, object model and programming language to succeed in the heterogeneity of the Web. Also, for XML Web services to enjoy the same widespread adoption as other Web-based technologies, they must abide to some rules. Want to know? Read on!

Read Related Content

Simple Web Services
7/3/2002
The most basic scenario fulfilled by XML Web services is that of providing some fundamental piece of functionality for its clients to use. For example, a challenge faced by e-commerce applications is the need to calculate charges for an assortment of shipping options. Such applications would require current shipping cost tables from each shipping company to use in these calculations.

Read Related Content

Using Web Services for Application Integration
7/1/2002
You can use XML Web services in a composite manner to integrate a seemingly disparate group of existing applications. The wide adoption of custom software throughout virtually every department of most companies has resulted in a vast array of useful but isolated islands of data and business logic. Due to the varied circumstances under which each was developed, and the ever-evolving nature of technology, it was a daunting task to create a functional assemblage from these applications.

Read Related Content

Now let's examine one last function that is required for managing content in a content management system: deleting the existing content.

Deleting the existing content

Deleting existing content involves a permission/security check as we did in the editing the existing content feature. The `EditContent.aspx` handles the delete functionality as well. Actually, `delete` is one of the options on the `EditContent.aspx` page when you are editing an existing content item. In case if you have forgotten, take a look at the following picture:

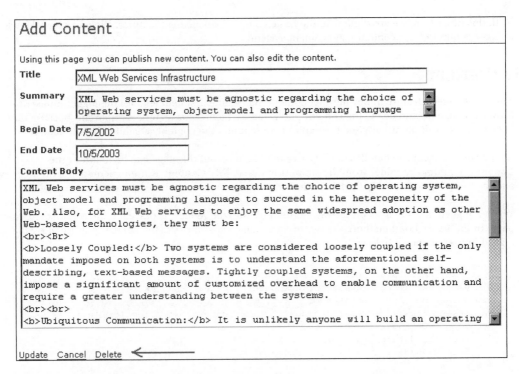

A click on the **Delete** button invokes the `deleteButton_Click` method from the `EditContent` page class. This method in turn calls the `DeleteContent` function of the `ContentManagement` class by passing the content `id` as an argument:

```
Private Sub deleteButton_Click(ByVal sender As System.Object, _
                ByVal e As System.EventArgs) Handles deleteButton.Click

    Dim cm As New ContentManagement.Components.ContentManagement()
    Dim result As Integer

    If itemId <> 0 Then

        result = cm.DeleteContent(itemId, Context.User.Identity.Name)
        If result >= 0 Then
            Response.Redirect(CType(ViewState("UrlReferrer"), String))
        Else
            ErrorMessage.Text = cm.ErrorMessage
        End If

    End If

    cm = Nothing

End Sub
```

With this discussion, we are done with the basic content management features. We will now take a look at other features of our content management system.

My Content

The 'My Content' feature in our intranet content management system enables the logged-in user to browse, read, edit, and delete the content published by them. This feature is important because the logged-in user will not usually see the expired content and the content scheduled for the future.

`MyContent.aspx` page handles the 'My Content' feature and this page can be found in the `ContentManagement` folder from the support material. 'My Content' is implemented at a module level and the hyperlink to view **My Content** is included in the module title user control.

When a logged-in user clicks on the **My Content** button, the request is passed to the `MyContent.aspx` page. In the `Page_Load` method, the `MyContent` page class retrieves the content published by the logged-in user as shown below:

```
'Get the contents and bind to the DataList Control
Dim cm As New ContentManagement.Components.ContentManagement()
Dim datareader As SqlDataReader
datareader = cm.ViewMyContent(moduleId, Me.Context.User.Identity.Name)
myDataList.DataSource = datareader
If IsNothing(datareader) Then
    ErrorMessage.Text = cm.ErrorMessage
Else
    myDataList.DataBind()
    datareader.Close()
End If
```

The `Page_Load` method calls the `ViewMyContent` function of the `ContentManagement` class.

So, a typical **My Content** page looks like as shown below:

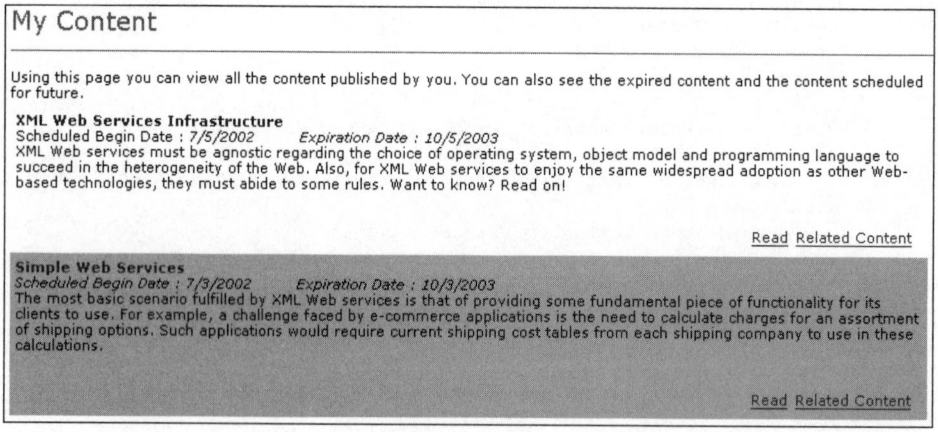

Each content item is displayed along with the Scheduled Begin Date and Expiration Date. Now the user has the ability to edit the content items that are expired (to reactivate the content) and to modify the content that is scheduled for the future.

Now let's take a look at another very important feature of the content management system – Searching.

Searching the Content

Like the My Content feature, searching is also a module level feature in our content management system. A user can search a module (category) for the content using a keyword. Let's see how to implement a simple Search functionality in order to search the modules with a keyword.

The search button is located in the Content Module Title control. When a user clicks on the search button, the request is forwarded to the ContentSearch.aspx page. This page implements the searching functionality in the content management system. This page can be found in the ContentManagement folder from the support material.

The following picture shows the search content page in a web browser:

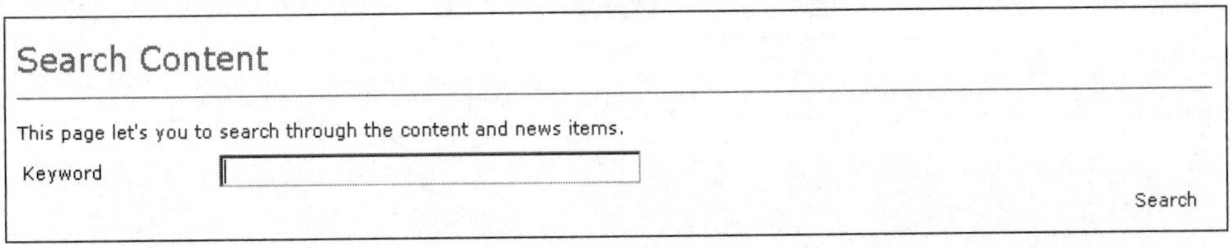

When the user types in a keyword and clicks on the Search button, the search_Click method of the ContentSearch page class is invoked to process the search request. The search_Click method is shown below:

```
Private Sub search_Click(ByVal sender As System.Object, _
                    ByVal e As System.EventArgs) Handles search.Click
    'Get the contents and bind to the DataList Control
    Dim cm As New ContentManagement.Components.ContentManagement()
    Dim datareader As SqlDataReader

    datareader = cm.SearchContent(KeyWord.Text, moduleId)

    If IsNothing(datareader) Then
        ErrorMessage.Text = cm.ErrorMessage
    Else
        myDataList.DataSource = datareader
        myDataList.DataBind()
        datareader.Close()
    End If
End Sub
```

The above method calls the `SearchContent` function of the `ContentManagement` class. The `SearchContent` function runs the SQL procedure `upContentManagement_SearchContent` to retrieve the content items that have a match with the keyword.

The following picture shows the search results for a search on the keyword "**Web Services**":

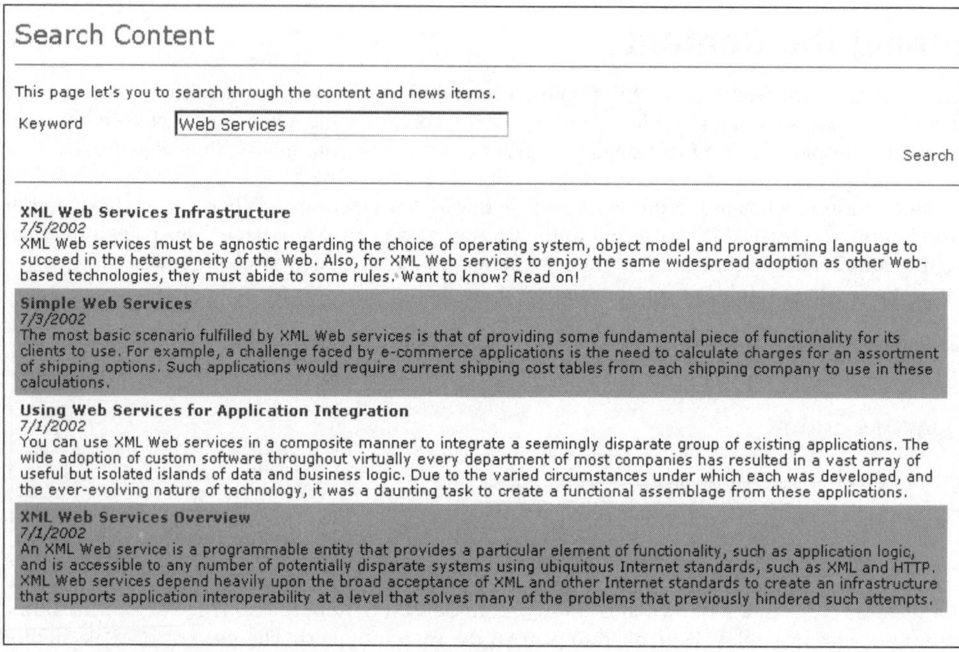

Another approach that can be implemented for search module is to create an extra column in the content table to hold the keywords for each content item. In this case, the keywords for the content item should be entered at the time of publishing the content item.

Searching is an important feature that actually decides the usability factor of the content in large content management systems.

Now let's look at the last but an important feature of the content management system: Content Targeting

Content Targeting

Fortunately, we do not need any additional code in order to provide targeted content! The `IBuySpy` architecture that we are using allows certain tabs to be available only to certain user roles. This, together with the fact that our module design allows multiple instances of our content management module means that we can create targeted content by placing content management module instances on different tabs.

To demonstrate Content Targeting, we have created a tab called Developer and assigned it to the Developer group:

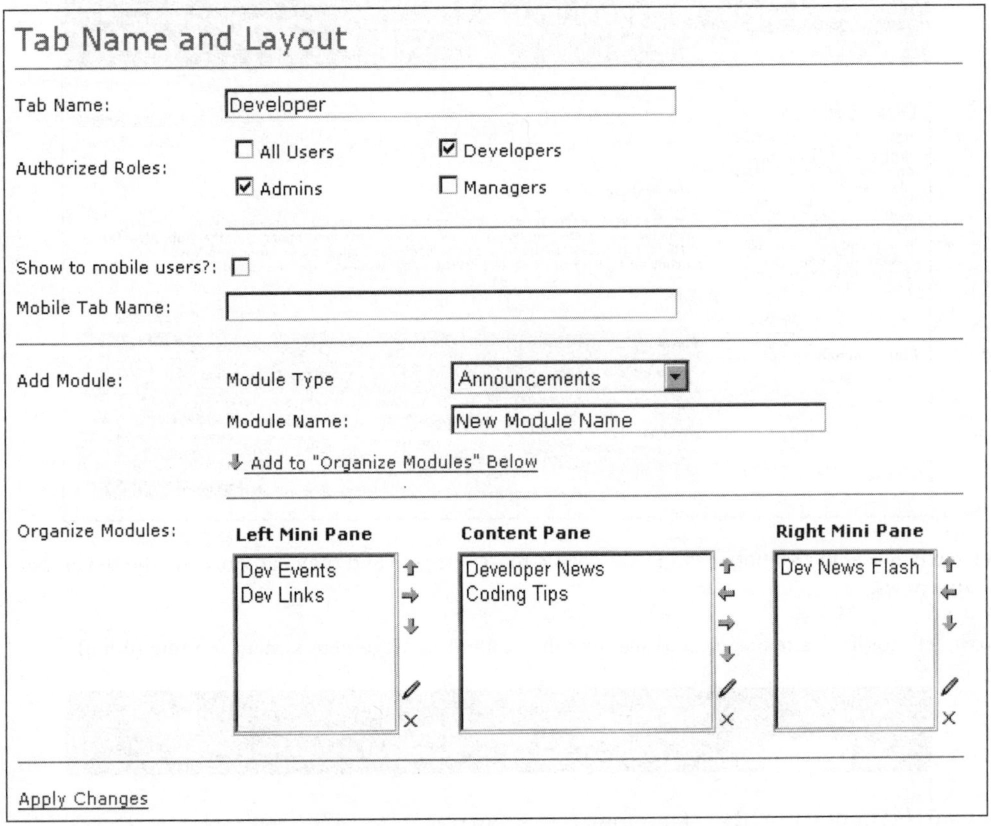

Tab Name and Layout

Tab Name: `Developer`

Authorized Roles:
☐ All Users   ☑ Developers
☑ Admins   ☐ Managers

Show to mobile users?: ☐
Mobile Tab Name:

Add Module:
Module Type   `Announcements` ▼
Module Name: `New Module Name`
⬇ Add to "Organize Modules" Below

Organize Modules:

Left Mini Pane	Content Pane	Right Mini Pane
Dev Events Dev Links	Developer News Coding Tips	Dev News Flash

Apply Changes

The content they see is all developer-related content such as Developer News and Coding Tips etc.

Then we have created a tab called Manager and assigned it to Managers group. The content in this category will all be related to the managers.

Now when a developer logs into the intranet this is how they view the content management system:

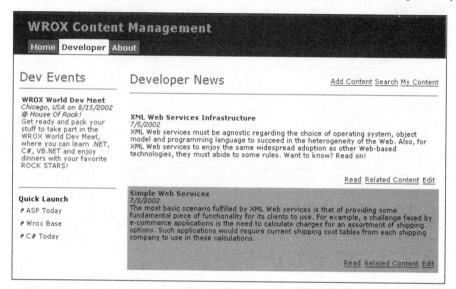

As you can see, the Manager tab is not visible to developers and they can only see the developer-related news.

Now, let's login as a manager, and see how the content management system is going to look:

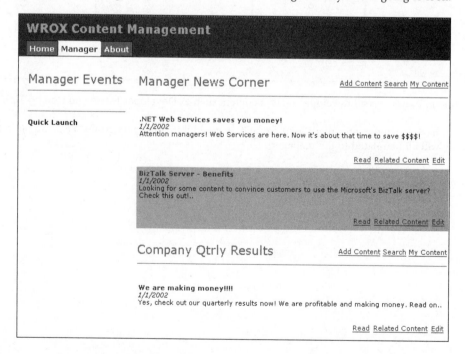

The logged in manager will not see the **Developer** tab and can only see the news and content items related to the managers group.

So a good design in roles in the organization makes it easy to implement the content targeting. As the Content targeting feature makes the intranet more relevant to and usable to different groups in the organization, a careful and well-thought-out role definition is needed.

Summary

In this chapter we have worked through the design and development of a new module for our intranet. The content management module that we created provides users with easier control over their content than any of the modules provided with IBuySpy.

We looked at:

❏ Designing the tables to store content and to relate content

❏ Building stored procedures that provide the access to the database that we need

❏ Creating a business component to link our database and our user interface

❏ Coding reusable controls for our user interface

❏ Building pages that allow users to manage their content

❏ Providing WYSIWYG editing through a custom server control

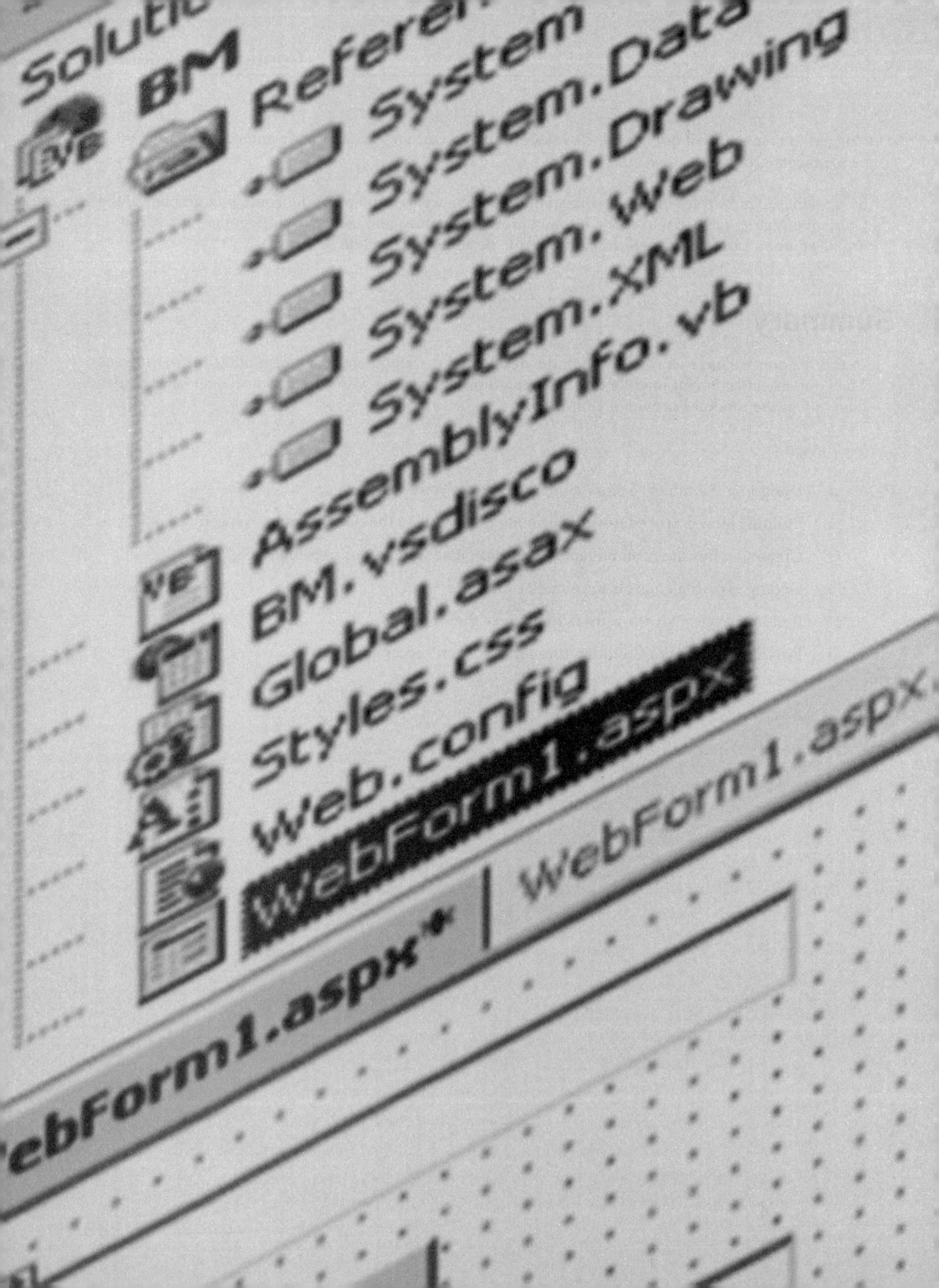

Solutio
BM Referen
System
System.Data
System.Drawing
System.Web
System.XML
AssemblyInfo.vb
Assembly
BM.vsdisco
Global.asax
Styles.css
Web.config
WebForm1.aspx

WebForm1.aspx

WebForm1.aspx* | WebForm1.aspx

8

Document Management

This chapter will build upon information covered in previous chapters to develop a document management solution that will plug into the **IBuySpy** framework that we are using for our intranet.

In this chapter, we will see:

- ❏ What we mean by document management
- ❏ What features a good document management system should have
- ❏ Storing documents and their meta data in our intranet database
- ❏ Coding stored procedures and triggers to provide access to the data
- ❏ Creating a set of business classes to abstract database access
- ❏ Building a set of pages and controls to provide an easy to use interface to our users

What Is Document Management?

The concept of Electronic Document Management Systems (also referred to as EDMS) is broad and difficult to define. Traditionally, Document Management Systems deal with the classification and management of documents of various types and the meta-information relating to those documents. Specifically, Document Management Systems are typically used to manage files that are created by other applications, for example Microsoft Word documents, Excel spreadsheets or even a PDF version of a signed contract.

The most common features for Document Management systems are:

- ❑ 'Checking Out' and 'Checking In'
- ❑ Versioning
- ❑ Access control
- ❑ Auditing

We'll discuss each of these in turn.

Checking Out and Checking In

When documents are stored centrally and multiple users are able to update them, it is important that conflicts do not arise in which more than one user tries to make changes to the same document at the same time. Imagine two users make changes to a document and then each submits an updated version. The user who submits their updated document second will overwrite the version submitted by the previous user and some changes will be lost.

Most document management systems seek to prevent this sort of problem by requiring users to 'Check Out' documents before making changes to them. Checking out a document marks it as unavailable for edits by other users (although they can still view it). When the user has completed their changes they 'Check In' the document and the new version will be available for checking out by other users.

Versioning

Versioning happens when a document is checked out of the system, modified and then checked back into the system. When the document is checked back in, the previous version is 'Versioned' and usually made available for viewing. When implemented in an application, Versioning allows users to view previous versions of documents.

Versioning is important in ensuring that users changes to documents only add information to the system. Without versioning, it would be possible for valuable information to be lost through mistaken edits to documents.

Access Control

It is important that access to documents stored in a document management system is controlled. If documents contain sensitive information, they should not be available for viewing by all. Also, we often want to control who is able to make changes to documents.

The way access is controlled to a document is by assigning permissions that require a level of authority for a user to perform actions on the document; unauthorized users are not allowed to perform actions in which they are unauthorized.

Auditing

When multiple users are collaborating on documents, we need to have records of who made which changes, and when changes were made. These sorts of record provide accountability for changes made to documents.

Auditing is the process of tracking what happens to a document, usually by implementing some type of logging mechanism.

Bringing It All Together

These four features are usually strongly linked to each other. For example, when a document is checked in an access control check will take place. If the check is successful, the document will be versioned and an entry added to the audit log of the user's activity.

Now that we have discussed some general concepts related to document management we can begin thinking about what we want from our application in a real world situation. For example, the following scenario is a typical situation that would require a Document Management solution. Bob is employed at the Marketing Department of Company X. Bob has a sales report that he needs to store in a shared location so that Frank in the Legal Department can access the document. However, Bob does not want other employees from Marketing to access the document. To further complicate the issue, Bob wants Frank to modify the document and replace his original document with the edited version while making previous versions available to other authorized users.

To implement this seemingly simple task in a traditional File Server environment could be quite cumbersome. A user must first make the file available in a shared resource that is accessible to authorized users - usually requiring intervention from a network administrator to assign appropriate permissions. Additionally, all authorized users must be notified of the network location so that they may access the file. However, a much easier solution is to develop or purchase a document management solution that provides the user with the desired functionality. This chapter will provide the requirements and the general steps necessary for developing such a solution as a module for our intranet.

Requirements for a Document Management Application

Let's start by establishing requirements for a basic Document Management application:

❑ Users should be able to store documents and assign permissions necessary to control access to any document. It is important to note that users should NOT need to have administrative access to a particular module in order to check a document in or out unless an administrator stipulates this. Authorized users should also be allowed to download a document for viewing without having to check the document out for modification.

❑ Documents can be checked in and out. When Documents are checked back in, the previous version of the document should be automatically versioned for archival purposes.

❑ Users should be able to view all versions of a document. However, only the current version may be checked in or out of the system.

❑ The system should identify the document originator who owns a document. When a document is checked out the application should also identify the user that initiated the check out request.

Looking to the IBuySpy Documents Module for Guidance

As a comparison to our stated requirements let's look at the Documents module provided in the IBuySpy solution to see if this out of the box example meets our needs. This is a fairly simple component allowing for documents to be uploaded and then displayed in the appropriate module from any of the selected tabs.

You may want to have a look at the IBuySpy Documents module yourself. Below is a screen shot of the Documents Module:

New Employee Documentation

Title	Owner	Area	Last Updated
Employee Handbook	JennaJ@ibuyspy.com	New Employee Info	12/20/2001
Annual Reviews	JennaJ@ibuyspy.com	New Employee Info	12/20/2001
Vacation Policy	JennaJ@ibuyspy.com	New Employee Info	12/20/2001

Right away we see that this example does not provide many of the common features of Document Management such as versioning, or the ability to check a document out of the system. The IBuySpy solution does, however, provide at least some of the functionality required for our application. For example, access to document submittals is controlled by the Security class that is built into IBuySpy. Only users who have edit permissions can upload documents to the system; unauthorized users can only download files.

Although this is a good start, we are still a long way from meeting the requirements of our application. Rather than building on top of the Documents Module we decided to start from scratch and loosely base the new application on the IBuySpy sample.

Planning our Project

Now that we have an idea of what we want from our application we should sketch out the steps that we will take to put theory into practice. The rest of this chapter will be divided into the following three sections:

❑ Designing the Database

❑ Creating the Business Layer

❑ Creating the Presentation Layer

Our database and Stored Procedures will be created in SQL Server. The remainder of the project we will create in the Visual Studio IDE. The business classes and the user pages will be created in a folder within the IBuySpy project as outlined in the section below.

Arranging the Project Files

So as not to confuse our content with the IBuySpy portal files, we will place our files in subdirectories under the existing project directories. The illustration below outlines the directory structure.

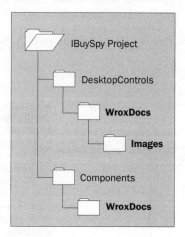

Designing the Database

The data layer in our application is the most important part of the application. Our stored procedures that add, edit and update our documents will be coded at this point. We will be adding our tables directly to the Portal database for our intranet.

> Note: the SQL script used to generate the tables and stored procedures for this example is included with the project Source Code. We suggest that you download the source code and install it to a working IBuySpy project. This will make it easier to follow along – especially since we have much to cover and not everything will be listed in detail. Consult the readme file in the source code for instructions on manually recreating the project in Visual Studio.

A Different Approach to Traditional File Storage

We need to decide how we will store our documents. There are a number of options here but we'll consider two: we can store the files in the **file system** on the server or we can store the files in an **image column** in SQL Server.

File Storage on the server's file system has the advantage of being simple to manage with a small number of files. However, when the number of documents starts to grow, file storage on the server's file system is no longer simple to manage, especially if we manage previous versions of a document. Since Access Control is a requirement of our application, we would need to manage many NTFS permissions to the files, which would incur more administrative overhead than the SQL Server approach, where we can use our own business logic to control access.

Storing the documents in our SQL Server database also has the advantage of storing them in the same place as the other information that is stored in the intranet. When the intranet database is backed up, the documents stored in our document management system will be included.

For these reasons, we decided to store our documents in the SQL Server database.

Below is our proposed Database structure:

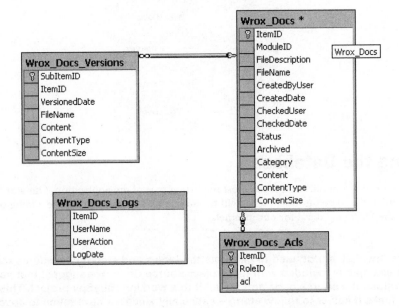

The Wrox_Docs Table

This table is the main store of user documents. The table contains meta-information about files and status information such as columns that indicate if a document is checked in or out of the system. The actual binary content of the files is stored in the table as well – although only for the most current version. When files are updated, the older versions will be moved to another table that is named `Wrox_Docs_Versions`. Moving the older versions to a separate table follows good database design - attempting to store too much information in one table can prevent the efficient and reliable management of the data in the table.

Column Name	Type	Size	Allow Null	Description
ItemID	Int-Identity Primary Key	4	No	The unique ID for any document.
ModuleID	Int	4	No	ID of IBuySpy module that the document is bound. This column determines the context that a record exists and allows us to have multiple instances of our component, potentially on the same page.
CreatedbyUser	Varchar	100	No	The name of document originator. This will be the Context.User.Identity.Name which is authenticated in the IBuySpy portal.
Created Date	Datetime	8	No	Date that a document was originally posted.
CheckedUser	Varchar	100	Yes	The user that performed the check in or out action. This will also be the Context.User.Identity.Name. The user is actually authenticated in the IBuySpy Portal site.
CheckedDate	Datetime	8	Yes	Date that document was checked in or out.
Status	Bit	1	No	Indicator of document status. '1' is status for checked in; '0' is the status for checked out.
Archived	Bit	1	No	Indicator of document archival status. '1' is status for Archived; '0' is status for a current document. The idea is to archive documents instead of deleting them from the system.
Category	Varchar	100	No	Document Category. This field is not really used in this example for any reason other than illustrating the updating of meta-information on a document. It could be used for future extensions.
Content	Image	16	No	This column holds the binary content of the document.
ContentType	Varchar	50	No	The MIME type (Multipurpose Internet Mail Extension) of a document. Takes the form of *application/type*. This is important because we will use it to tell the users browser which type of document they are downloading.
ContentSize	Int	4	No	The length of a document in bytes.

The Wrox_Docs_Versions Table

The purpose of this table is to control document versioning and to allow users to download a previous version of any document for which they have permissions. Information about the document such as title and current status is appropriately maintained in the parent table.

Column Name	Type	Size	Allow Null	Description
SubItemID	Int-Identity Primary Key	4	No	The unique ID for any child document.
ItemID	Int	4	No	The foreign key for the parent document.
Versioned Date	Datetime	8	No	Date that the document was versioned as a result of a newer document being checked into the system.
FileName	Varchar	255	No	The filename of the document version.
Content	Image	16	No	This column holds the binary content of the document.
ContentType	Varchar	50	No	The MIME type (Multipurpose Internet Mail Extension) of a document. Takes the form of *application/type*.
ContentSize	Int	4	No	The length of a document in bytes.

The Wrox_Docs_Acls Table

This table is a junction table that maps a particular document to a specific role. The Acl field in this table controls the access that a role has to a document. This junction allows us to control access at the document level, giving us finer granularity in assigning permissions. Taking this approach allows us to implement a hypothetical scenario such as giving 'Group A' edit rights to a particular document; while assigning 'Group B' limited access to the same document; and finally giving 'Group C' no access to the document at all.

The Acl column maps to an enumeration in our WroxDocSecurity security class that allows us to do document security checks before users perform actions on any document. We will look at the enumeration later when we code the business layer.

Column Name	Type	Size	Allow Null	Description
ItemID	Int-Foreign Key	4	No	The ID of a document in the Wrox_Docs table.

Column Name	Type	Size	Allow Null	Description
RoleID	Int-Foreign Key	4	No	The ID of a role. This is a foreign key into the portal's Roles table.
Acl	Int	4	No	The particular permission assigned to the document and role combination. The permissions are set from an enumeration that we will create later.

Notice that the combination of the ItemID and RoleID make up the Primary Key of the Wrox_Docs_Acls table

The Wrox_Docs_Logs Table

This table stores auditing information and will be updated based on Table Triggers that fire automatically when documents are updated or archived. We will code the trigger after we finish looking at our stored procedures below.

Column Name	Type	Size	Allow Null	Description
ItemID	Int	4	No	The ID of a document in the Wrox_Docs table
UserName	Varchar	100	Yes	The identity of the logged on user that originated an action.
UserAction	Varchar	100	No	Text describing the action that was performed.
LogDate	Datetime	8	Yes	The Date and time of the entry.

The Stored Procedures

As with the other modules in our intranet, our document management module will make all database calls through a set of stored procedures.

Stored Procedure	Parameters	Description
upDMS_GetWroxDocs	@ModuleID	Returns a listing of documents for a specific module from the `Wrox_Docs` table.
upDMS_GetChildWroxDocs	@ItemID	Returns all child versions of a document that match the @ItemID parameter from the `Wrox_Docs_Versions` table.
upDMS_GetSingleWroxDoc	@ItemID	Returns a single document that matched the @ItemID parameter from the `Wrox_Docs` table.
upDMS_UploadWroxDoc	@ItemID @ModuleID @FileName @FileDesc @UserName @Category @Content @ContentType @ContentSize @Status	Submits a new document to the system. The document is stored in the `Wrox_Docs table`. The document is associated to a particular module with the @ModuleID parameter.
upDMS_UpdateWroxDoc	@ItemID @FileDesc @Category	Performs an update on the meta data of a particular document. In our example there are only two columns that are being updated to keep things simple.
upDMS_RenderWroxDoc	@ItemID @Table	Streams a file to the browser based on the file's MIME type. The @Table parameter determines if the document is pulled from the parent table, `Wrox_Docs` or from the child table `Wrox_Docs_Versions`.
upDMS_ArchiveWroxDoc	@ItemID @ArchivedBit	Archives a document by changing the `Archived` column in the `Wrox_Docs` table.
upDMS_CheckInWroxDoc	@ItemID @FileName @UserName @Content @ContentType @ContentSize	Checks a document into the system by changing the `Status` column of an existing document. The previous version of the document is inserted into the `Wrox_Docs_Versions` table.

Stored Procedure	Parameters	Description
upDMS_CheckOutWroxDoc	@ItemID @UserName	Checks a document out of the system by changing the Status field in the Wrox_Docs table.
upDMS_WroxDocsHasAcls	@User @ItemID @TargetAcl	Verifies that a user has certain permissions for a document.
upDMS_UpdateWroxDocPermission	@ItemID @RoleID @Acl	Updates permissions for a particular document.
upDMS_AddWroxDocAcls	@ItemID @RoleID @Acl	Adds permissions to a particular document.
upDMS_DeleteWroxDocAcls	@ItemID @RoleID	Deletes permissions from a document.
upDMS_GetWroxDocPermissions	@ItemID	Gets All Permissions for a document.

Coding the Stored Procedures

In this section we will look at the code for our stored procedures in some detail. For brevity we will not discuss every procedure in equal detail. Moreover, some procedures are actually similar in structure or are fairly straightforward in approach and therefore should require very little explanation. You can see the full code for all of the stored procedures in the code download for the book.

upDMS_GetWroxDocs

Below is the code to return a list of all documents for a particular module.

```
CREATE PROCEDURE upDMS_GetWroxDocs
(
    @ModuleID int
)
AS

SELECT
    ItemID,
    FileName,
    FileDescription,
    CreatedByUser,
    CreatedDate,
    CheckedUser,
    Category,
    ContentType,
    Status,
    ContentSize,
    (SELECT COUNT(*) FROM Wrox_Docs_Versions WHERE ItemID = Wrox_Docs.ItemID) AS
VersionCount
```

```
FROM
    Wrox_Docs

WHERE
    ModuleID = @ModuleID AND Archived <> 1
ORDER by CreatedDate DESC
GO
```

The procedure returns all documents for a particular module, excluding documents that are archived. We also return a VersionCount column that is created from a COUNT(*) command:

```
(SELECT COUNT(*) FROM Wrox_Docs_Versions WHERE ItemID = Wrox_Docs.ItemID) AS
VersionCount
```

This count represents the number of previous document versions for the record that are contained in the child table Wrox_Docs_Versions, and will enable our interface to let users know whether previous versions exist.

Note that we do not return the Content column – we will not need the binary content of the documents to create a list, so it would be very inefficient to return the full content of all documents from this procedure.

upDMS_GetChildWroxDocs

This procedure returns all versions listed under a particular document from the Wrox_Docs_Versions table.

```
CREATE PROCEDURE upDMS_GetChildWroxDocs
(
    @ItemID int
)
AS

DECLARE @Counter int

SELECT
    SubItemID,
    ItemID,
    FileName,
    VersionedDate,
    ContentType,
    ContentSize

FROM
    Wrox_Docs_Versions

WHERE
    ItemID = @ItemID

ORDER BY VersionedDate
GO
```

As with the previous procedure, we do not return the Content column.

upDMS_GetSingleWroxDoc

This procedure returns a single document from the Wrox_Docs table that matches the ItemID parameter.

```
CREATE PROCEDURE upDMS_GetSingleWroxDoc
(
    @ItemID int
)
AS

SELECT
    FileName,
    CreatedByUser,
    CreatedDate,
    FileDescription,
    Category,
    ContentSize,
    ContentType

FROM
    Wrox_Docs

WHERE
    ItemID = @ItemID
GO
```

Even though we are only selecting a single document, we still do not return Content – this is a procedure for retrieving the metadata for the document. The upDMS_RenderWroxDoc procedure will provide access to the binary content.

upDMS_UploadWroxDoc

This procedure stores a new document to the system. The @Status parameter defaults to '1' which indicates that the document is "Checked in" and available for check out by authorized users.

```
CREATE PROCEDURE upDMS_UploadWroxDoc
(
    @ItemID            int,
    @ModuleID          int,
    @FileName          varchar(255),
    @FileDesc          varchar(255),
    @UserName          varchar(100),
    @Category          varchar(50),
    @Content           image,
    @ContentType       varchar(50),
    @ContentSize       int,
    @Status            bit = 1
)

AS

INSERT INTO Wrox_Docs
```

```
(
    ModuleID,
    FileName,
    FileDescription,
    CreatedByUser,
    CreatedDate,
    Status,
    Category,
    Content,
    ContentType,
    ContentSize
)

VALUES
(
    @ModuleID,
    @FileName,
    @FileDesc,
    @UserName,
    GetDate(),
    @Status,
    @Category,
    @Content,
    @ContentType,
    @ContentSize
)
GO
```

upDMS_UpdateWroxDoc

This procedure updates the meta data for a document in the Wrox_Docs table. Again, for simplicity in our example we have only two columns FileDescription and Category that are updated. In your own deployment you may well want to add more columns to describe your documents.

```
CREATE PROCEDURE upDMS_UpdateWroxDoc
(
    @ItemID          int ,
    @FileDesc        varchar(255),
    @Category        varchar(50)
)
AS

/* An Update Action is being performed */

BEGIN

UPDATE
    Wrox_Docs

SET
    Category          = @Category,
    FileDescription   = @FileDesc
```

```
WHERE
     ItemID = @ItemID

END
GO
```

upDMS_RenderWroxDoc

This procedure returns a single document to be rendered in the client's browser. If the @Table parameter passes 'parent' the document is pulled from the Wrox_Docs table; if not then the document comes from the child table Wrox_Docs_Versions. This will allow us to view either a current document version or a child version depending on which one the user requested from our application. We look at how users view documents when we code our presentation layer.

```
CREATE PROCEDURE upDMS_RenderWroxDoc
(
     @ItemID int,
     @Table char(10)
)
AS

IF (@Table = 'parent')
BEGIN
SELECT
   Content,
   ContentType,
   ContentSize,
   FileName
FROM Wrox_Docs
WHERE ItemID = @ItemID
END

ELSE
/* Render a child document */
BEGIN
SELECT
   Content,
   ContentType,
   ContentSize,
   FileName
FROM Wrox_Docs_Versions
WHERE SubItemID = @ItemID

END
GO
```

upDMS_ArchiveWroxDoc

This procedure archives a document by changing the Archived column to '1' in the Wrox_Docs table. Note that this procedure could also be used to "unarchive" a document simply by passing a '0' in the @ArchivedBit parameter.

```
CREATE PROCEDURE upDMS_ArchiveWroxDoc
(
    @ItemID      int ,
    @ArchivedBit bit = 1
)
AS

BEGIN

UPDATE
    Wrox_Docs

SET
    Archived = @ArchivedBit

WHERE
    ItemID = @ItemID

END
GO
```

upDMS_CheckInWroxDoc

This procedure checks a document into the system and places the previous version in the Wrox_Docs_Versions table. The procedure is performed in a transaction that will roll back any inserts if either the update or insert fails.

```
CREATE PROCEDURE upDMS_CheckInWroxDoc
(
    @ItemID          int ,
    @FileName        varchar(255),
    @UserName        varchar(100),
    @Content         image,
    @ContentType     varchar(50),
    @ContentSize     int
)

AS

BEGIN TRANSACTION CheckIn

/* Perform an Insert */
INSERT INTO Wrox_Docs_Versions
(
    ItemID,
    FileName,
    VersionedDate,
    Content,
    ContentType,
    ContentSize
)
```

```
SELECT
    ItemID,
    FileName,
    GETDATE(),
    Content,
    ContentType,
    ContentSize
FROM Wrox_Docs
WHERE ItemID = @ItemID

/* Perform an Update */
UPDATE
    Wrox_Docs
SET
    FileName          = @FileName,
    CheckedDate       = GETDATE(),
    CheckedUser       = @UserName,
    Content           = @Content,
    ContentType       = @ContentType,
    ContentSize       = @ContentSize,
    Status            = 1

WHERE
    ItemID = @ItemID

IF @@ERROR > 0
    BEGIN
    RAISERROR('Check In Failed',16,1)
    ROLLBACK TRANSACTION CheckIn
    RETURN 99
    END

COMMIT TRANSACTION CheckIn
GO
```

upDMS_CheckOutWroxDoc

This procedure changes the Status column to indicate that a document has been checked out of the system. Users will not be able to check the document out until it is checked back in by the originator, or by a user with Edit rights to the module.

```
CREATE PROCEDURE upDMS_CheckOutWroxDoc
(
    @ItemID       int,
    @UserName     varchar(100)
)

AS

UPDATE Wrox_Docs
SET   status     = 0,
      CheckedDate = GETDATE(),
      CheckedUser = @UserName
WHERE ItemID = @ItemID
GO
```

upDMS_WroxDocHasAcls

This procedure determines if a user has appropriate permissions on a document, such as the ability to check out or download a document. The @TargetAcl parameter represents the permission that is being checked. The UserRoles and Roles tables are part of the IBuySpy Portal database and are used in this procedure to resolve the logged on User to a RoleID.

The procedure returns the @@ROWCOUNT variable from the select statement, which represents the number of rows that were returned. If a user's role has the appropriate permissions then the @@ROWCOUNT will be greater than 0.

```
CREATE PROCEDURE upDMS_WroxDocsHasAcls
(
    @User nvarchar(100),
    @ItemID int,
    @TargetAcl int
)

AS

BEGIN
SELECT

    Roles.RoleID,
    Wrox_Docs_Acls.Acl

FROM
    UserRoles

  INNER JOIN
    Users ON UserRoles.UserID = Users.UserID
  INNER JOIN
    Roles ON UserRoles.RoleID = Roles.RoleID
  INNER JOIN
    Wrox_Docs_Acls ON Roles.RoleID = Wrox_Docs_Acls.RoleID

WHERE
    Users.Email = @User AND Wrox_Docs_Acls.ItemID = @ItemID
    AND Wrox_Docs_Acls.Acl >= @targetAcl

RETURN @@ROWCOUNT

END
GO
```

upDMS_UpdateWroxDocPermission

This procedure updates permissions on a single document in the Wrox_Docs_Acls table.

```
CREATE PROCEDURE upDMS_UpdateWroxDocPermission
(
    @ItemID  int,
```

```
        @RoleID  int,
        @Acl     int
)

AS

UPDATE Wrox_Docs_Acls SET
Acl = @Acl
WHERE ItemID = @ItemID AND RoleID = @RoleID

GO
```

upDMS_AddWroxDocAcls

This procedure first verifies if a particular role is listed in Wrox_Docs_Acls table. If the role is not in the table already, it is added.

```
CREATE PROCEDURE upDMS_AddWroxDocAcls
(
        @ItemID int,
        @RoleID int,
        @Acl   int  = 3
)

AS

IF  NOT EXISTS (
    SELECT
        *
    FROM
        Wrox_Docs_Acls
    WHERE
        ItemID = @ItemID AND  RoleID = @RoleID
)

BEGIN
INSERT INTO Wrox_Docs_Acls
    (ItemID,
     RoleID,
     Acl
     )
VALUES
    (
     @ItemID,
     @RoleID,
     @Acl
     )
END
ELSE
RETURN -1
GO
```

Creating Triggers to Enable Auditing

The final task for our Database is to enable an automated auditing process. What we are looking for is a way to add an entry to the Wrox_Docs_Logs table every time a record is updated, inserted or archived. We could easily add insert statements to any of our stored procedures, but this approach will leave us with bits of code in multiple places that could break if any of our tables change. Our solution is to create **Triggers** that perform the updates for our application automatically. A trigger is a procedure that will execute automatically when an UPDATE, INSERT, or DELETE statement is issued against a table.

> *Note: to create a trigger open SQL Enterprise Manager right-click over the* Wrox_Docs *table and choose* All Tasks / Manage Triggers. *The Triggers may then be coded and saved.*

Coding the update_log Trigger

The trigger fires when Wrox_Docs is updated, at which point a record is inserted into the Wrox_Docs_Logs table. When the Archived column is updated an entry is made indicating that the document was archived; if the Status column is updated the trigger checks the value of the inserted.Status column and then makes an entry indicating a check in or check out action.

```
CREATE TRIGGER update_log
ON dbo.Wrox_Docs
FOR UPDATE
AS
IF UPDATE(archived)
BEGIN

INSERT Wrox_Docs_Logs (ItemID, UserName,LogDate,UserAction)
SELECT ItemID, CreatedByUser, GETDATE(), 'Document Archived'
FROM inserted
END

ELSE
IF UPDATE(status)
BEGIN

DECLARE @StatusText char(20)
DECLARE @Statuscode int

SELECT @StatusCode = status FROM inserted
  IF (@StatusCode = 1)
      SET @StatusText = 'Document Checked In'
      ELSE
      SET @StatusText = 'Document Checked Out'

INSERT Wrox_Docs_Logs (ItemID, UserName,LogDate,UserAction)
SELECT ItemID, CheckedUser, GETDATE(),@StatusText
FROM inserted
END
```

The trigger starts by defining that it will react to updates being made to the Wrox_Docs table:

```
CREATE TRIGGER update_log
ON dbo.Wrox_Docs
FOR UPDATE
AS
```

It then specifies that if the Archived column is updated, an appropriate entry should be added to Wrox_Docs_Logs:

```
IF UPDATE(archived)
BEGIN

INSERT Wrox_Docs_Logs (ItemID, UserName,LogDate,UserAction)
SELECT ItemID, CreatedByUser, GETDATE(), 'Document Archived'
FROM inserted
END
```

If the archived column was not updated, the trigger checks for whether the Status column was changed (i.e. a document has been checked in or out). If this is the case, a further check is performed for what exactly the status code is, in order that the correct log can be made.

```
ELSE
IF UPDATE(status)
BEGIN

DECLARE @StatusText char(20)
DECLARE @Statuscode int

SELECT @StatusCode = status FROM inserted
  IF (@StatusCode = 1)
      SET @StatusText = 'Document Checked In'
      ELSE
      SET @StatusText = 'Document Checked Out'
```

An entry is then added to the Wrox_Docs_Logs table:

```
INSERT Wrox_Docs_Logs (ItemID, UserName,LogDate,UserAction)
SELECT ItemID, CheckedUser, GETDATE(),@StatusText
FROM inserted
END
```

The following screen shot is an example of Wrox_Docs_Logs entries. Notice that there are several entries that indicate the various actions that have been logged. For example the highlighted row indicates that the user "guest" checked out a document that has an ItemID of 5.

ItemID	UserName	UserAction	LogDate
14	guest	Document Archived	7/14/2002 5:13:36
5	guest	Document Checked In	7/14/2002 5:07:40
5	guest	Document Checked Out	7/14/2002 5:08:46
6	joe	Document Checked In	7/14/2002 5:10:08
5	joe	Document Checked In	7/14/2002 5:10:43

Designing the Business Layer

Now that we have finished designing our databases we can move on to coding our business classes. Our business classes are written in Visual Basic.Net and will provide our application access to the logic that will run our application. Calls to our stored procedures are neatly wrapped in our classes. Remember, most of the code that accesses our stored procedures is similar so we will not be covering each method in great detail.

There are 3 classes that constitute the business layer:

❑ **WroxDocsDB** – This class wraps all of our Database calls to the stored procedures by calling the `Database` class that we used earlier in the book.

❑ **WroxDocUtilBiz** – Contains utility functions that the application will use.

❑ **WroxDocSecurity** – Class that wraps our application's security functions such as verifying a user's access to a document. This class inherits from IBuySpy's `PortalSecurity` class.

We also define one enumeration, `DocumentPermissions`, to specify the permissions that can be granted.

```
Public Enum DocumentPermissions
        CheckInOutRights     = 3     'check in/out ability
        DownloadandViewOnly  = 2     'no check in/out ability
        ViewListingOnly      = 1     'same as anonymous users
End Enum
```

This enumeration will be used throughout the rest of the code when permissions for documents must be specified.

The WroxDocsDB Class

Of all our classes this is the most important. This class wraps all the database calls to our stored procedures through the `Wrox.Intranet.DataTools.Database` class, making it much easier to maintain our application if the database should ever change. Because most of the methods are almost identical to each other and each one calls the equivalent stored procedure we have not listed all methods in their entirety. Again, we recommend that you download the source code for this chapter and examine the code as you move through this chapter. This will supplement your understanding of what each section is accomplishing.

Method	Description
GetDocuments	Returns a `DataSet` object of documents.
GetSingleDocument	Returns a single document as a `SqlDataReader object`.
GetChildDocuments	Returns all versions of a document from the `Wrox_Docs_Versions` table. Return type is a DataSet.
CheckDocumentIn	Checks a document back into the system.
CheckDocumentOut	Checks a document out of the system.
UploadDocument	Stores a new document in the system.
RenderDocument	Streams the document down to the client's browser.

Looking at the code in the WroxDocsDB Class

Below is the `GetDocuments` method that returns a `DataSet` to the calling function for a particular module. We will later use this method to display our documents in a `DataGrid`. We are returning a `DataSet` so that we can use the default paging feature in our `DataGrids`.

```
Public Function GetDocuments(ByVal ModuleID As Integer) As DataSet

        Dim db As New Wrox.Intranet.DataTools.Database()
        Dim ds As New DataSet()
        Dim params(0) As SqlParameter

        Try
            params(0) = db.MakeParameter("@ModuleId", ModuleID)
            db.RunProcedure("upDMS_GetWroxDocs", params, ds)
            If ds Is Nothing Then
                _errorMessage = db.ErrorMessage
            End If
        Catch e As Exception
            _errorMessage = "Unable to retrieve documents[" & e.Message & "]"
            ds = Nothing
        End Try

        Return ds
    End Function
```

Remember that we are using the common `Database` class for data access. More details on this class can be found in Appendix A.

The other method of interest in the `WroxDocsDB` class is the `RenderDocument` method that streams a document to the client's browser. Notice in the code listed below that the `Response` object is passed by reference as a parameter to the function. The document's content is then read into a `Byte` array and written directly into the `Response.Output` stream. What we want to happen at this point is for the user to be prompted with a "**Save As**" dialog in the browser. The way we accomplish this is by adding the `Content-Disposition` header and by setting the file name so that the "**Save As**" dialog will list the actual file's name and not the name of the `aspx` file that is serving the document to the user. The `strTable` parameter determines which table the document is pulled from, `Wrox_Docs` or `Wrox_Docs_Versions`.

```
Public Function RenderDocument(ByVal ItemID As Integer, ByVal strTable As String, _
ByRef response As HttpResponse) As Integer

        Dim db As New Wrox.Intranet.DataTools.Database()
        Dim dr As SqlDataReader
        Dim params(1) As SqlParameter

        Try
            params(0) = db.MakeParameter("@ItemID", ItemID)
            params(1) = db.MakeParameter("@Table", strTable)
            db.RunProcedure("upDMS_RenderWroxDoc", params, dr)
            If dr Is Nothing Then
                _errorMessage = db.ErrorMessage
            End If
        Catch e As Exception
            _errorMessage = "Unable to retrieve the document [" & e.Message & "]"
            dr = Nothing
        End Try

        dr.Read()

        response.AddHeader("Content-Disposition", _
          "inline;filename=" & dr("filename"))
        'NOTE: could also use "attachment" instead of "inline"

        response.ContentType = CType(dr("ContentType"), String)
        response.OutputStream.Write(CType(dr("Content"), Byte()), _
          0, CInt(dr("ContentSize")))

        dr.Close()
        response.End()

End Sub
```

As stated earlier, the remainder of the methods in the `WroxDocsDB` class calls the equivalent stored procedure for each method and is not listed here for brevity.

The WroxDocUtilBiz Class

This class has two fundamental methods. The `GetImageFromMime` method resolves a MIME type to an image file name for the purpose of displaying an icon in the main listing of documents that matches the document type. For example, if the file is a Microsoft Word document then a MS Word icon will be displayed. It will be used in our `.aspx` pages later. The other utility type method is the `HandleItemBound` method that is used with several `DataGrids` in our pages.

Method	Description
GetImageFromMime	Returns a `string` that represents an image filename.
HandleItemBound	Allows us to access a data item before it is displayed in the grid.

We will look at the `HandleItemBound` later when we code our DataGrids. The `GetImageFromMime` method is listed below. This method is what enables any document type to display the appropriate icon. If a MIME type is not recognized, the `default.gif` image will be displayed.

In order to identify other types of images (not listed below) you will want to modify the method. You could even recode the method so that the types are not hard coded, perhaps using a configuration file. This is an example of how abstracting the process of linking MIME types to image files into a method like this gives us the flexibility to change how we carry it out:

```
Public Function GetImageFromMime(ByVal strMimeType As String) As String

    Select Case strMimeType
        Case "application/pdf"
            Return "pdfsmall.gif"
        Case "application/msword"
            Return "wordsmall.gif"
        Case "application/vnd.ms-excel"
            Return "excelsmall.gif"
        Case "application/x-zip-compressed"
            Return "zipsmall.gif"
        Case Else
            Return "default.gif"
    End Select

End Function
```

The WroxDocSecurity Class

This class will be used any time we need to verify the permissions that a user has on a specific document. The class actually inherits from the `PortalSecurity` class that is defined by the IBuySpy Framework and described in Chapter 4. Again, these methods are similar to each other in that they call their counterpart stored procedures. Therefore we will not look at each method in great detail.

Method	Description
HasDocPermissions	Returns a Boolean value to determine if a user's role has appropriate permissions to a document.
UpdateDocAcls	Updates the permissions for a document based on user's role membership.
DeleteDocAcls	Deletes the permissions for a specific RoleID on a document.
AddDocAcls	Adds permissions for a specific RoleID on a document.
GetDocAcls	Returns the permissions for a specific document as a DataSet.

The HasDocPermisions method is listed below. It calls the upDMS_WroxDocsHasAcls stored procedure that we listed earlier. This method is used when we need to verify a user's permission on a document. For example, when a user attempts to check out or download a document, this method will determine if the user is authorized to perform the action:

```
Public Function HasDocPermissions(ByVal Acls As DocumentPermissions, _
                                  ByVal ItemID As Integer) As Boolean
    Dim result As Integer
    Dim db As New Wrox.Intranet.DataTools.Database()
    Dim context As HttpContext = HttpContext.Current

    Dim params(2) As SqlParameter

    Try
        params(0) = db.MakeParameter("@ItemID", ItemID)
        params(1) = db.MakeParameter("@User", context.User.Identity.Name)
        params(2) = db.MakeParameter("@TargetAcl", CType(Acls, Integer))


        result = db.RunProcedure("upDMS_WroxDocsHasAcls", params)
        If result <= 0 Then
            _errorMessage = db.ErrorMessage
        End If
    Catch e As Exception
        _errorMessage = "Unable to verify the permission [" & e.Message & "]"
        result = -1
    Finally
        db = Nothing
    End Try

    Return result

End Function
```

Notice that we are obtaining the user's logged on name from the HttpContext class by accessing the User.Identity.Name property.

Creating the Presentation Layer

Now that we have reviewed the Business layer we can move on to the final section. Our user interface will be created in Visual Studio and consists of 4 `aspx` pages and 5 `ascx` User Controls. Rather than creating each file in the exact order listed below we will follow a more functional approach beginning with the Upload and Edit process. Next we will code the Display and Select Process that is responsible for displaying and selecting documents. Then we will code the Check out and in process. We will eventually touch on each of the files listed below in some detail.

The User Controls

❑ `DisplayFull.ascx` – This is our main control that manages documents submitted by users. It is hosted in the `DesktopDefault.aspx` page from the IBuySpy Portal.

❑ `DisplaySummary.ascx` – A scaled down version of the main control (listed above) designed to be used in an area of the portal site where space is limited. For example in the right or left column of the IBuySpy site.

❑ `DocumentDetails.ascx` – This control is embedded in the two main controls (listed above) and is used to display the child versions of any given document..

❑ `WroxDocAcls.ascx` – This control is a DataGrid that enables a user to manage permissions on a document. This control is embedded in our Edit page, `WroxDocEdit.aspx`.

❑ `WroxDocsTitle.ascx` – Displays the module title and displays the Edit, Search and Add Document links in each of our controls.

The aspx Pages

❑ `WroxDocEdit.aspx` – This page submits new documents to the system and edits existing meta-information pertaining to documents when an authorized user clicks the edit button.

❑ `WroxDocAction.aspx` – This page checks documents in and out of the system.

❑ `ServeWroxDocument.aspx` – This page downloads a file to the user's computer.

❑ `SearchWroxDocs.aspx` – Searches for a particular document.

Below is a diagram that illustrates how our main pages fit together. Notice that the `DisplayFull.ascx` control is our main control in which all document actions are performed. The controls that are not listed on the diagram, such as `DocumentDetails.ascx` and `WroxDocAcls.ascx`, are helper controls that are embedded inside of either the main control or in our `.aspx` pages and will be explained in more detail later in the text.

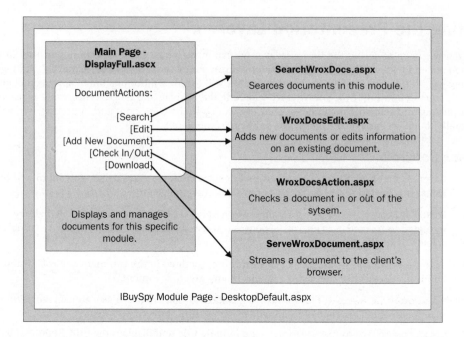

IBuySpy Module Page - DesktopDefault.aspx

Coding the Upload and Edit Process

First we need a way for users to place files into the system. Once files are in the system we must then provide a means to edit the information related to the posted files. Both of these tasks are accomplished in the `WroxDocEdit.aspx` file. To keep this example as brief as possible we have limited the number of input fields on the form to three: Title, Category and the actual file to upload. You will no doubt want to add more fields to the form in your own production environment.

Below is the form performing an upload action:

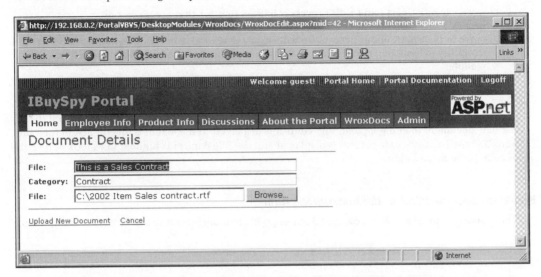

Again the same form but this time performing an update on an existing record. The information that can be edited is in the FileDescription, Category and Acl columns.

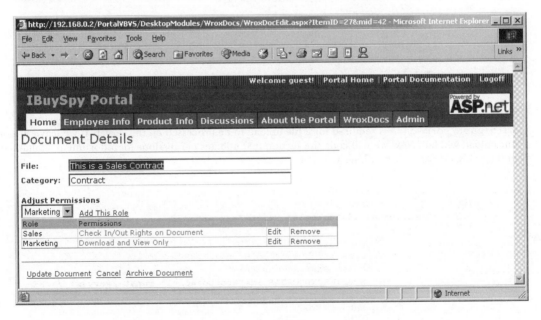

> Access to our Upload and Edit process is limited to users that are given Edit permissions in the IBuySpy Administrative Module for a specific module. When we move to the Check in/out process we will ensure that we give our application more flexibility in assigning permissions at the document level – rather than for the entire module.

You probably noticed that the form looked very different in both of the screen shots above. This is because content is dynamically hidden or displayed depending on the action. For example if the action is a new document then the Upload File control is displayed. If the action is an edit action then the WroxDocsAcls.ascx user control is displayed and the File control is hidden. Let's look at how this is done in more detail below:

Breaking down the HTML in the Edit/Upload form

The first task is to create the WroxDocEdit.aspx file and begin coding the HTML to build the form.

```
<FORM encType="multipart/form-data" runat="server">
         
        <TABLE cellSpacing="0" cellPadding="0" width="100%" border="0">
          <TBODY>
            <TR vAlign="top">
            <TD colSpan="2">
            <portal:banner id="SiteHeader" runat="server" />
            </TD>
            </TR>
          </TBODY>
        </TABLE>
    ...
```

The most significant detail about this form is the enctype property of the <Form> tag. Specifying multipart/form-data is required for a file upload to be processed on the server. If we leave this out our upload will fail. Next we will code the section that updates permissions for a document, contained in the WroxDocsAcls.ascx User Control.

```
        ...
            <!-- Acls Panel -->
            <asp:panel id="pnlAcls" Runat="server">
              <TR>
                <TD width="14"> </TD>
                <TD class="subhead" colSpan="2"><BR>
                  Adjust Permissions<BR>
                  <Wrox:WROXDOCACLS id="WroxDocAcls1" runat="server" /><BR>
                </TD>
                <TD> </TD>
              </TR>
            </asp:panel>
            <!-- End Acls Panel -->
            <!--Begin File Panel -->
            <asp:panel id="pnlFile" Runat="server">
```

```
        <TR>
            <TD width="14"> </TD>
            <TD class="subhead">File:</TD>
            <TD>
                <INPUT id="Upload"
                style="WIDTH: 353px; FONT-FAMILY: verdana"
                type="file" name="Upload" runat="server" width="300">
            </TD>
            <TD> </TD>
        </TR>
    </asp:panel>
    <!-- End File panel -->

...
```

Note the use of `Panel` objects in our HTML above. Panels act as containers for other objects and are generally useful when dealing with dynamic processing of controls. The highlighted lines show the two panel objects named `pnlAcls` and `pnlFile`. Panels are used because we want to show and hide areas in the HTML when the document is rendered. Also take note of the other highlighted lines that show the `WroxDocAcls` user control that we will code in the next few paragraphs.

> *Visible Panels are rendered as `<div>` tags in the client's browser when the page is processed. If a Panel's `Visible` property is set to false it will not be rendered in the client.*

The last few items to code are the Update, Cancel and Archive `LinkButtons`.

```
    <TR>
        <TD width="14"> </TD>
        <TD colSpan="2">
            <HR>
            <asp:linkbutton class="CommandButton" id="UploadButton"
                runat="server" Text="Upload New Document" /> 
            <asp:linkbutton class="CommandButton" id="UpdateButton"
                runat="server" Text="Update Document" /> 
            <asp:linkbutton class="CommandButton" id="CancelButton"
                runat="server" Text="Cancel" CausesValidation="False" />
                 
            <asp:linkbutton class="CommandButton" id="ArchiveButton"
                runat="server" Text="Archive Document" /></TD>
        <TD> </TD>
    </TR>
    </TABLE>
    </FORM>
    </BODY>
</HTML>
```

We have added our command buttons above together in one table cell. We will also hide and display these depending on what action is being performed. For example if the action is an upload we will only show the `UploadButton` and `CancelButton` since these are appropriate to that particular action. This is done in the codebehind for this page.

Coding the Codebehind File for our Upload/Edit Process

Let's start by looking at the Page_Load event in the WroxDocsEdit.aspx.vb file.

```
        Private ItemID As Integer = 0
        Private ModuleID As Integer = 0

    Private Sub Page_Load(ByVal sender As System.Object, ByVal e As _
      System.EventArgs) Handles MyBase.Load

            ' Grab the module ID of this particuar module
            ModuleID = Int32.Parse(Request.Params("Mid"))

            ' Verify that the current user has access to edit this module
            If PortalSecurity.HasEditPermissions(ModuleID) = False Then
                Response.Redirect("~/Admin/EditAccessDenied.aspx")
            End If

            ' Determine ItemID of Document to Update
            If Not (Request.Params("ItemID") Is Nothing) Then
                ItemID = Int32.Parse(Request.Params("ItemID"))
            End If
        ...
```

Several things are going on at this point in the page. We are assigning the ModuleID and ItemID to a set of private variables. We are also calling the HasEditPermissions function in the PortalSecurity class. This class is part of the IBuySpy Framework and tells us if the current user is in the administrator role or has been given edit rights to the particular module. If the user is unauthorized the page is routed to a generic access denied page.

```
    ...
    If Not IsPostBack Then

            If Not (Request.Params("ItemID") Is Nothing) Then    'Update Action

                ' Obtain a single row of document information
                Dim DocsDB As New WroxDocsDB()

                'dont show the file upload on edits
                pnlFile.Visible = False
                pnlAcls.Visible = True
                UploadButton.Visible = False
                ArchiveButton.Attributes.Add("onclick", _
                "return (confirm('Are you sure you want to archive _
                this document?'));")

                Dim dr As SqlDataReader = DocsDB.GetSingleDocument(ItemID)
                ' Load first row into Datareader
                dr.Read()
                txtDes.Text = CStr(dr("FileDescription"))
                txtCat.Text = CStr(dr("Category"))
                dr.Close()
```

```
            Else
...
```

In the code above we are checking that an `ItemID` is being passed to the page. If not then we can assume that the action is a new file to be uploaded and we hide and display our panel accordingly.

Also take note of the `ArchiveButton`. Since an archive action is permanent, we want to verify the user's intent in case a link was accidentally clicked. We can accomplish this by adding a JavaScript confirmation. We do this by adding the code to the `Attributes` collection of the `ArchiveButton` control:

```
ArchiveButton.Attributes.Add("onclick", _
"return (confirm('Are you sure you want to archive _
this document?'));")
```

If the user clicks **OK**, the click event will fire, else the user will be returned to the form and the event will not fire.

If the `ItemID` parameter is passed then we call the `GetSingleDocument` method from our `WroxDocsDB` business class and fill the fields on the form.

The other item of interest is the addition of the `UrlReferrer` to the `ViewState` object. This will enable us to send the user back to the referring page if cancel is clicked.

```
            'The action is a new document
            pnlAcls.Visible = False
            pnlFile.Visible = True
            UpdateButton.Visible = False
            ArchiveButton.Visible = False

        End If

        ' Store URL Referrer to return to portal
        ViewState("UrlReferrer") = Request.UrlReferrer.ToString()

    End If

End Sub
```

Processing the UploadButton_Click event

When the user clicks the `Upload` Button the `Click` event for the button is fired and the process of adding the file to the database is initiated.

```
Private Sub UploadButton_Click(ByVal sender As System.Object, ByVal e As
System.EventArgs) Handles UploadButton.Click

        Dim DocsDB As New WroxDocsDB()

        ' Determine whether a file was uploaded
        If Not (Upload.PostedFile.ContentLength = 0) Then

            'parse path out of filename
            Dim filename As String = _
            Upload.PostedFile.FileName.Substring _
            (Upload.PostedFile.FileName.LastIndexOf("\") + 1)

            'get the byte array and len
            Dim length As Integer = CInt(Upload.PostedFile.ContentLength)
            Dim contentType As String = Upload.PostedFile.ContentType
            Dim content(length) As Byte

            'read into the byte array
            Upload.PostedFile.InputStream.Read(content, 0, length)
        ...
```

Listed above we obtain the filename from the `Upload` file field and parse out the directory information, leaving us with the file name and file extension. We then set the `ContentType` and the length of the file in bytes. A `Byte` array is created and filled with the uploaded file. Next we call our `UploadDocument` method in our `WroxDocsDB` business class and send the user back to the originating page.

If the length of the file is 0 then we set an error message in the page and return from the method.

```
        ...
                ' Upload a new document with a file attached
                DocsDB.UploadDocument(ModuleID, _
                                            ItemID, _
                                            Context.User.Identity.Name, _
                                            filename, _
                                            txtDes.Text, _
                                            txtCat.Text, _
                                            content, _
                                            length, _
                                            contentType)
            Else
                ErrorMessage.Text = "You  must select a valid file to upload."
                Return
            End If

            ' go back to the portal home page
            Response.Redirect(CType(ViewState("UrlReferrer"), String))

        End Sub
```

The remaining methods in the `WroxDocsEdit.aspx.vb` file are `Click` events for the `ArchiveButton` and `UpdateButton` buttons and are relatively straightforward. Notice that the `UpdateButton` does not submit a file, but rather only updates the other two fields on our form. This is because we will later implement the check in and out process that will handle this functionality.

```
Private Sub UpdateButton_Click(ByVal sender As Object, ByVal e As
System.EventArgs) Handles UpdateButton.Click
        If Not (Request.Params("ItemID") Is Nothing) Then

            Dim DocsDB As New WroxDocsDB()

            ' Update information about a document
            DocsDB.UpdateDocument(ItemID, _
                                    txtDes.Text, _
                                    txtCat.Text)

            ' go back to the portal home page
            Response.Redirect(CType(ViewState("UrlReferrer"), String))
        End If
    End Sub


    Private Sub ArchiveButton_Click(ByVal sender As Object, ByVal e _
    As System.EventArgs) Handles ArchiveButton.Click
        If Not (Request.Params("ItemID") Is Nothing) Then

            Dim DocsDB As New WroxDocsDB()
            DocsDB.ArchiveDocument(ItemID)

        End If

        ' Redirect back to the portal home page
        Response.Redirect(CType(ViewState("UrlReferrer"), String))
    End Sub
```

Coding the WroxDocsAcls.ascx Permissions control

This control is embedded inside the `WroxDocsEdit.aspx` form and is only displayed on an `Edit` action. The idea is that permissions can be assigned according to individual documents rather than by module. This allows for more flexibility than the existing solution offered by IBuySpy, which requires giving `Edit` rights per entire module for any user that needs to perform an action on a specific document.

Remember that we defined an enumeration in the `WroxDocSecurity.vb` file that represents the following document level permissions that may be assigned to any given document. As it is short, we'll show it again here to remind ourselves of its members:

```
Public Enum DocumentPermissions
        CheckInOutRights      = 3    'check in/out ability
        DownloadandViewOnly   = 2    'no check in/out ability
        ViewListingOnly       = 1    'same as anonymous users
End Enum
```

The highest level of permissions is a 3, allowing for a document to be checked in or out of the system. A level 2 only allows files to be downloaded. Level 1 is the most restrictive and allows users to view the listing of documents but will not allow any documents to be downloaded to the client's computer. If a user's role is granted `Edit` permissions in the IBuySpy administrative tab, the user can perform all actions on a document by default. We will see this in greater detail in the next few pages.

Below is the HTML for our permissions DataGrid, named `dgRoles`:

```
<%@ Control Language="vb" AutoEventWireup="false" Codebehind="WroxDocAcls.ascx.vb"
Inherits="ASPNetPortal.WroxDocAcls" %>
<asp:dropdownlist id="DlRoles" runat="server" DataTextField="RoleName"
DataValueField="RoleID" /> 
<asp:linkbutton class="CommandButton" id="AddRoleButton" runat="server" text="Add
This Role" /><BR>
<asp:datagrid id="dgRoles" runat="server" Width="500px"
AutoGenerateColumns="False" OnCancelCommand="CancelCommand"
OnEditCommand="EditCommand" OnUpdateCommand="UpdateCommand"
OnDeleteCommand="DeleteCommand" DataKeyField="RoleID" CssClass="normal">
    <EditItemStyle BackColor="LightYellow" />
    <HeaderStyle ForeColor="Black" BackColor="Silver" />
    <Columns>
        <asp:BoundColumn DataField="RoleName" ReadOnly="True" HeaderText="Role" />
        <asp:TemplateColumn HeaderText="Permissions">
            <ItemTemplate>
                <asp:Label id="lblAcls" runat="server" />
            </ItemTemplate>
            <EditItemTemplate>
                <asp:DropDownList id="dlPermissions" runat="server">
                    <asp:ListItem Value="1">View Listing Only</asp:ListItem>
                    <asp:ListItem Value="2">View and Download Only</asp:ListItem>
                    <asp:ListItem Value="3">Check In/Out Rights</asp:ListItem>
                </asp:DropDownList>
            </EditItemTemplate>
        </asp:TemplateColumn>
        <asp:EditCommandColumn ButtonType="LinkButton"
            UpdateText="Update" CancelText="Cancel" EditText="Edit" />
        <asp:ButtonColumn Text="Remove" CommandName="Delete" />
    </Columns>
</asp:datagrid>
<asp:label id="lblMsg" runat="server" Visible="False" CssClass="NormalRed"
text="** There are no Roles Associated with this Document yet **" />
```

Notice in the bold code above that we are defining handlers for any `Edit`, `Update`, `Cancel` and `Delete` command initiated by the user. These handlers are coded in the codebehind for this control and will be discussed next. The other item of interest is the addition of a drop-down column in the `EditItemTemplate` column of the datagrid, which is what is displayed when a user clicks on the `Edit` column. This allows a user to select permissions from the drop-down list when in edit mode; when not in edit mode a label is displayed that shows the permission. You can see examples of both item templates in the graphic below. The item selected for edit is for the Marketing role on a particular document.

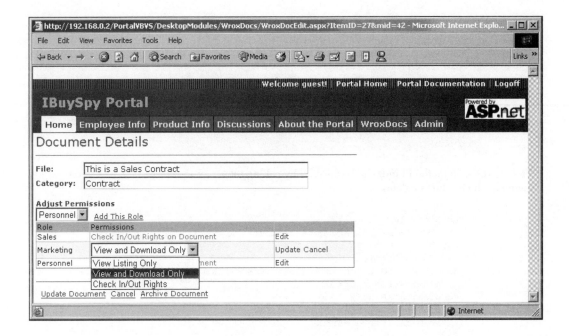

Inheriting our Control from the PortalModuleControl Class

All of our user controls will inherit from the `PortalModuleControl` control. As we saw in Chapter 3, inheriting from the `PortalModuleControl` gives us access to the IBuySpy parent class that controls how all User Controls behave in the portal.`Namespace ASPNetPortal`

```
Public MustInherit Class WroxDocAcls
    Inherits ASPNetPortal.PortalModuleControl
```

Codebehind for the WroxDocsAcls.ascx control

This is the first User Control that we have created in the project.
The first item to code is the `Page_Load` event. We will want to fill our DataGrid with any roles that may be associated with the document that is loaded into the edit form. We are also filling the drop down list of roles with all available roles that are stored in the Portal by calling the `AdminDB.GetPortalRoles` method.

```
    Private Sub Page_Load(ByVal sender As System.Object, ByVal e _
As System.EventArgs) Handles MyBase.Load
        'Put user code to initialize the page here
        If Page.IsPostBack = False Then

            Dim _portalSettings As PortalSettings = _
            CType(Context.Items("PortalSettings"), PortalSettings)
            Dim tab As TabSettings = _portalSettings.ActiveTab
```

```
              Dim admin As New AdminDB()
              Dim roles As SqlDataReader = _
              admin.GetPortalRoles(_portalSettings.PortalId)

              DlRoles.DataSource = roles
              DlRoles.DataBind()

              BindRoles()
         End If
      End Sub
```

The `BindRoles` method binds the `DataGrid` by calling the `WroxDocSecurity.GetDocAcls` method, which returns a dataset.

```
Private Sub BindRoles()
        Dim DocsDB As New WroxDocSecurity()

        Dim ds As DataSet
        ds = DocsDB.GetDocAcls(Request.Params("ItemID"))
        dgRoles.DataSource = ds
        dgRoles.DataBind()
        If ds.Tables(0).Rows.Count = 0 Then
            lblMsg.Visible = True
        Else
            lblMsg.Visible = False
        End If

    End Sub
```

It is necessary to populate our drop down list when the user clicks `Edit` in our `DataGrid`. We are also formatting several items at run time in our grid to display a more descriptive label for the `Acl` column. Remember that this column matches up with the `DocumentPermissions` enumeration. However it is not recommended to display a numeric value that represents the permission for a role. The chosen solution to this is to hook into the `ItemDataBound` which fires when a row of the `DataGrid` is bound to an item of the associated data source. This way we may substitute the numeric value of the permission with a text description that is easier to understand such as "Download and View Only."

```
Sub dgRoles_ItemDataBound(ByVal sender As Object, ByVal e As
System.Web.UI.WebControls.DataGridItemEventArgs) Handles dgRoles.ItemDataBound

        'If row is not in edit mode and not a pager or header bar
        If e.Item.ItemType = ListItemType.Item Or _
        e.Item.ItemType = ListItemType.AlternatingItem Then
            Dim Acl As DocumentPermissions
            Dim lblAcl As Label
            lblAcl = CType(e.Item.Cells(1).FindControl("lblAcls"), Label)
            lblAcl.ForeColor = Color.Red

            Select Case DataBinder.Eval(e.Item.DataItem, "Acl")
                Case Acl.ViewListingOnly
                    lblAcl.Text = "View Listing Only"
                Case Acl.DownloadandViewOnly
```

```
                        lblAcl.Text = "Download and View Only"
                  Case Acl.CheckInOutRights
                        lblAcl.Text = "Check In/Out Rights on Document"

            End Select

      End If

      ' handle the edit state
      If e.Item.ItemType = ListItemType.EditItem Then
         Dim dlAcls As DropDownList
         dlAcls = _
            CType(e.Item.Cells(1).FindControl("dlPermissions"), DropDownList)
         dlAcls.SelectedIndex = _
         dlAcls.Items.IndexOf(dlAcls.Items.FindByValue(e.Item.DataItem("Acl")))
      End If

   End Sub
```

The remainder of the codebehind in this control is the event handlers that provide the Add, Edit, and Update functionality of the grid. Notice that we are hiding columns depending on what is clicked. For example when Edit is clicked we hide the 'Remove column.

```
' Editcommand - fires when Edit is clicked
Sub EditCommand(ByVal Sender As Object, ByVal E As DataGridCommandEventArgs)
      dgRoles.EditItemIndex = E.Item.ItemIndex

      'hide the remove column while in edit mode
      dgRoles.Columns(3).Visible = False
      BindRoles()
End Sub

' Updatecommand - fires when Update is clicked
Sub UpdateCommand(ByVal Sender As Object, ByVal E _
As DataGridCommandEventArgs)
      Dim DocsDB As New WroxDocSecurity()

      Dim dlAcls As DropDownList
      dlAcls = CType(E.Item.Cells(1).FindControl _
      ("dlPermissions"), DropDownList)
      DocsDB.UpdateDocAcls(Request.Params("ItemID"), _
                              dgRoles.DataKeys(E.Item.ItemIndex), _
                              dlAcls.SelectedItem.Value)
      'Deselect the grid
      dgRoles.EditItemIndex = -1

      'show the remove column
      dgRoles.Columns(3).Visible = True
      BindRoles()
End Sub

' Cancelcommand - fires when cancel is clicked
Sub CancelCommand(ByVal Sender As Object, ByVal E _
```

```
         As DataGridCommandEventArgs)
             dgRoles.Columns(3).Visible = True
             dgRoles.EditItemIndex = -1
             BindRoles()
      End Sub

      ' Deletecommand - fires when Remove is clicked
      Sub DeleteCommand(ByVal Sender As Object, ByVal E As DataGridCommandEventArgs)
             Dim DocsDB As New WroxDocSecurity()
             DocsDB.DeleteDocAcls(Request.Params("ItemID"), _
             dgRoles.DataKeys(E.Item.ItemIndex))
             BindRoles()
      End Sub

      ' AddRoleButton_Click - fires when Add this Role is clicked
      Sub AddRoleButton_Click(ByVal sender As System.Object, ByVal e As
      System.EventArgs) Handles AddRoleButton.Click
             Dim DocsDB As New WroxDocSecurity()
             If DocsDB.AddDocAcls(Request.Params("ItemID"), _
             DlRoles.SelectedItem.Value) Then BindRoles()
      End Sub
```

Coding the Display and Select Process

Now that we have a method for users to place files into the system we need to create the
DisplayFull.ascx User Control that will display documents for a module and will allow users to
edit, select or check documents in and out of the system. Below is a screen shot of what our application
will look like:

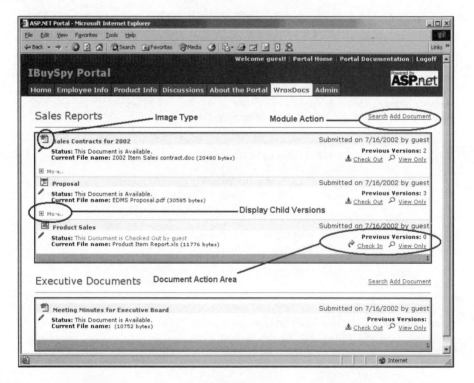

In the screen shot above there are two instances of our module on one page: one titled Sales Reports and one named Executive Documents. The documents are associated to each module with by the `ModuleID` column in our `Wrox_Docs` table. This enables us to compartmentalize our documents and to keep Edit permissions managed by module. Let's discuss the circled areas in the screen shot and then we will code the page.

Features of DisplayFull.ascx User Control

❑ **Image Type Icon** – this icon represents the type of document. This icon is set by calling the `WroxDocUtilBiz.GetImageFromMime` function in our code.

❑ **Module Action** – This portion of the page comes from the `WroxDocsTitle.ascx` control, which shows the module title and displays action links for the module. If a user has `Edit` access to the module, the **Add Document** link will be shown. The **Search** link will be shown for all users and will allow users to search for documents in a specific module.

❑ **Display Child Documents** – If a document has more than one version the plus sign will be displayed on the report. Clicking on the plus sign will display a datagrid with the child versions. We will discuss this in more detail shortly.

❑ **Document Action Area** – The links displayed in this section perform the check in and out actions. The View link will download a copy of the file to the user's browser but will not check the document out.

Showing document versions is handled by embedding a child datagrid as seen in the graphic below. The child grid itself is a User Control named `DocumentDetails.ascx`. It is rendered in the grid through the use of the `EditItemTemplate` which isn't rendered in the `HTML` until a specific `ItemCommand` is fired and the `EditItemIndex` is set to the current row.

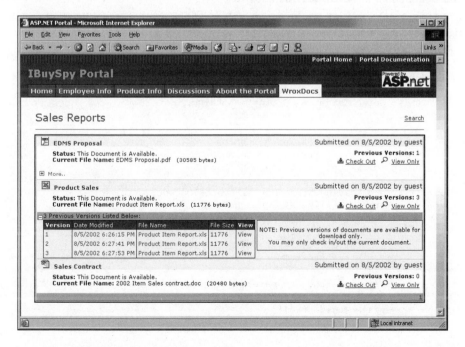

Creating the WroxDocsTitle.ascx User Control

This control will display the module title and will enable authorized users to add documents to the system. The control is embedded in the main `DisplayFull.ascx` control. In the screen shot above this control is the section that displays the **Sales Report** text and the **Search** link.

```
<%@ Control Language="vb" AutoEventWireup="false"
Codebehind="WroxDocsTitle.ascx.vb" Inherits="ASPNetPortal.WroxDocsTitle" %>
<TABLE width="100%" cellspacing="0" cellpadding="2">
    <TR>
        <TD align="left">
            <asp:label id="ModuleTitle" cssclass="Head"
            EnableViewState="false" runat="server" />
        </TD>
        <TD align="right" nowrap>
            <asp:hyperlink id="SearchButton" cssclass="CommandButton"
            EnableViewState="false" runat="server" />
            <asp:hyperlink id="EditButton" cssclass="CommandButton"
            EnableViewState="false" runat="server" />
        </TD>
    </TR>
    <TR>
        <TD colspan="4">
            <HR noshade size="4">
        </TD>
    </TR>
</TABLE>
```

Coding the Codebehind in WroxDocsTitle.ascx.vb

The codebehind in this control sets the module title and hides or displays the Edit button if the user has edit rights to the module.

```
    'Search Text
    Public SearchText As String = Nothing
    Public SearchUrl As String = Nothing
    Public SearchTarget As String = Nothing

    'Add Document text
    Public EditText As String = Nothing
    Public EditUrl As String = Nothing
    Public EditTarget As String = Nothing

Private Sub Page_Load(ByVal sender As System.Object, ByVal e _
    As System.EventArgs) Handles MyBase.Load

        ' Obtain PortalSettings from Current Context
        Dim _portalSettings As PortalSettings = _
            CType(HttpContext.Current.Items("PortalSettings"), PortalSettings)

        ' Obtain reference to parent portal module
        Dim portalModule As PortalModuleControl = CType(Me.Parent, _
            PortalModuleControl)
```

```
        ' Display Module Title and Buttons
        ModuleTitle.Text = portalModule.ModuleConfiguration.ModuleTitle

        ' Display the Edit button if the parent portalmodule has configured
        ' the PortalModuleTitle User Control
        ' to display it -- and the current client has edit access permissions
        If _portalSettings.AlwaysShowEditButton = True Or _
          (PortalSecurity.IsInRoles _
          (portalModule.ModuleConfiguration.AuthorizedEditRoles)) Then

            'Set the Add Document Button
            If Not IsNothing(EditText) Then
                EditButton.Text = EditText
                EditButton.NavigateUrl = EditUrl + "?mid=" + _
                  portalModule.ModuleId.ToString()
                EditButton.Target = EditTarget
            End If

        End If

        'Set the Search Button
        If Not IsNothing(SearchText) Then
            SearchButton.Text = SearchText
            SearchButton.NavigateUrl = SearchUrl + "?mid=" + _
              portalModule.ModuleId.ToString()
            SearchButton.Target = SearchTarget
        End If

    End Sub
```

Coding the DisplayFull.ascx Control

Our `DisplayFull.ascx` User Control consists of one `DataGrid` for the parent documents and one child grid embedded in a row of the parent grid. Because we wanted to format our grid with rich markup we coded the grid as one `ItemTemplate` column. The choice of using a `DataGrid` instead of a `DataList` control was made because of the automatic paging that is built into the `DataGrid` control. If we chose a `DataList` we would have to manually implement paging for our control.

```
<asp:datagrid id="dgListing" runat="server" CssClass="normal" Width="100%"
Height="101px" AutoGenerateColumns="False" AllowPaging="True"
OnItemCommand="SelectItemCommand" PageSize="5" OnPageIndexChanged="PageChange"
ShowHeader="False" DataKeyField="ItemID">
        <FooterStyle BackColor="Silver" />
        <Columns>
          <asp:TemplateColumn>
            <ItemTemplate>
```

We have several events handled in the `DataGrid` above: the `OnPageIndexChanged` will fire when a user clicks any of the paging buttons located at the bottom of the grid. We set the paging on the grid to display only five records at a time. The other event that has a handler in our codebehind file is `OnItemCommand`, which fires when a **command** button is clicked from inside our `ItemTemplate` column. The command buttons have a `CommandArgument` and `CommandName` property that will identify the particular command so we will know which button was pressed and what to do with the command.

Next we code the HTML that displays document icons and other information such as the date that a document was submitted and which user posted the document.

```
...
<!-- table begin -->
<TABLE cellSpacing="0" cellPadding="0" width="100%" bgColor="#eeeecc" border="0">
   <TR>
      <TD class="SubHead" colSpan="2"> 
         <asp:Image id="imgFormat" runat="server"
            ImageUrl="images/wordsmall.gif" /> 
         <B><%# Container.DataItem("FileDescription") %> </B>
      </TD>
      <!-- submitted date -->
      <TD align="right">
         <FONT size="2">Submitted on <%# DataBinder.Eval(Container.DataItem,
            "CreatedDate", "{0:d}") %> by
            <%# Container.DataItem("CreatedbyUser") %>
         </FONT><BR>
      </TD>
   </TR>
</TABLE>
...
```

The next section of HTML is the table that displays other document information, such as the current status, file name, and the number of previous versions that are listed for the document. The action buttons that perform check in and out actions are also defined.

```
<TABLE cellSpacing="0" cellPadding="0" width="100%" bgColor="#ffffff" border="0">
   <TR>
      <TD width="100%">
         <TABLE width="100%">
            <TR>
               <TD vAlign="top" width="20">
                  <asp:HyperLink id=lnkEdit runat="server"
                     ImageUrl="~/images/edit.gif"
                     NavigateUrl=
                     '<%# "~/DesktopModules/WroxDocs/WroxDocEdit.aspx?ItemID="
                     &amp; Container.DataItem("ItemID")  &amp; "&amp;mid="
                     &amp; ModuleId %>' Visible="<%# IsEditable %>" /><BR>
               </TD>
               <TD vAlign="top" align="right">
                  <!-- Middle Table -->
                  <TABLE class="normal" width="100%">
                     <TR>
```

```
                    <TD><B>Status:</B>
                        <asp:Label id="lblStatus" runat="server" /> 
                        <BR>
                        <B>Current File Name:</B>
                        <%# Container.DataItem("FileName") %>
                          <FONT size="1">
                        (<%# Container.DataItem("ContentSize") %> bytes)
                        </FONT>
                    </TD>
                    <TD vAlign="top" align="right"><B>Previous Versions:</B>
                        <asp:Label id="lblVersions" runat="server"
                          EnableViewState="False"
                          text = '<%# Container.DataItem("VersionCount") %>'
                        /><BR>
                        <asp:ImageButton id="ImgCheck" runat="server"
                          ImageUrl="images/checkin.gif"
                          commandname="DocumentAction" />
                        <asp:LinkButton id="CheckButton" runat="server"
                          CssClass="CommandButton"
                          commandname="DocumentAction"
                          text="Check Out" />  
                        <asp:Image id="ImgView"
                           ImageUrl=
                           "~/DesktopModules/WroxDocs/images/Browsesmall.gif"
                           border="0" Runat="server" />
                        <asp:hyperlink id=lnkView runat="server"
                           CssClass="CommandButton" NavigateUrl='<%#
                    "~/DesktopModules/WroxDocs/ServeWroxDocument.aspx?ItemID="
                    &amp; Container.DataItem("ItemID")
                    &amp; "&amp;mid=" &amp; ModuleId & "&key=" &
                    Container.DataItem("ItemID")%>' Target="_blank"
                    text="View Only" />
                    </TD>
                </TR>
            </TABLE>
        </TD>
    </TR>
    <TR>
        <TD colSpan="2">
            <asp:ImageButton id=PlusButton runat="server"
              ImageUrl="images/plus.gif" Visible='<%#
              Container.DataItem("VersionCount") %>'
              CommandName="View" />
            <asp:Label id=Label1 runat="server" Visible='<%#
              Container.DataItem("VersionCount") %>'>
            <font color="red" size="1">More..</font></asp:Label>
        </TD>
    </TR>
  </TABLE>
 </TD>
 </TR>
 </TABLE>
 <!-- End of Table -->
</ItemTemplate>
```

Listed above is the `ItemTemplate`, which is a non-selected row in our `DataGrid`. Next we will code the `EditItemTemplate`, which will display our child `DataGrid`.

Notice that the HTML is the same as when we coded in the `ItemTemplate` column except that the control names have _Edit appended to distinguish the controls in the `EditItemTemplate` from the controls in the `ItemTemplate` column. This is done so that the selected row will display the same information as a non-selected row in addition to the child `DataGrid` of previous document versions.

```
<EditItemTemplate>
  <!-- Child Table begin -->
  <TABLE cellSpacing="0" cellPadding="0" width="100%"
    bgColor="#eeeecc" border="0">
    <TR>
        <TD class="SubHead" colSpan="2"> 
            <asp:Image id="imgFormat_Edit" runat="server"
                ImageUrl="images/wordsmall.gif" /> 
                <B><%# Container.DataItem("FileDescription") %></B>
        </TD>
        <!-- submitted date -->
        <TD align="right">
        <FONT size="2">
          Submitted on
          <%# DataBinder.Eval(Container.DataItem, "CreatedDate", "{0:d}") %>
          by
          <%# Container.DataItem("CreatedbyUser") %> </FONT><BR>
        </TD>
    </TR>
  </TABLE>
  ...
```

Again, this HTML is the same as in the `ItemTemplate` column except for the control names and the addition of the child `DataGrid`.

```
        ...
        <TABLE cellSpacing="0" cellPadding="0" width="100%"
          bgColor="#ffffff" border="0">
          <TR>
              <TD width="100%">
                  <TABLE width="100%">
                    <TR>
                        <TD vAlign="top" width="20">
                            <asp:HyperLink id=lnkEdit_Edit runat="server"
                                ImageUrl="~/images/edit.gif" NavigateUrl='<%#
                                "~/DesktopModules/WroxDocs/WroxDocEdit.aspx?ItemID="
                                &amp; Container.DataItem("ItemID")  &amp;
                                "&amp;mid=" &amp; ModuleId %>'
                                Visible="<%# IsEditable %>" /><BR>
                        </TD>
                        <TD vAlign="top" align="right">

                        <!-- Middle Table -->
                        <TABLE class="normal" width="100%">
                          <TR>
```

```
<TD><B>Status:</B>
  <asp:Label id="lblStatus_Edit"
    runat="server" />  <BR>
  <B>Current File Name:</B>
  <%# Container.DataItem("FileName") %>
    <FONT size="1">
  (<%# Container.DataItem("ContentSize") %> bytes)
  </FONT>
</TD>
<TD vAlign="top" align="right">
  <B>Previous Versions:</B>
  <asp:Label id="lblVersions_Edit"
    runat="server" EnableViewState="False"
    text = '<%# Container.DataItem("VersionCount")%>'
    /><BR>
<asp:ImageButton id="ImgCheck_Edit"
  runat="server" ImageUrl="images/checkin.gif"
  commandname="DocumentAction" />
<asp:LinkButton id="CheckButton_Edit" runat="server"
  CssClass="CommandButton"
  commandname="DocumentAction" text="Check Out"
  />  
<asp:Image id="ImgView_Edit"
  ImageUrl="~/DesktopModules/WroxDocs/images/
  Browsesmall.gif" border="0" Runat="server" />
<asp:hyperlink id=lnkView_Edit runat="server"
  CssClass="CommandButton" NavigateUrl='<%#
  "~/DesktopModules/WroxDocs/ServeWroxDocument.aspx
  ?ItemID=" &amp; Container.DataItem("ItemID") &amp;
  "&amp;mid=" &amp; ModuleId & "&key=" &
  Container.DataItem("ItemID")%>' Target="_blank"
  text="View Only" />
</TD>
        </TR>
    </TABLE>
    </TD>
  </TR>
</TD>
</TR>
</TABLE>

<!-- Marker for Child Grid -->
<TABLE cellSpacing="0" cellPadding="0" width="100%" bgColor="lightyellow">
  <TR>
    <TD bgColor="silver" align="center">
      <asp:ImageButton id="ImgMinus" runat="server"
        ImageUrl="images/minus.gif" CommandName="View" />
    </TD>
    <TD align="left" bgColor="silver" Class="normal">
      <%# Container.DataItem("VersionCount") %>
      Previous Versions Listed Below:
    </TD>
  </TR>
  <TR>
    <TD> </TD>
```

Below is the child grid User Control. Notice the parameters that we are setting. The `DocumentID` parameter is used inside the child grid when data is bound to the grid. We will cover that control in full shortly.

```
...
    <Wrox:DocumentDetails id=Documentdetails2 runat="server"
        mid='<%# moduleID %>'
        DocumentID='<%# Container.DataItem("ItemID") %>' />
...
```

The remainder of the HTML code is mostly the closing tags for our `DataGrid`.

```
...
            <asp:Panel id="Panel1" runat="server" CssClass="normal"
                Height="59px" BackColor="#FFFFC0" BorderWidth="1"
                BorderColor="Maroon">
            <BR>NOTE: Previous versions of documents are available for
            download only.<BR>You may only check in/out the current document.
            </asp:Panel>
        </TD>
      </TR>
    </TABLE>
  </EditItemTemplate>
</asp:TemplateColumn>
<asp:BoundColumn Visible="False" DataField="ContentType" />
</Columns>
<PagerStyle HorizontalAlign="Right" BackColor="Silver" Mode="NumericPages" />
</asp:datagrid>
```

Coding the Codebehind for the DisplayFull.ascx User Control

We have several tasks to accomplish in the codebehind for this control. First we need to format the icons in our DataGrid to reflect the type of document that is stored in the database. Next we need to set the Check in and out buttons according to the current state of the document. However, before we do that let's walk through the code in the `DisplayFull.aspx.vb` file.

First, we define some class members that will be available in the rest of our code:

```
Dim DocsDB As New WroxDocsDB()
Dim DocsUtil As New WroxDocUtilBiz()
Dim DocsSec As New WroxDocSecurity()
Dim IsAnonymous As Boolean
Dim HasDownloadRights As Boolean
```

Next, we add a `Page_Load` event handler that populates the `IsAnonymous` member we just defined and calls `BindMasterGrid` to do our databinding (we'll look at this method next). We only want to do these things if the current request is not a postback.

```
    Private Sub Page_Load(ByVal sender As System.Object, ByVal e _
As System.EventArgs) Handles MyBase.Load
        If Not Page.IsPostBack Then

            IsAnonymous = Not (context.User.Identity.IsAuthenticated())
            BindMasterGrid()
        End If

    End Sub
```

The `BindMasterGrid` method calls the `GetDocuments` method of our business class and also includes some code to deal with errors and to display a message if there are no documents for display.

```
    Sub BindMasterGrid()

        Dim ds As New DataSet()
        ds = DocsDB.GetDocuments(ModuleId)

        If IsNothing(ds) Then
            ErrorMessage.Text = DocsDB.ErrorMessage
            Exit Sub
        End If

        Dim dv As DataView = ds.Tables(0).DefaultView

        If dv.Count = 0 Then
            ErrorMessage.Text = "No Documents Listed Yet!"
        Else
            dgListing.DataSource = dv
            dgListing.DataBind()
        End If

    End Sub
```

Next, let's look at how we changed the icons and command buttons in response to the status of each document in the `ItemDataBound` event:

```
    Sub dgListing_ItemDataBound(ByVal sender As Object, ByVal e As _
    System.Web.UI.WebControls.DataGridItemEventArgs) Handles dgListing.ItemDataBound

        DocsUtil.HandleItemBound(e, IsAnonymous)

    End Sub
```

A call is made to the `WroxDocUtilBiz.HandleItemBound` function that takes care of the formatting. We placed the function in the `WroxDocUtilBiz` class. This allows us to reuse the code in our other `DataGrids` later without having duplicate code floating around. Now, let's jump to that class and look at the code, listed below:

```
Sub HandleItemBound(ByRef e As System.Web.UI.WebControls.DataGridItemEventArgs,
ByVal IsAnonymous As Boolean)
If e.Item.ItemType = ListItemType.Item
Or e.Item.ItemType = ListItemType.AlternatingItem
Or e.Item.ItemType = ListItemType.EditItem Then

Dim ControlName As String = ""

            'since we are using the EditItemTemplate to display
            'our child grid, we need to distinguish the control names
            'to avoid duplicate names
            If e.Item.ItemType = ListItemType.EditItem Then
                ControlName = "_Edit"
            End If

            'Set the image icon to match the format
            Dim img As WebControls.Image
            img = CType(e.Item.Cells(0).FindControl("imgFormat" & ControlName) _
                , WebControls.Image)
            If Not (img Is Nothing) Then img.ImageUrl = "images/" & _
                Me.GetImageFromMime(e.Item.DataItem("ContentType"))

            'Now set the imagebutton to indicate check in/out
            Dim imgCheck As ImageButton
            imgCheck = CType(e.Item.Cells(0).FindControl("imgCheck" & _
                ControlName), ImageButton)

            'Check out / in command
            Dim lnkCheck As LinkButton
            lnkCheck = CType(e.Item.Cells(0).FindControl("CheckButton" & _
                ControlName), LinkButton)

            'Check out / in command
            Dim lblMsgs As Label
            lblMsgs = CType(e.Item.Cells(0).FindControl("lblStatus" & _
                ControlName), Label)
```

At this point we need to set our buttons and images according to the Status column of the document, which tells us if the document is checked in or out of the system. If the document is checked out, then the row is formatted accordingly by setting the lblMsgs.ForeColor property to red and listing the user name that checked the document out of the system. The appropriate icon is also displayed.

```
            'Set buttons and imgages according to Status
            If e.Item.DataItem("Status") <> "1" Then
                ' the document is checked out
                lblMsgs.ForeColor = Color.Red
                lblMsgs.Text = "<font color='red'>This Document is Checked _
                    Out by " & _
                DataBinder.Eval(e.Item.DataItem, "CheckedUser") & "</font>"

                If Not (imgCheck Is Nothing) Then
                    imgCheck.ImageUrl = "images/checkin.gif"
```

```
            imgCheck.CommandArgument = "checkin"
        End If

        If Not (lnkCheck Is Nothing) Then
            lnkCheck.CommandArgument = "checkin"
            lnkCheck.Text = "Check In"
        End If
```

Now we need to code the section that does our first level of permissions checking. If the user is not logged in then the click event is set to display a JavaScript alert telling the user that they must log in.

```
        'disable link if anonymous
        If IsAnonymous Then
            If Not (imgCheck Is Nothing) Then
                imgCheck.Attributes.Add("onclick", _
                "alert('You are not authorized to Check this document _
                    in. \nTry again after Logging in." & "');return false")
            End If

            If Not (lnkCheck Is Nothing) Then
                lnkCheck.Attributes.Add("onclick", _
                "alert('You are not authorized to Check this document _
                    in. \nTry again after Logging in." & "');return false")
            End If

        End If
```

We do the same as above, but this time for documents that are checked into the system.

```
        Else ' else document is checked in
            lblMsgs.Text = "This Document is Available."
            lblMsgs.ForeColor = Color.Black

            If Not (imgCheck Is Nothing) Then
                imgCheck.ImageUrl = "images/checkout.gif"
                imgCheck.CommandArgument = "checkout"
            End If

            If Not (lnkCheck Is Nothing) Then
                lnkCheck.CommandArgument = "checkout"
                lnkCheck.Text = "Check Out"
            End If

            If IsAnonymous Then
                If Not (imgCheck Is Nothing) Then
                    imgCheck.Attributes.Add("onclick", _
                    "alert('You are not authorized to Check this document _
                        out. \nTry again after Logging in." & "');return false")
                End If

                If Not (lnkCheck Is Nothing) Then
```

```
                            lnkCheck.Attributes.Add("onclick", _
                            "alert('You are not authorized to Check this document _
                                out. \nTry again after Logging in." & "');return false")
                    End If
                End If
            End If
        End If


    End Sub
```

The next section code in the `DisplayFull.aspx.vb` file is the `SelectItemCommand` handler that processes the click events from our command buttons. The `DocumentAction` command names represent the Check in and out buttons. The View command corresponds to the plus sign that a user clicks to expand the child datagrid.

```
Public Sub SelectItemCommand(ByVal source As System.Object, ByVal e As
System.Web.UI.WebControls.DataGridCommandEventArgs)
        Select Case e.CommandName
            Case "DocumentAction"
                Dim ItemID As Integer
                ItemID = dgListing.DataKeys(e.Item.ItemIndex)
                'perform check in/out Action
                Select Case e.CommandArgument
                    Case "checkin"
                    'check in
    Response.Redirect("~/DesktopModules/WroxDocs/WroxDocAction.aspx?ItemID=" & _
                    ItemID & "&Action=checkin&mid=" & ModuleId)
                    Case "checkout"
                    'check out
                        Response.Redirect("~/DesktopModules/WroxDocs/ _
                        WroxDocAction.aspx?ItemID=" & _
                        ItemID & "&Action=checkout&mid=" & ModuleId)
                    Case Else
                        'nothing
                End Select


            Case "View"
                ' Plus sign clicked, activate child grid
                If Not (dgListing.EditItemIndex = e.Item.ItemIndex) Then
                    dgListing.EditItemIndex = e.Item.ItemIndex
                Else
                    'minus sign, deselect child grid
                    dgListing.EditItemIndex = -1
                End If
                BindMasterGrid()
            Case Else

        End Select
End Sub
```

The final piece of code handles the paging of our display, ensuring that our `DataGrid` moves to the correct page and that no item is selected.

```
'hook into Page Change
Public Sub PageChange(ByVal source As System.Object, ByVal e _
As System.Web.UI.WebControls.DataGridPageChangedEventArgs)
        dgListing.CurrentPageIndex = e.NewPageIndex
        dgListing.SelectedIndex = -1
        BindMasterGrid()
End Sub
```

Rendering the File in the User's Browser

If a user clicks the `View` link from the document listing, the file is served to the user's browser by calling the `ServeWroxDocument.aspx` page. The codebehind in `ServeWroxDocument.aspx.vb` listed below demonstrates how this is done. By default only authorized users will be able to download documents. If this is too restrictive and you wish to allow all users (including anonymous users) the ability to download files simply comment out the `If` statement that checks the user's access to a document.

Notice that the script is checking first for the `ItemID` parameter. If this is passed then the `strTable` string is set to parent and the document will be streamed from the parent table `Wrox_Docs`. If, however, the `SubItemID` is passed then the document is streamed from the child table `Wrox_Docs_Versions`.

```
Private Sub Page_Load(ByVal sender As System.Object, ByVal e As System.EventArgs)
Handles MyBase.Load

  Dim ItemID As Integer = -1
  Dim strTable As String = "parent"
  Dim DocsSec As New WroxDocSecurity()

  'comment this check if you don't want to lock down the download process
  If Not (DocsSec.HasDocPermissions _
   (DocumentPermissions.DownloadandViewOnly, Request.Params("key"))) _
   And Not (PortalSecurity.HasEditPermissions(Request.Params("mid"))) Then

     Response.Write("<script>alert('You do not have authority to download _
       files.')</script>")
     Response.End()
     End If

     If Not (Request.Params("ItemID") Is Nothing) Then
         ItemID = Int32.Parse(Request.Params("ItemID"))
       ElseIf Not (Request.Params("SubItemID") Is Nothing) Then
          ItemID = Int32.Parse(Request.Params("SubItemID"))
           strTable = "child"
     End If

     If ItemID <> -1 Then
```

```
        ' Obtain Document Data from Documents table
        Dim DocsDB As New WroxDocsDB()
        DocsDB.RenderDocument(ItemID, strTable, Response)

        End If

    End Sub
```

Coding the Check in and out Process

The `WroxDocAction.aspx` page will handle both the check in and check out process. For a check out, the Status column is changed, while for a check in action a file is uploaded and will replace the current version and the status column is changed. We followed the same approach as in the earlier Upload/Update process in that we used one form for two different actions and used panels to hide or display regions depending on the action that occurs.

Below is a screen shot of the check in form.

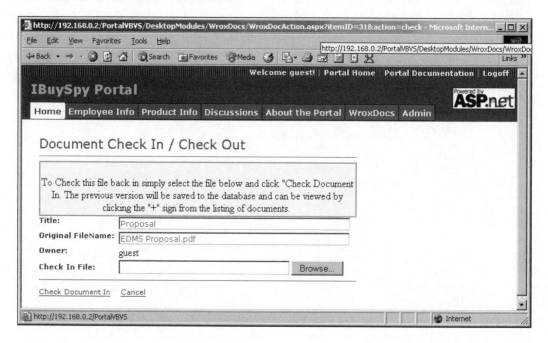

Below is a screen shot of the check out form.

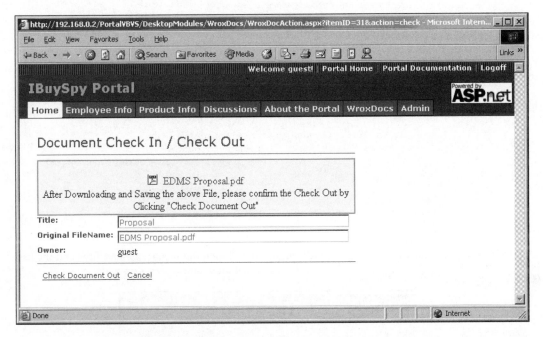

The HTML for the form is similar to the `WroxDocEdit.aspx` form so we will not show it here. All source code is available for download if you wish to look at any of the code listed here in more detail.

Verifying the User's access to a document

We need to verify that a user can check a document in or out of the system. This is accomplished with the `WroxDocSecurity.HasDocPermissions` and the `PortalSecurity.HasEditPermissions` functions. The excerpt below from the `Page_load` event of the `WroxDocAction.aspx` file illustrates how this is done.

```
Private Sub Page_Load(ByVal sender As System.Object, ByVal e As System.EventArgs)
Handles MyBase.Load
        Dim DocsSec As New WroxDocSecurity()

        If Not (Request.Params("ItemID") Is Nothing) Then
            ItemID = Int32.Parse(Request.Params("ItemID"))
        End If

        If Not IsPostBack Then
            If Not (Request.Params("ItemID") Is Nothing) Then
                'Run our custom permission checks
                If Not (DocsSec.HasDocPermissions(_
                  DocumentPermissions.CheckInOutRights, ItemID)) _
                And Not _
                (PortalSecurity.HasEditPermissions(Request.Params("mid"))) Then
```

```
                    'send the user back with a javascript alert
                    Response.Write("<script>_
                    alert('You do not have authority to perform this Action.');" _
                    & "location.replace('" & _
                    Request.UrlReferrer.ToString() & "');</script>")
                End If

                Dim documents As New WroxDocsDB()
                Dim dr As SqlDataReader = documents.GetSingleDocument(ItemID)
                dr.Read()

                SetForm(CStr(Request.Params("Action")), dr)
                ' Store URL Referrer to return to portal
                ViewState.Add("UrlReferrer", Request.UrlReferrer.ToString())
            End If
        End If

    End Sub
    ...
```

If a user does not have permissions to perform the action then the JavaScript alert fires and the user is routed back to the referring page. Below is the alert that an unauthorized user will receive.

If a user is authenticated we process the document action depending on a check out or check in action. The following code checks a document out by calling the `WroxDocsDb.CheckOutDocument` method.

```
Private Sub CheckOutButton_Click(ByVal sender As System.Object, ByVal e As
System.EventArgs) Handles CheckOutButton.Click
        Dim documents As New ASPNetPortal.WroxDocsDB()
        documents.CheckOutDocument(Int32.Parse( _
            Request.Params("ItemID")), context.Current.User.Identity.Name)
        Response.Redirect(CType(ViewState("UrlReferrer"), String))
End Sub
```

Next, the code listed below checks a document back into the system. Notice that it is similar to the code that uploads a new document to the system.

```
Private Sub CheckInButton_Click(ByVal sender As System.Object, ByVal e As
System.EventArgs) Handles CheckInButton.Click
        If Page.IsValid = True Then

            Dim documents As New WroxDocsDB()
```

346

```
        ' Determine whether a file was uploaded
        If Not (txtFile.PostedFile.ContentLength = 0) Then

            'parse path out of filename
            Dim filename As String = _
            CStr(txtFile.PostedFile.FileName.Substring _
            (txtFile.PostedFile.FileName.LastIndexOf("\") + 1))

            'get the byte array and len
            Dim length As Integer = CInt(txtFile.PostedFile.ContentLength)
            Dim contentType As String = txtFile.PostedFile.ContentType
            Dim content(length) As Byte

            'read into the byte array
            txtFile.PostedFile.InputStream.Read(content, 0, length)

            ' Update the document within the Documents table
            documents.CheckInDocument(ItemID, _
                                Context.User.Identity.Name, _
                                filename, _
                                content, _
                                length, _
                                contentType)

        Else
            ' no file selected display error message
            ErrorMessage.Text = "You must choose a file to check back in."
            Return

        End If

        ' go back to the portal home page
        Response.Redirect(CType(ViewState("UrlReferrer"), String))

    End If
End Sub
```

Adding the Search Page

The screen shot below shows what our Search page looks like.

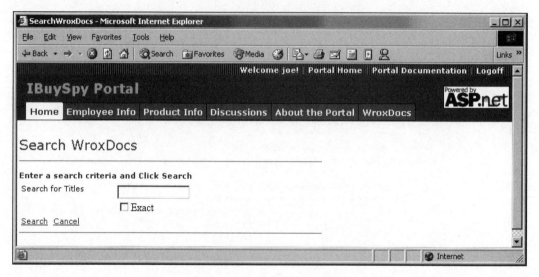

The `SearchWroxDocs.aspx` page is almost identical to the main document listing that we coded in the `DisplayFull.ascx` control except for the Search area that has been added to the top of the page. Below is the HTML portion in the `SearchWroxDocs.aspx` file that includes our search form. The search form consists of one text control named `txtFilter`, one check box control named `chkExact` and one `LinkButton` named `SearchButton`. Again, the remainder of the HTML is the same as the `DisplayFull.ascx` code that contains our main `DataGrid` so we are only showing the portion that is different.

```
...
<TABLE width="100%">
    <TR>
        <TD class="Normal" vAlign="top" width="141">
            Search for Titles
        </TD>
        <TD>
            <asp:textbox id="txtFilter" runat="server" width="108px"
                columns="20" cssclass="NormalTextBox" /> 
            <asp:requiredfieldvalidator id="RequiredFieldValidator1"
                runat="server" ErrorMessage="You must enter a Search Term"
                ControlToValidate="txtFilter" /><BR>
            <asp:checkbox id="chkExact" runat="server" Text="Exact" />
    <TR>
        <TD class="Normal" width="141">
            <asp:linkbutton id="SearchButton" runat="server" Width="4px"
                CssClass="commandbutton" text="Search" /> 
            <asp:linkbutton id="CancelButton" runat="server" Width="4px"
                CssClass="commandbutton" CausesValidation="False" text="Cancel" />
        </TD>
```

```
            <TD></TD>
        </TR>
    </TABLE>
    ...
```

Coding the Codebehind for the SearchWroxDocs.aspx Page

The only difference in the codebehind in the search page and the codebehind for our main control is that we have added the following code to the click event of the search button to process the search request.

When the Search button is clicked, a string variable that represents a search filter is added to the `ViewState` collection for later retrieval.

If the `chkExact` checkbox is checked then we assume that the user wants records filtered that exactly match the search criteria; otherwise we include the `LIKE` syntax in the filter which will filter records that are similar to the search criteria specified.

```
Private Sub SearchButton_Click(ByVal sender As System.Object, ByVal e As
System.EventArgs) Handles SearchButton.Click
        Dim SearchFilter As String

    If txtFilter.Text <> "" Then
        Dim SearchWild As String = ""
        Dim SearchLike As String = "="

        If Not chkExact.Checked Then
        SearchWild = "*"
        SearchLike = "LIKE"
        End IF

        SearchFilter = "FileDescription " & SearchLike & " '" &
        SearchWild &  txtFilter.Text & SearchWild & "'"
    End If
    ' add to the page viewstate
    ViewState.Add("filter", SearchFilter)

    BindMasterGrid()
End Sub
```

In the `BindMasterGrid` method, we use the `SearchFilter` from the viewstate to set the `RowFilter` property of the default `DataView` for our main `DataSet`. This will filter the `datagrid` to show only the records that match the filter expression.

We can look at the code in `BindMasterGrid` method below to see how the filter property is retrieved from the `ViewState` collection and then assigned to the `RowFilter` property of the `DataView` object.

```
Sub BindMasterGrid()

        Dim ds As New DataSet()
        ds = DocsDB.GetDocuments(ModuleID)

        If IsNothing(ds) Then
           ErrorMessage.Text = DocsDB.ErrorMessage
           Exit Sub
        End If

        Dim dv As DataView = ds.Tables(0).DefaultView

        dv.RowFilter = ViewState("filter")

        If dv.Count = 0 Then
           ErrorMessage.Text = "No Documents Listed Yet!"
           dgListing.DataBind()
        Else
           dgListing.DataSource = dv
           dgListing.DataBind()
        End If

    End Sub
```

Adding the compact DisplaySummary.ascx User Control

This control is also similar to the `DisplayFull.ascx` except that it is designed to fit in a smaller screen area. In fact, the only difference in this control is that only the icons are shown for various actions and not the textual links such as Check In or View Document. The screen shot below shows how it is used in a smaller screen area in the portal site.

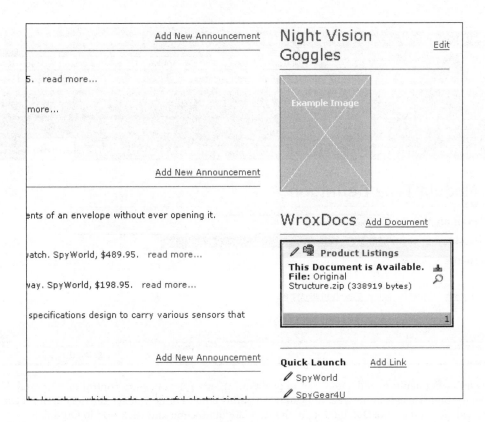

Plugging the Application into IBuySpy

We are now ready to plug our application into the IBuySpy portal. Remember that IBuySpy handles all of the dirty work of inserting our application into the page programmatically. It is necessary for us to add the module to the portal framework by clicking the online Administrators Tab. Click on the **Add New Module Type** link to bring up the page shown below. Enter the information for the new module and click **Update**.

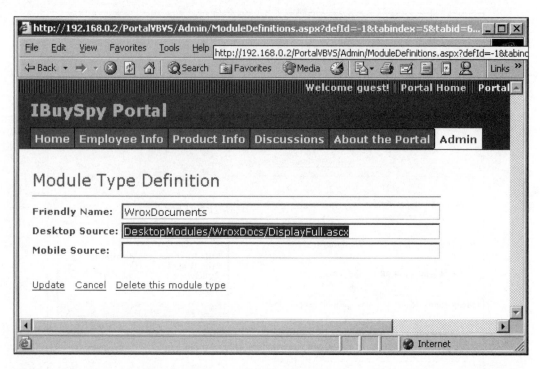

The following step is to add a new Tab to insert our `DisplayFull.ascx` control to the portal. If you need to control access to the Tab you can do so at this point. For now, leave the default of All Users selected. Select the WroxDoc module in the Add Module section and click Add to Organize Modules Below.

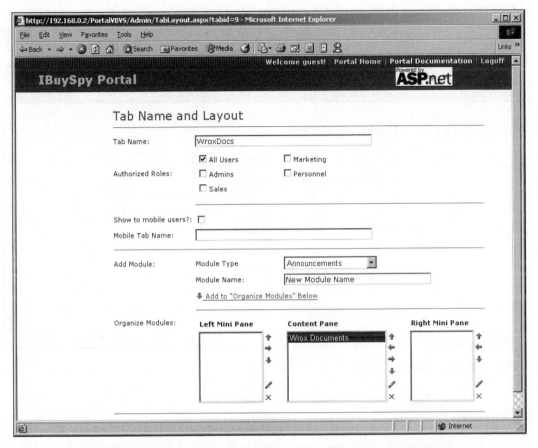

Then, click on the edit icon next to the module name. Choose a title such as **Sales Reports**. Set the roles that can edit content by clicking the checkbox next to the role that you wish to have edit rights. Since this module is titled "**Sales Reports**" we will give the Sales role edit access. This will enable USERS in the Sales role to add new documents to the system.

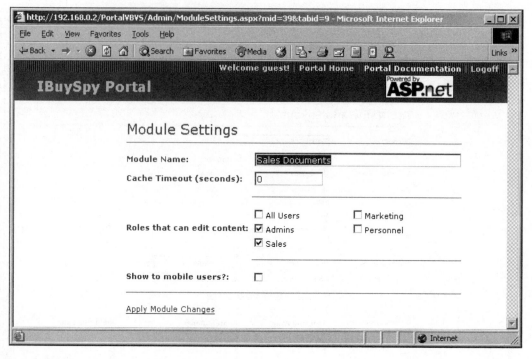

Finally, click on **Apply Changes**.

Summary

In brief, this chapter outlined the general steps necessary to build a Document Management solution from the ground up and plug it into the IBuySpy Framework. We took the following steps to accomplish this:

- ❑ We created a database and a set of stored procedures in SQL Server that handled the adding, editing and archiving of documents. We took the approach of storing the binary contents of the documents as an image column in our database.

- ❑ We then created a set of business classes that performed the business logic in our application. Some of the features that we added include versioning, the ability to check documents in and out of the system, and assigning access control per document.

- ❑ Finally, we created the user controls and .aspx pages that serve as the front end for our application. These pages display our documents and present the user with the forms to manage documents in the system.

Although our sample is somewhat simplistic, it allows for customization. For example, adding a workflow process would be a useful addition that could easily be integrated into an application such as the one described in this chapter. Another useful addition would be to add some level of file compression for the documents that are being stored in the SQL Server. This would ease the storage burden on SQL Server by reducing the size of the documents that are stored in the database.

Solutio
BM
Referel
System
System.Data
System.Drawing
System.Web
System.XML
AssemblyInfo.vb
Assemb
BM.vsdisco
Global.asax
Styles.css
Web.config
WebForm1.aspx

WebForm1.aspx* | WebForm1.aspx

ebForm1.aspx*

9

Human Resources Information System

In this chapter, we will present the development of an ASP.NET Human Resources Information System, referred to as the HRIS in the remainder of the chapter. While the HRIS application is central to most organizations, it is often visible only to a dedicated Human Resources department. So before we go on to the technical implementation details let's take a step back and look at exactly what an HRIS is and what functionality we will provide in our Wrox intranet HRIS.

What is an HRIS?

An HRIS for a large enterprise will typically be made up of several distinct functional modules including:

- ❑ Employee Information
- ❑ Organizational Mapping
- ❑ Training

The Employee Information module stores the personal details of all employees in the company. It is used to record any employee specific information such as salary, health notes, the name, and address of the employee's doctor, social security number, and contract. This module also feeds the payroll system.

The Training module includes functionality to record the list of available internal training courses, details of external training companies and their courses, information on the training courses employees have attended or are scheduled to attend and recommended training structure for individual job roles.

The Organizational Mapping module is used to map every position within the company. It stores details about each job within the organization and the requisite skills for that job. Each job within the system has documented roles and responsibilities. The storage of job information at this level is necessary in large organizations for organizational design, and efficient recruitment practices. Every job has a unique number, and the status of the position is reflected in the Employee Information module.

Building an Employee Information Module for Our Intranet

This chapter will focus on the development of a complete Employee Information module with the following features:

- ❑ Enable the Employee Handbook to be referenced and searched, by all employees, through the intranet.
- ❑ Notify all employees of new recruits.
- ❑ Enable staff to browse through the business-relevant details of each employee.
- ❑ Enable an employee to easily gain read access to any information the company stores about them.

The HRIS application should provide you with a base HR system that can be used as-is or tailored to the specific requirements of any organization. The primary focus of the chapter is not the HRIS itself but rather the discussion of the techniques and technologies that were used in its development that are useful in the design and development of any intranet applications. Some of the topics that we will be covering are:

- ❑ Configuring and using Full-text Searches on:
  - ❑ The File system
  - ❑ Database Contents
  - ❑ Unified Searches on both File and Database
- ❑ Caching
- ❑ Techniques for Auditing
- ❑ Configuring Visual SourceSafe Shadow folders
- ❑ Error Handling
- ❑ Implementing Paging and Sorting

The **Human Resources Information System** is comprised of several components that work together to provide the required functionality. Each of these components is built around a 3-tier model as shown in the diagram below.

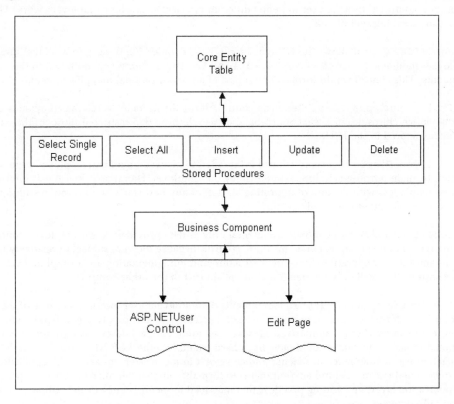

The HRIS is made up of five such components and two further entity models with no user interface.

- ❑ Job Titles component (HrisJobTitles)
- ❑ Sites component (HrisSites)
- ❑ Employees Display Full (HrisEmployeesDisplayFull)
- ❑ Employees Display Summary (HrisEmployeesDisplaySummary)
- ❑ Employees Search (HrisEmployeesDisplaySearchResults)
- ❑ EthnicOrigins (no UI provided)
- ❑ Statuses (no UI provided)

Before we go on to walk through the development of each of these modules, and show how they work together in our intranet to provide the Human Resources Employee system, we will describe the functionality each module provides and how they integrate. This high-level overview will help put each of the ensuing module discussions in context; and therefore clarify our objectives.

The `EmployeesDisplayFull` control is the heart of the HRIS. It provides a means of entering, updating, and browsing information on all of the staff currently employed by the company.

The `Sites` control allows the user to define different physical sites where employees work. This is very much a standard intranet module.

The `JobTitles` control allows the HR manager to keep detailed job descriptions on the intranet. The Employees modules (`EmployeesDisplayFull` and `EmployeesSummary`) both link to the `JobTitles` documents. This control would form a central part of an organizational mapping system.

The `EmployeesDisplaySearchResults` control allows the users to search the companies Employee Handbook (which resides in Visual SourceSafe) or search through a restricted subset of the employee information stored in the HRIS.

The `EmployeesDisplaySummary` control is intended to be used on a main employee page within the intranet. Its main purpose is to link to and display the Employee Handbook. It also lists information on any new employees with the aim of informing all staff of any new starts, their position within the company and any other applicable details.

The `JobTitles` and `Sites` controls are integral only as data providers to the employee controls. A user interface has been implemented for these controls because they are subject to relatively frequent updates and user configuration. Since their structure and implementation are a simplified version of the other controls, they will only be mentioned in the context of the other controls.

The `EthnicOrigins` and `Statuses` components do not have a user interface because of the static nature of the information they represent. The `EthnicOrigins` are usually prescribed by law and are therefore only entered once; similarly, `JobStatuses` are high-level descriptive groupings with no functional impact. The values could have been hard coded into the ASP.NET forms themselves, but this approach causes maintenance headaches and can result in inconsistencies across the application. One of the fundamental reasons behind any intranet is to formalize and standardize the business processes and communication layer; any coding practices that may lead to inconsistency or inflexibility should be strongly discouraged.

Hopefully, the above has provided a basic overview of the structure of the HRIS, so let's look at the implementation of the HRIS; starting with the Data Layer.

The Data Layer

The Data Layer underpins almost any intranet module. It is typically the starting point of all development. The table diagram below shows the database schema for the HRIS module in its entirety.

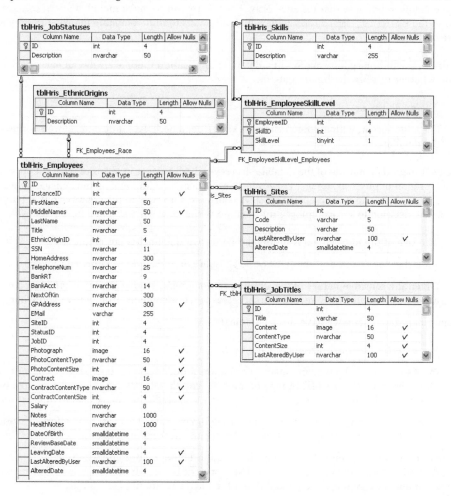

The Database Tables

The following section describes the complete table structure for our Human Resources module.

The Employees Table (tblHris_Employees)

The tblHris_Employees stores all the information about the company's employees. The key considerations in the design of this table relate to the scope of the module and the storage of binary data.

When designing the HRIS we had to consider whether or not the HRIS would be managed centrally or regionally. If the module was to be managed centrally then any instances of an `Employee` control should have access to all of the information within the table. If, however, a regional implementation was required then it should be possible to create two or more instances of the HRIS each of which shows employee details relating to that instance only. For this reason we have included an `InstanceID` column in the `tblHris_Employees` table which allows us to limit available information to a single instance of the HRIS.

When dealing with binary information in a database application there is always an early decision to be made on whether to store the binary data in:

❑ The database, or

❑ On a file server, with a pointer of some kind (filename, URL, index etc) stored within the database.

Storing the binary data outside of the database has several advantages in terms of retrieval optimization and configuration of physical storage. However, it introduces an additional maintenance overhead (ensuring binary data and database links are always in sync) and adds to the security configuration required. The decision to store employee information in the database was taken for the following reasons:

❑ The size of the binary data is minimal, one or two documents per employee.

❑ Both the `Contract` and the `Photograph` relate to one, and only one, employee.

❑ Given the sensitive nature of the `Contract` document, storing the information in a database allows us to more easily record who accesses what documents, from where and when.

For each binary document, we have three columns:

❑ `Binary Data` – the document or file itself

❑ `ContentType` – the type of binary information stored, e.g. jpeg, doc, xls etc. This not only allows us to specify the MIME type of the data, and thereby stream the document to a browser window, it also allows us to enable index server to include the binary data in full-text searches.

❑ `ContentLength` – the length in bytes of the binary data. This eases the effort of sizing the destination byte array when retrieving the document from SQL Server.

We have also included columns for storing who last altered the record and when (`LastAlteredByUser` and `AlteredDate`). The `AlteredDate` column has a default of `getdate` to ensure that it always contains the date and time of the last alteration.

The Periphery Tables

The tables `tblHris_Sites`, `tblHris_JobTitles`, `tblHris_JobStatuses` and `tblHris_EthnicOrigins` contain descriptive representations of business entities or business descriptors.

The tables `tblHris_Skills` and `tblHris_EmployeeSkillLevel` are used to describe the skill sets within the company and link to individual employee details to show what level of skill each employee has.

These tables are very simple in structure and are briefly described here in order to present a clear picture of their function.

The Sites Table (tblHris_Sites)

The `tblHris_Sites` table is used to store the description of a physical location. This could be an office, a city, or any other regional description. The information is useful within the HRIS to see where an employee is based.

The Job Titles Table (tblHris_JobTitles)

The `tblHris_JobTitles` table is used to store a full job description, including roles and responsibilities for every job type within the organization. The job description document is stored in the table in an image column to simplify access to the document across the enterprise, and to enable future integration with the search full-text search module.

The Skills Table (tblHris_Skills)

The `tblHris_Skills` table is used to store a description of each skill relevant to the company's business.

The Employee Skills Level Table (tblHris_EmployeeSkillLevel)

The `tblHris_EmployeeSkillLevel` table provides a m:m (many-to-many) link to the `Skills` table, and is used to store an employee's level of expertise in any specified skill.

The Job Statuses Table (tblHris_JobStatuses)

The `tblHris_JobStatuses` table stores descriptions of the various bands of seniority or section (e.g. Company Director, Senior Manager, Technical Lead, etc).

The `JobStatuses` are included in the HRIS with an eye on the bigger picture of payroll integration. Typically, salary increases are applied across the board by job status, e.g. Directors receive an 8% pay increase while Senior Managers receive a 6.5% pay increase. By storing the status of each employee, we are able to apply these blanket calculations should the HRIS ever be used to feed a payroll system.

The Ethnic Origins Table (tblHris_EthnicOrigins)

The `tblHris_EthnicOrigins` table stores descriptions of the ethnic origin categories prescribed by the company/government for classification of an employee's ethnic origin.

The Stored Procedures

For each of the tables in the HRIS we have defined a set of stored procedures that handle all data access, one for each of the following functions:

❑   `Select All` – Used to populate the main control

❑   `Select Single` – Used to populate the Edit page

❑   `Insert`

❑   Update

❑   Delete

The structure of the stored procedures is almost identical for each of the tables (The generation of these stored procedures can very easily be automated, because of their similarity, through the use of templates.) For this reason, we will only examine the set of stored procedures for the `tblHris_Employees` table. In addition to the standard stored procedures there are other function-specific stored procedures used by the HRIS, which are described in full in this section.

Select All

The `Select All` stored procedure `up_Hris_Get` is used to return all records or all records for a particular control instance. The `up_Hris_GetEmployees` procedure is shown below

```
CREATE PROCEDURE up_Hris_GetEmployees
/*
Procedure to return all of the Employees in the tblHris_Employees table.
*/
(
   @InstanceID int
)
AS

SELECT
  ID,
  FirstName,
  MiddleNames,
  LastName,
  Title,
  EthnicOriginID,
  SSN,
  HomeAddress,
  TelephoneNum,
  BankRT,
  BankAcct,
  NextOfKin,
  GPAddress,
  EMail,
  SiteID,
  StatusID,
  JobID,
  Photograph,
  PhotoContentType,
  PhotoContentSize,
  Contract,
  ContractContentType,
  ContractContentSize,
  Salary,
  Notes,
  HealthNotes,
  DateOfBirth,
  ReviewBaseDate,
  LeavingDate
```

```
FROM
    tblHris_Employees
WHERE
    InstanceID = @InstanceID
```

For the `tblHris_Employees` table the procedure takes a single parameter, which limits the returned result set to only those records with an `InstanceID` equal to the `@InstanceID` parameter.

Select Single

The `Select Single` stored procedure `up_Hris_GetSingle` is used to return all information stored about a single entity (e.g. `Employee`). The `up_Hris_GetSingleEmployee` procedure is shown below

```
CREATE PROCEDURE up_Hris_GetSingleEmployee
/*
Procedure to return a single Employee from the tblHris_Employees table.
*/
(
    @ID int
)
AS

SELECT
    FirstName,
    MiddleNames,
    LastName,
    str(Datediff(yyyy, DateOfBirth, getdate())) as 'Age',
    tblHris_Employees.Title as 'Title',
    EthnicOriginID,
    tblHris_EthnicOrigins.Description as 'EthnicOrigin',
    SSN,
    HomeAddress,
    TelephoneNum,
    BankRT,
    BankAcct,
    NextOfKin,
    GPAddress,
    EMail,
    SiteID,
    tblHris_Sites.Description as 'SiteDescription',
    StatusID,
    tblHris_JobStatuses.Description as 'StatusDescription',
    JobID,
    JobTitles.Title as 'JobTitle',
    Photograph,
    PhotoContentType,
    PhotoContentSize,
    Contract,
    ContractContentType,
    ContractContentSize,
    Salary,
    Notes,
    HealthNotes,
```

```
    DateOfBirth,
    ReviewBaseDate,
    CASE WHEN dateadd(yyyy,datediff(yyyy, Convert(smalldatetime,ReviewBaseDate),
getdate()), ReviewBaseDate) < getdate()        then dateadd(yyyy, datediff(yyyy,
Convert(smalldatetime,ReviewBaseDate), getdate()) + 1,ReviewBaseDate)
    ELSE    dateadd(yyyy,datediff(yyyy, Convert(smalldatetime,ReviewBaseDate),
getdate()), ReviewBaseDate)
    END AS    'NextReviewDate',
    LeavingDate,
    tblHris_Employees.LastAlteredByUser,
    tblHris_Employees.AlteredDate

FROM
    tblHris_Employees INNER JOIN tblHris_Sites
    ON SiteID = tblHris_Sites.ID
    INNER JOIN tblHris_JobTitles JobTitles
    ON JobID = JobTitles.ID
    INNER JOIN tblHris_JobStatuses
    ON tblHris_JobStatuses.ID = StatusID
    INNER JOIN tblHris_EthnicOrigins
    ON tblHris_EthnicOrigins.ID = EthnicOriginID

WHERE
    tblHris_Employees.ID = @ID
```

The Select Single style stored procedure will usually take the primary key of the underlying table as a single input parameter (as in the above tblHris_Employees.ID). This ensures that the required record is identified and returned to the business layer.

In the above procedure, you can also see that we have used T-SQL to supplement the information stored in the database by returning the employee's age,

```
    str(Datediff(yyyy, DateOfBirth, getdate())) as 'Age',
```

as well as the date of their next review;

```
    CASE WHEN dateadd(yyyy,datediff(yyyy, Convert(smalldatetime,ReviewBaseDate),
getdate()), ReviewBaseDate) < getdate()        then dateadd(yyyy, datediff(yyyy,
Convert(smalldatetime,ReviewBaseDate), getdate()) + 1,ReviewBaseDate)
    ELSE    dateadd(yyyy,datediff(yyyy, Convert(smalldatetime,ReviewBaseDate),
getdate()), ReviewBaseDate)
    END AS    'NextReviewDate',
```

Insert

The Insert stored procedure up_Hris_Insert is used to add a new record to the underlying table. The up_Hris_InsertEmployee procedure is shown below:

```
CREATE PROCEDURE up_Hris_InsertEmployee
/*
Procedure to Insert Employee details in the tblHris_Employees table.
```

```
*/
(
    @ID int OUTPUT,
    @InstanceID int,
    @FirstName nvarchar(50),
    @MiddleNames nvarchar(50),
    @LastName nvarchar(50),
    @Title nvarchar(5),
    @EthnicOriginID int,
    @SSN nvarchar(11),
    @HomeAddress nvarchar(300),
    @TelephoneNum nvarchar(25),
    @BankRT nvarchar(9),
    @BankAcct nvarchar(14),
    @NextOfKin nvarchar(300),
    @GPAddress nvarchar(300),
    @EMail varchar(255),
    @SiteID int,
    @StatusID int,
    @JobID int,
    @Photograph image,
    @PhotoContentType nvarchar(50),
    @PhotoContentSize int,
    @Contract image,
    @ContractContentType nvarchar(50),
    @ContractContentSize int,
    @Salary money,
    @Notes nvarchar(1000),
    @HealthNotes nvarchar(1000),
    @DateOfBirth smalldatetime,
    @ReviewBaseDate smalldatetime,
    @LeavingDate smalldatetime,
    @UserName nvarchar(100)
)
AS

NSERT INTO tblHris_Employees
    (
    InstanceID,
    FirstName,
    MiddleNames,
    LastName,
    Title,
    EthnicOriginID,
    SSN,
    HomeAddress,
    TelephoneNum,
    BankRT,
    BankAcct,
    NextOfKin,
    GPAddress,
    EMail,
    SiteID,
```

```
            StatusID,
            JobID,
            Photograph,
            PhotoContentType,
            PhotoContentSize,
            Contract,
            ContractContentType,
            ContractContentSize,
            Salary,
            Notes,
            HealthNotes,
            DateOfBirth,
            ReviewBaseDate,
            LeavingDate,
            LastAlteredByUser,
            AlteredDate
            )
        VALUES
            (
            @InstanceID,
            @FirstName,
            @MiddleNames,
            @LastName,
            @Title,
            @EthnicOriginID,
            @SSN,
            @HomeAddress,
            @TelephoneNum,
            @BankRT,
            @BankAcct,
            @NextOfKin,
            @GPAddress,
            @EMail,
            @SiteID,
            @StatusID,
            @JobID,
            @Photograph,
            @PhotoContentType,
            @PhotoContentSize,
            @Contract,
            @ContractContentType,
            @ContractContentSize,
            @Salary,
            @Notes,
            @HealthNotes,
            @DateOfBirth,
            @ReviewBaseDate,
            @LeavingDate,
            @UserName,
            getdate()
            )

        SELECT @ID = @@Identity
```

The `Insert` stored procedure returns the primary key of the newly inserted record. This is handled through the `@ID` output parameter, and the use of `@@IDENTITY`.

```
@ID int OUTPUT,
```

Since the `ID` field of the `tblHris_Employees` table is an identity column we can use `@@IDENTITY` (a pre-defined SQL Server session level variable that returns the last identity value assigned for any table within the current session) to return the `ID` of the newly inserted record.

The SQL function `getdate` is used in the `insert` to record the date and time that the record was inserted.

Update

The `Update` stored procedure `up_Hris_Update` is used to update an existing record to the underlying table. The `up_Hris_UpdateEmployee` procedure is shown below:

```
CREATE PROCEDURE up_Hris_UpdateEmployee
/*
Procedure to Update Employee details on the tblHris_Employees table.
Input: The Identity column from the tblHris_Employees table (ID)
  All other fields in the table
*/
(
@ID   int,
@InstanceID int,
@FirstName nvarchar(50),
@MiddleNames nvarchar(50),
@LastName nvarchar(50),
@Title nvarchar(5),
@EthnicOriginID int,
@SSN nvarchar(11),
@HomeAddress nvarchar(300),
@TelephoneNum nvarchar(25),
@BankRT nvarchar(9),
@BankAcct nvarchar(14),
@NextOfKin nvarchar(300),
@GPAddress nvarchar(300),
@EMail varchar(255),
@SiteID int,
@StatusID int,
@JobID int,
@Photograph image,
@PhotoContentType nvarchar(50),
@PhotoContentSize int,
@Contract image,
@ContractContentType nvarchar(50),
@ContractContentSize int,
@Salary money,
@Notes nvarchar(1000),
@HealthNotes nvarchar(1000),
@DateOfBirth smalldatetime,
```

```
@ReviewBaseDate smalldatetime,
@LeavingDate smalldatetime,
@UserName nvarchar(100)
)
AS
-- If the record exists for this employee thenUpdate the details
-- otherwise  INSERT the new employee record
IF EXISTS (SELECT * FROM tblHris_Employees WHERE ID = @ID) BEGIN
UPDATE
    tblHris_Employees

-- InstanceID is not updated since it should never change
SET
  FirstName = @FirstName,
  MiddleNames = @MiddleNames,
  LastName = @LastName,
  Title = @Title,
  EthnicOriginID = @EthnicOriginID,
  SSN = @SSN,
  HomeAddress = @HomeAddress,
  TelephoneNum = @TelephoneNum,
  BankRT = @BankRT,
  BankAcct = @BankAcct,
  NextOfKin = @NextOfKin,
  GPAddress = @GPAddress,
  EMail = @EMail,
  SiteID = @SiteID,
  StatusID = @StatusID,
  JobID = @JobID,
/* 000001 The File Uploads are Handled as part of a subsequent update */
  Salary = @Salary,
  Notes = @Notes,
  HealthNotes = @HealthNotes,
  DateOfBirth = @DateOfBirth,
  ReviewBaseDate = @ReviewBaseDate,
  LeavingDate = @LeavingDate,
  LastAlteredByUser = @UserName,
  AlteredDate = getdate()

WHERE
    ID = @ID
  END
ELSE BEGIN
    INSERT INTO tblHris_Employees
    (
  InstanceID,
  FirstName,
  MiddleNames,
  LastName,
  Title,
  EthnicOriginID,
  SSN,
  HomeAddress,
```

```
TelephoneNum,
BankRT,
BankAcct,
NextOfKin,
GPAddress,
EMail,
SiteID,
StatusID,
JobID,
/* 000001 */
Salary,
Notes,
HealthNotes,
DateOfBirth,
ReviewBaseDate,
LeavingDate,
LastAlteredByUser,
AlteredDate
   )
  VALUES
  (
@InstanceID,
@FirstName,
@MiddleNames,
@LastName,
@Title,
@EthnicOriginID,
@SSN,
@HomeAddress,
@TelephoneNum,
@BankRT,
@BankAcct,
@NextOfKin,
@GPAddress,
@EMail,
@SiteID,
@StatusID,
@JobID,
/* 000001 */
@Salary,
@Notes,
@HealthNotes,
@DateOfBirth,
@ReviewBaseDate,
@LeavingDate,
@UserName,
getdate()
   )

-- 000002
-- This is required because we later update the binary large object fields
-- ONLY if the ContentSize is > 0
  SELECT @ID = @@IDENTITY
END
```

```
-- The Employee record now exists in the DB, any existing documents still exist
-- but have not yet been updated.
```

```
-- Update the Photograph if a file has been uploaded
IF @PhotoContentSize > 0 BEGIN
   UPDATE     tblHris_Employees
   SET    Photograph = @Photograph,
     PhotoContentType = @PhotoContentType,
     PhotoContentSize = @PhotoContentSize
   WHERE
         ID = @ID
END


-- Update the Contract if a file has been uploaded
IF @ContractContentSize > 0 BEGIN
   UPDATE     tblHris_Employees
   SET    Contract = @Contract,
     ContractContentType = @ContractContentType,
     ContractContentSize = @ContractContentSize
   WHERE
         ID = @ID
END
```

The Update procedure shown above handles both Insert and Update. The merging of these functions is very common, as it removes the need for the business or presentation layer to know categorically whether the record is an insert or update.

The updating of binary documents within a stored procedure throws up some interesting problems. In our HRIS module, and in most web applications, if the user edits a record they do not expect to have to re-upload any binary information – especially if it has not changed. However, because of the way the binary document upload is handled within ASP.NET that is exactly what they would be required to do, otherwise when the update ran it would overwrite the stored binary information with an empty byte array.

To solve this problem, the binary files are handled as updates after the main INSERT / UPDATE. The reason for this is that there are a number of upload combinations (some of which are listed below):

❑   Update details but not photo

❑   Update details and photo but not contract

❑   Update all

❑   Update contract but not photo, etc.

Rather than code separate `update` and `insert` statements for each combination (remembering if the content size is `zero` we do not want to update the binary field as this will effectively delete the existing binary data), we chose to handle the binary data as separate updates. (We store the `@@IDENTITY` value from the `INSERT` to allow subsequent updates.) This is a cleaner solution for future maintenance since, if we were to later add an additional set of columns for another binary file, we need only add another bounded `update` statement; whereas if we were to write SQL to handle each combination, the number of options would increase by a factor of two for every binary field we add. The second advantage to this approach is that the binary data, which could be very large, does not have to be retrieved for the edit page; instead, it is only retrieved for display purposes in a series of specialized `HrisView....aspx` pages.

Auditing

In the `Insert` and `Update` procedures of the HRIS system, we have implemented very basic auditing of any changes to the data (DML changes). We store the username of the person who last edited or added a record, and the exact date and time at which the modification took place. The logic for this level of auditing is very straightforward; we simply pass the `username` as a parameter to the `add` and `update` methods of the appropriate business object. The stored procedures then use the `getdate` function to insert the date and time into the record.

```
CREATE PROCEDURE up_Hris_InsertEmployee
(
    @ID int OUTPUT,
    ...
    @ReviewBaseDate smalldatetime,
    @LeavingDate smalldatetime,
    @UserName nvarchar(100)
)
    AS

INSERT INTO tblHris_Employees
    (
    InstanceID,
    ...
    LeavingDate,
    LastAlteredByUser,
    AlteredDate
    )
VALUES
    (
    @InstanceID,
    ...
    @LeavingDate,
    @UserName,
    getdate()
    )
SELECT @ID = @@Identity
```

When we edit a record, we are then presented with this information in brief at the bottom of the page.

<u>Update</u>   <u>Cancel</u>   <u>Delete this item</u>

Created by SSchubert@alphatec.net on 07/09/2001

There are however many cases where a more advanced auditing structure would need to be in place. These typically involve changes to documents, details, or workflow (versioning). The most important point in any auditing system is to ensure that all changes are recorded; for this reason the auditing is rarely performed in the business layer as any direct access to the database would by-pass the auditing procedure. The advantage of placing the audit logging at the database level is that we do not have to remember to implement the auditing logic within business objects or data access classes. Similarly, any alterations to the logic should not affect numerous classes across many applications and possibly many development teams. Instead, by recording the change details using triggers on the tables we can ensure that any alterations by any classes or even by direct SQL execution against the DB will be logged. Typically, all log requests are fed to a single table, which feeds reports to a central administrative application.

In SQL Server, triggers can be created on a table that execute for Update, Insert or Delete. We could use a trigger for UPDATE on the Employees table that logged all changes to Salary.

```
CREATE TRIGGER tU_Employees_Salary
ON tblHris_Employees
FOR UPDATE
AS
IF (COLUMNS_UPDATED() & 8388608) > 0 BEGIN
    INSERT LogTable (LogDate, UserName, Description)
    SELECT getdate(),inserted.LastAlteredByUser, 'Salary altered for ' +
        inserted.FirstName + ' ' + inserted.LastName + ' from ' +
        convert(varchar,deleted.Salary) + ' to ' +
        convert(varchar,inserted.Salary)
    FROM inserted INNER JOIN deleted ON inserted.ID = deleted.ID
END
```

A couple of things in the above trigger are worth explaining for those unfamiliar with triggers. The COLUMNS_UPDATED function returns a numeric column mask of the columns that were updated. The mask is calculated by summing the values of 2 to the power of (column number updated -1).

For example, we wanted to only log salary updates. The Salary column in the tblHris_Employees table is column 24. To calculate the mask we calculated 2 to the power of (24 - 1) which equals 8388608. The logical AND'ing of the masks then lets us see whether the Salary column was updated.

In triggers, we have access to two special temporary tables, the inserted table holds the values (note this can be more than one row) to be inserted, while the deleted table holds the values that will be replaced or deleted (in a FOR DELETE trigger).

In most cases, if we are implementing a sophisticated auditing process then we will also not be deleting records after a `delete` request. Instead, we will mark the record as deleted by use of an `IsDeleted` bit field on the relevant table. All queries feeding the UI would then only return records where `IsDeleted = 0`, making the front end application behave in exactly the same way while ensuring that all changes and deletions were recorded, audited and possibly even reversible.

> **Triggers should be used judiciously, as inefficient or unnecessary code in a trigger can have a major impact on the performance of an application.**

Delete

The `Delete` stored procedure `up_Hris_Delete` is used to delete a record from the underlying table. The `up_Hris_DeleteEmployee` procedure is shown below

```
CREATE PROCEDURE up_Hris_DeleteEmployee
/*
Procedure to Delete Employee details from the tblHris_Employees table.
Input: The Identity column from the tblHris_Employees table (ID)
*/
(
    @ID int
)
AS

DELETE FROM
    tblHris_Employees

WHERE
    ID = @ID
```

The procedure simply deletes the record with the specified ID from the table.

The stored procedures relating to the other tables have the same structure. There are however, as always, some additional stored procedures to handle the data requests of for more specific functions. Let's now look at some of these.

Get Employee Information for Browsing (up_Hris_GetEmployeesFull)

The `up_Hris_GetEmployeesFull` stored procedure is used to retrieve a subset of the employee information for the presentation layer. The `up_Hris_GetEmployeesFull` procedure is shown below

```
CREATE PROCEDURE up_Hris_GetEmployeesFull
/*
Procedure to return basic details on all of the Employees in the tblHris_Employees
table.
*/
(
@InstanceID int
)
AS
```

```
SELECT Emp.ID, Emp.Title as 'EmpTitle', FirstName, LastName,
   Code as 'SiteCode',    -- Site Code
   JobID,
   JobTitles.Title as 'JobTitle',
   str(Datediff(yyyy, ReviewBaseDate, getdate())) + ' Years' as 'Service',
   EMail,
   CASE WHEN Photograph IS NULL THEN '' ELSE 'Show Photo' END as 'PhotoAvail'
FROM
   tblHris_Employees Emp INNER JOIN tblHris_Sites
     ON SiteID = tblHris_Sites.ID
   INNER JOIN tblHris_JobTitles JobTitles
     ON JobID = JobTitles.ID
WHERE InstanceID = @InstanceID
```

Since the `Employee` table contains binary information and numerous fields, we do not want to retrieve any information that is not required. For this reason, we have defined the `up_Hris_GetEmployeesFull` stored procedure to return only the information required to populate the user controls in the presentation layer.

In the case of the photograph field, we return the text 'Show Photo' only if a photograph exists for the employee. This enables the UI to present a link to `Employee` `photographs` in the main HRIS control without the overhead of retrieving the binary information until it is required.

Get Information on New Employees (up_Hris_GetNewEmployees)

The stored procedure `up_Hris_GetNewEmployees` is used to return the limited details on any employees who have started within the last few months. The number of months used to qualify an employee as new is passed into the stored procedure in the `@Months` parameter. The `up_Hris_GetNewEmployees` procedure is shown below

```
CREATE PROCEDURE up_Hris_GetNewEmployees
/*
Procedure to return basic details on all newly started Employees in the
tblHris_Employees table. The ReviewBaseDate is treated
as the start date.
*/
(
@Months int = 3
)
AS

SELECT Emp.ID, Emp.Title as 'EmpTitle', FirstName, LastName,
   Code as 'SiteCode',    -- Site Code
   JobID,
   JobTitles.Title as 'JobTitle',
   str(Datediff(yyyy, ReviewBaseDate, getdate())) + ' Years' as 'Service',
   EMail,
   CASE WHEN Photograph IS NULL THEN '' ELSE 'Show Photo' END as 'PhotoAvail'
FROM
   tblHris_Employees Emp INNER JOIN tblHris_Sites
     ON SiteID = tblHris_Sites.ID
```

```
    INNER JOIN tblHris_JobTitles JobTitles
      ON JobID = JobTitles.ID
WHERE datediff(mm,ReviewBaseDate, getdate()) < @Months
```

Search (up_Hris_SearchEmployeesFT)

The stored procedure up_Hris_SearchEmployeesFT is used to perform a full-text search on the tblHris_Employees table. The stored procedure text is shown below;

```
CREATE PROCEDURE up_Hris_SearchEmployeesFT
/*
Procedure to perform a full text search on the Employees table using CONTAINSTABLE
*/
(
@SearchText varchar(1000)
)
AS
DECLARE @sql varchar(3000)


SELECT @sql = 'Select key_tbl.RANK, ft_tbl.[ID], ft_tbl.[Title] as ''EmpTitle'',
ft_tbl.[FirstName],  ft_tbl.[LastName], Code as ''SiteCode'', JobID,
JobTitles.Title as ''JobTitle''  from tblHris_Employees as ft_tbl inner join
CONTAINSTABLE(tblHRIS_Employees, *, ''' + @SearchText  + ''') as key_tbl on
ft_tbl.[ID] = key_tbl.[KEY]  INNER JOIN tblHris_Sites ON SiteID = tblHris_Sites.ID
INNER JOIN tblHris_JobTitles JobTitles ON JobID = JobTitles.ID order by
key_tbl.RANK desc'
EXEC (@sql)
```

This procedure uses CONTAINSTABLE to perform a full-text search on the information within the table. The details of CONTAINSTABLE syntax and Full-Text configuration are covered in the configuration section at the end of this chapter.

Now that we have built our data layer, let's look at the development of the business layer that services each of the following controls

❑ HrisEmployeesDisplayFull

❑ HrisEmployeesDisplaySummary

❑ HrisEmployeesDisplaySearchResults

The Business Layer

In the previous section, we built the sets of SQL stored procedures that act as our data layer. For each of the core tables in the HRIS there was a set of these T-SQL stored procedures. Similarly for each set of stored procedures, there is a corresponding business layer class. The classes in the HRIS modules are listed below:

❑ EmployeesBiz

❑ EmployeesSkillLevelBiz

❑ EthnicOriginsBiz

377

❑ `JobStatusesBiz`

❑ `SitesBiz`

❑ `SkillsBiz`

The Business Layer in our HRIS is predominantly made up of .NET wrapper functions for each of the stored procedures we defined in the data layer. Consequently, the structure and code involved in one business class is almost identical to the code in each of the other classes. For this reason, we will focus this section on the `EmployeesBiz` class that services our three main user controls:

❑ `HrisEmployeesDisplayFull.ascx`

❑ `HrisEmployeesDisplaySummary.ascx`

❑ `HrisEmployeesDisplaySearchResults.ascx`

Understanding construction of this class will provide all the necessary detail to understand any of the other HRIS business layer classes.

EmployeesBiz

As mentioned above, the `EmployeesBiz.vb` class provides a callable wrapper around the SQL Server stored procedures related to the `tblHris_Employees` table. The purpose of each of the methods is described in the following table.

Public Methods	Description	Returns
`DeleteEmployee`	Deletes an `Employee` record from the `tblHris_Employees` table.	
`UpdateEmployee`	Updates or Inserts (if the employee does not already exist) an `employee` record with the provided information.	
`AddEmployee`	Provided for completeness but not used in the current implementation because of the way in which the intranet handles updates. See the `HrisEditEmployess` section.	`Integer`. The `@@IDENTITY` value of the newly added record.
`GetEmployees`	Returns all information about all employees.	`DataSet`
`GetSingle Employee`	Gets all information about a single Employee.	`SqlDataRea der`
`GetBrowsePathDet ails`	A `Helper` function that is used to control the pages used to view employee details.	`String`

Public Methods	Description	Returns
GetEmployees Summary	Returns a `DataSet` containing only the columns required to populate the `EmployeeFull` controls `DataGrid`.	DataSet
GetNewEmployees	Returns a `DataSet` containing limited details on all employees who have started working for the company within the last number of specified months (as configured in `web.config`).	DataSet
SearchEmployees	Returns the Search results.	DataSet

Since the `EmployeesBiz` class itself has no object state, the methods have been implemented with a scope of `shared` (`static` in C#), enabling the methods to be called without first creating an instance of the class (all of the Business layer classes in the HRIS module are similar in this respect).

The GetEmployees Method

```
'*********************************************************************
' GetEmployees Method
'
' The GetEmployees method returns a DataSet containing all of the
' Entities for a specific portal module from the Hris
' database.
'
'*********************************************************************
Public Shared Function GetEmployees(ByVal InstanceID As Integer) As DataSet

    ' Create and Fill the DataSet
    Dim myDataSet As New DataSet()
    Dim db As New Database()
    Dim params(0) As SqlParameter

    params(0) = db.MakeParameter("@InstanceID", InstanceID)
    db.RunProcedure("up_Hris_GetEmployees", params, myDataSet)

    'Since the Database class traps all data exceptions we can pass
    'the ErrorMessage back to the user controls
    If myDataSet Is Nothing Then
        Throw New Exception(db.ErrorMessage)
    End If

    ' Return the DataSet
    Return myDataSet
End Function
```

This enables the user controls to call the method using code such as:

```
myDataGrid.DataSource = EmployeesBiz.GetEmployees(InstanceId)
```

The `EmployeesBiz` methods, and all of the HRIS business layer class methods, make use of the `Wrox.Intranet.DataTools.Database` class for all of their ADO.NET calls. There are more details about this class and why we decided to use it in Appendix A.

The `GetEmployees` method shows how we use the Database class to call a stored procedure and return the results. In the Wrox intranet, we have used MS SQL Server as our database, for this reason we have used the `System.Data.SqlClient` namespace object to query the database. When working with any other OLE DB compliant database the mechanisms are almost identical and in many cases the code can be converted by simply using the `System.Data.OleDbClient` namespace and the classes within that namespace, most of which are identical in both name and function to the `SqlClient` classes-e.g. `OleDbConnection`.

Firstly, we create an instance of the Database class.

```
Dim db As New Database()
```

Next, we must create an array of `SqlParameter` objects. This array will contain one item for each parameter in the called stored procedure.

```
Dim params(0) As SqlParameter
```

This creates an array capable of holding one item (with index 0). The `Database` class contains the `MakeParameter` helper methods, which simplify our task of defining the `SqlParameter`. The following line creates a `SqlParameter` and adds it to our array:

```
params(0) = db.MakeParameter("@InstanceID", InstanceID)
```

This creates an `input` parameter with the value of `InstanceID` (the `ID` of the specific instance of the HRIS control) and named `@InstanceID`. The name must correspond exactly to the name of the parameter in the stored procedure.

All that is left now is to use `Database.RunProcedure` method to execute the `up_Hris_GetEmployees` stored procedure and populate a DataSet containing our results (a list of all employees details for the specified `InstanceID`).

```
db.RunProcedure("up_Hris_GetEmployees", params, myDataSet)
```

This procedure handles the creation of the connection and command objects for us. The third parameter of the `RunProcedure` is passed by reference.

Therefore, the `myDataSet` variable will contain the results of the stored procedure if the call has been successful.

The `Database` class traps any exceptions that may occur during the stored procedure call and populates the `ErrorMessage` property with the value of `Exception.Message`. In the business layer of the HRIS, we check the success of the call and raise an exception to the presentation layer in the event of an error.

```
'Since the Database class traps all data exceptions we can pass
'the ErrorMessage back to the user controls
If myDataSet Is Nothing Then
    Throw New Exception(db.ErrorMessage)
End If
```

The `Database` class provides several overloaded `RunProcedure` methods. These allow us to either `ExecuteScalar`, execute the stored procedure and return a dataset, or execute the stored procedure and return a `sql datareader`. The means of checking for the success of each of these is slightly different. For this reason, we have chosen to handle the check for success within the business object and raise an exception to the presentation layer in the event of an unsuccessful execution. This simplifies the code in the presentation layer by standardising the handling of the calls to the business layer. Two alternative approaches to this are to:

❑ Have the Database class bubble the exception through the business layer

❑ Add a Boolean Success property to the Database class which indicates whether or not the call succeeded

Finally, we return the populated DataSet.

```
' Return the DataSet
Return myDataSet
```

GetEmployeesSummary, GetNewEmployees, and SearchEmployees

The `GetEmployeesSummary`, `GetNewEmployees` and `SearchEmployees` methods, shown below, are identical in code structure to the `GetEmployees` method described above.

❑ GetEmployeesSummary

```
'*********************************************************************
' GetEmployeesSummary Method
'
' The GetEmployeesSummary method returns a DataSet containing all of the
' some of the details about an Employee
'
'*********************************************************************
Public Shared Function GetEmployeesSummary(ByVal InstanceID As Integer) _
    As DataSet

    ' Create and Fill the DataSet
    Dim myDataSet As New DataSet()
    Dim db As New Database()
    Dim params(0) As SqlParameter
```

```
        params(0) = db.MakeParameter("@InstanceID", InstanceID)
        db.RunProcedure("up_Hris_GetEmployeesFull", params, myDataSet)

        'Since the Database class traps all data exceptions we can pass the
        'ErrorMessage back to the user controls
        If myDataSet Is Nothing Then
            Throw New Exception(db.ErrorMessage)
        End If

        ' Return the DataSet
        Return myDataSet
    End Function
```

❑ GetNewEmployees

```
'**********************************************************************
' GetNewEmployees Method
'
' The GetNewEmployees method returns a DataSet containing all of the
' details about newly employed Employees. The stored procedure
' accepts a single parameter of the number of months for which an employee
' is treated as new (it defaults to 3)
'
'**********************************************************************
Public Shared Function GetNewEmployees(ByVal Months As Integer) As DataSet

    ' Create and Fill the DataSet
    Dim myDataSet As New DataSet()
    Dim db As New Database()
    Dim params(0) As SqlParameter

    params(0) = db.MakeParameter("@Months", Months)
    db.RunProcedure("up_Hris_GetNewEmployees", params, myDataSet)

    'Since the Database class traps all data exceptions
    'we can pass the ErrorMessage back
    'to the user controls
    If myDataSet Is Nothing Then
        Throw New Exception(db.ErrorMessage)
    End If

    ' Return the DataSet
    Return myDataSet

End Function
```

❑ SearchEmployees

```
'**********************************************************************
' SearchEmployees Method
'
' The SearchEmployees method returns a DataSet containing the search results
```

```
' from a full text search on the Employees table.
'
'*********************************************************************
Public Shared Function SearchEmployees(ByVal SearchText As String) As DataSet

    ' Create and Fill the DataSet
    Dim myDataSet As New DataSet()
    Dim db As New Database()
    Dim params(0) As SqlParameter

    params(0) = db.MakeParameter("@SearchText", SearchText)
    db.RunProcedure("up_Hris_SearchEmployeesFT", params, myDataSet)

    'Since the Database class traps all data exceptions we can pass the
ErrorMessage back
    'to the user controls
    If myDataSet Is Nothing Then
        Throw New Exception(db.ErrorMessage)
    End If

    ' Return the DataSet
    Return myDataSet

End Function
```

Each of these methods return a `Dataset` to enable the presentation layer to work with paging and sorting the DataGrid through the `ICollection` interface.

The *GetSingleEmployee* Method

The `GetSingleEmployee` method is used to return the details of a single employee. The information returned is used to populate individual HTML controls and server controls. We can therefore return the information as a `SqlDataReader`, which is less resource hungry than the `DataSet` class. The code to execute our stored procedure and return a `DataReader` is almost identical to that used to return a `DataSet`, thanks to our `Database` helper class.

```
'*********************************************************************
' GetSingleEmployee Method
'
' The GetSingleEmployee method returns a SqlDataReader containing details
' about a specific Employee from the tblHris_Employees database table.
'*********************************************************************
Public Shared Function GetSingleEmployee(ByVal itemId As Integer) As SqlDataReader

    ' Create and Fill the DataReader
    Dim myDataReader As SqlDataReader
    Dim db As New Database()
    Dim params(0) As SqlParameter

    params(0) = db.MakeParameter("@ID", itemId)
    db.RunProcedure("up_Hris_GetSingleEmployee", params, myDataReader)
```

```
          'Since the Database class traps all data exceptions we can pass the
          ' ErrorMessage back to the user controls
          If myDataReader Is Nothing Then
               Throw New Exception(db.ErrorMessage)
          End If

          ' Return the DataSet
          Return myDataReader
    End Function
```

The Database class provides several overloads for the `RunProcedure` method. In this case, we are passing the `SqlDataReader` by reference and calling the `up_Hris_GetSingleEmployee` stored procedure.

The *AddEmployee* Method

All of the methods in our business class discussed so far have dealt only with input parameters. The `AddEmployee` method of the `EmployeesBiz` class must however return the `ID` of the `Employee` record just inserted. To return single values from a stored procedure we can use output parameters. These must be defined within the stored procedure as output:

```
  @ID int OUTPUT,
```

The use of output parameters within .NET is specified by setting the `SqlParameter.Direction` value. The `database` class provides an overload of the `MakeParameter` function, which allows us to specify the direction of a parameter.

```
    Public Function MakeParameter(ByVal ParamName As String, ByVal Direction As _
        ParameterDirection, ByVal Value As Object) As SqlParameter
        Dim param As SqlParameter

        param = New SqlParameter(ParamName, Value)
        param.Direction = Direction

        Return param

    End Function
```

Our code for the `AddEmployee` method becomes:

```
          '*********************************************************************
          ' AddEmployee Method
          '
          ' The AddEmployee method adds a new Employee to the tblHris_Employees
          ' database table, and returns the ItemId value as a result.
          '*********************************************************************
          Public Shared Function AddEmployee(ByVal InstanceID As Integer, _
              ByVal FirstName As String, ByVal MiddleNames As String, _
              ByVal LastName As String, ByVal Title As String, _
              ByVal EthnicOriginID As Integer, ByVal SSN As String, _
```

```
        ByVal HomeAddress As String, ByVal TelephoneNum As String, _
        ByVal BankRT As String, ByVal BankAcct As String, _
        ByVal NextOfKin As String, ByVal GPAddress As String, _
        ByVal EMail As String, ByVal SiteID As Integer, _
        ByVal StatusID As Integer, ByVal JobID As Integer, _
        ByVal Photograph() As Byte, ByVal PhotoContentType As String, _
        ByVal PhotoContentSize As Integer, ByVal Contract() As Byte, _
        ByVal ContractContentType As String, _
        ByVal ContractContentSize As Integer, ByVal Salary As Single, _
        ByVal Notes As String, ByVal HealthNotes As String, _
        ByVal DateOfBirth As String, ByVal ReviewBaseDate As String, _
        ByVal LeavingDate As String, ByVal UserName As String) As Integer

    ' Create and Fill the DataReader
    Dim myDataReader As SqlDataReader
    Dim db As New Database()
    Dim params(30) As SqlParameter
    Dim itemId As Integer

    params(0) = db.MakeParameter("@ID", ParameterDirection.Output, _
        itemId)
    params(1) = db.MakeParameter("@InstanceID", InstanceID)
    params(2) = db.MakeParameter("@FirstName", FirstName)
    params(3) = db.MakeParameter("@MiddleNames", MiddleNames)
    params(4) = db.MakeParameter("@LastName", LastName)
    params(5) = db.MakeParameter("@Title", Title)
    params(6) = db.MakeParameter("@EthnicOriginID", EthnicOriginID)
    params(7) = db.MakeParameter("@SSN", SSN)
    params(8) = db.MakeParameter("@HomeAddress", HomeAddress)
    params(9) = db.MakeParameter("@TelephoneNum", TelephoneNum)
    params(10) = db.MakeParameter("@BankRT", BankRT)
    params(11) = db.MakeParameter("@BankAcct", BankAcct)
    params(12) = db.MakeParameter("@NextOfKin", NextOfKin)
    params(13) = db.MakeParameter("@GPAddress", GPAddress)
    params(14) = db.MakeParameter("@EMail", EMail)
    params(15) = db.MakeParameter("@SiteID", SiteID)
    params(16) = db.MakeParameter("@StatusID", StatusID)
    params(17) = db.MakeParameter("@JobID", JobID)
    params(18) = db.MakeParameter("@Photograph", Photograph)
    params(19) = db.MakeParameter("@PhotoContentType", _
        PhotoContentType)
    params(20) = db.MakeParameter("@PhotoContentSize", _
        PhotoContentSize)
    params(21) = db.MakeParameter("@Contract", Contract)
    params(22) = db.MakeParameter("@ContractContentType", _
        ContractContentType)
    params(23) = db.MakeParameter("@ContractContentSize", _
        ContractContentSize)
    params(24) = db.MakeParameter("@Salary", Salary)
    params(25) = db.MakeParameter("@Notes", Notes)
    params(26) = db.MakeParameter("@HealthNotes", HealthNotes)
    params(27) = db.MakeParameter("@DateOfBirth", DateOfBirth)
    params(28) = db.MakeParameter("@ReviewBaseDate", ReviewBaseDate)
```

```
        If UserName.Length < 1 Then
            UserName = "unknown"
        End If
        params(29) = db.MakeParameter("@UserName", UserName)
        Try
            If IsDate(LeavingDate) Then
                params(30) = db.MakeParameter("@LeavingDate", LeavingDate)
            Else
                params(30) = db.MakeParameter("@LeavingDate", _
                        System.DBNull.Value)
            End If
        Catch
            params(30) = db.MakeParameter("@LeavingDate", _
                    System.DBNull.Value)
        End Try

        db.RunProcedure("up_Hris_InsertEmployee", params, myDataReader)

        'Since the Database class traps all data exceptions we can pass
        'the ErrorMessage back to the user controls
        If myDataReader Is Nothing Then
            Throw New Exception(db.ErrorMessage)
        End If

        ' Return the ID Value
        Return CInt(params(0).Value)
    End Function
```

Firstly, don't let the number of parameters or the size of the method signature cloud this key points. The AddEmployee function returns an integer. This integer value is the ID of the employee record just inserted. This is very useful for the presentation layer as it is now able to execute any additional queries or perform any additional actions against the database that relate to the newly inserted record. The output parameter is added to our parameter array in the following line of code

```
params(0) = db.MakeParameter("@ID", ParameterDirection.Output, itemId)
```

Unlike the RunProcedure methods, the itemId parameter is not passed by reference. Therefore, to get the resultant value from the SQL output parameter we need to interrogate the parameter collection, as shown below:

```
Return CInt(params(0).Value)
```

This will return the value of the output parameter to the presentation layer.

The *UpdateEmployee* Method

The UpdateEmployee method of EmployeesBiz is identical to the AddEmployee method except that it does not return any ID value because the ID value is passed into the method in order to identify the record to be updated. The code for the UpdateMethod is shown below:

```
'*********************************************************************
' UpdateEmployee Method
'
' The UpdateEmployee method updates an Employee to the tblHris_Employees
' database table
'*********************************************************************
Public Shared Sub UpdateEmployee(ByVal InstanceID As Integer, _
        ByVal ID As Integer, ByVal FirstName As String, _
        ByVal MiddleNames As String, _
        ByVal LastName As String, ByVal Title As String, _
        ByVal EthnicOriginID As Integer, ByVal SSN As String, _
        ByVal HomeAddress As String, ByVal TelephoneNum As String,_
        ByVal BankRT As String, ByVal BankAcct As String, _
        ByVal NextOfKin As String, ByVal GPAddress As String, _
        ByVal EMail As String, ByVal SiteID As Integer, _
        ByVal StatusID As Integer, ByVal JobID As Integer, _
        ByVal Photograph() As Byte, ByVal PhotoContentType As String, _
        ByVal PhotoContentSize As Integer, ByVal Contract() As Byte, _
        ByVal ContractContentType As String, _
        ByVal ContractContentSize As Integer, ByVal Salary As Single, _
        ByVal Notes As String, ByVal HealthNotes As String, _
        ByVal DateOfBirth As String, ByVal ReviewBaseDate As String, _
        ByVal LeavingDate As String, ByVal UserName As String)

    Dim result As Integer
    Dim db As New Database()
    Dim params(30) As SqlParameter

    params(0) = db.MakeParameter("@ID", ID)
    params(1) = db.MakeParameter("@InstanceID", InstanceID)
    params(2) = db.MakeParameter("@FirstName", FirstName)
    params(3) = db.MakeParameter("@MiddleNames", MiddleNames)
    params(4) = db.MakeParameter("@LastName", LastName)
    params(5) = db.MakeParameter("@Title", Title)
    params(6) = db.MakeParameter("@EthnicOriginID", EthnicOriginID)
    params(7) = db.MakeParameter("@SSN", SSN)
    params(8) = db.MakeParameter("@HomeAddress", HomeAddress)
    params(9) = db.MakeParameter("@TelephoneNum", TelephoneNum)
    params(10) = db.MakeParameter("@BankRT", BankRT)
    params(11) = db.MakeParameter("@BankAcct", BankAcct)
    params(12) = db.MakeParameter("@NextOfKin", NextOfKin)
    params(13) = db.MakeParameter("@GPAddress", GPAddress)
    params(14) = db.MakeParameter("@EMail", EMail)
    params(15) = db.MakeParameter("@SiteID", SiteID)
    params(16) = db.MakeParameter("@StatusID", StatusID)
    params(17) = db.MakeParameter("@JobID", JobID)
    params(18) = db.MakeParameter("@Photograph", Photograph)
```

```
params(19) = db.MakeParameter("@PhotoContentType", PhotoContentType)
params(20) = db.MakeParameter("@PhotoContentSize", PhotoContentSize)
params(21) = db.MakeParameter("@Contract", Contract)
params(22) = db.MakeParameter("@ContractContentType", ContractContentType)
params(23) = db.MakeParameter("@ContractContentSize", ContractContentSize)
params(24) = db.MakeParameter("@Salary", Salary)
params(25) = db.MakeParameter("@Notes", Notes)
params(26) = db.MakeParameter("@HealthNotes", HealthNotes)
params(27) = db.MakeParameter("@DateOfBirth", DateOfBirth)
params(28) = db.MakeParameter("@ReviewBaseDate", ReviewBaseDate)

If UserName.Length < 1 Then
    UserName = "unknown"
End If
params(29) = db.MakeParameter("@UserName", UserName)
Try
    If IsDate(LeavingDate) Then
        params(30) = db.MakeParameter("@LeavingDate", LeavingDate)
    Else
        params(30) = db.MakeParameter("@LeavingDate", System.DBNull.Value)
    End If
Catch
    params(30) = db.MakeParameter("@LeavingDate", System.DBNull.Value)
End Try

result = db.RunProcedure("up_Hris_UpdateEmployee", params)
If result < 0 Then
    Throw New Exception(db.ErrorMessage)
End If
End Sub
```

These add and update methods demonstrate how we use the Database class to execute an ExecuteScalar command, as used by the RunProcedure function overload. The value returned by ExecuteScalar is stored in the result variable and used to check whether the Add/Update was successful.

```
result = db.RunProcedure("up_Hris_UpdateEmployee", params)
If result < 0 Then
    Throw New Exception(db.ErrorMessage)
End If
```

One point to note here is that the Database class uses a value of -1 to report an exception. When using the Database class we must be aware of any stored procedures that will return a negative number as a successful result, e.g. retrieving sales growth etc.

The add and update methods shown above have to deal with the possibility of null values. This requires some care in how it is coded. The following section discusses how to handle nulls.

Handling NULLs

Database NULLs cause almost every database developer a headache or two at some point. Within queries the most common problem is that since null equates to unknown then any comparison or concatenation involving a null results in null (see note on Database Settings for NULL).

> **Database Settings for NULL** – When you concatenate null values, either the concat null yields null setting of sp_dboption or SET CONCAT_NULL_YIELDS_NULL determines the behavior when one expression is NULL. With either concat null yields null or SET CONCAT_NULL_YIELDS_NULL enabled ON, 'string' + NULL returns NULL. If either concat null yields null or SET CONCAT_NULL_YIELDS_NULL is disabled, the result is 'string'.

The nature of the HRIS is such that this is not too much of a problem, the SQL involved in this application is basic insert, update and delete statements. The problem arises when a value is passed to the Biz component that is not of the required type and is not a required field. This is best illustrated with an example.

In tblHris_Employees the LeavingDate should be of type smalldatetime but can be null (since not all employees are leaving the company). The web form can use validation controls to check for a valid DateTime but if no value is acceptable then what should the code do. There are two main options:

❑ Overload the Add / Update method of the business component so that it can accept fewer parameters (i.e. a different method signature is used when the LeavingDate is null).

❑ Check the validity of the field value and set the value to null if either an exception occurs or the value is not of the required type.

In EmployeesBiz.vb we chose the second option. The reason for this is twofold, firstly we wanted to show how to conditionally set a field to null, and secondly the first method is a clean, correct solution to use when there are a relatively small number of parameters with only one or two possible nulls. Where there are a large number of parameters with various possible null value combinations the number of overloads grows factorially, resulting in a cumbersome interface.

Here is how we handle the possibility of a null value LeavingDate in the UpdateEmployee method

```
Try
    If IsDate(LeavingDate) Then
        parameterLeavingDate.Value = LeavingDate
    Else
        parameterLeavingDate.Value = System.DBNull.Value
    End If
Catch
    parameterLeavingDate.Value = System.DBNull.Value
End Try
```

The first thing we do is to embed the logic within a `try catch` statement. This ensures that any exception raised within the code results in the `Catch` code being run which sets the `parameterLeavingDate.Value` to `System.DBNull.Value`.

The second part of the logic checks to see if the value is of the type we are expecting, in this case `Date`. This lets us use valid values and default to `System.DBNull.Value` for invalid values or exceptions.

The `DeleteEmployee` Method

The `DeleteEmployee` method is identical in structure to the `UpdateEmployee` method, only with far fewer parameters.

```
'**********************************************************************
' DeleteEmployee Method
'
' The DeleteEmployee method deletes the specified Employee from
' the Employees database table.
'**********************************************************************
Public Shared Sub DeleteEmployee(ByVal itemID As Integer)

    Dim result As Integer
    Dim db As New Database()
    Dim params(0) As SqlParameter

    params(0) = db.MakeParameter("@ID", itemID)
    result = db.RunProcedure("up_Hris_DeleteEmployee", params)
    If result < 0 Then
        Throw New Exception(db.ErrorMessage)
    End If
End Sub
```

The `GetBrowsePathDetails` Helper Function

We have now covered all the standard set of database wrapper methods (together with the employee specific `SearchEmployees` method) that are used in the business objects of the HRIS module. The `EmployeesBiz` class also contains a helper function for configuration of the pages used to browse binary data (`GetBrowsePathDetails`).

The `GetBrowsePathDetails` function is shown below:

```
Public Shared Function GetBrowsePathDetails(ByVal Entity As String, ByVal ID As
Integer) As String
    ' if there is content in the database, create an
    ' url to browse it
    Select Case Entity
        Case "Employee"
        Return "~/DesktopModules/ViewHrisEmployeeDetails.aspx?ID=" & ID.ToString()
        Case "JobTitle"
```

```
            Return "~/DesktopModules/ViewHrisJobTitles.aspx?ID=" & ID.ToString()
        Case "Photo"
            Return "~/DesktopModules/HrisViewPhoto.aspx?ID=" & ID.ToString()
        Case "Contract"
            Return "~/DesktopModules/HrisViewContract.aspx?ID=" & ID.ToString()
    End Select
End Function
```

It is used by the user control code to determine which page to use to view binary large object (BLOB) information. While the information could just as easily have been stored within the `web.config` file `appSettings` key, the information returned by this function is not customizable or user configurable, rather it is fixed at application development time and as such should be altered only as part of an application upgrade or version release.

> **BLOB or Binary Large Object is a term used to describe binary documents that are stored as an array of bytes within a DB column. In SQL Server the image datatype is normally used to store BLOBs, e.g. the `tblHris_Employees`. Photograph column can be used to store a picture (.bmp, .gif, .jpg etc) of the employee. The handling of binary large objects is covered in the `HrisEmployeesDisplayFull.ascx` section.**

We have now seen how the `EmployeesBiz.vb` class is structured, and examined some general techniques for querying a SQL Server database.

Now that we have a business component that allows us to query the database through stored procedures, let's look at how we leverage the `IBuySpy` Portals infrastructure to create the presentation layer of our HRIS module.

The Presentation Layer

The presentation layer consists of the visible user interface of our HRIS module. This consists of a user control and an edit page for each component of our HRIS module. As with the earlier sections on the data layer and business layer; the discussion of the presentation layer will focus on the employee related UI.

❑ `HrisEmployeesDisplayFull.ascx`

❑ `HrisEmployeesDisplaySummary.ascx`

❑ `HrisEmployeesDisplaySearchResults.ascx`

The presentation layer for the other components is a very basic subset of the user interface used for the `EmployeesDisplayFull` control. As a result, a discussion of these components in turn would not add any value to this chapter.

EmployeesDisplayFull

The `EmployeesDisplayFull` allows users with the appropriate permission to `edit`, `update` and `browse` information on all of the staff currently employed by the company. This control can safely be visible to all employees.

Only the members of the HRAdmin role (see the Configuration section at the end of this chapter for more details on the HRAdmin role) are able to add new employees details or edit existing employees' details. However, other employees are able to browse limited, non-sensitive, details about each employee. The main user control is shown below

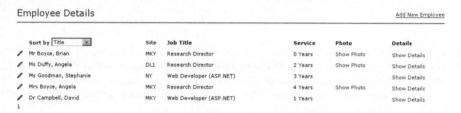

The corresponding data entry page, (HrisEditEmployees.aspx) shown below, for employees is also discussed in this section.

Employee Details

Title:	Mr
First Name:	Brian
Middle Names:	G
Last Name:	Boyce
Ethnic Origin:	Caucasian
SSN:	555-11-2222
Home Address:	10 Wilson Court
Telephone:	01908 266152
Bank RT:	831234123
Bank Account:	12341234512342
Next of Kin:	J Boyce
GP Address:	Dr Barckin
E-Mail:	BBoyce@alphat
Site:	Milton Keynes
Status:	Director
Job Title:	Research Director
Photograph:	☐ Upload photo to database (will overwrite existing photo) Browse...
Contract:	☐ Upload Contract to database (will overwrite existing Contract) Browse...
Salary:	12000
Notes:	Ambition
Health Notes:	Alergic to X
Date of Birth:	03/02/1972
Start Date:	06/06/2002
Leaving Date:	

Update Cancel Delete this item

Created by guest on 10/07/2002

Technology Summary

In the implementation of the `EmployeesDisplayFull` component, we demonstrate how to use the following ASP.NET features:

❑ Sorting

❑ Paging data

❑ Customizing the Datagrid

❑ ASP.NET Validation Controls

❑ Using Javascript Attributes to control server side events

❑ Creating and populating ASP.NET forms

HrisEmployeesDisplayFull.ascx

The IBuySpy portal framework allows for the development and integration of user controls through its `Admin` tab. The only requirement that the framework imposes on the developer is that he/she must create a user control that inherits from the `ASPNetPortal.PortalModuleControl` class.

```
Namespace ASPNetPortal.Hris
```

```
    Public MustInherit Class HrisEmployeesDisplayFull
        Inherits ASPNetPortal.PortalModuleControl
```

The `PortalModuleControl` class (declared in `DesktopPortalControls.vb`) defines a base class containing several module specific properties. Since the user controls we develop for the intranet inherit from this class, these properties should be used within the code in order to control the behavior of the control. Similarly, any enhancements you make to the framework which affect the module definitions should include corresponding changes to the base classes, in order to fully utilize the enhancements made.

The `HrisEmployeesDisplayFull.ascx` user control allows the user to browse through and display appropriate details for any of the employees within the organization. The information is presented using an ASP.NET DataGrid control.

Sorting the DataGrid

Sorting in a `DataGrid` can be enabled on all columns or on a selection of columns. To enable sorting on all columns set the `AllowSorting` property to `true` and associate a subroutine with the `SortCommand` event. This causes the `HeaderText` to be rendered as a hyperlink that will trigger the `SortCommand` when clicked.

In the `HrisEmployeeDisplayFull` control, we enabled sorting on four fields in two columns. To limit the sort to certain columns we set the `SortExpression` property only on those columns we wish to sort.

```
<asp:datagrid id="myDataGrid" runat="server" EnableViewState="false"
  AllowSorting="True"    AutoGenerateColumns="false" width="100%" Border="0"
  AllowPaging="True"     OnPageIndexChanged="Employees_PageIndexChanged"
```

```
PageSize="5">
<Columns>
   <asp:TemplateColumn>
      <ItemTemplate>
    <asp:HyperLink ImageUrl="~/images/edit.gif" NavigateUrl='<%#
"~/DesktopModules/HrisEditEmployees.aspx?ItemID=" &
DataBinder.Eval(Container.DataItem,"ID") & "&mid=" & ModuleId %>' Visible="<%#
IsEditable %>" runat="server" />
      </ItemTemplate>
   </asp:TemplateColumn>
   <asp:TemplateColumn SortExpression="*" HeaderText="Sort by ">
      <HeaderStyle CssClass="NormalBold"></HeaderStyle>
      <ItemStyle CssClass="Normal"></ItemStyle>
      <ItemTemplate>
      <asp:Label runat="server" Text='<%#
DataBinder.Eval(Container.DataItem,"EmpTitle") & " " &
DataBinder.Eval(Container.DataItem,"LastName") & ", " &
DataBinder.Eval(Container.DataItem,"FirstName")%>' />
      </ItemTemplate>
   </asp:TemplateColumn>
   <asp:BoundColumn DataField="SiteCode" SortExpression="SiteCode"
HeaderText="Site">
      <HeaderStyle CssClass="NormalBold"></HeaderStyle>
      <ItemStyle CssClass="Normal"></ItemStyle>
   </asp:BoundColumn>
   <asp:BoundColumn DataField="JobTitle" HeaderText="Job Title">
      <HeaderStyle CssClass="NormalBold"></HeaderStyle>
      <ItemStyle CssClass="Normal"></ItemStyle>
   </asp:BoundColumn>
```

The code above shows how we have set the SortExpression on both the Name column and the Site column. The Site column is the most straightforward, and has set the SortExpression equal to "SiteCode", SiteCode being the name of the field in the DataTable populated by up_Hris_GetEmployeesFull. Sorting by a column defined in this way is as simple as setting the DataViews Sort property to the DataGridSortCommandEventArgs.SortExpression in the SortCommand event.

```
Public Sub Employees_SortCommand(ByVal sender As System.Object, ByVal e As
DataGridSortCommandEventArgs) Handles myDataGrid.SortCommand

    Dim dv As New DataView()
    If Cache.Item(CachedDataViewName) Is Nothing Then
        dv = _ EmployeesBiz.GetEmployeesSummary(ModuleId).Tables(0).DefaultView()
        Cache.Add(CachedDataViewName, dv, Nothing, _
            DateTime.Now.AddSeconds(20), Cache.NoSlidingExpiration, _
            Caching.CacheItemPriority.Normal, Nothing)
    Else
        dv = CType(Cache.Item(CachedDataViewName), DataView)
    End If

    myDataGrid.DataSource = dv

    If e.SortExpression <> "*" Then
```

```
                dv.Sort = e.SortExpression
                ViewState("SortExpression") = e.SortExpression.ToString()


        Else
            Dim dgItem As DataGridItem = CType(e.CommandSource, DataGridItem)
            Dim ddl1 As DropDownList = CType(dgItem.FindControl("SortNameDDL"),
    DropDownList)

            ' Get the selected sort expression from the list
            dv.Sort = ddl1.SelectedItem.Value
            ViewState("SortExpression") = ddl1.SelectedItem.Value

            ' Store the currently select sort expression from the dropdownlist
            myDataGrid.Attributes("SortFieldIndex") = CStr(ddl1.SelectedIndex)
            ViewState("SortFieldIndex") = ddl1.SelectedIndex

        End If

        myDataGrid.DataBind()

    End Sub
```

The `Template` column for the `Name` column sets the `SortExpression="*"`. This is a placeholder used to indicate that the column should behave like a sortable column but that we will handle the setting of the `SortExpression` in the `SortCommand` event. This is necessary because we are going to customize the `DataGrid` header by placing a drop-down list box in the column header. By handling the `ItemCreated` event, we are able to customize any row in the resulting table (`DataGrid`) by checking the `ListItemType` of the item and adding content to the appropriate cell in the table row.

```
    Public Sub Employees_ItemCreated(ByVal sender As System.Object, ByVal e As _
            DataGridItemEventArgs) Handles myDataGrid.ItemCreated
        Dim lit As System.Web.UI.WebControls.ListItemType = e.Item.ItemType

        If lit = ListItemType.Header Then
            Dim SortNameDDL As New DropDownList()
            SortNameDDL.CssClass = "Normal"
            SortNameDDL.ID = "SortNameDDL"
            Dim li1 As New ListItem("Title", "EmpTitle")
            SortNameDDL.Items.Add(li1)

            Dim li2 As New ListItem("Last Name", "LastName")
            SortNameDDL.Items.Add(li2)

            Dim li3 As New ListItem("First Name", "FirstName")
            SortNameDDL.Items.Add(li3)

            If ViewState("SortFieldIndex") = Nothing Then
                SortNameDDL.SelectedIndex = _
                    Int(myDataGrid.Attributes("SortFieldIndex"))
            Else
                SortNameDDL.SelectedIndex = CInt(ViewState("SortFieldIndex"))
```

```
        End If

        'Add the Drop down list to the Header cell
        Dim cell As New TableCell()
        cell = e.Item.Controls(1)
        cell.Controls.Add(SortNameDDL)
    End If
End Sub
```

In the above code, we create a new `DropDownList` control and populate it with a series of `ListItems` that represent the constituent fields in the employee's name. The `if` statement ensures that the `DropDownList` is only created for the `ListItemType.Header` row. We then gain a reference to the second column in the `DataGrid` (index of 1) and add the `DropDownList` control to it. The screenshot below shows the outcome of this procedure.

Employee Details   Add New Employee

	Sort by	First Name ▼	Site	Job Title	Service	Photo	Details
✎	Ms Duffy	Title	DL1	Research Director	2 Years	Show Photo	Show Details
✎	Mrs Boyce	Last Name	MKY	Research Director	4 Years	Show Photo	Show Details
✎	Mr Boyce, Brian	First Name	MKY	Research Director	0 Years	Show Photo	Show Details
✎	Ms Burton, Michelle		NY	Web Developer (ASP.NET)	1 Years	Show Photo	Show Details
✎	Ms Goodman, Stephanie		NY	Web Developer (ASP.NET)	3 Years	Show Photo	Show Details

1 2

This is sufficient for custom sorting of the `DataGrid`. However, when we add paging capabilities to the control the selected index of the `DropDownList` is lost on the change of a page. Luckily, ASP.NET lets us make use of `ViewState` to preserve information across `postbacks`. The `SelectedIndex` information is preserved by `ViewState` in the following code.

```
    If ViewState("SortFieldIndex") = Nothing Then
        SortNameDDL.SelectedIndex = Int(myDataGrid.Attributes("SortFieldIndex"))
    Else
        SortNameDDL.SelectedIndex = CInt(ViewState("SortFieldIndex"))
    End If
```

In the `ItemCreated` event we store the `SelectedIndex` of the `DropDownList` control so that after a page move the `DropDownList` continues to show the correct value.

DataGrid Paging

There are two forms of paging available for use with the `DataGrid`.

❑   Built-in Paging

❑   Custom Paging

The `DataGrid`'s built-in paging works best with small datasources, and is the method used in the HRIS module. This is because the data is retrieved each time the `CurrentPageIndex` is changed. To make use of built-in paging we simply set `AllowPaging` equal to `true` and the `PageSize` property of the `DataGrid` to the number of records we wish to display on a single page. Then we handle the `PageIndexChanged` event to set the `CurrentPageIndex` to the value passed in by `DataGridPageChangedEventArgs.NewPageIndex`.

```
Public Sub Employees_PageIndexChanged(ByVal sender As System.Object, _
    ByVal e As DataGridPageChangedEventArgs) _
    Handles myDataGrid.PageIndexChanged

  myDataGrid.CurrentPageIndex = e.NewPageIndex
  BindGrid()
End Sub
```

In most cases you will want to create a small subroutine that can be called to rebind the `DataGrid` after the `CurrentPageIndex` is changed.

```
'Common routine to bind the datagrid to the Employees dataset
Private Sub BindGrid()
   Dim dv As New DataView()

   If Cache.Item(CachedDataViewName) Is Nothing Then
       dv = EmployeesBiz.GetEmployeesSummary(ModuleId).Tables(0).DefaultView()
       Cache.Add(CachedDataViewName, dv, Nothing, DateTime.Now.AddSeconds(20),
Cache.NoSlidingExpiration, Caching.CacheItemPriority.Normal, Nothing)
   Else
       dv = CType(Cache.Item(CachedDataViewName), DataView)
   End If

   myDataGrid.DataSource = dv

   'Set the Sort criteria, otherwise it is lost across the paging
   If ViewState("SortExpression") <> Nothing Then
      dv.Sort = ViewState("SortExpression").ToString()
   End If

   myDataGrid.DataBind()
End Sub
```

The above code is used to rebind the `Datagrid` in order to reflect changes to sorting or paging. Now that we are able to sort and page through our employee information we can turn our hand to improving the efficiency of the control through caching.

Using Caching to Improve Performance

The `HrisEmployeesDisplayFull.ascx` control uses data caching in order to reduce the number of requests sent to the SQL server. We take advantage of the fact that the employee information is relatively static to improve the performance of the built-in paging by caching the employee details. Data Caching allows us to assign objects to the cache and retrieve them when required.

We can add items to the cache object by assigning a value to the cache's `item` property, as follows:

```
Cache.Item("myStringKey") = myObject
```

Or

```
Cache("myStringKey") = myObject
```

Retrieving items is only slightly more involved. As with page caching and fragment caching, even if we add an item to the cache it is not guaranteed to remain there until it is removed; since the ASP.NET framework may reclaim some resources by removing items from the cache. We must therefore always check that the item exists in the cache before working with it.

```
If Cache.Item(CachedDataViewName) Is Nothing Then
    dv = EmployeesBiz.GetEmployeesSummary(ModuleId).Tables(0).DefaultView()
    Cache.Add(CachedDataViewName, dv, Nothing, DateTime.Now.AddSeconds(20), _
        Cache.NoSlidingExpiration, Caching.CacheItemPriority.Normal, Nothing)
Else
    dv = CType(Cache.Item(CachedDataViewName), DataView)
End If
```

As the above code shows, if the item does not exist within the cache, then we must re-create the item, and optionally add it to the cache.

```
dv = EmployeesBiz.GetEmployeesSummary(ModuleId).Tables(0).DefaultView()
Cache.Add(CachedDataViewName, dv, Nothing, DateTime.Now.AddSeconds(20), _
    Cache.NoSlidingExpiration, Caching.CacheItemPriority.Normal, Nothing)
```

Items are returned from the cache as type `object`. Therefore, we must always convert the returned cache object to the proper type.

```
dv = CType(Cache.Item(CachedDataViewName), DataView)
```

Within our intranet framework, we must always bear in mind that a single `.ascx` can be presenting different information in different module instances. If we were to use a simple string literal to key the data cache, different module instances could end up displaying information for the wrong module. We can work around this by incorporating the `ModuleId` of the current instance into the cache key, as shown in the `HrisEmployeesDisplayFull.ascx`.

```
CachedDataViewName = "EmployeesFull" & CType(ModuleId, String)
```

Through the admin pages of the IBuySpy PORTAL, we can also define the Duration value of the fragment caching for any user control (custom module) we add, as shown below

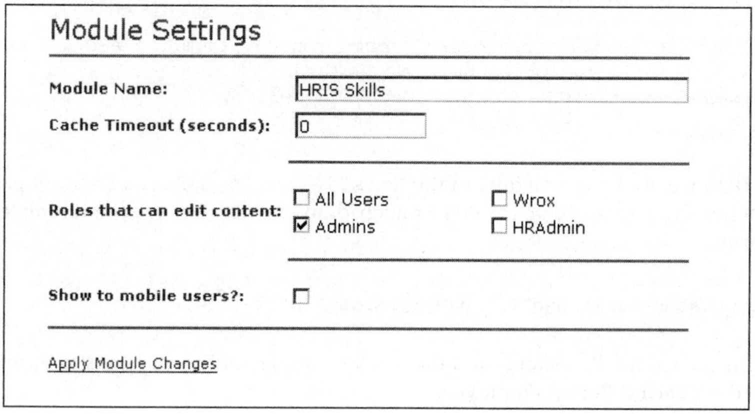

Module Settings

Module Name:	HRIS Skills
Cache Timeout (seconds):	0

Roles that can edit content: ☐ All Users ☐ Wrox ☑ Admins ☐ HRAdmin

Show to mobile users?: ☐

Apply Module Changes

This setting is used to alter the Duration property of caching for this particular instance of the .ascx by using the following code:

```
Protected Overrides Sub Render(ByVal output As HtmlTextWriter)

    ' If no caching is specified, render the child tree and return
    If _moduleConfiguration.CacheTime = 0 Then
        MyBase.Render(output)
        Return
    End If

    ' If no cached output was found from a previous request, render
    ' child controls into a TextWriter, and then cache the results
    ' in the ASP.NET Cache for future requests.
    If _cachedOutput Is Nothing Then
        Dim tempWriter = New StringWriter()
        MyBase.Render(New HtmlTextWriter(tempWriter))
        _cachedOutput = tempWriter.ToString()

        Context.Cache.Insert(CacheKey, _cachedOutput, Nothing, _
            DateTime.Now.AddSeconds(_moduleConfiguration.CacheTime), _
            TimeSpan.Zero)

    End If

    ' Output the user control's content
    output.Write(_cachedOutput)

End Sub
```

As the above code shows, a value of 0 in the Intranet Admin will not make use of the output caching built into the intranet framework.

The `CreateChildControls` method then attempts to reload any cached output from the user control.

```
Protected Overrides Sub CreateChildControls()

    ' Attempt to resolve previously cached content from the ASP.NET Cache
    If _moduleConfiguration.CacheTime > 0 Then
        _cachedOutput = CStr(Context.Cache(CacheKey))
    End If
```

Within the HRIS we used page caching in the `HrisViewEmployeeDetails.aspx` page. This page is linked within the `EmployeesDisplayFull` datagrid, to enable users to see more detail about any given employee.

```
<%@ OutputCache Duration="15" VaryByParam="ID" %>
```

The details are cached for 15 seconds and the `VaryByParam` setting allows us to ensure that a separate page is cached for each different employee.

> **Pages are not guaranteed to stay in the cache for the cache duration. If resources are low, the ASP.NET Framework will remove some information from the cache.**

Conditional Column Formatting

The Photo column of the `HrisEmployeesDisplayFull.ascx` has to show a hyperlink to the `HrisViewPhoto.aspx` page only if the photograph is available in the database.

The photograph is not returned with the employee details that populate the `DataGrid` in order to keep the size of the information to a minimum. Instead, we return the string text for the hyper link column using a `T-SQL CASE` statement to determine whether the photograph is available for the employee.

```
SELECT Emp.ID, Emp.Title as 'EmpTitle', FirstName, LastName,
    Code as 'SiteCode',    -- Site Code
    JobID,
    JobTitles.Title as 'JobTitle',
    str(Datediff(yyyy, ReviewBaseDate, getdate())) + ' Years' as 'Service',
    EMail,
    CASE WHEN Photograph IS NULL THEN '' ELSE 'Show Photo' END as 'PhotoAvail'
FROM
    tblHris_Employees Emp INNER JOIN tblHris_Sites
```

The hyperlink column for the main `Datagrid` in the `HrisEmployeesDisplayFull.ascx` is then implemented as follows;

```
<asp:HyperLinkColumn Target="_new" DataNavigateUrlField="ID"
DataNavigateUrlFormatString="javascript:window.open('DesktopModules/HrisViewPhoto.
aspx?ID={0}','_new','width=400;height=400;');" DataTextField="PhotoAvail"
HeaderText="Photo" DataTextFormatString="{0}">
    <HeaderStyle CssClass="NormalBold"></HeaderStyle>
    <ItemStyle CssClass="Normal"></ItemStyle>
</asp:HyperLinkColumn>
```

The `DataNavigateUrlField` and the `DataNavigateUrlFormat` string are used together to create the URL. The `DataNavigateUrlField` identifies the field from the `DataGrid DataSource` to be used to create the URL. The `DataNavigateUrlFormat` property is used to format the URL. In the above piece of code, we use the `DataNavigateUrlFormatString` to insert some JavaScript into the HTML sent to the client that will open a new window.

Similarly, the `DataTextField` and the `DataTextFormatString` are used together to create the text for the hyperlink. The `DataTextField` identifies the field in the `DataGridsDataSource` and the `DataTextFormatString` controls the formatting of the text for display.

We have now seen how to create a user control for integration into the IBuySpy Framework that effectively and efficiently displays information from our SQL Server database. That still leaves the question of how we get the information into the Database.

Data Entry – HrisEditEmployees.aspx

In general, each modular addition to the intranet will include a user control to display and interact with the information and, at least, one further page to edit the information. The HRIS is no exception, and provides the `HrisEditEmployees.aspx` page to allow the users to edit existing employee information and to add new employee information to the HRIS.

The data entry form is key to the module. Its usability and robustness will determine the user's satisfaction with the application. If a data entry screen is awkward to use or, worse still, prone to crashing then users will gradually stop using the system no matter how good the rest of the system functionality is. This is another reason why each of the application modules provided within the IBuySpy Framework, and even those we have developed in the course of this book, maintains a certain look and feel across modules. This consistency helps the user to feel confident with new modules. It is worth setting up a new tab with limited role access and having some users work with the new application before putting it on a widely accessible tab to gain feedback on usability.

The screenshot below shows how the main data entry screen looks for the `HrisEditEmployees aspx` page. We have submitted the form with no information, in order to show the validation control messages.

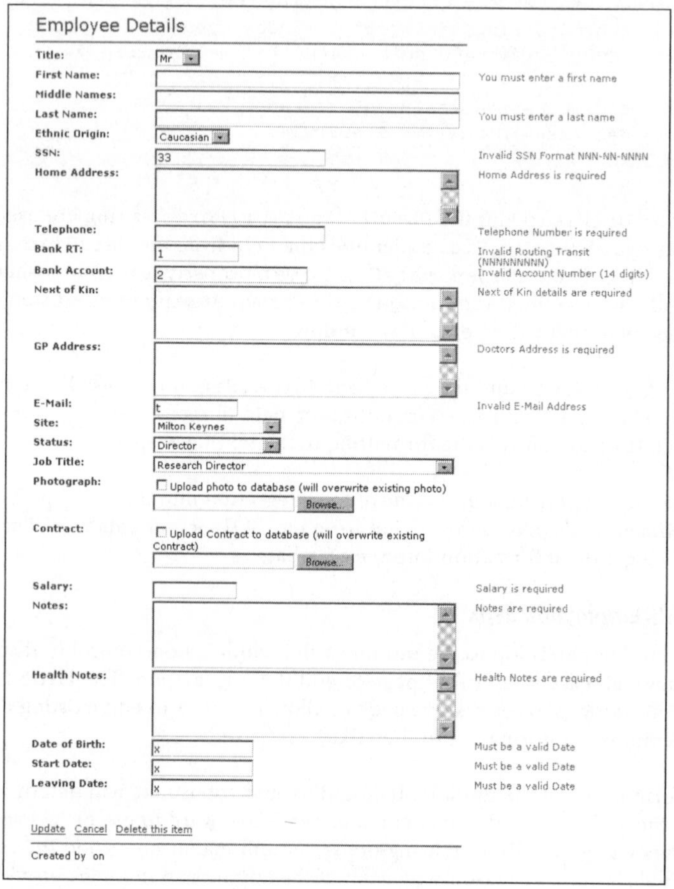

Validating the user's Input

The ASP.NET validation controls provide an extremely powerful and simple means of improving the quality of data entry from both a user interface and a back-end system standpoint. The validation controls are used between <FORM> tags in a web form to validate the data that a user enters against set criteria or behaviors. The required fields in `HrisEditEmployees.aspx` are all enforced using the `<asp:RequiredFieldValidator>`, as shown in the following section;

```
<td>
    <asp:textbox id="LastNameField" runat="server" maxlength="50" Columns="28"
width="353" cssclass="NormalTextBox"></asp:textbox>
</td>
<td class="Normal" width="250">
    <asp:requiredfieldvalidator id="Requiredfieldvalidator2" runat="server"
```

```
ControlToValidate="LastNameField" ErrorMessage="You must enter a last name"
Display="Static"></asp:requiredfieldvalidator>
</td>
```

The `RequiredFieldValidator` even allows us to set an `InitialValue`, e.g. **Please enter your first name only.** `IsValid` will only return `true` if a value is entered by the user and it is different from the `InitialValue`.

The required field validator is used to force the user to enter information in the following fields:

❑ First Name

❑ Last Name

❑ Home Address

❑ Telephone Number

❑ Next of Kin

❑ Doctors Address

❑ Salary

❑ Notes

❑ Health Notes

We also use the `CompareValidator` control to compare the entered value with either a constant, the value of another control or a type. This control is extremely useful for ensuring that a value entered is consistent with another value entered, e.g. the employee start date must be greater then the employee's date of birth.

The `Operator` property is used to control the function of the `CompareValidator` control. The settings are summarized below:

Operator	Description
Equal	The values should equal one another.
GreaterThan	The `ControlToValidate` value must be greater than the `ControlToCompare` or `ValueToCompare` value.
GreaterThanEqual	The `ControlToValidate` value must be greater than or equal to the `ControlToCompare` or `ValueToCompare` value.
LessThan	The `ControlToValidate` value must be less than the `ControlToCompare` or `ValueToCompare` value.

Operator	Description
LessThanEqual	The `ControlToValidate` value must be less than or equal to the `ControlToCompare` or `ValueToCompare` value.
NotEqual	The `ControlToValidate` value must not be equal to the `ControlToCompare` or `ValueToCompare` value.
DataTypeCheck	The `ControlToValidate` value must be of the same type or convertible to the same type as the `ControlToCompare` or `ValueToCompare` data type.

When we are using the `DataTypeCheck` operator, we can specify any one of the `ValidationDataType` enumerations:

- ❏ String
- ❏ Integer
- ❏ Double
- ❏ Date
- ❏ Currency

In `HrisEditEmployees` the `CompareValidator` is used to ensure that the dates entered are valid dates.

```
<td>
    <asp:textbox id="LeavingDateField" runat="server" Columns="28" width="120"
cssclass="NormalTextBox"></asp:textbox>
</td>
<td class="Normal" width="250">
    <asp:comparevalidator id="Comparevalidator4" runat="server"
ControlToValidate="LeavingDateField" ErrorMessage="Must be a valid Date"
Display="Dynamic" Operator="DataTypeCheck" Type="Date">
</asp:comparevalidator>
</td>
```

We have also used the `CompareValidator` to check that nobody entered a salary of over `100000`.

```
<asp:comparevalidator id="CompareValidator3" runat="server" Display="Dynamic"
ErrorMessage="Salary cannot be more than 100000" ControlToValidate="SalaryField"
Operator="LessThanEqual" ValueToCompare="100000">
</asp:comparevalidator>
```

The `CompareValidator` is used to validate the following fields:

❑ `Salary` –as shown above

❑ `Date of Birth` – to ensure that value entered is a valid date

```
<td>
    <asp:textbox id="DateOfBirthField" runat="server" cssclass="NormalTextBox"
width="120" Columns="28"></asp:textbox>
</td>
<td class="Normal" width="250">
    <asp:comparevalidator id="CompareValidator1" runat="server" Display="Static"
        ErrorMessage="Must be a valid Date" ControlToValidate="DateOfBirthField"
Type="Date" Operator="DataTypeCheck">
    </asp:comparevalidator>
</td>
```

❑ `Annual Review Base Date` – to ensure that value entered is a valid date as shown above for Date of Birth

❑ `Leaving Date` – to ensure that value entered is a valid date as shown above for Date of Birth

Another validation control we make use of in the `HrisEditEmployees.aspx` page is the `RegularExpressionValidator` control. The `RegularExpressionValidator` is one of the most powerful validation controls available to developers in .NET. It allows us to specify a regular expression, which the value entered into the `ControlToValidate` must match.

Regular expressions can be used to model quite complex character and textual patterns (the `Systems.Text.RegularExpressions` namespace and the `RegEx` class in .NET allow us to work with regular expressions within our own classes). The `HrisEditEmployees.aspx` page makes use of the `RegularExpressionValidator` to check that the e-mail address entered is a syntactically correct e-mail address:

```
<td>
    <asp:textbox id="EMailField" runat="server" cssclass="NormalTextBox"
width="100" Columns="28" maxlength="255"></asp:textbox>
</td>
<td class="Normal" width="250">
    <asp:regularexpressionvalidator id="Regularexpressionvalidator5"
Display="Static" ErrorMessage="Invalid E-Mail Address"
ControlToValidate="EMailField" Runat="server" ValidationExpression=" \w+([-
+.]\w+)*@\w+([-.]\w+)*\.\w+([-.]\w+)*"></asp:regularexpressionvalidator>
</td>
```

And we ensure that the social security number entered is of the form nnn-nn-nnnn:

```
<td>
    <asp:textbox id="SSNField" runat="server" cssclass="NormalTextBox" width="200"
Columns="28" maxlength="12"></asp:textbox>
</td>
```

```
<td class="Normal" width="250">
    <asp:regularexpressionvalidator id="RegularExpressionValidator1"
Display="Static" ErrorMessage="Invalid SSN Format NNN-NN-NNNN"
ControlToValidate="SSNField" Runat="server" ValidationExpression="^\d{3}-\d{2}-
\d{4}$"></asp:regularexpressionvalidator>
</td>
```

While regular expressions appear complicated at first glance, when they are broken into their constituent parts they are relatively easy to follow, e.g. the regular expression we used to validate the e-mail address "\w+([-+.]\w+)*@\w+([-.]\w+)*\.\w+([-.]\w+)*" can be easily understood when we know that:

> \w means any word character

> + means match one or more instances

> * indicates zero or more matches

> [] indicates the character must match one of the characters within the brackets.

These are best followed by explaining the constituent parts:

> \w+ matches one or more characters

> ([-+.]\w+)* matches zero or more strings of one of a -, + or . followed by one or more characters

> @ matches an @ sign

> \. Matches a fullstop

Our regular expression was chosen from the list of standard regular expressions Visual Studio .Net provides for the regular expression validator. There are a number of sites and articles on the Internet about regular expressions, and even whole books devoted to the subject. One site that springs to mind is Steve Smith's www.regexlib.com which lists several sample regular expressions and even includes the option of testing the regular expressions or adding your own regular expressions.

By using the validator controls provided by .NET we can ensure clean data is being passed through to our application layer and also, as importantly, provide a responsive user interface for our users. While the data entry access is controlled through the intranet framework's security model, the nature of the information warrants additional control and reporting.

We have now covered most aspects of data entry. However, one aspect of the data entry form (HrisEditEmployee.aspx) we have not covered is the uploading of employee photographs and contract documents. This is covered in the next section on uploading and displaying binary data in web forms.

HrisViewEmployeeDetails.aspx

The HrisViewEmployeeDetails page (shown below) is intended to be used to provide detailed information about each employee. The HrisViewEmployeeDetails.aspx page is displayed whenever a user clicks on the Show Details link of the HrisEmployeesDisplayFull (or the HrisEmployeesDisplaySummary) datagrid.

This section demonstrates working with binary large objects (BLOBs), such as images and office documents. We also discuss how to interact with the intranet's Security framework in order to limit access to these files. Although this section is titled HrisViewEmployeeDetails.aspx, we will also be discussing the HrisViewContract.aspx and HrisViewPhoto.aspx pages, as there is a lot of overlap in their functional implementation.

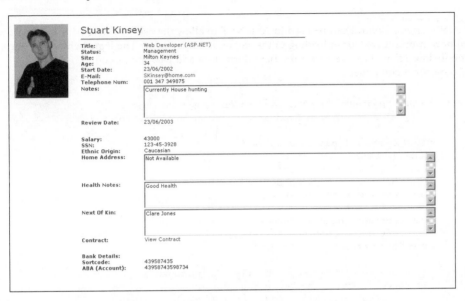

Working with BLOBs

Within the HRIS we wanted to store non-textual information about each employee, including their photograph and a copy of their current contract in word format. Binary documents of this type are stored in SQL Server image columns. In order to store binary data for successful retrieval and formatting we define the binary data columns as shown below:

Photograph	image	16	✓
PhotoContentType	nvarchar	50	✓
PhotoContentSize	int	4	✓
Contract	image	16	✓
ContractContentTy	nvarchar	50	✓
ContractContentSi	int	4	✓
Salary	money	8	

The binary document is stored in an image column, the content type column stores the mime-type of the document (e.g. image/jpeg, application/msword) and the content size column stores the length (in bytes) of the binary data.

Let's start by looking at how we get binary information into the database. The
`HrisEditEmployees.aspx` page contains a checkbox and an `HTML Input` control.

Photograph:

The `HTML Input` Control can be used in ASP.NET to allow the user to select a file on their accessible
(local or network) drives for uploading to the server as a byte array. The logic behind the `update`
button (below) shows how we access the file information and pass it on to our
`EmployeesBiz` component.

```
Private Sub UpdateBtn_Click(ByVal sender As System.Object, _
        ByVal e As  System.EventArgs) Handles updateButton.Click

    'Only Update if Input Data is Valid
    If Page.IsValid = True Then
        Dim PhotoLength As Integer
        Dim PhotoContentType As String
        Dim PhotoContent() As Byte

        Dim ContractLength As Integer
        Dim ContractContentType As String
        Dim ContractContent() As Byte


        ' Determine whether a photo file was uploaded
        If chkUploadPhoto.Checked = True And Not _
            (PhotographField.PostedFile Is Nothing) Then

            ' Loading to the server for security and web farm support
            PhotoLength = CInt(PhotographField.PostedFile.InputStream.Length)
            ReDim PhotoContent(PhotoLength)
            PhotoContentType = PhotographField.PostedFile.ContentType

            PhotographField.PostedFile.InputStream.Read(PhotoContent, 0, _
                PhotoLength)
        Else
            ' Setup acceptable 0 values for the Photo
            PhotoLength = 0

            'Create a zero length byte array
            ReDim PhotoContent(0)
            PhotoContentType = ""
        End If

        ' Determine whether a Contract file was uploaded
        If chkUploadContract.Checked = True And Not _
            (ContractField.PostedFile Is Nothing) Then
            ' Loading to the server for security and web farm support
            ContractLength = CInt(ContractField.PostedFile.InputStream.Length)
            ReDim ContractContent(ContractLength)
            ContractContentType = ContractField.PostedFile.ContentType

            ContractField.PostedFile.InputStream.Read(ContractContent, 0, _
```

```
                    ContractLength)
            Else
                ' Setup acceptable 0 values for the Photo
                ContractLength = 0

                'Create a zero length byte array
                ReDim ContractContent(0)
                ContractContentType = ""
            End If

            Try
                ' Update the Employee information within the Employees table
                EmployeesBiz.UpdateEmployee(moduleId, itemId, FirstNameField.Text, _
                    MiddleNamesField.Text, LastNameField.Text, _
                    TitleDDL.SelectedItem.Text, _
                    Int(EthnicOriginDDL.SelectedItem.Value), _
                    SSNField.Text, HomeAddField.Text, _
                    TelephoneNumField.Text, BankRTField.Text, BankAcct.Text, _
                    NextOfKinField.Text, GPAddressField.Text, _
                    EMailField.Text, CInt(SiteDDL.SelectedItem.Value), _
                    CInt(StatusDDL.SelectedItem.Value), _
                    CInt(JobTitleDDL.SelectedItem.Value), _
                    PhotoContent, PhotoContentType, PhotoLength, ContractContent, _
                    ContractContentType, ContractLength, SalaryField.Text, _
                    NotesField.Text, _
                    HealthNotesField.Text, DateOfBirthField.Text, _
                    ReviewBaseDateField.Text, LeavingDateField.Text, _
                    Context.User.Identity.Name)

                ' Redirect back to the portal home page
                Response.Redirect(CType(ViewState("UrlReferrer"), String))
            Catch exc As Exception
                lblError.Text = _
                    "Update failed. Please check the values you entered.(" _
                    & exc.Message.ToString() & ")"
            End Try
        End If

    End Sub
```

The file posted to the `Input` control is accessed through the `PostedFile` class. From this we are able to:

Read the `ContentType`:

```
PhotoContentType = PhotographField.PostedFile.ContentType
```

Determine the length of the file (`ContentSize`):

```
PhotoLength = CInt(PhotographField.PostedFile.InputStream.Length)
```

Create a byte array of length, `ContentSize`, to hold the file:

```
ReDim PhotoContent(PhotoLength)
```

Finally, stream the file contents into the newly dimmed byte array:

```
PhotographField.PostedFile.InputStream.Read(PhotoContent, 0, _
    PhotoLength)
```

The resulting details can now be passed through to the `EmployeesBiz.UpdateEmployee` method where the information is passed as parameter values:

```
Dim parameterPhotograph As New SqlParameter("@Photograph", _
    SqlDbType.Image)
parameterPhotograph.Value = Photograph
myCommand.Parameters.Add(parameterPhotograph)

Dim parameterPhotoContentType As New SqlParameter("@PhotoContentType", _
    SqlDbType.NVarChar, 50)
parameterPhotoContentType.Value = PhotoContentType
myCommand.Parameters.Add(parameterPhotoContentType)

Dim parameterPhotoContentSize As New SqlParameter("@PhotoContentSize", _
    SqlDbType.Int, 4)
parameterPhotoContentSize.Value = PhotoContentSize
myCommand.Parameters.Add(parameterPhotoContentSize)
```

through to the SQL stored procedure `up_Hris_UpdateEmployee`. This procedure inserts a new employee record or updates an existing record if the employee's details already exist on the database. If we look back at the screenshot of the `input` control, we can see that a checkbox has been added. Given that the `Input` control's `PostedFile` class is not updated when we retrieve existing information from the database, what would happen if we were to edit an employee's details, change a value and click update? The `PostedFile` class would be `Nothing` and any previously uploaded photograph/contract would be lost. For this reason we have included some additional logic that will allow our users to either blank out previously uploaded data or replace this data with a new file.

```
If chkUploadPhoto.Checked = True And Not _
    (PhotographField.PostedFile Is Nothing) Then
```

We only read in the posted file information if the user has checked the option to upload a file and has used the input control to select a file.

```
Else
    ' Setup acceptable 0 values for the Photo
    PhotoLength = 0

    'Create a zero length byte array
    ReDim PhotoContent(0)
    PhotoContentType = ""
End If
```

Otherwise, we create a `zero byte` array and set the `ContentSize` to 0. Within the stored procedure, there is further logic to control this upload.

```sql
CREATE PROCEDURE up_Hris_UpdateEmployee
(
    @ID  int,
    ...
    @Photograph image,
    @PhotoContentType nvarchar(50),
    @PhotoContentSize int,
    @Contract image,
    @ContractContentType nvarchar(50),
    @ContractContentSize int,
    ...)
AS
-- If the record exists for this employee thenUpdate the details
-- otherwise  INSERT the new employee record
IF EXISTS (SELECT * FROM tblHris_Employees WHERE ID = @ID) BEGIN
    UPDATE
        tblHris_Employees

    -- InstanceID is not updated since it should never change
    SET
        FirstName = @FirstName,
        ..
    WHERE
        ID = @ID
    END
ELSE BEGIN
    INSERT INTO tblHris_Employees
    (
        InstanceID,
        ...
        AlteredDate
    )
    VALUES
    (
        @InstanceID,
        ...
        getdate()
    )

    -- This is required because we later update the binary large object fields
    -- ONLY if the ContentSize is > 0
    SELECT @ID = @@IDENTITY
END

-- The Employee record now exists in the DB, any existing documents still
-- exist but have not yet been updated.

-- Update the Photograph if a file has been uploaded
IF @PhotoContentSize > 0 BEGIN
    UPDATE    tblHris_Employees
    SET    Photograph = @Photograph,
```

```
        PhotoContentType = @PhotoContentType,
        PhotoContentSize = @PhotoContentSize
    WHERE
            ID = @ID
END
```

```
-- Update the Contract if a file has been uploaded
IF @ContractContentSize > 0 BEGIN
    UPDATE      tblHris_Employees
    SET     Contract = @Contract,
        ContractContentType = @ContractContentType,
        ContractContentSize = @ContractContentSize
    WHERE
            ID = @ID
END
```

We now know how to handle the upload of binary information to our database but, without knowing how to retrieve this information and display it, this is of limited value to us. So let's now examine the HrisViewPhoto.aspx (the code for this page is almost identical to the HrisViewContract.aspx and HrisViewJobTitles.aspx pages).

The HrisViewPhoto.aspx page accepts the employee ID as its single integer parameter.

```
' Obtain image data from the Employees table
Dim dBContent As SqlDataReader = EmployeesBiz.GetSingleEmployee(EmployeeId)
dBContent.Read()
```

```
' Serve up the file by name
Response.AppendHeader("content-disposition", "filename=" & _
    CStr(dBContent("FirstName")))
```

```
' set the content type for the Response to that of the
' document to display. For example. "application/msword"
Response.ContentType = CType(dBContent("PhotoContentType"), String)
```

```
' output the actual contents to the response output stream
Response.OutputStream.Write(CType(dBContent("Photograph"), Byte()), 0, _
    CInt(dBContent("PhotoContentSize")))
```

```
' end the response
Response.End()
```

```
' close the SqlDataReader
dbContent.Close()
```

The `filename` property does not have to be set. It is used in the optional download dialog box that asks the user to confirm a binary download (see screenshot below). We can therefore choose the most meaningful field, or a string literal for the filename.

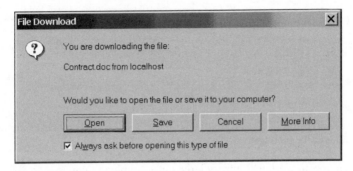

The most important actions are to:

❑ Set the `Response.ContentType` to tell the browser that the content is, for example, a jpeg

```
Response.ContentType = CType(dBContent("PhotoContentType"), String)
```

❑ Stream the contents of the image field byte array to the `Response.OutputStream`

```
Response.OutputStream.Write(CType(dBContent("Photograph"), Byte()), 0, _
    CInt(dBContent("PhotoContentSize")))
```

The photograph is now sent back to the browser as an image, not as an HTML page with an `<img>` tag. This is important and the significance of this distinction will become clearer when we show how to display the `Employee` image within a `.aspx` page such as the `HrisViewEmployeeDetails.aspx`.

Setting the `Response.Content` type to the appropriate `mime` type allows the browser to load the appropriate viewer, e.g. when we use the `HrisViewContract.aspx` page the contract is displayed with the appropriate office application embedded in the browser, as shown below.

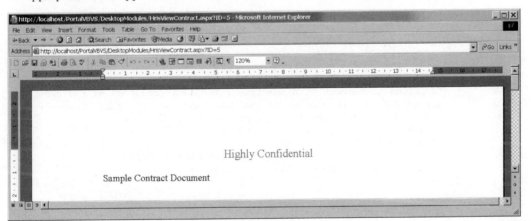

This ability to stream binary data of a specified type to the browser enables us to use .aspx pages as the url for <img> tags, as demonstrated by the HrisViewEmployeeDetails.aspx page which loads the employee's picture with the code.

```
Image1.ImageUrl = EmployeesBiz.GetBrowsePathDetails("Photo", itemId)
```

Which sets the ImageUrl to:

```
"~/DesktopModules/HrisViewPhoto.aspx?ID=" & ID.ToString()
```

We have used an .aspx page to return an image. This technique is very powerful in a number of scenarios, and is often used to generate simple bar chart, jpegs, or gifs dynamically using GDI+ and to generate button images for web sites.

We have now seen how to work with binary large objects, upload them to a database (being careful in our updates not to overwrite existing information), and retrieve and display the information within the browser. However, we have yet to cover how to use full-text indexing in conjunction with database image columns. While the HRIS does not index the contract information for security reasons, enabling full-text indexing on image data will be discussed as part of the HrisEmployeeSearchResults.ascx control a fuller discussion of full-text indexing.

Security and Electronic Data Concerns

The information within a Human Resources application is by definition of both a personal and sensitive nature. In most countries there are strict laws relating to the storage of personal information on computer systems. The legal implications of this are, in general, best handled as part of the employees' contracts, which should have a section that explicitly asks the employees' permission to hold information pertinent to their employment on computer.

The information that is stored about employees must only be available to those with sufficient security access to view the information. Fortunately, the intranet framework provides an in-built role-based security system. The HRIS takes advantage of this by allowing unrestricted access to information only to members of the HRAdmin role. The name of this role can be changed in the web.config file.

```
<!-- application specific settings -->
<appSettings>
    <add key="ConnectionString" value="server=localhost;
      Trusted_Connection=true; database=portal" />
    <!--The Human Resources Information System has restricted certain
        functions to members of a specific role (Administrators of the HRIS
        system). Rather than hardcode the role name into the code, the code
    will pick up the rolename from the HRISAdminRole key -->
        <add key="HRISAdminRole" value="HRAdmin" />
        <add key="HRISEmployeeHandbookPath"
             value="C:\PortalVBVS\PortalVBVS\Data\HRISDocs" />
        <add key="HRISNewEmployeeMonths" value="3" />
</appSettings>
```

This key setting is used in both the `HrisViewContract.aspx` to ensure that only an HRAdmin role member or the employee themselves (the code currently checks that the e-mail address of the employee is the same as the current users username) can view the contract and the full employee details.

> **Important**: Members of the HRAdmin role have access to everyone's information in the HRIS.

There is a business benefit in enabling non-sensitive information to be viewed by all other employees. This can be used to find contact details, interests, skill sets etc. A non-HRAdmin role member will see the following fields in the `HrisViewEmployeesDetails.aspx`.

HrisEmployeesDisplaySummary.ascx

The `display summary` control is intended to provide users with an immediate window into a limited area of the HRIS application.

HRIS Summary

New Employees

Sort by [Last Name ▾]

	Site	Job Title	Service	Photo	Details
Mr Boyce, Brian	MKY	Research Director	0 Years	Show Photo	Show Details
Mr Kinsey, Stuart	MKY	Web Developer (ASP.NET)	0 Years	Show Photo	Show Details
1					

Employee Handbook

Business Travel.doc	(Last written to on: 11/07/2002 15:30:10)
Data Protection.doc	(Last written to on: 11/07/2002 15:31:30)
HEALTH & SAFETY.doc	(Last written to on: 11/07/2002 15:32:52)

Rather than showing a smaller subset of the same information shown in the display full control, the control is used to provide access to the Employee Handbook and a list of all employees (with links to their details) who have joined the company in the last three months (the `HRISNewEmployeeMonths` key controls the number of months). The `New Employee` portion is identical in implementation to the `EmployeeDisplayFull` control. The only difference is that the `EmployeesBiz.GetNewEmployees` function returns only those employees who have joined in the last x months (the default is `three`).

Displaying the Employee Handbook on the intranet is one of the most legally compelling reasons for an intranet. If the Employee Handbook is available to all authorized intranet users then no employee can ever claim against (or sue) the company claiming not to know the conditions of their employment. The intranet also enables the HR department to ensure that the copy of the Employee Handbook being read by employees is always the most up-to-date. This gives the company a great deal of legal protection through explicit compliance with obligations to communicate conditions of employment to all employees in an unprejudiced form.

The Employee Handbook could have been implemented as a series of links using the `quicklinks` module or as documents or indeed as a custom module with documents uploaded to the server. All of these are viable options and each has particular pros and cons. However, we have implemented the Employee Handbook portion of the display summary control by having the control read a directory specified in the `web.config` file and displaying the documents it contains. The reason for this approach was to demonstrate another very useful technique for content control – integration with version control software.

Visual Source Safe Shadow Folders

In many organizations, and in particular software companies, the use of version control software is prevalent. In this section, we will show how to configure Microsoft's Visual SourceSafe to create what is called a shadow folder. A shadow folder is a read-only folder on a drive (usually under a network share) that contains a copy of all of the most recent (checked-in) versions of the documents in a project. The following walk-through shows how to set-up a shadow folder for a project:

❑ Open up the VSS Admin with the correct database and select Tools I Options

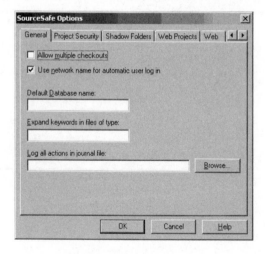

❑ Select the **Shadow Folders** tab and under "Set shadow folder for project" browse to the VSS folder you wish to shadow. Next, under "Set shadow folder to", browse to the folder which you want to use as your current copy of the checked-in files (this can be a new folder if you wish).

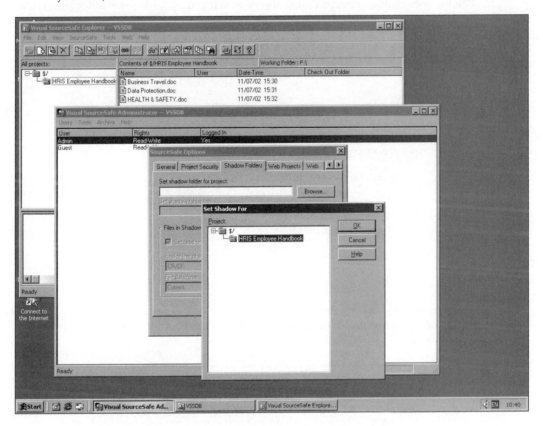

> **The folder that you are configuring as the shadow folder must be accessible from the intranet server or the display summary control will not be able to browse the directory. (The ASP.NET account must have sufficient access to read from this folder.)**

At this point, the shadow folder will contain a read-only copy of the documents from the source safe project. The following steps are necessary however to ensure that the contents of the shadow folder are kept coordinated with the VSS projects checked-in files.

❑ The set `read-only` flag for all files is selected by default. This is the correct setting. Next select **OK** and exit the **VSS Admin** application.

❑ Go back into **VSS**. Right-click on your folder and select "Get Latest Version".

❑ In the 'To' box, browse to find the shadow folder (the folder that will be read by the display summary module) and select the 'Recursive' checkbox. Then select the 'Build Tree' checkbox and click the OK button.

❑ Edit the web.config file and change the value of the HRISEmployeeHandbookPath key to the UNC of the shadow folder.

The HrisEmployeesSummary control will now browse this directory for files using the following code:

```
Private Sub Page_Load(ByVal sender As System.Object, ByVal e As System.EventArgs)
Handles MyBase.Load

        ' Obtain Employee information
        ' and bind to the DataGrid Control
        Months = CInt(ConfigurationSettings.AppSettings("HRISNewEmployeeMonths"))
        If Not Page.IsPostBack Then
            DocPath = _
                ConfigurationSettings.AppSettings("HRISEmployeeHandbookPath")
            Dim dInfo As DirectoryInfo = New DirectoryInfo(DocPath)

            dlHandbookFiles.DataSource = dInfo.GetFiles("*.*")
            dlHandbookFiles.DataBind()

        End If
        BindGrid()
End Sub
```

The DataList is bound to the IList interface of the array of FileInfo returned by GetFiles. The DataList template then uses hyperlink controls to display hyperlinks to the documents in the Employee Handbook.

> **The DataList Template Trap!** When setting up templates for the DataList we must ensure that we define both an ItemTemplate and an AlternatingItemTemplate otherwise, we will simply not display every second item from our DataSource.

```
<ItemTemplate>
<tr>
   <td>
      <asp:HyperLink id=HyperLink2 CssClass="Normal" Target="_new" runat="server"
Text='<%# DataBinder.Eval(Container.DataItem,"Name") %>' NavigateUrl='<%#
DataBinder.Eval(Container.DataItem,"FullName") %>'>
      </asp:HyperLink>
   </td>
   <td align="right">
      <asp:Label CssClass="Normal" id="Label3" Text='<%#   " (Last written to on: "
& Cstr(DataBinder.Eval(Container.DataItem,"LastWriteTime")) & ")" %>'
runat="server">
      </asp:Label>
   </td>
```

```
    </tr>
  </ItemTemplate>

  <AlternatingItemTemplate>
  <tr>
     <td>
        <asp:HyperLink CssClass="Normal" id=Hyperlink3 Target="_new" runat="server"
Text='<%#  DataBinder.Eval(Container.DataItem,"Name") %>' NavigateUrl='<%#
DataBinder.Eval(Container.DataItem,"FullName") %>'>
        </asp:HyperLink>
     </td>
     <td align="right">
        <asp:Label CssClass="Normal" id="Label4" Text='<%#  " (Last written to on: "
& Cstr(DataBinder.Eval(Container.DataItem,"LastWriteTime")) & ")" %>'
runat="server">
        </asp:Label>
     </td>
  </tr>
  </AlternatingItemTemplate>
```

This section has demonstrated a useful technique for linking to the most recent checked-in documents in Visual Sourcesafe. The control could easily be adapted to a more generic shadow folder display module. We now have a useful human resources intranet application for storing and displaying employee related information. However, we are currently limited to browsing for information. The next control in the HRIS will show how we can use the Microsoft Indexing Service to enable full-text indexing and full-text searching of our employee information.

HrisEmployeesDisplaySearchResults.ascx

The HRIS search control allows the user to search either the Employee Handbook or the employee information stored in the database. In this section, we will explain how to configure full-text searching (using the MS Indexing Service) on both SQL Server and the file system. Although the HRIS treats these as two distinct searches, the search function can be combined; and we will show how the results of a search on the file system can be linked to database information to supplement the result set.

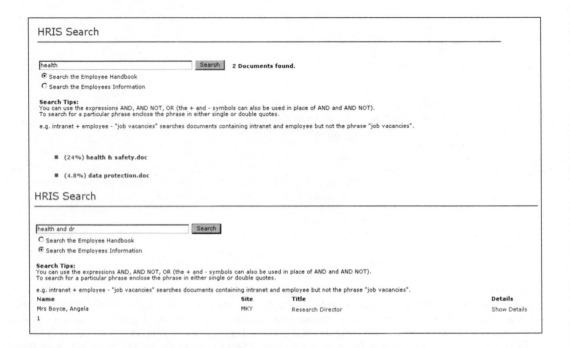

A Brief Overview of the MS Indexing Service

The MS Indexing Service (often referred to as the MS Search Service) is an installable service (on Windows NT, 2000 and XP) that sits outside of SQL Server and can be used to build full-text indexes on a data store. The Indexing Service can be installed as part of SQL Server 2000 Standard or Enterprise edition, and is installed as part of the Windows 2000 operating system. The diagram below shows how the Indexing Service interacts with SQL Server.

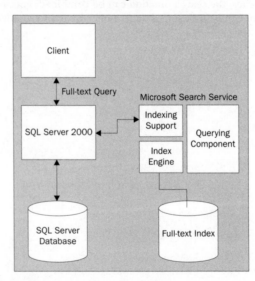

The Indexing Service works by creating indexes on the contents and properties of the data stores entities. With regard to files, it works by creating indexes of all non-noise words in the documents, and then uses these indexes to support linguistic searches and proximity searches. The indexing of files is handled by filters. SQL Server 2000 contains filters for .doc, .xls, .ppt, .txt, and .htm files (any non-supported file extension is treated as though it were a .txt file). It is possible to create custom filters for other types of files; the Platform SDK contains examples of how to do this (search on "custom filters").

The noise words used for each of the different languages can be found in the directory listed below:

```
C:\Program Files\Microsoft SQL Server\<<instance
name>>\FTDATA\SQLServer$<<instance name>>\Config
```

The files are called Noise. *<lang>* where *<lang>* is an extension indicating the language with which the file is associated for full-text indexing purposes. If the information we are indexing has industry or business-specific noise words then these could be added to the appropriate noise file for the language in order to ignore those words for indexing purposes.

For details on configuring the Indexing Service for the HRIS module, see the Configuration section at the end of this chapter. In this next section we walkthrough the configuration of the Indexing Service for the HRIS application.

In the HRIS application we do not use full-text search to index the contract data because we do not want contract information becoming visible to unauthorized users through a search. We do however index the following fields of the Employee information:

❑ FirstName

❑ LastName

❑ Title

❑ SSN

❑ HomeAddress

❑ GPAddress

❑ Email

❑ Notes

❑ HealthNotes

Before we can query the full-text catalog, we must populate the index. There are a number of different types of population.

❑ Full Population

A full population can be executed on either a table or a catalog. It will rebuild the index entries for all the rows in the table or catalog tables respectively. This is typically only performed when a catalog or index is first populated, thereafter the indexes can be maintained using change or incremental populations.

421

❑   Change Tracking Population

SQL Server maintains a record of the rows that have been modified and propagates the changes to the full-text index either in the background, on demand or on a scheduled basis.

❑   Incremental Population

This option adjusts the index entries for any records that have been inserted, deleted, or modified since the last population. This option requires that the table has a column of type `timestamp`. If we request an incremental population on a table that does not have a timestamp column the index will undergo a full population. A request for an incremental population will also result in a full population if any of the meta-data relating to the table has been altered. This includes altering column, index, or full-text index definitions.

Scheduling the Index Population can be configured through SQL Server's Enterprise Manager (see Configuration section for a full walkthrough).

Querying Full-text Indexes

SQL Server provides a number of T-SQL constructs that allow us to query full-text information. This, in conjunction with the distributed query functionality, allows for interrogation of SQL Server-based indexes, file system indexes and even queries performing joins across database and file system.

The four T-SQL statements for querying full-text indexes are outlined below:

❑   `FREETEXT`

`Freetext` is used to search columns containing character-based data types for values that match the meaning rather than the exact wording of the words in the search condition. The results of a `freetext` query are less precise than those from the `CONTAINS` predicate.

```
SELECT FirstName, LastName, GPAddress FROM tblHris_Employees
    WHERE FREETEXT(*, 'boyce')
```

❑   `CONTAINS`

`Contains` is used to search columns containing character-based data for precise or fuzzy matches. For example, `Contains` can search for:

❑   A word or phrase
❑   The prefix of a word or phrase
❑   A word with same inflectional stem as another word (e.g. fly, flies, flying)
❑   A word that has a higher designated weighting than another

```
SELECT FirstName, LastName, GPAddress FROM tblHris_Employees
    WHERE Contains(*, '"Health Centre" near "Dunn"')
```

❏   FREETEXTTABLE

FreeTextTable returns a table of zero, one or more rows of results that satisfy the freetext query. Since the FREETEXTTABLE returns a table it can be used in joins, and even provides two special columns to enhance this function. The KEY column contains the unique value (primary key or unique constraint column defined as part of the original index definition) associated with a row. The RANK column contains a relevance rating for the row that can be used to order the result set.

```
SELECT key_tbl.RANK, ft_tbl.[ID], ft_tbl.[Title] as 'EmpTitle',
    ft_tbl.[FirstName],  ft_tbl.[LastName], Code as 'SiteCode',
    JobID, JobTitles.Title as 'JobTitle'
FROM tblHris_Employees as ft_tbl
    INNER JOIN FREETEXTTABLE(tblHRIS_Employees, *, '"Dr Berkin"') as key_tbl
        ON ft_tbl.[ID] = key_tbl.[KEY]
    INNER JOIN tblHris_Sites
        ON SiteID = tblHris_Sites.ID
    INNER JOIN tblHris_JobTitles JobTitles
        ON JobID = JobTitles.ID
ORDER BY key_tbl.RANK DESC
```

❏   CONTAINSTABLE

CONTAINSTABLE returns a table of zero, one or more rows of results that satisfy the CONTAINS query. Since the CONTAINSTABLE returns a table it can be used in joins, and even provides two special columns to enhance this function. The KEY column contains the unique value (primary key or unique constraint column defined as part of the original index definition) associated with a row. The RANK column contains a relevance rating for the row that can be used to order the result set.

```
SELECT key_tbl.RANK, ft_tbl.[ID], ft_tbl.[Title] as 'EmpTitle',
    ft_tbl.[FirstName],  ft_tbl.[LastName], Code as 'SiteCode',
    JobID, JobTitles.Title as 'JobTitle'
FROM tblHris_Employees as ft_tbl
    INNER JOIN CONTAINSTABLE(tblHRIS_Employees, *, '"Angela" OR "Bo*"') as key_tbl
        ON ft_tbl.[ID] = key_tbl.[KEY]
    INNER JOIN tblHris_Sites
        ON SiteID = tblHris_Sites.ID
    INNER JOIN tblHris_JobTitles JobTitles
        ON JobID = JobTitles.ID
ORDER BY key_tbl.RANK DESC
```

The File System indexes are interrogated using the OPENQUERY statement to pass the query through to the linked server, as follows:

```
SELECT * FROM OPENQUERY(HRIS, 'SELECT FileName, Size, DocAuthor FROM SCOPE()
    WHERE FREETEXT(''health'') > 0 ORDER BY RANK DESC')
```

The File System provides a large number of properties that we can retrieve on any file. These properties can then be used to join the results back to database information, e.g. joining the results to an authors table based on the DocAuthor property of the file.

In our HRIS we did not include the `Contract` field in the full-text index. The decision not to include this field was made because of the nature of the document. The indexing of binary data stored within a SQL Server column is no more difficult than indexing any other character-based column. The only extra requirement is that the table must contain a column that indicates the type of document stored in the image field. The indexing service requires this column to store the content type in the format `'doc'`, `'ppt'`, or `'txt'` The screenshot below shows how to configure this option within the full-text indexing service wizard.

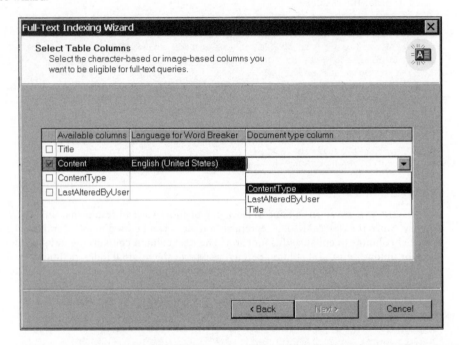

That concludes our examination of the HRIS system. The other modules shown in the application map at the start of the chapter were developed using the same principals and are used to enhance the usability of the three main employee modules – `DisplayFull`, `DisplaySummary` and `DisplaySearchResults`.

We felt it better to devote the chapter to the three core modules and cover the techniques in greater depth, than to skim over all modules in the HRIS. To finish the chapter we have included a section on installing and configuring the HRIS and a few ideas for extending the Human Resources Information System further.

Adding the HRIS to the Intranet

The following section covers the configuration of the `web.config` file and the MS Indexing Service to support the HRIS module.

Configuring the Human Resources Information System

This section covers how to:

❑ Set-up and configure the HRIS module on our intranet, and;

❑ Configure MS Indexing Service to enable full-text searching through SQL Server

Application Settings

When designing the HRIS system we added some application specific keys to the `web.config` file to control the availability of confidential information and to allow for simple configuration of the location of the Employee Handbook. The following listing shows the relevant `web.config` entries.

```
<!-- application specific settings -->
<appSettings>
    <add key="ConnectionString" value="server=localhost;
      Trusted_Connection=true; database=portal" />
    <!--The Human Resources Information System has restricted certain
        functions to members of a specific role (Administrators of the HRIS
        system). Rather than hardcode the role name into the code, the code
    will pick up the rolename from the HRISAdminRole key -->
        <add key="HRISAdminRole" value="HRAdmin" />
        <add key="HRISEmployeeHandbookPath"
               value="C:\PortalVBVS\PortalVBVS\Data\HRISDocs" />
        <add key="HRISNewEmployeeMonths" value="3" />
</appSettings>
```

The `HRISAdminRole` allows the intranet administrator to define which role has complete access to all HRIS functionality. The role name has been stored in the `web.config` file to allow it to be changed in accordance with the roles active in each organization.

The `HRISEmployeeHandbookPath` should be set to point to a network share which all users have access to. The reasons for using a network share are expanded on in the section on the `EmployeeSummary` control. The `Data\HRIS` folder within the intranet web application contains some sample HR-related documents that can be used for testing.

The `HRISNewEmployeeMonths` key determines how long new employees' details are shown on the `EmployeeSummary` control.

The configuration of the full-text indexing will be explained when we present the `EmployeeDisplaySearchResults` user control.

Full-Text Searching

Configuring the Indexing Service for File System Indexing

The first step is to ensure that the Indexing Service is running.

1. Right-click on My Computer and choose Manage

2. Expand the Services and Applications node

3. Select the Indexing Service

4. Click the Start Indexing Button if it is not already started (the play arrow on the toolbar)

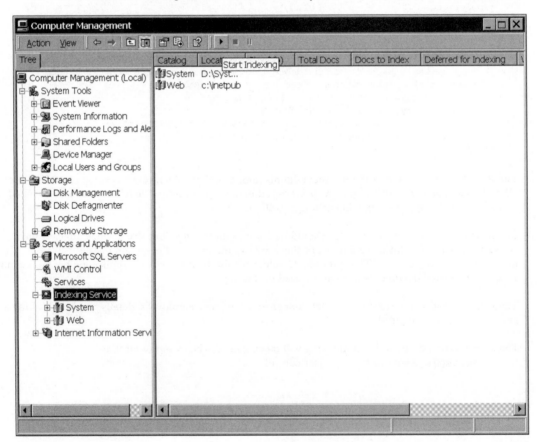

Next we need to create the catalog to store our full-text indexes. We could simply add another directory to the system or web catalogs, but we have chosen to create a new catalog in order to separate the content that is accessible through the intranet.

5. Right-click on the Indexing Service and choose New | Catalog

6. Enter the Name of the catalog (this can be anything but should correspond to the name of the catalog we specify when we add the Indexing Service to SQL Server as a linked server later on), and browse to the shadow folder that contains the HR documents. (If you have not created a shadow folder then select the folder that contains the Employee Handbook documents.)

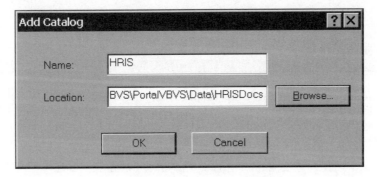

The Index Server will now warn us that the catalog will remain offline until the indexing service is restarted. Click OK.

7. Expand the HRIS catalog and right-click on the Directories node. Select New | Directory. Enter the Path and UNC of the shadow folder (or the folder containing the Employee Handbook documents).

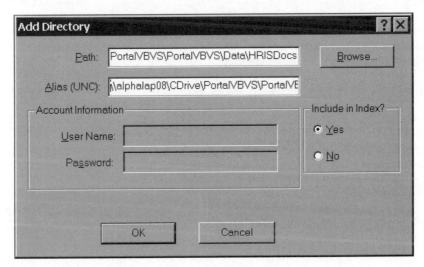

8. Finally, in the **Computer Management** console select the **Indexing Service** node and **stop** and **start** the service. The Indexing Service will now index the documents in that folder. This may take a few minutes depending on the number and size of the documents in the folder.

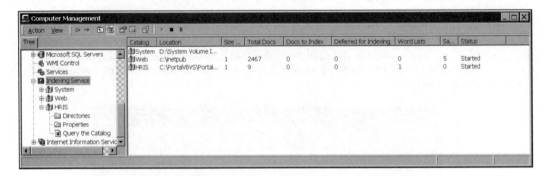

9. We need to be able to query this catalog from ADO.NET. Thanks to SQL Servers distributed query ability we can interrogate the Indexing Service's OLE DB interface through SQL server by treating the service as a linked server. We add the linked server by executing the following SQL:

```
exec sp_addlinkedserver HRIS, 'Index Server', 'MSIDXS', 'HRIS'
```

This adds the OLE DB Provider for the Indexing Service (MSIDXS) as 'HRIS' and points to the HRIS catalog.

We can test that this has been successful by executing the following SQL in **Query Analyzer**.

```
select FILENAME from openquery(HRIS, 'SELECT FileName from scope()')
```

This should return a list of all of the files in the indexed directory. In the above query, we returned the `FileName`. The MS Indexing Service provides access to over 50 document properties (see Windows 2000 Help for a complete list of document properties).

We have now configured the Indexing Service for the files. Creating full-text information on database fields is a lot simpler.

Configuring the Full-text Indexing on SQL Server Data

In the HRIS application, we do not use full-text search to index the `Contract` data because we do not want contract information becoming visible to unauthorized users through a search. We do however index the basic text fields of the employee information.

To set-up `Full-Text Search` on the `Employees` table use the following SQL (which is also listed in the comments portion of the `up_Hris_SearchEmployeesFT` stored procedure).

Enable `Full-Text Searching` on the current database.

```
if (select DATABASEPROPERTY(DB_NAME(), N'IsFullTextEnabled')) <> 1
exec sp_fulltext_database N'enable'
GO
```

Create the `HRISEmployees` full-text catalog if it does not already exist.

```
if not exists (select * from dbo.sysfulltextcatalogs where name =
N'HRISEmployees')
    exec sp_fulltext_catalog N'HRISEmployees', N'create'
```

Add the Table to the `HRISEmployees` catalog for full-text indexing. We must also specify a unique index or `primary` key on the table for the index server to work with.

```
exec sp_fulltext_table N'[dbo].[tblHris_Employees]', N'create', N'HRISEmployees',
N'PK_Employees'
```

Define the columns on the table that we wish to have indexed (the 1033 refers to the Unicode Collation to be used for the linguistic analysis – 1033 is General Unicode).

See MDSN Topic 'International Features in Microsoft SQL Server 2000' for more details and a complete list of Locale ID's.

```
exec sp_fulltext_column N'[dbo].[tblHris_Employees]', N'FirstName', N'add', 1033
exec sp_fulltext_column N'[dbo].[tblHris_Employees]', N'LastName', N'add', 1033
exec sp_fulltext_column N'[dbo].[tblHris_Employees]', N'Title', N'add', 1033
exec sp_fulltext_column N'[dbo].[tblHris_Employees]', N'SSN', N'add', 1033
exec sp_fulltext_column N'[dbo].[tblHris_Employees]', N'HomeAddress', N'add', 1033
exec sp_fulltext_column N'[dbo].[tblHris_Employees]', N'GPAddress', N'add', 1033
exec sp_fulltext_column N'[dbo].[tblHris_Employees]', N'EMail', N'add', 1033
exec sp_fulltext_column N'[dbo].[tblHris_Employees]', N'Notes', N'add', 1033
exec sp_fulltext_column N'[dbo].[tblHris_Employees]', N'HealthNotes', N'add', 1033
GO
```

Activate the Indexing:

```
exec sp_fulltext_table N'[dbo].[tblHris_Employees]', N'activate'
GO
```

Before we can query the full-text catalog, we must populate the index. There are a number of different types of population, these are described in the section on the `HrisEmployeesDisplaySearchResults.ascx` control, for just now choose Full Population.

Scheduling the index population can be configured by right-clicking on the table in Enterprise Manager and choosing Full-Text Index Table | Schedules…

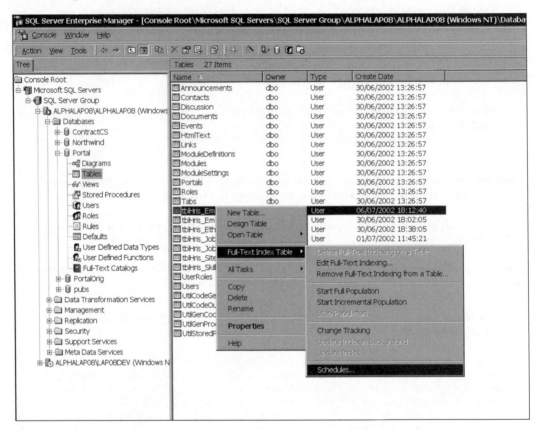

This allows you to easily set-up a recurring repopulation of the appropriate indexes. The options available are shown below.

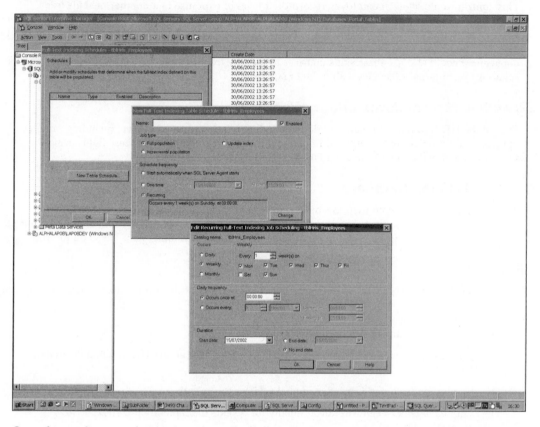

Once this configuration has been performed, all that remains is to query the data and display the search results.

Ideas on the Extension of the HRIS Application

The HRIS presented in this chapter is intended to be used as a base system. There are a number of ways in which this system could be extended, some of which are presented below along with some ideas on implementation to help kick-start the development.

New Employee Checklist

This could be a checklist or set of actions (e.g. configuration of exchange account, add entry to intranet contacts, etc.) to be completed whenever a new employee either leaves or joins the company. This could even be used to add items, configure the new users account details, and add/remove permissions.

An Employee Skills Database

This control would let each employee record their level of expertise in a number of skills (see HrisSkills.ascx). While the Skills control is supplied in the HRIS, it is not currently linked to the Employee controls to enable employees to record their skills profile. This information could be used by delivery managers within the organization to identify resources for up-coming projects. The HR department could also use these skills matrices to identify training requirements and assess a candidate's suitability for internal vacancies within the organization.

Expanding the Employee Information

Extend the HRIS so that it contains all documentation relating to an employee, including minutes of appraisals, disciplinary letters etc. and implement full-text searching on the these fields using the techniques outlined in the Configuring Full-Text Search section above.

Create a Training Database

The training database can be used to store details of all available courses, course schedules, and employee feedback on courses attended as well as professional certificate gained. This will link into the employee details, and can be useful in identifying skill gaps and training plans based on job role.

HRIS Alerts

Extend the HRIS to include an Admin control that allows the HR department to configure or subscribe to alerts such as:

❑   End of a new employee's probationary period.

❑   Notification of an employee's notice period ending. This allows HR to schedule an exit review.

❑   Employees A, B, and C are due annual reviews this month.

❑   Employee D has been with the company for 5 years on September 5, 2002.

These are just some sample alerts that would help streamline the functions of the HR office.

Summary

In this chapter, we have seen how easy it is to write a complete intranet application comprising several modules. We have covered various applicable techniques including:

❑   DataGrid Paging, both standard and custom.

❑   Advanced DataGrid Sorting.

❑   Use client side Javascript to provide confirmation dialog boxes.

❑   Creation of Shadow folders.

❑   Configuration of MS Index Server.

❑   Full-text indexing of character-based data, files and BLOBs.

- ❑ Using CONTAINSTABLE to provide a unified search facility.

- ❑ Configuring page, fragment and data caching.

- ❑ Altering the content-type of an .aspx page to return images and other binary file types.

- ❑ Using the ASP.NET Validator controls.

- ❑ Auditing considerations.

- ❑ Implications of storing personal information on computer systems.

While we have not had the space to cover every single technical feature in depth, hopefully the code presented here covers the most common aspects of intranet module development and will provide ideas and techniques that will prove useful in the development of your own modules.

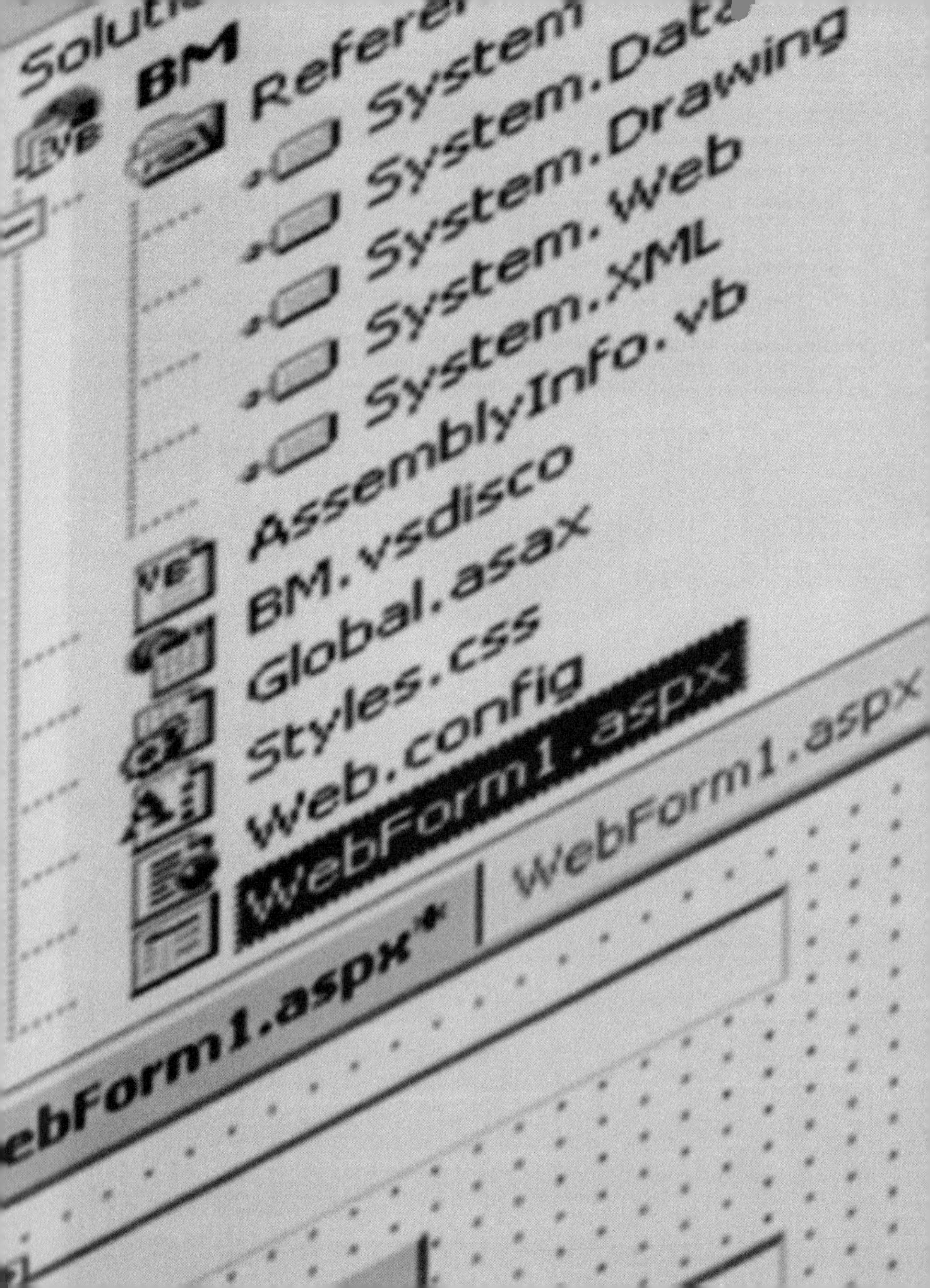

Solutio
BM   Referer
System.Data
System.Drawing
System.Web
System.XML
AssemblyInfo.vb
Assembly
BM.vsdisco
Global.asax
Styles.css
Web.config
WebForm1.aspx

WebForm1.aspx* | WebForm1.aspx

ebForm1.aspx*

A Common Data Access Class

In any software system, there will be a set of common tasks that will be performed from several different places in different components. Let's take a simple example of running a stored procedure: this is a task that we need to perform almost everywhere in an intranet to access the database to manipulate the data. So, this task could be encapsulated into a component as a generic function that accepts a stored procedure name as a string and other SQL parameters. This design will save a lot of time during the application development because you're-using the packaged functionality repeatedly instead of reinventing the wheel!

In this short Appendix, we will take a look at the `Database` class that is used in several chapters of this book to handle data access.

The `Database` Class

This class encapsulates the functionality related to database access. This class can be found in the support material in the `Components` folder, with the name `Database.vb`. It belongs to the namespace `Wrox.Intranet.DataTools`.

The following table gives you an overview of all the members that are exposed by the Database class.

Member Name	Member Type	Functionality
ErrorMessage	Public Property	This public property gives the error message as a string from the last exception.
LastException	Public Property	This public property holds the last exception in the DataTools class. The return type is System.Exception.
RunProcedure	Public Method	This is an overloaded method that can take a stored procedure name and SQL parameters as input arguments and returns an integer, a SQLDataReader or a Dataset.
MakeParameter	Public Method	This is an overloaded method that is used to prepare SQL parameters that are intended to pass in as arguments for the stored procedures.
Close	Public Method	This method closes the SQL connection that is used by the DataTools class instance.
Dispose	Public Method	This method is an implementation of the interface IDisposable. This method disposes the SQL Connection that is used by the DataTools class instance.
_errorMessage	Private Field	A private field that holds the last error message.
_exception	Private field	A private field that holds the last exception.

Implementing IDisposable

The class implements the IDisposable interface as shown below:

```
Namespace Wrox.Intranet.DataTools

    Public Class Database
        Implements IDisposable
```

Classes that require releasing unmanaged resources should implement the IDisposable interface. In our case the Database class implements IDisposable interface to release the SQLConnection that is used by the members of the class. Here is the implementation of the Dispose method in the Database class:

```
Public Sub Dispose() Implements IDisposable.Dispose
    'Check if the connection object still exists
    If (con Is Nothing) Then
    Else
```

```
            con.Dispose()
            con = Nothing
        End If
        'Suppress the finalization process
        System.GC.SuppressFinalize(Me)
End Sub
```

Exposing the Connection String

The Database class exposes a shared property called ConnectionString that returns the database connection string from the Web.Config file.

```
Public Shared ReadOnly Property ConnectionString() As String
    Get
        Return System.Configuration.ConfigurationSettings.AppSettings _
                                        ("ConnectionString")

    End Get
End Property
```

This property can be used to retrieve the connection string from the Web.Config file from your application code if needed.

Our Database class provides a lot of functionality for running stored procedures, so most code should not need to use the connection string directly. However, it is always wise to plan for the unexpected so the ConnectionString property allows code that needs to talk to the database directly to use the same connection string as the Database class.

Running Stored Procedures

Most of the methods of the Database class are concerned with allowing stored procedures to be run. They abstract the database connection, providing a layer between it and the code that uses it.

Why Abstract Stored Procedure Execution?

To understand why it is useful to do this, consider the following scenario:

You need to run a stored procedure up_UserLogon with parameters @UserId and @Password from your application. This stored procedure returns an integer indicating whether the logon is successful or not.

To achieve the above functionality, you would usually do something like the example below (assuming that you have imported the System.Data and System.Data.SqlClient namespaces):

```
Dim result As Integer
Dim cmd As SqlCommand
Dim con As SqlConnection

Try

    con = New SqlConnection("your connection string")
    con.Open()

    cmd = New SqlCommand("up_UserLogon", con)
    cmd.CommandType = CommandType.StoredProcedure

    cmd.Parameters.Add("@UserId", "username")
    cmd.Parameters.Add("@Password", "password")

    result = CType(cmd.ExecuteScalar(), Integer)

Catch(e As Exception)
    . . .
Finally
    con.Close()
End Try
```

What if we need to run a different stored procedure, with a different set of parameters from your application? You will have to repeat the above code to run the other stored procedure again. Since most of the applications that we develop spend a lot of time manipulating data, data access code will be present in almost every function.

To avoid repeatedly re-inventing the wheel, we need to package the task of running a stored procedure into a re-usable method. Thats what we did in the Database class. If you use the Database class to achieve the same functionality that we have discussed above, the code will reduce to:

```
Dim result As Integer
Dim db As New Wrox.Intranet.DataTools.Database()
Dim params(1) As SqlParameter

params(0) = db.MakeParameter("@UserId", "username")
params(1) = db.MakeParameter("@Password", "password")
result = db.RunProcedure("up_UserLogon", params)
db = Nothing
```

As you can see, running a stored procedure from your application component is now independent of the data access code. This has three big advantages:

❑   We need less code to manipulate data

❑   All parts of our application will use consistent data access code

❑   If we want to change our data access code, we only need to do it in one place

The Methods For Executing Stored Procedures

The key methods from the example in the previous section are `MakeParameter` and `RunProcedure`.

The `MakeParameter` method is shown below:

```
Public Function MakeParameter(ByVal ParamName As String, _
                   ByVal Value As Object) As SqlParameter
   Dim param As SqlParameter

   param = New SqlParameter(ParamName, Value)
   param.Direction = ParameterDirection.Input

   Return param
End Function
```

As you can see, the method simply creates a `SQLParameter` object and sets its direction to `Input`.

`MakeParameter` has another overload that takes in an extra argument to decide the direction of the SQL parameter so that you can mark the parameter as an `OUTPUT` parameter if needed. The signature of the method is shown below:

```
Public Function MakeParameter(ByVal ParamName As String, _
                   ByVal Direction As ParameterDirection, _
                   ByVal Value As Object) As SqlParameter
```

The `RunProcedure` method handles the actual execution of a stored procedure. Here is one of its overloads:

```
Public Function RunProcedure (ByVal procName As String, _
                   ByVal prams As SqlParameter()) As Integer
      Dim result As Integer
      Dim cmd As SqlCommand

      Try
         cmd = CreateCommand(procName, prams)
         result = cmd.ExecuteScalar()
      Catch e As Exception
         result = -1
         _errorMessage = e.Message
      Finally
         Me.Close()
      End Try
      Return result
End Function
```

This function is also overloaded for all kinds of data-access scenario such as running procedures with no parameters and running procedures that return records. The overloaded signatures of this method are shown below:

For running procedures that return a scalar value:

```
Public Function RunProcedure(ByVal procName As String) As Integer

Public Function RunProcedure(ByVal procName As String, _
    ByVal prams As SqlParameter()) As Integer
```

For running procedures that return records and returning these records as a `SqlDataReader`:

```
Public Sub RunProcedure(ByVal procName As String, ByRef dataReader _
    As SqlDataReader)

Public Sub RunProcedure(ByVal procName As String, _
    ByVal prams As SqlParameter(), ByRef dataReader As SqlDataReader)
```

For running procedures that return records and returning these records as a `DataSet`:

```
Public Sub RunProcedure(ByVal procName As String, _
    ByVal prams As SqlParameter(), ByRef ds As DataSet)

Public Sub RunProcedure(ByVal procName As String, ByRef ds As DataSet)
```

Handling Errors

What about if an exception occurs in the `Database` class? How does our application know about the error? The `Database` class takes care of this issue too.

The `Database` class exposes a public property called `ErrorMessage` as a string that passes the exception message to the application component. So, if your application receives an unexpected value (such as a procedure returning a result –1 after running it), you should check for the `ErrorMessage` property of the Database class to see whether there is any error message present. Not only that, if you need to investigate more about the exception, you can also gain access to the last exception by probing the public property `LastException`. This property exposes the last exception instance (returns `System.Exception` instance) so that you can get more information about the exception.

So lets take a look at the example of running the up_UserLogon stored procedure again. But this time, were going to add the error checking process. This time, were checking the `ErrorMessage` property of the Database class instance to check the error message in case of an exception:

```
Dim result As Integer
Dim db As New Wrox.Intranet.DataTools.Database()
Dim params(1) As SqlParameter
Dim errorMessage As String

params(0) = db.MakeParameter("@UserId", ModuleID)
params(1) = db.MakeParameter("@Password", Title)

result = db.RunProcedure("up_UserLogon", params)
```

```
If result < 0 Then
    errorMessage = db.ErrorMessage
    'Do your error processing
End If
```

```
db = Nothing
```

A Problem With the Database Class

Have you spotted the problem with the way this class handles errors? It uses the return value to let calling code know that there was an error. For example, in the RunProcedure method that we looked at above, we execute the following code when there is an error:

```
Catch e As Exception
    result = -1
    _errorMessage = e.Message
```

What if -1 is a desired result? For example, if the procedure we are calling returns the balance of a users account, the result may well be negative.

We do not need such negative results in our intranet application, so this does not cause us any immediate problems, but it is a weakness of this data access class that should be understood. A better solution for error handling might be to throw exceptions to inform calling code that there was an error, rather than using the return value.

As we have seen in many parts of this book, code can almost always be improved in some way. We should always be prepared to take another look at code that we have written to see whether it has weaknesses.

Solutio...
BM Referen...
    System
      System.Data
      System.Drawing
      System.Web
      System.XML
      AssemblyInfo.vb
    BM.vsdisco
    Global.asax
    Styles.css
    Web.config
    WebForm1.aspx

WebForm1.aspx* | WebForm1.aspx

ebForm1.aspx*

Index

A Guide to the Index

The index is arranged hierarchically, in alphabetical order, with symbols preceding the letter A. Most second-level entries and many third-level entries also occur as first-level entries. This is to ensure that users will find the information they require however they choose to search for it.

V

W

X

Y

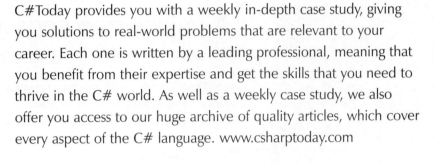

wrox

Programmer to Programmer™

Registration Code: | 749307CYZNL7UI01 |

Wrox writes books for you. Any suggestions, or ideas about how you want
information given in your ideal book will be studied by our team.
Your comments are always valued at Wrox.

Free phone in USA 800-USE-WROX
Fax (312) 893 8001

UK Tel.: (0121) 687 4100   Fax: (0121) 687 4101

Building An ASP.NET Intranet – Registration Card

Name _____

Address _____

_____

_____

City _____ State/Region _____

Country _____ Postcode/Zip _____

E-Mail _____

Occupation _____

How did you hear about this book?

☐ Book review (name) _____

☐ Advertisement (name) _____

☐ Recommendation _____

☐ Catalog _____

☐ Other _____

Where did you buy this book?

☐ Bookstore (name) _____ City_____

☐ Computer store (name) _____

☐ Mail order _____

☐ Other _____

What influenced you in the purchase of this book?

☐ Cover Design   ☐ Contents   ☐ Other (please specify):

How did you rate the overall content of this book?

☐ Excellent   ☐ Good   ☐ Average   ☐ Poor

What did you find most useful about this book? _____

_____

What did you find least useful about this book? _____

_____

Please add any additional comments. _____

_____

What other subjects will you buy a computer book on soon?

_____

What is the best computer book you have used this year?

_____

Note: This information will only be used to keep you updated
about new Wrox Press titles and will not be used for
any other purpose or passed to any other third party.

wrox

Programmer to Programmer™

Note: If you post the bounce back card below in the UK, please send it to:

Wrox Press Limited, Arden House, 1102 Warwick Road,
Acocks Green, Birmingham B27 6HB. UK.

Computer Book Publishers

NO POSTAGE
NECESSARY
IF MAILED
IN THE
UNITED STATES

BUSINESS REPLY MAIL

FIRST CLASS MAIL   PERMIT#64   CHICAGO, IL

POSTAGE WILL BE PAID BY ADDRESSEE

WROX PRESS INC.,
29 S. LA SALLE ST.,
SUITE 520
CHICAGO IL 60603-USA